PRAISE FOR A DAILY COMPANION TO MY UTMOST FOR HIS HIGHEST

"Oswald Chambers' *My Utmost for His Highest* is an old friend that I've returned to again and again over a period of forty years. But it has always seemed a bit ethereal—the powerful insights plucked from the air by a listening prophet. In *A Daily Companion to My Utmost for His Highest*, Jed and Cecilie Macosko sharpen the familiar daily lessons and set them firmly in the context of Chambers' biography, of Scripture, and of personal application—and they are much the richer for it! 'Like apples of gold in settings of silver,' Chambers' timeless wisdom has never been presented so beautifully."

Erick Schenkel, Executive Director, The JESUS Film Project

"*My Utmost for His Highest* has enriched, confronted, and lifted many of us year after year, decade after decade. This rich guide that includes thoughtful biblical insights plus relevant facts from Chambers' life provides new freshness and depth."

Harold Myra, CEO of Christianity Today International from 1975 to 2007 and author of *The One Year Book of Encouragement*

"A fantastically useful companion to Oswald Chambers' classic work. The mountain of wisdom may be Chambers', but Jed and Cecilie Macosko are the Sherpas guiding us to the top."

Phil Vischer, creator of VeggieTales and What's in the Bible?

"As an author of devotionals myself, I marvel at what Jed and Cecilie Macosko have done to enhance Oswald Chambers' *My Utmost for His Highest*. They have made a sometimes-challenging classic easily accessible to a new generation of Chambers' readers."

F. LaGard Smith, compiler of *The Daily Bible: In Chronological Order*

THE FOLLOWING OSWALD CHAMBERS BOOKS ARE AVAILABLE FROM DISCOVERY HOUSE PUBLISHERS:

Fresh Insights for
Oswald Chambers' Timeless Classic

A DAILY COMPANION

to

MY UTMOST

for

HIS HIGHEST

Dr. Jed Macosko
& Dr. Cecilie Macosko

DISCOVERY HOUSE
PUBLISHERS®

A Daily Companion to My Utmost for His Highest:
Fresh Insights for Oswald Chambers' Timeless Classic

© 2014 by Jed Macosko and Cecilie Macosko

Discovery House is affiliated with RBC Ministries, Grand Rapids, Michigan.

Requests for permission to quote from this book should be directed to: Permissions Department, Discovery House Publishers, P.O. Box 3566, Grand Rapids, MI 49501, or contact us by e-mail at permissionsdept@dhp.org

Interior design by Michelle Espinoza

ISBN 978-1-62707-071-3

Printed in the United States of America

First printing in 2014

To J, K, L, C & M.
We love you!

FOREWORD

A little over fifteen years ago, I was having the time of my life fulfilling my calling: writing about Darwinism and giving lectures all over the world. Meanwhile, Jed Macosko, a PhD candidate in biophysical chemistry, lived in the basement of our house in Berkeley, California. Around the same time, Cecilie—still an Olsson and home from Princeton for the summer—worked in Jed's lab. It was an exciting time for all of us in each of our callings. I treasure the memories I have of Jed and Cecilie from before they were even engaged.

After a decade and a half, two strokes, and nerve-damaging surgery, I have a new calling. Now it's not about the intellectual battles I have fought, but about encouraging the successes of my friends. The book that follows this foreword is a superb example of one such success, one that I (and others like me) have needed.

Since 1978, when I put my faith in Christ, people have recommended that I read Oswald Chambers' classic devotional. But every time I picked up *My Utmost for His Highest*, it didn't seem to connect with my life. My wife, Kathie, and I have friends who read it every day. This only made me more perplexed. "What do people get out of this little book?" I wondered. It always seemed to me to be a perfect daily devotional for young people wanting to be missionaries—not for a law professor like me.

As I near my seventy-fourth birthday, my dear friends Jed and Cecilie have put together a wonderful tool for all of us. Their explanations of each *Utmost* reading clearly show how Oswald Chambers' message is not just for soon-to-be-missionaries, but for anyone who faces everyday struggles. As Chambers puts it, "The greatest test of Christianity is the wear and tear of daily life."

My daily life has changed dramatically over the past fifteen years. The challenge of writing op-eds for international audiences has given way to the ordeal of walking around part of the block with a cane in one hand and a helper at my side. But through all the changes, I have consistently tried to answer the question: Is Christianity true, or is it not?

A related question is this: Does Jesus Christ really provide supernatural strength to overcome daily struggles? In my darkest times, I'm afraid to ask myself that question, since I fear that my answer may not be the resounding "Yes!" I want it to be.

It's in dark times like those when *My Utmost for His Highest* with *A Daily Companion* can help. I can open up both books to June 18, for example, and see that I'm not alone in my doubts about Christ's power. Even the apostle Peter had the same doubts; and in the midst of his struggle, he learned the secret to overcoming.

Whether we venture bravely to the mission field or fight against unsound philosophies or struggle to climb a flight of stairs, we all need to know the secret of overcoming our daily battles. Oswald Chambers' timeless words remind us of that secret: We must focus on Christ while doing whatever is the next thing He wants us to do. *A Daily Companion* amplifies this profound message. It is an excellent resource for all of us. May God use it to encourage you, just as He has used its authors to encourage me in my darkest days.

Phillip E. Johnson
Author, *Darwin on Trial, The Wedge of Truth, Reason in the Balance*

INTRODUCTION

As a husband-wife writing team, creating *A Daily Companion to My Utmost for His Highest* was a labor of love for us in many ways. We love devotionals, and since Oswald Chambers' classic has been our favorite, we wanted to help others experience this timeless and powerful masterpiece as never before. We also love the reward of working together as best friends and were especially drawn to *Utmost*, which is the loving creation of perhaps the greatest husband-wife writing team ever—Oswald and Biddy Chambers. As we juggle two careers (Jed is a physics professor and Cecilie is a family doctor) and raise five young children, the *Daily Companion* project brought us closer as a couple. Faced with a challenging goal—to make each *Utmost* reading come alive in a new way—we discovered that many of the daily readings ministered to us with an unexpected freshness. Neither of us knew how much it would take to be *our* utmost for God's highest as we embarked on this project. If we did, we might never have started!

The same may be true for you. If God told you right now what will happen to you as you complete Oswald Chambers' one-year spiritual expedition with *A Daily Companion* as your map, you might lose heart. Giving our utmost for God's highest disrupts our whole lives, since our lives are not yet the highest God wants them to be. Despite this unsettling truth, let us be of good cheer. Each reading comes in its own time. There will be a time to plant new habits and a time to uproot old ones. There will be a time to tear down idols and a time to build altars to remember God's provision. There will be a time to weep over sin and a time to laugh in the joy of God's goodness. God will make each season of this one-year devotional beautiful in its time. And before you know it, you will be a changed person; you will be your utmost for our high and mighty King.

HOW TO USE THIS STUDY GUIDE

The full 366 days of Oswald Chambers' hard-hitting truths overwhelm, inspire, and transform. The key is to experience *all* 366 days. *A Daily Companion*'s most basic goal is to help you read the devotional of the day for an entire year. In doing that, you can achieve the far more important goal of living your uttermost best for the sake of God's highest glory. Thus, the best way to use *A Daily Companion* is whatever way helps you faithfully read each day's Scripture portion and devotional thought.

The following guidelines may come in handy as you use *A Daily Companion*. Each page matches a reading in *Utmost* and displays the same title and date. First, the **BACKGROUND** introduces the topic that Oswald Chambers covers on that day and sets the scene to prepare you for what he will say. Along with the Background, there are occasionally cross-references (indicated by month and day, not by page number) to other parts of *A Daily Companion,* and there is always a short summary of the devotional set off from the text just below the title. These pithy summaries were the first piece of the *Daily Companion* that we wrote. For several years before we wrote the rest of the study guide, these summaries proved helpful keys to Chambers' teaching.

After the Background, the **SCRIPTURAL CONTEXT** section points you to the Bible and helps you learn the context of the verse or verses that Chambers quotes. As you already know, or will soon see, the structure of every reading in *Utmost* begins with the title and date, followed by a Scripture quote, followed by a devotional. Each Scripture quote is extremely short, and to fully grasp the meaning of the devotional it is essential that you know the context. If you have the whole Bible memorized, you can read the short quote and be on your way! If not, you will want to have three books (or reading devices) in front of you: the Bible, a copy of *Utmost*, and *A Daily Companion*.

Once you have found the context verses, you are ready to dive into the devotional. The section labeled **WHAT'S THE DEVOTIONAL SAYING?** is designed to help you explore the meaning of the devotional. There are questions to ask yourself about parts of the devotional that you might easily miss. Combined with the summary, this section will allow you to tighten your grip on the essence of each daily reading.

Finally, in the **APPLICATION** section *A Daily Companion* will help you apply what you have learned to your current situation. One of Oswald Chambers' recurring themes is that we cannot learn anything new from God until we apply what He has already taught us (see, for example, the *Utmost* devotion on March 27). The Application section, then, is most important. Here is where you have space to write down a few notes to yourself about what you need to change in your life (if you like to write a lot, you may want to add a fourth book to your pile—a journal—or get the journaling version of *Utmost*). This section is also where you will be encouraged to finish a prayer that we have started for you about what you learned and what you plan to change. A devotional book will discourage you if you try to apply what it says by your own power. But when God's power is let loose in your life by prayer, there is no telling what good things will happen!

Each of Oswald Chambers' devotionals, as edited and presented by his wife, Biddy, is like an exquisite entrée or a rich dessert. Your spiritual taste buds thrill as you read it. To enjoy a full meal, however, you need the quoted Scripture *with* its full context. *A Daily Companion*, with its four place settings of Background, Scriptural Context, What's the Devotional Saying? and Application, will help you connect each devotional to its quoted Scripture and then to specific applications in your life. Even the most sensuous meal is meant not just to please our palette, but also to nourish us, giving us energy to be who God wants us to be. So also, the purpose of Chambers' masterpiece, *My Utmost for His Highest*, is to give us spiritual energy to be our best for God. *A Daily Companion* will help you better digest Chambers' teaching on the Scriptures and will better aid the Holy Spirit as He uses these Bible passages to make radical changes in your life.

LET US KEEP TO THE POINT

Has God sent you a crisis?
Give Him what He's asking for: your Utmost for His Highest!

BACKGROUND Wouldn't it have been amazing to listen to Mr. Chambers speak at the weekly Devotional Hour in the Bible Training College? From 1911 to 1915, Chambers taught in the Clapham district of south-central London. Biddy, Oswald Chambers' wife, said these devotionals "marked an epoch" in students' lives. Chambers' words transformed souls back then; how will they change your life today?

My Utmost for His Highest, the title Biddy chose, comes straight from today's devotional. Thus, it's absolutely crucial for us to grasp Chambers' point. A short summary of the main idea can be found, as always for this study guide, at the top of the page.

SCRIPTURAL CONTEXT Chambers based this reading on Philippians 1:20, which he took from James Moffatt's 1913 translation (see the Classic Edition of *Utmost*). Chambers usually quoted from the King James Version, so the differences between Moffatt ("that now as ever I may do honour to Christ in my own person by fearless courage") and the King James ("that with all boldness, as always, so now also Christ shall be magnified in my body") must be significant. Which version puts greater emphasis on *Paul's* responsibility to magnify Christ's glory? Read the full context of this quote (Philippi-ans 1:1–26 and 4:2–3). What crisis did God send to Paul? What crisis did He send to the Philippians?

WHAT'S THE DEVOTIONAL SAYING? The first part of the devotional tells us that we have a choice. We can either give our all to God (which is the point of today's message), or we can be ashamed. The choice can't be made merely by debating the pros and cons. It has to be made as an act of will, a commitment to give our all to God no matter what the cost. Chambers warns us that when we say we are worried about what it costs *others*, we are really thinking about *ourselves*. Don't be fooled!

In the end, what could giving your all to God cost you? Death? The second part of the devotional says that not even *that* ultimate cost deterred Paul. But how can mere mortals like us have that kind of courage?

Chambers explains that we gain courage when God sends us a crisis. When does He send it? Right as we are debating and reasoning ourselves out of whatever it is He wants us to do! Our God-given crisis is what compels us to finally cast off our comfortable-but-worldly state of affairs and to surrender to our bridegroom Jesus, no matter what the cost. Will you keep to this all-important point today?

APPLICATION
What is stopping you from being your utmost for His highest?
What crises are causing you to decide for or against God?
Finish this prayer: "Today, Lord, I will keep myself before you by . . ."

⟜ JANUARY 2 ⟞
WILL YOU GO OUT WITHOUT KNOWING?

When were you close to God?
If you still feel that closeness, you'll be winsome for God!

Charming

BACKGROUND When was the last time you did something for God that was "crazy"? Oswald Chambers' students at the Bible Training College were people preparing for a life of ministry at a small, recently opened school. Surely their parents asked them, "But what do you expect to *do* with the training you are getting?"

To prepare his students for these and other challenges, Chambers taught them to trust God even when all else was crashing down around them. It wasn't enough just to feel close to God in London. How would they fare near a brutal World War I battlefield? Today's summary at the top of the page reminds us that our strength in the trenches comes from clinging as closely to God there as we do in quieter moments. Circumstances may change, but *He* never does!

SCRIPTURAL CONTEXT Can you guess which Bible character in Hebrews 11 went out "not knowing where"? Are you surprised to see Barak, Samson, and Jephthah also mentioned, despite their many flaws? Even Abraham had just as many downs as ups in his spiritual journey. So what makes him an example we should follow? How was Abraham's going out similar to what Chambers' students did?

Chambers also quotes Luke 12:22. Read the context of this quote (verses 13–53). How would you feel reading this passage if you were in Chambers' college training to be a missionary? How do you feel about this passage in your current situation?

WHAT'S THE DEVOTIONAL SAYING? In the process of compiling *Utmost*, Biddy rearranged her husband's devotional talks into an order that made sense to her. Consequently, today's devotional follows fast on yesterday's heels; if we are going to live our utmost for God's highest, it will often mean we must go out without knowing. Chambers helps us "go out" in our daily lives by clearing the air of our biggest smokescreen—asking to know God's will.

We need not ask His will, because He never tells us (at least not when we use this smokescreen). Instead, He shows us that He is still the mysterious, miracle-working God we knew that time when we felt closest to Him. Chambers wants us to have the sublime charm that God loves to see in His children. This winsome quality comes from complete trust in Him—like Abraham had in his journey to Canaan and like Chambers demonstrated when he left for Egypt in 1915. Chambers was a man who practiced what he preached!

APPLICATION

What stops you from daily going out and placing your confidence in God?

How has God responded to your questions and worries about what He is going to do?

Finish this prayer: "God, I'm learning to go out, trusting you, in the area of . . ."

ᴏᴡᴡᴏ JANUARY 3 ᴏᴡᴡᴏ
CLOUDS AND DARKNESS

Do you think you know God?
He's utterly incomprehensible, but the Spirit reveals Him to us.

BACKGROUND Oswald Chambers experienced a four-year period of clouds and darkness starting when he was twenty-three years old. Though distressing, this darkness ushered in a spiritual renewal in his life, which began when he read Luke 11:13. This verse promises the good gift of the Holy Spirit, not because we deserve Him in our lives but because of Christ's righteousness credited to us. As Chambers put it, "I had to claim the gift from God on the authority of Jesus Christ."

In today's devotional, Chambers urges us not to assume we know God but to recognize that He is shrouded in mystery. Yet despite God's unfathomability, we can still know Him through the Word by the Holy Spirit, as the summary above reminds us.

SCRIPTURAL CONTEXT Psalm 97 gives us an amazing picture of God's power, righteousness, and justice. Based on this Psalm, how does C. S. Lewis' quote about Aslan in *The Lion, the Witch and the Wardrobe*—"He isn't safe. But he's good"— apply to God? How might this quote help you when you're experiencing clouds and darkness?

Now read Exodus 3. How would you feel if God said to you what He said to Moses in verse 5? Finally, read Luke 11:11–13. How could this passage help someone who, like Chambers did, struggles to experience true Christianity?

WHAT'S THE DEVOTIONAL SAYING?
Interestingly, Chambers begins this devotional by explaining that clouds and darkness are signs that we are baptized in the Spirit. So even though these dark times distress us, they give testimony to the Spirit's important work. His work is to throw off the casual, earthly reasons we follow Jesus, just as He did in John 6. People were following Jesus to see if He would make more earthly bread appear—ignoring that He himself was the true bread from heaven.

Chambers quotes John 6:63 to show us that after clouds and darkness, Jesus speaks words of spirit and life. Darkness is lifted from our hearts as we realize that *who* God is and *what* He will do (as we saw yesterday) will remain wonderfully impenetrable this side of heaven.
↳cannot be pierced

APPLICATION
How does knowing Jesus differ from knowing what He does?
In what ways have you, now or in the past, experienced clouds and darkness about who Jesus is?
Finish this prayer: "After meditating on your Word today, Lord Jesus, I better understand that . . ."

ᘉᘓ JANUARY 4 ᘓᘉ
WHY CAN I NOT FOLLOW YOU NOW?

Do you see a trial looming?
The real test will surprise you. Look to God before you leap!

➤

BACKGROUND Oswald Chambers freely admitted it when he had misunderstood God's voice. For example, he was sure, as sure as any of his "intuitions born in communion with God," that World War I would end by the close of 1916. On December 9 of that year he wrote that his error was "just another indication of how little we dare trust anything but our Lord himself."

Today's devotional advises humility when we sense that God wants us to do something. God's tests require not only "going out without knowing" (*Utmost*, January 2), but also waiting for God's timing. If we don't wait, we will be surprised by these tests, just as Peter was surprised by a test on the night he denied Jesus.

SCRIPTURAL CONTEXT What could be more tragic than a betrayal? Peter thought he understood what Christ was saying in John 13:38. He probably figured that since he had followed Christ when others turned away (as we read yesterday in John 6), he was sure to pass the test. Poor Peter! In many ways, his denial was more heartbreaking than Judas' betrayal of Christ. Peter wanted so badly to pass his test, but he didn't think to wait on God—even when Jesus asked him to do exactly that (Mark 14:34)!

WHAT'S THE DEVOTIONAL SAYING? Based on the number of copies in print, we've always known that *Utmost* connects with people as no other devotional book does. But now, thanks to the digital age, we can pinpoint the exact parts that people find most helpful. If you have *Utmost* on Kindle, you can turn on Popular Highlights and see that today's reading contains one of the most frequently highlighted lines in the whole book: "Never run before God's guidance. If there is the slightest doubt, then He is not guiding. Whenever there is doubt—don't." Think how many people would be spared broken hearts and disappointment if they were to follow these three sentences!

Chambers says there are two parts to every test: the decision to obey God (*Utmost*, January 1) and the wisdom to know when to act (today's topic). When we pass the first part of a test, our "natural devotion" to Jesus makes us want to leap forward to obey. But true devotion, which is supernatural, helps us wisely wait and pass the second part of the test.

Should we always wait before we obey? Not at all! If you think Chambers is saying that, you may have missed the last sentence of the second paragraph. The "providential will of God" is quite different from His moral will. If you are tested on a moral issue, obey at once!

resulting from divine interverl

APPLICATION
What is God providentially (through circumstances) calling you to do?
What could you wait to see before you take the next steps?
Finish this prayer: "In my natural devotion to you, Jesus, I've made rash decisions that . . ."

ᚙ JANUARY 5 ᚙ
THE LIFE OF POWER TO FOLLOW

We follow Christ, amazed.
We continue on, invaded by the Holy Spirit!

◄

BACKGROUND The "◄" symbol at the top of this page shows that this devotional continues yesterday's theme. Yesterday we learned that Peter had "natural devotion" for Christ but that this caused him to jump the gun.

When Oswald Chambers was in his twenties, he thought God was calling him to evangelize artists by being an artist himself. He didn't fail any tests by going down that road, but there was still a sense that in his heart he had gotten ahead of God's plan.

Thankfully, God uses the times when our hearts get ahead of Him to draw us closer. Indeed, our natural devotion for Jesus makes us take action; and as we move forward, God can cause us to stumble, thereby showing us that we are not yet held tightly in the Spirit's grip.

SCRIPTURAL CONTEXT Although the quoted text is again from John 13, today's message is equally based on Matthew 4:18–22 and John 21:15–19. After reading these two passages, how would you describe Peter's change between his two callings? What do John 13:36, 20:22, and Matthew 26:69–75 have to do with this change? How did Jesus move Peter from natural devotion to Holy Spirit invasion?

WHAT'S THE DEVOTIONAL SAYING?
The main point today is that God uses our failures to give us the Spirit's power, which often comes to us only *after* we fail. Additionally, Chambers points out the difference between why we first follow Jesus (because He amazes us) and why we keep following Him (because the Holy Spirit invades us). Invasion by the Spirit happens only when we get to the end of ourselves, and, if we are like Peter, that happens through our spectacular failures.

What do you think Chambers meant when he said, "There is no figure in front now saving the Lord Jesus Christ."? (The Updated Edition of *Utmost* renders this sentence, "Now no one is in front of Peter except the Lord Jesus Christ.") Certainly, Peter needed to get himself out of the way so he could properly follow Jesus. But he also needed to get his "figure" of Jesus out of the way. Is our "figure" of Jesus built more on our amazement of Him than on who He really is and on the Spirit He gives?

Chambers compares this attitude of trusting Christ alone to having a single navigation star. Nowadays it would be like having a GPS system with only one destination. Are you willing to set your coordinates on Jesus and on nothing or no one else?

APPLICATION
How can you move from an external devotion for Jesus to an internal martyrdom and yielding to Him?
How does it make you feel to know that you cannot accomplish this move yourself?
Finish this prayer: "Holy Spirit, I'll come to the end of my self-sufficiency by . . ."

JANUARY 6
WORSHIP

Give God your best, or it will rot away.

BACKGROUND On Oswald Chambers' way to Egypt, the ship was so crowded with soldiers and supplies that his only quiet refuge was in a lifeboat. There he spent his mornings reading the Bible and talking to God.

Today we get Chambers' twofold definition of worship: giving back to God the gifts He gives, and daily spending quiet time with Him in the midst of the world. Chambers lived out both his definitions. Not only did he find a lifeboat where he could be alone with God, but he also gave back his spiritual gift of teaching—even to us a century later!

SCRIPTURAL CONTEXT What exactly does a person *do* as the father of God's people? Abraham, Isaac, and Jacob (and Noah, for that matter) filled their roles one altar at a time. Genesis 12:1–9 tells us about Abram's call and the first two altars he built to the Lord.

What does an altar have to do with Chambers' definition of worship? First, it's where you give up your prized possessions. Second, it

takes you away from the busyness of the world. Third, it forces you to think about what you will give up.

If you were an altar-builder, where would your worship begin? Would it begin when you gather the altar stones? When you work hard to multiply your flocks in hopes of finding a flawless lamb? For a lamb-finder like Abram, or for a lifeboat-finder like Chambers, worship never ends.

WHAT'S THE DEVOTIONAL SAYING? We've already seen Chambers' twofold definition of worship; now let's see his threefold warning. First, when we withhold our best, God makes it rot. Second, there are two extremes: rushing like the world (Ai), and resting as if there were no world (Bethel). Finally, uniting worship, waiting, and work in an unhurried but relentless way is difficult; and it requires discipline over the long haul. Are you willing to cultivate this kind of true worship?

APPLICATION

What are some of the blessings God has given you, and how have you given them back?

Why is your public activity for God dependent on your private communion with Him?

Finish this prayer: "God, when it comes to worship, waiting, and work, I've been learning . . ."

◦﹏◦ JANUARY 7 ◦﹏◦
INTIMATE WITH JESUS

The aim: intimacy with Jesus. Its fruit: calm balance.
Let Him satisfy your depths!

BACKGROUND Oswald and Biddy Chambers married in 1910, just before Oswald began the Bible Training College and the devotional sessions we read in *Utmost*. So when he talks about friendship in today's reading, he is speaking with the knowledge of his intimacy with Biddy.

Chambers' closeness to Biddy reflected his deep intimacy with Jesus. He spent his whole life striving to know his Savior, and his close relationships with others flowed out of this deep oneness (as it does for any true follower of Jesus!).

SCRIPTURAL CONTEXT How would you compare the disciples' fruit—before and after Pentecost? Before, they were able to "conquer demons and to bring about a revival." But after, they brought the gospel to the whole world! This greater fruit came from a deeper intimacy, which Jesus gave them when He departed and sent His Spirit.

Read as much of John 14–16 as you can right now, paying special attention to the verses Chambers quotes (John 14:9, 15:1–4, 15, and 16:7). Next, read Luke 10:18–20, which shows the fruit the disciples already had reaped before they were given even greater intimacy with Jesus.

WHAT'S THE DEVOTIONAL SAYING? Today's reading helps us better understand Jesus' tone in John 14:9. The same encouraging, gentle tone Jesus used with Philip extends to us two thousand years later. He wants us to be intimate with Him, identifying with Him in thought, heart, and spirit. He uses all of life's experiences, especially the discipline of difficult circumstances, to draw us closer to Him. As a result of this intimacy, we will "never draw attention to [ourselves] but will only show the evidence of a life where Jesus is completely in control." We all desire lives that point to Jesus and not ourselves, yet we are so tempted to do anything and everything that draws attention to ourselves. We need to let *Jesus* satisfy every area of life—down to our deepest, darkest depths.

APPLICATION

What makes true friendship so rare, and is this the same obstacle that prevents your intimacy with Jesus?

What is the purpose of the whole "experience" [or "discipline"—*Utmost* Classic Edition] of life?

Finish this prayer: "Jesus, I want to be satisfied by you in every area of my life, so today I will . . ."

JANUARY 8
IS MY SACRIFICE LIVING?

Give your talents to God. That is the best offering.

BACKGROUND Do you think Oswald Chambers should have stayed in London in 1915? He was having an amazing influence at the Bible Training College. Did he go against what he is saying in today's devotional by giving something up just to give it up?

Chamber's decision to close the college and move to Egypt wasn't easy. He needed to be sure that his desire to go wasn't just his own "restlessness." In the end, Chambers' decision to give up the college, far from contradicting today's devotional, lends him all the more authority. Out of his wrestling with God flows today's profound insight.

SCRIPTURAL CONTEXT Genesis 22:9 continues the altar-building theme, in which altars teach us about the all-encompassing enterprise of worship (see January 6, *Companion*). But this time we see Abraham building his final and most important altar. Here he shows his willingness to offer his son Isaac, and God mercifully intervenes to prevent him from doing so. Chambers uses this familiar Bible story to teach us an important lesson about how we ought to give things up to God.

WHAT'S THE DEVOTIONAL SAYING? A question to ask is this: "Why didn't Biddy put today's reading next to the one from January 6?" Perhaps this is the same order Chambers used when he gave his talks, but that still leaves us wondering how yesterday's lesson is connected to the two on either side. The key is Chambers' phrase, "life with Himself." As you read this phrase and its context, think about how our worship and the sacrifices we lay on the altar affect our intimacy with Jesus. What prevents you from drawing closer to Him? Yesterday we saw that all of life's experiences are designed to bring us closer to Him. Today we understand more clearly the nature of life's discipline: It's about the times we have to give up something.

Chambers further explains that we shouldn't give something up just to give it up but to gain closeness to Jesus. The very things that most hinder our closeness—our gifts, talents, and powers—are what God will use in His kingdom once we give them up to Him. God asks us to do what Jesus did when, in His death, He laid down His life, glory, and strength.

APPLICATION

What is the difference between a one-time death and the sacrifice of Romans 12:1?
Describe some of the "bands," as Chambers suggests, that are hindering your spiritual walk with Jesus.
Finish this prayer: "Father, the 'bands that hinder' in my life are loosened when I . . ."

᠀ JANUARY 9 ᠀
PRAYERFUL INNER-SEARCHING

God purifies rotten motives. He cleans our unknown sin!

BACKGROUND Oswald Chambers' four-year inner battle (1897–1901) was fueled by his recognition of his sinful hidden motives. Are your motives like bad apples—shiny on the outside but rotten to the core? If so, today's reading comes as a huge relief. For Chambers, the key to purifying our motives is, as he put it, the "mysterious work of the Holy Spirit." Once he accepted by faith that the Spirit was at work in him, his four-year battle was over; he had confidence that he was no longer condemned in God's sight for his less-than-perfect motives or for the sins that dulled his senses.

SCRIPTURAL CONTEXT Today Chambers paraphrases Psalm 139 for us. Read this psalm and compare it to Chambers' first paragraph. How does Psalm 139 make you feel? An alternate translation of verse 17 is, "How precious are your thoughts concerning me." Do you really think God obsesses over us like that—with more thoughts about us than there are grains of sand (verse 18)?

In addition to Psalm 139, Chambers quotes 1 Thessalonians 5:23 and 1 John 1:7. The latter says God cleanses all our sin, while the former reminds us that He cleanses our *whole* spirit:

both the conscious and unconscious parts. Based on the context verses (1 Thessalonians 5:12–28 and 1 John 1:5–2:2), what is the relationship between sanctification and walking in the light? How do these verses highlight for us God's role in our sanctification and cleansing?

WHAT'S THE DEVOTIONAL SAYING?
Chambers interprets Psalm 139 in the following way: When David says that he flees to heavens, depths, distant shores, and darkness, he means there are parts of a person's soul that are more hidden than any of those places. Yet God will find those hidden parts and "see if there is any offensive way" in them. Chambers takes comfort in the "massive truth" that God knows more about our hearts than we can ever know.

Our one responsibility in the cleansing process is to "walk in the light." Since not much is said in this devotional about how to do that, the Application section focuses on this requirement. If you are confused, remember how Chambers could finally obey God and walk in the light: He claimed God's gift of the Holy Spirit on Christ's authority, and he accepted by faith that the Spirit was at work in him.

APPLICATION
What is involved in walking in the light?
How are you tempted to step out of God's light?
Finish this prayer: "Lord, I want to stay open and honest in your presence by . . ."

JANUARY 10
THE OPENED SIGHT

Sanctification is giving Jesus your rights—
becoming one mind and heart with God.

BACKGROUND Oswald Chambers' final victory in his four-year inner battle was won at a League of Prayer meeting. There he claimed the gift of the Holy Spirit from the promise in Luke 11:13. Chambers later became a regular speaker at League events. Founded in 1891, the League prayed for three things: for the Holy Spirit to fill every Christian, for churches to be revived, and for scriptural holiness to spread. This emphasis on the Spirit's filling, church revival, and biblical sanctification forms a backdrop for what we will learn about today.

SCRIPTURAL CONTEXT Chambers focuses on just one verse today: Acts 26:18, which is the climax of Paul's speech to King Agrippa. As you read the whole chapter, notice Jesus' response to Paul in verses 15–18. How are these verses, especially verse 18, the climax and a transition from Paul's conversion story to the gospel presentation he gave Agrippa?

WHAT'S THE DEVOTIONAL SAYING? Do you think a believer can be sinless? What about blameless? During his four-year struggle, Chambers lamented the sinful condition of his heart. When he obtained victory, he wrote, "The power and the tyranny of sin is gone." His first love, Chrissie Brain, whose hand in marriage he felt that God asked him to release during this time, would later say that Chambers was "not faultless, but blameless."

In today's devotional, we read that the first step to blamelessness is opened eyes. Once our eyes are opened by a gospel presentation, we can receive salvation as a free gift from God. The second step (also God's gift) is sanctification. This is when saved people deliberately give Jesus their rights to themselves and are caught up in God's great plans for mankind. One reason *Utmost* is loved by so many is that it puts aside the controversial questions about whether a believer can be sinless and focuses us on sanctification: giving God *all* our rights.

APPLICATION
When (and why) have you failed in your "personal Christian life"?
What is the difference between conversion, salvation, and sanctification?
Finish this prayer: "Father, I know I'm born again because . . ."

JANUARY 11
WHAT MY OBEDIENCE TO GOD COSTS OTHER PEOPLE

Do friends suffer for you?
God will provide for them; you just focus on Him.

BACKGROUND Until Oswald Chambers married, he never had a steady income. His hand-to-mouth lifestyle meant many others also suffered financially. For example, when Chambers' father asked him for "money help" (money sent home to help the family), he replied, "What is money help compared to the eternal assistance I am enabled to give here to souls. In heaven, you will thank God for the life so few of you deem more than foolishness."

Chambers resisted the temptation to alleviate his family's financial hardships, since doing so would take his focus away from God. And in the end, God richly provided for all those who suffered from what others thought was merely Chambers' "foolishness."

SCRIPTURAL CONTEXT In Chambers' response to his father, he also pointed to Mary Magdalene's "waste" of pure spikenard (Mark 14:5). Today he highlights two other examples: Simon of Cyrene (Luke 23:26) and the women who supported Jesus' ministry (Luke 8:2–3). Read these passages and also Mark 15:21, which adds the fact that Simon was the father of Rufus, possibly a friend of Paul (Romans 16:13). Which of the three examples—Mary, Simon, and the women—obeyed in a way that cost others? Which ones suffered because of Jesus' obedience? Were all those who suffered believers? What happened to them in the end? Who else suffered because of Jesus? (See John 7:5 and Mark 3:21, 6:3, and 3:31.)

WHAT'S THE DEVOTIONAL SAYING? When we follow God, others will suffer, and that is how God intends it to be. Chambers also gives two related issues that are slightly less clear. First, people ridicule Christianity because we make our friends suffer. Second, we are tempted to stop following God, not just to prevent our friend from suffering but also because we are prideful and don't like being dependent on anyone. The reason these two issues are difficult is because the former seems counter-productive to God's plan, while the latter addresses our hidden motives, which are never crystal clear. It's important that we meditate on these more difficult issues so we are not derailed from following God when we hear the ridicule or when we are tempted to be "Lone Ranger" Christians.

APPLICATION
What happened the last time somebody's plans were upset because you followed God?
How did God take care of that person's suffering?
Finish this prayer: "By following you right now, God, it seems I will hurt . . ."

⚬⚬⚬ JANUARY 12 ⚬⚬⚬
HAVE YOU EVER BEEN ALONE WITH GOD?

Have you been embarrassed?
In this, God reveals your heart and molds it to His purpose.

➢

BACKGROUND During Oswald Chambers' four-year inner battle, God used the embarrassing incident of a false accusation to reveal to Chambers the deep, hidden nooks and crannies of his character. Only after this incident—with the dark depths of his soul that it revealed—could he know to his core his complete unworthiness. Today's devotional speaks about truths he may have gleaned during this dark time.

SCRIPTURAL CONTEXT In Mark 4:1–34, we see Jesus' parables and the disciples' responses. Tomorrow we will see Jesus' solitude and the disciples' questions (verses 10–13), but today Chambers focuses on the solitude of the disciples and the way Jesus taught them (verses 33–34). Jesus' teaching had three unique features. First, He taught only as much as His audience could understand (verse 33). Second, He used parables for the crowds but taught even deeper truths to His disciples (verse 34). Third—and this is the connection to tomorrow's devotional—Jesus made sure His students were alone (verse 34).

WHAT'S THE DEVOTIONAL SAYING? Chambers takes each of these three characteristics of Jesus' teaching and draws parallels to our lives. First, Jesus teaches us only what we are ready to obey. This is a theme that we will see over and over in *Utmost*: We get our second lesson only after we obey the first.

Second, Jesus still tells parables; but now He tells them through the lives of people around us. He also expects His disciples to understand the meaning of these life-parables; namely, He wants us to deeply examine and know ("spell out" is how Chambers phrased it) our own souls. This is difficult because we think we already know our souls. How wrong we are! We don't fully know our souls until we get to the point where we wouldn't dream to say that we are unworthy because it's so blatantly obvious to us.

Third, He gets us alone through the heartbreak and disappointment of embarrassment and wounded pride. Have you felt that recently? We hear pastors, teachers, and friends telling us that there are hidden sins in our lives. But until God "gets us alone over them" through heartache and pain, their words are only like classroom lectures and have no effect.

APPLICATION

What have you learned from God about all the nooks and crannies of your life?

What has upset or embarrassed you lately, and how has God used these experiences to teach you?

Finish this prayer: "God, you're dealing with me over the issue of . . ."

JANUARY 13
HAVE YOU EVER BEEN ALONE WITH GOD?

If wants are thwarted, rejoice!
Closed doors show us who we are and soften stubborn souls.

◄

BACKGROUND For more than seven years, Oswald Chambers probably thought he would marry his dear friend Chrissie Brain. Then, at the age of twenty-five, he broke off communication with her. It would be almost nine more years before he would fall in love with Gertrude "Biddy" Hobbs. His broken friendship with Chrissie contributed to his four-year period of darkness when God cornered him and made him absolutely alone. The pain of this loss revealed Christ—a recurring theme that we see in today's devotional.

SCRIPTURAL CONTEXT Today's reading is from a two-day set that began yesterday. Besides the continuing theme about how Jesus teaches us away from the crowds, there is the secondary point about asking Jesus too many questions. In Mark 4:10 we see the disciples asking Jesus about each of His parables. Then in 4:13 Jesus asks them how they expect to understand each of His parables if they can't even catch the meaning of His simplest one: the parable of the sower. In other words, the disciples shouldn't have been asking about the other parables until they mastered the easiest

one. Thankfully, as Chambers points out, the Holy Spirit later taught them *all* things, reminding them of *everything* Jesus said (John 14:26).

WHAT'S THE DEVOTIONAL SAYING? In Chambers' mind, parables nowadays are the real-life stories from other people and (especially) from our own lives. When Jesus causes something to happen to us or to someone we know, He is teaching us through parables. We often don't understand what He's saying, and we ask Him a flurry of questions. But when He goes on to thwart our plans and send us heartbreak, we get "alone" with Him and stop asking questions. He then explains some of the parables—the ones that deal with the softening of our own stubborn souls (the parables about other people's struggles remain mysteries to us).

Sometimes Jesus does explain parables to us while we are still asking questions, as He did with the disciples. But like them, we won't understand the meaning until much later, when the Holy Spirit reminds us and teaches us. If you are puzzling over the strange parables God is creating with your life, quiet your noisy intellectual questions and get alone with Him!

APPLICATION

What has God taught you through negative circumstances?

How does God deal with your soul?

Finish this prayer: "Jesus, I am stubborn and ignorant, but you can quiet my questions about . . ."

CALLED BY GOD

If we see God face-to-face, we'll gladly say,
"Send me!" He never begs us to say it.

BACKGROUND Oswald Chambers' first major evangelistic calling was to fellow artists. But this never materialized the way he had hoped (see January 5, *Companion*). His last major calling was to Egypt, and there was a point at which God "indicated" to Chambers that he should go (see January 8, *Companion*). This calling was realized when Chambers went there—becoming his final calling on earth.

SCRIPTURAL CONTEXT Isaiah 6 is an amazing chapter. Here we read about how the prophet Isaiah was called to his ministry. As Jerry Bridges discusses in *The Transforming Power of the Gospel*, this passage contains the progression from guilt (verse 5) to gospel (verse 7) to gratitude (verse 8). Our gratitude about the good news of God's forgiveness is what opens our ears to hear God's call.

WHAT'S THE DEVOTIONAL SAYING? Chambers dispels the notion that God forces His call on us. Nowadays, people don't have a firm grasp on "God's call." (Someone might ask, "Are we talking about a *phone* call, or what?") But back in Chambers' day, if people did something out of the ordinary—and they did it because they were Christians—they would likely say that they had heard "God's call."

Although some people may have abused this concept of calling, it helped Christians consider the possibility that God could call them to a radically different life trajectory. In today's reading, Chambers doesn't fault people for attributing their new trajectory to God's voice. He merely encourages them not to wait for God to call them individually, forcefully, or pleadingly, since the examples in Isaiah 6 and Matthew 4:18–22 are the opposite; the call is global, gentle, and open-ended. We have total freedom to say "no," though it would rob us of the ultimate joyful adventure!

APPLICATION

In what ways might you be expecting God to *compel* you to follow Him?

How do you think God might enable you to prove yourself a chosen one (Matthew 22:14)?

Finish this prayer: "Father, my attitude right now about 'going' is . . ."

༄ JANUARY 15 ༄
DO YOU WALK IN WHITE?

No need to strive. Just die to your old life—what can stop you then?

BACKGROUND Oswald Chambers loved poetry, and until the end of his four years of darkness he often composed a dozen or more poems a year. He also extensively quoted poetry in his devotional talks. Today he quotes a memorable part of Tennyson's poem to Queen Victoria on the occasion of her daughter's wedding. Describing the wedding as a "white funeral" was shocking to the queen—and shocking to us, as we think of our need to die to our old way of living.

SCRIPTURAL CONTEXT Are you refusing to think seriously about your Christianity, or do you *really* want to live a sanctified, holy life? That's Chambers' message today and also Paul's point in Romans 6. As you read that chapter, imagine a church full of Roman Christians who were in many ways identical to their non-Christian neighbors. They still fed their lusts, made money in less-than-honest ways, and justified their actions with pious Christian lingo about how their sins made God's grace increase. Paul's words in 1 Thessalonians 4 show that lust and dishonest gain were problems in the whole Roman Empire. And they are obviously still problems today!

WHAT'S THE DEVOTIONAL SAYING? Chambers is telling us bluntly that our Christianity is nothing unless it's born out of death—the death of our old lives. He challenges us to make today the day we give our lives over to death. As Chambers puts it, "Death means you stop being." What kind of Christian are you "being"? A striving one? An earnestly intense one? If you have truly understood God's unstoppable will—His desire to give you the gift of His Holy Spirit—you will not intensely strive. You will enter into sanctification as naturally as can be. You will be the consecrated life that God wants you to be. Nothing and no one will be able to topple you. All that could ever be defeated has already died!

APPLICATION

If you've had a "white funeral" experience, why was it necessary? (If not, what is holding you back?)

Has God placed you in circumstances that keep you from striving? How?

Finish this prayer: "Lord, I'm ready, by Christ's authorization, to accept your gift of the Spirit, even if those closest to me see my . . ."

JANUARY 16
THE VOICE OF THE NATURE OF GOD

Crisis tunes our heart to God and to His plan for us.

➤

BACKGROUND Today's devotional picks up on the theme "Called by God" from two days ago. It's as if Oswald Chambers started speaking about God's call to his students and then realized they had not yet experienced their "white funeral." So he challenged them to stop playing the Christian game and to accept God's gift of the Holy Spirit—no matter what might happen next.

At his own "white funeral" in 1901, Chambers thought God would expose his sin to those who knew him best. Initially, he "was not willing to be a fool for Christ's sake." Thankfully, his utter despair finally got him to say, "I did not care whether everyone knew how bad I was, I cared for nothing on earth, saving to get out of my present condition."

SCRIPTURAL CONTEXT Are you so sick of the fake parts of your Christian life that you don't care what people find out about you? Can you say with Isaiah, "Woe is me, for I am undone! Because I am a man of unclean lips" (6:5)? The crisis Isaiah faced is what we all must face if we will see God and hear His call. Read Isaiah 6. What uncleanness keeps *you* from hearing God's call?

WHAT'S THE DEVOTIONAL SAYING? Ernest Shackleton, the polar explorer, was born a few months before Chambers and died just a few years after him. Shackleton received a calling from what Chambers refers to (in the Classic Edition) as "the great ice barriers." Something deep within Shackleton made him respond to Antarctica's call, despite his repeated brushes with icy death. The same could be said for those few who hear the call of the world's tallest mountains or roughest seas. When you imagine being called by nature in these exotic ways, does it help you think about God's calling? Or is God's calling an equally foreign concept for you?

In today's devotional, Chambers warns against thinking about your own inclinations when trying to hear God's call. The only thing that helps us hear God's call is a closer relationship with God, and that happens when we hit a crisis, as Isaiah did and as Chambers did in 1901. Are the voices in your mind all about yourself? Or are you feeling a crisis that has begun to tune your heart to what God wants you to do?

APPLICATION

How do we hear the call of God?

What strand or thread of God's call is He weaving in you right now?

Finish this prayer: "One thing that I need to change in order to better hear your call, God, is . . ."

JANUARY 17
THE CALL OF THE NATURAL LIFE

God's call resonates in lives tuned to His nature, each with its own unique tone.

BACKGROUND At eight years old, Oswald Chambers began studies at Sharp's Institution (now Perth Academy) in Scotland. His artistic talent was soon noticed by his teachers, and art became his focus for the next fourteen years. Although he abandoned a career in art when he was twenty-two, on his forty-third (and final) birthday he wrote that his old delight in art had come "back in a glorious edition deluxe . . . which is truly the receiving of a hundredfold more."

Do you have a passion for something? Have you had to abandon it? Chambers would say that this is because our calling is not to a particular goal but to a personal God. And this God has promised to give back a hundredfold whatever you've had to give up.

SCRIPTURAL CONTEXT Paul's goal was to preach the gospel to Gentiles. But he makes it clear in Galatians 1 that God called him to Jesus, not to this goal. Read this chapter and describe what motivated Paul's various goals before and after he met Christ.

WHAT'S THE DEVOTIONAL SAYING? For the third time in four days, Chambers addresses the topic of God's call. He wants to make it amply clear that God's call is only about God, not about us.

So what is about us? What makes my Christian life different from yours? Today Chambers tells us that our *service* is what is particular to us. He explains that God's calling doesn't tell us which service we must do. Our particular type of service can change from day to day and from year to year, as circumstances change. But it will always be motivated by a close love for God and not the result of following some mystical calling.

APPLICATION

When did you first realize what you desire to do for God?

How is He preparing you to serve Him in the future?

Finish this prayer: "Lord, my desires are resonating now with your heart for . . ."

ᓕᔑᔧ JANUARY 18 ᓕᔑᔧ
"IT IS THE LORD!"

Want to be satisfied?
Here's what Jesus wants: lives poured out to Him!

BACKGROUND In his early twenties, Oswald Chambers' goal was to serve God through art. But when his career opportunities were thwarted by what Chambers called "the repeated and pointed shutting of doors that seemed just opening," he gave up. As biographer David McCasland put it, "His aim had once been art for God. Now it was only God."

Today's devotional warns us of confusing our loyalty to God with our loyalty to our service for God. Service can be wonderful, such as evangelizing the artistic world. But if it takes us away from pouring out our lives to Jesus, it's a deadly trap.

SCRIPTURAL CONTEXT For such a short devotional, there are lots of verses for you to track down! Start with John 20. How does Thomas demonstrate uncompromising devotion to Jesus? Read the next chapter in John and find today's title, "It is the Lord!" Who said this? How did Peter show his devotion? Now flip back to chapter 4 and read how the woman at the well showed her devotion and was used by God in His battles. Finally, read Acts 1:6–9. How does being Jesus' witnesses ("witnesses unto me") differ from just being witnesses *about* Jesus?

WHAT'S THE DEVOTIONAL SAYING? The first part of today's reading urges us not to become lazy Christians—always taking in but never pouring back to God. In our world of mid-week Bible studies, podcasts, and Christian bookstores (and daily devotionals like this one!), Chambers' words are more needed than ever. And you? Are you feeding your faith or just *fattening* it?

In the second paragraph, Chambers warns us of the first trap we fall into as we pour ourselves out in Christian service. Oh, how easy it is to make service our false god! How will you avoid this today?

APPLICATION
In general,
  How can you be more devoted to God?
  How can you satisfy Jesus today?
Finish this prayer: "Lord, I want you to use me in your battles; so I will . . ."

VISION AND DARKNESS

Has God made it dark?
God quenches your lights so you'll see only His.

BACKGROUND The biography *Oswald Chambers: Abandoned to God* says that during his four years of darkness, Chambers was conscious of God speaking personally to him only three times. Have you ever been conscious of God's voice? Ordinary Christians might be glad to hear God speak three times in four years, but Chambers thought this number was small!

If you're an ordinary Christian, today's lesson is for you. It will give you the insight you need to wait during periods of God's silence. When you come through your darkness, you'll be ready to hear God speak.

SCRIPTURAL CONTEXT Comparing the Classic and Updated editions of *Utmost* is eye opening. If you read the Classic Edition, the Updated Edition will help you, for example, to know what *El-Shaddai* means (and where in the Bible it first appears). If you read the Updated Edition, the original language might surprise you. For example, today Chambers talks about the "Father-Mother God." What do you think he means? Perhaps he had in mind Deuteronomy 32:18, where the two parallel lines of Hebrew poetry alternately describe God creating His people in the male and female sense (in the ESV, "fathered" and "gave birth").

Can you find all the other biblical quotes and references for today? Don't forget Genesis 17:1 and Philippians 3:4!

WHAT'S THE DEVOTIONAL SAYING?

Out of his own times of darkness and from the wellspring of his scriptural knowledge, Chambers shares a profound insight today: God's silence is often the best discipline. No one enjoys being disciplined. As Hebrews 12:11 puts it, "Discipline always seems for the time to be a thing of pain, not of joy" (Moffatt). Thus, Chambers urges us not to pretend it is a joy. He also warns us against listening to "good advice" and putting your trust in books when you are going through a time of God's silence. All these interfere with the goal of God's discipline, which is to make you dependent only on Him.

Is your silent darkness the result of having the bright light of receiving God's vision? Or it is something else? A good question to ask yourself is this: "Has God given me a vision?" If not, you may need to get closer to God first. Your silence might be the silence of never having heard in the first place. But if you did receive His vision and now are in darkness, wait for God to finish disciplining you. Place your confidence in God alone, not in your own light.

APPLICATION

Describe a vision for your life that you feel God has given you.
How is God dealing with any self-sufficiency in your life?
Finish this prayer: "God, you are more real to me now than ever before because . . ."

JANUARY 20
ARE YOU FRESH FOR EVERYTHING?

Are you frantic?
Your busyness is a Band-Aid for the hurts that God wants to heal.

BACKGROUND How often do you have to polish your shoes? What about cleaning your boots or, worse yet, someone else's? In Oswald Chambers' day, with horse-drawn carriages and livestock clogging the streets, cleaning boots was a mucky, smelly job. It closely paralleled first-century foot washing. Just as Jesus asked His disciples to wash each other's grimy feet, so Chambers urged his students to be "fresh" to do even the most menial tasks. Chambers laid down only one house rule for his students at the college: "All service ranks the same with God. You are requested to kindly do your part in keeping this room tidy. If you do not, someone else will have to." But how do you think he wanted his students to keep their rooms tidy? With a bounce in their step? Or out of obligation?

SCRIPTURAL CONTEXT All the scriptural references today are from the apostle John. First, read John 3, paying special attention to Jesus' description of the wind and the Spirit (these two words are identical in Greek). Then read John 17:20–23 and 1 John 1:5–7. How do these verses describe a person "born of the Spirit"?

WHAT'S THE DEVOTIONAL SAYING? Today Chambers explains the difference between obedience and being born of the Holy Spirit. The Spirit gives us vitality and godly exuberance. Obedience "keeps us in the light," which is a theme in *Utmost* (see, for example, January 9, *Utmost*). Our problem is that we put the cart before the horse. We frantically look for ways to obey God (though we rarely look for boots to clean!). But we don't first look to God for the Spirit. As a result, we get stale, and we lack the vitality that the Spirit always brings.

In the second half of the devotional, Chambers warns that if we prop ourselves up with anything but God, it will ruin our oneness with Him. Oneness with God through the Spirit is far more than just having our sins forgiven and getting into heaven. Our Spirit-given oneness is the only way for us to be "fresh" each day. What are your props? What hurts are you trying to fix by staying busy? How will God heal you today?

APPLICATION

Are you feeling fresh or frantically searching for something to do? In what ways?

Is there an area of your life where you are not open to God? Is it where you are strong?

Finish this prayer: "Lord, I really want to open all of my life to you by . . ."

JANUARY 21
RECALL WHAT GOD REMEMBERS

Where's your love of God?
Admit your cold heart, and He'll make it new.

BACKGROUND In the devotional from three days ago, Oswald Chambers said we ought to be "satisfying" Jesus. He continues this theme by asking us today if our lives brighten God's heart. But how can anything in our lives bless God? God doesn't need us for anything!

Long before his own daughter was born, Chambers loved to romp on the floor with small children. The image of God romping around with us shows us how we can satisfy God and also gets at the heart of today's devotional.

SCRIPTURAL CONTEXT In each paragraph we find a key verse. First is John 4:7, which we also saw on January 18. Jeremiah 2:2 comes second. Chambers explains that these are God's words to His people. Read all of Jeremiah 2, paying special attention to verse 13. Third, we see 2 Corinthians 7:10, which talks about "godly sorrow." Read verses 8–13. What is the right response when we realize our wrong?

WHAT'S THE DEVOTIONAL SAYING The three verses Chambers quotes go along with three questions: First, are we "satisfying" Jesus and being kind to God? In other words, do we avoid complaining and live honorably? Second, do we remember when we were deeply in love with God? Jeremiah 2:2 tells us that God remembers and treasures this thought. Third, will we embrace the shame and humiliation of realizing that we don't love God as we used to love Him? The shame of having a cold heart can bring godly sorrow, which is the way God brings the repentance that saves us from ourselves.

Children romping with their dad have no thought for who respects them or for "man's wisdom." They don't become "wise over loving" their dad. They just love him and pour out constant, overflowing extravagant love. And for that, they bless their father, though he doesn't need anything they have to offer.

APPLICATION

What is one area where you are kind to God?

What are some things in your life that keep you from being extravagant in your love for God?

Finish this prayer: "Lord, I want to love you like I did before, but I've got mixed-up priorities, such as . . ."

JANURAY 22
AM I LOOKING TO GOD?

Is there some phantom Christian you want to be like?
Focus on God! He saves you for real.

➤

BACKGROUND Oswald Chambers' brother Arthur was thirteen years older than Oswald, and he was Clarence and Hannah's eldest child. At Oswald's memorial service in London on December 5, 1917, Arthur recalled what the thirty-three-year-old Oswald had said to him as he slapped down a half crown coin (which would be like our twenty-dollar bill). "I've been 'round the world, all-found, on no-pence a week, and have half-a-crown left."

That was Oswald's way of telling Arthur that by looking to God, not money, he "found" all that God wanted him to find, *and* God took care of his needs. Today's devotional warns us how God's blessings and what we long for (such as having money and becoming a "better" Christian) can take our focus from God.

SCRIPTURAL CONTEXT Isaiah 45 is a conversation, first between God and Cyrus, then between God and idolaters. What do the idolaters look at in order to find satisfaction? Are you one of them? In the Sermon on the Mount (Matthew 5–7), Jesus tells us to focus on God, not material things that have become our idols. Read 6:19–24. What is your treasure? Do you consider it God's blessing? Keep reading through verse 34. Are you worried about what you will do this summer or even tomorrow?

WHAT'S THE DEVOTIONAL SAYING? Besides urging us to look to God, not His blessings, Chambers also teaches us two other lessons. First, he emphasizes the *be* in "and *be* saved," reminding us that our salvation is in the present tense. It's not something we strive for in the future by constantly comparing ourselves to a "phantom" Christian (who doesn't even exist!). It's what we have as soon as we look to God and stop comparing ourselves to others.

Second, Chambers remarks that troubles, more than blessings, make us look to God. We can't expect God to save us (not just from our sin, but also from our myriad of daily problems) by sending us blessings. The only way He saves us is when we look to Him. Are you looking to Him today?

APPLICATION

Are you looking for things you want from God, or are you looking to God himself? How?

What problems, blessings, or expectations keep you from focusing on God?

Finish this prayer: "Lord, the things I want to thank you for and give back to you are . . ."

JANUARY 23
TRANSFORMED BY BEHOLDING

Are you doing what's best or only what's good?
Mere good dulls Christ's glory.

‹

BACKGROUND Yesterday we saw that blessings can be traps that keep us from looking to God. Today we will see how blessings can keep us not only from looking to God but also from reflecting His glory. We need to reflect God's glory so others can also look to Him.

SCRIPTURAL CONTEXT The main verse for today is from 2 Corinthians 3. Read the context (7–18) noticing the words *glory, veil,* and *Spirit.* Who removes the veil? Who transforms us? Does He give us glory or is His *work* glorious? Now flip to Colossians 3 and read 1–17. What does a life hidden with Christ look like? How might this life be a "mirror for others"?

WHAT'S THE DEVOTIONAL SAYING? How does today's devotional differ from yesterday's? We learned yesterday that our twofold temptation is the following: (1) to look at our blessings and (2) to look at a mental picture of what we think a "good" Christian ought to be. We also learned that the reward of looking to God is immediate freedom from worry. Today our warning is against hurry and busyness, and our reward is a life that reflects God's glory and that points people to Him.

How about you? Are you setting aside work, clothes, food, and other things and focusing 100 percent on God? Only the Spirit can transform us so we can focus on God.

APPLICATION

What good thing is hindering you from the very best that God has for you?

How can you better learn the discipline of keeping your focus "above"?

Finish this prayer: "Today, Lord, I will make an effort to wait for your best by . . ."

JANUARY 24
GOD'S OVERPOWERING PURPOSE

Are you addicted to Jesus?
Don't just know about Him. Desire Jesus himself.

BACKGROUND Malcolm Gladwell's 2010 article in *The New Yorker* ("Small Change: Why the Revolution Will Not Be Tweeted") says that social media is incapable of bringing about big changes because it does not foster deep personal relationships. Oswald Chambers shared a similar insight one hundred years earlier. He said that nothing except a "personal relationship" with Jesus matters. No noble cause will give us the endurance to hold on tightly to our visions, dreams, and goals. Chambers understood this truth and thus sought a deeper personal relationship with Jesus above all else.

SCRIPTURAL CONTEXT Chambers quotes Acts 26:16 and 19, verses that straddle Paul's climactic verse 18, which was our theme on January 10. These two verses mention the vision God gave Paul. Do you have a vision for your life? As you may have done two weeks ago, read all of chapter 26. What do you notice about how Paul responded to the vision he received? How is he responding to it even as he speaks to King Agrippa?

Chambers also quotes from John 15 and 1 Corinthians 2. Who chooses our vision for us? What is the essence of our vision? Read the end of Acts 26:16 again. Jesus asked Paul to appear on the witness stand, as it were. Of *what* was Paul a witness?

WHAT'S THE DEVOTIONAL SAYING? The message today is as follows: God's overpowering purpose is to subdue us by an overpowering relationship with Jesus. From that relationship flow all our other purposes, aims, goals, and visions. And *only* through that relationship will we have the power to accomplish our vision.

What are you hoping might happen to your life today, tomorrow, or this year? Do you think any of those things are visions from God? Do you believe they can be accomplished? Even though we are only twenty-four days into *Utmost*, Chambers might already sound like a broken record. But have you mastered what he is teaching us? Are you willing to live for nothing but Christ and be "addicted" to Him alone? Are you willing to *be* absolutely Christ's?

APPLICATION
Are you ready to be overpowered by God? How do you know?
Right now what are your ends, your aims, and your purposes?
Finish this prayer: "Lord, I want to deepen my relationship with you today by . . ."

༄ JANUARY 25 ༄
LEAVE ROOM FOR GOD

Do you put God in a box?
God shatters our notions and gives us perfect gifts.

BACKGROUND Oswald Chambers took a round-the-world tour that had a stopover in the United States. There he taught at God's Bible School in Cincinnati for six months and participated in the school's Christmas Convention. He wrote later about the convention: "Many were the signs of God's mighty presence—the full altars, the spontaneous freedom, and the prominent place the Bible received, but perhaps the most significant sign to some of us was the opening of God's truth to us and the ability granted us by the Holy Spirit to understand and grip the Lord's vital truth." Chambers appreciated balance between "spontaneous freedom" and "vital truth." In today's devotional, he urges us to expect unexpected leadings of the Holy Spirit.

SCRIPTURAL CONTEXT Why did Jesus wait so long to appear to Paul? If Jesus had revealed himself to Paul in a blinding light just a day or two before Stephen was stoned to death, wouldn't countless Christian lives have been spared? Read Galatians 1 and decide what you think about God's timing. We may never know *why* God does what He does when He does it, but we know for sure that He has perfect timing.

WHAT'S THE DEVOTIONAL SAYING? The main point of today's lesson is clear and simple. Chambers says that we should make space in our daily routine for God to do whatever he wants to do. (He's especially talking to Christian workers, but it's applicable to all of us.) Easier said than done! We spin so many plates—and pile so much on each one. With all that we do, it's no wonder we don't notice when God does something. What a shame! God is waiting to help us "understand and grip" His vital truth, and we are not even looking.

Perhaps it's time right now to make space for God in whatever things you have left to do today, including finishing today's devotional! Has your quest for insight from *Utmost* become a chore? Remember, it's not your *quiet time with God* that's important but God who is important. He is your Abba, the Father of lights, who will give you the perfect gift today.

APPLICATION

Describe a time when you prayed—expecting God to answer in a certain way.

How did He (or did He not) answer in the way you expected?

Finish this prayer: "God, because you see the bigger picture, I can let go of . . ."

JANUARY 26
LOOK AGAIN AND CONSECRATE

God handles everything. Our only job is to live the simple life of the Spirit.

➤

BACKGROUND Four days ago, Oswald Chambers taught us about looking to God. He continued the next day with a lesson about how, by looking to God, we reflect His glory. Today and tomorrow we find "Look Again" in the title, but this time Chambers is asking us to look at creation—not to become nature-worshipers but to gain wisdom.

Chambers, always an artist at heart, loved the outdoors. His journals are full of sublime descriptions of sunrises, mountains, billowing waves, and even the wildlife he encountered on his travels. Thus, today's insights flow from his careful attention to the birds of the air and the lilies of the field.

SCRIPTURAL CONTEXT Today and tomorrow we are treated to Chambers' commentary on Matthew 6:25–34. Read these verses and imagine being a bird or a lily. What would be your daily routine? Now turn to Matthew 13 and read the parable of the sower. How would it feel being a plant choked by thorny weeds?

WHAT'S THE DEVOTIONAL SAYING? The first paragraph tells us that we need to live a simple life by relying on God for everything. In the second paragraph, we gain wisdom from birds: We need to follow the Spirit in us, just as birds follow the instincts in them. The final paragraph makes two points. First, we must be like lilies and stay where God puts us. It's difficult to do, especially when we feel gifted for far "better" things. Second, we must be consecrated, which means cutting out of our lives everything but what God wants us to do.

Are you asking God questions about what you should be doing? Perhaps that's better than not caring about His will at all! But we must guard against asking for His will just to get out of doing what He has already told us to do. Once we realize that when we bloom where He plants us we are more beautiful than Easter lilies in God's eyes, we will cease worrying about the material things that matter so little.

APPLICATION

When was the last time you lost fellowship with Jesus because of earthly cares?

What makes it difficult to be simple and trust God for provision?

Finish this prayer: "Today, Lord, I'll keep my feathers from being ruffled by . . ."

JANUARY 27
LOOK AGAIN AND THINK

Do your worries crowd out Jesus?
Let his rich provision entice you to trust in Him.

◄

BACKGROUND After nearly two decades of wandering Great Britain and the world, Oswald Chambers married Biddy Hobbs and suddenly found himself charged with the weighty responsibilities of being a husband. Three years later, to the day, he and Biddy found themselves blessed with the new and exciting responsibility of parenting a daughter. How could Chambers, the man who had lived on "no-pence a week" (see January 22, *Companion*), not worry?

The answer to that question, and the key to today's devotional, was that God had richly blessed Chambers all his life. It was no struggle, then, for Chambers to trust Him with each new phase of life.

SCRIPTURAL CONTEXT We return to the same two chapters in Matthew that we saw yesterday. As you reread these familiar verses, what stands out to you in a fresh way? What does Chambers emphasize today compared to yesterday? Which phrase does he repeat again, and why is it so important?

WHAT'S THE DEVOTIONAL SAYING? Today's devotional, like yesterday's, is a pithy commentary on the "do not worry" part of Jesus' Sermon on the Mount. Do you resonate with the first paragraph? Aren't there endless needs that tempt us to worry?

The second paragraph warns us, in typical Chambers' fashion, against common sense. What is your common sense telling you to be concerned about right now?

In the final paragraph, we see what we *should* be thinking about: "Look again and think." Can you spot what we need to keep our minds focused on?

APPLICATION

How does it make you feel to know that we are never free from the temptation to worry?

What causes you to worry? (Perhaps uncertain or overturned plans, money, friends, circumstances.)

Finish this prayer: "Jesus, the concerns that most compete with my relationship to you are . . ."

JANUARY 28
HOW COULD SOMEONE SO PERSECUTE JESUS!

Insisting on your rights grieves Jesus. Be one with Him instead.

➤

BACKGROUND "I can brush my teeth *myself*," yells a spunky three-year-old. This might save her parents time and effort, but how do her teeth feel about it? In the same way, we want to serve God the way *we* want to serve Him. But how does the Holy Spirit in us feel about our stubbornness?

In today's devotional, Oswald Chambers reminds us that when we try to serve God our own way, we grieve the Holy Spirit and persecute Jesus. Whenever we serve God by our own power, we end up relying on our own dignity and self-respect. This is a recipe for disaster, as Chambers so clearly explains.

SCRIPTURAL CONTEXT To understand today's lesson, think about the full context of Paul's life. He served God in his own way from his early youth until he was converted (perhaps in his late twenties). And his service to God after Stephen's stoning mainly involved threatening Christians with murder! So for Paul the link between serving God in one's own way and persecuting Jesus was very tight.

Another key to today's devotional is Matthew 11:25–30. Chambers quotes the familiar verse 29, but he also refers to the oneness between the Father and the Son that is discussed in verse 27. This oneness is what God "revealed to little children" like us, so that we could have the same oneness.

WHAT'S THE DEVOTIONAL SAYING? The two paragraphs today give different but complementary truths. First, Chambers tells us that when we serve God by our own power and do the things *we* think are best, we persecute Jesus. Second, self-driven service is a sham, especially when our service is teaching the Word.

So how can we serve and teach? Chambers says we need to have "perfect oneness" with God. However, this oneness is not for the faint of heart. When we are one with God, people will use us, ignore us, "over-reach" us, and take advantage of us.

Interestingly, all of these unpleasant results of our oneness give us a precious gift. Chambers recognized this benefit when he quoted a line from an 1863 poem by Henry Alford: "What thou hast not by suffering bought, presume thou not to teach." To teach the Word, we need to suffer. By relinquishing our rights and by tossing out our self-driven efforts to be a good boy or girl, we are sure to suffer at the hands of those around us. It's as if God tests us to see if we really have given up our self-will.

APPLICATION

Just how well does what you preach match what you do?

One way you're relying on self-respect is _____. As you trust in self-respect, how does this grieve the Spirit?

Finish this prayer: "How I long to prevent your persecution today, Jesus, by . . ."

HOW COULD SOMEONE BE SO IGNORANT!

Are you overconfident in serving God?
He'll humble you so you can serve with delight.

◄

BACKGROUND Yesterday we saw how serving God in our own way is the same as persecuting Jesus. Today we learn more about what is at the root of this persecution. Oswald Chambers says our *ignorance* underlies our insistence on serving God in our own overconfident way.

SCRIPTURAL CONTEXT When Jesus appeared to Saul, the two traded questions. Jesus' question for Saul was yesterday's theme, and today we see Saul's question to Jesus. The questions revealed, first, how Saul persecuted Jesus; and second, how he didn't know Jesus. Chambers says that these two things are *still* true about us Christians.

Chambers refers to four other parts of Scripture. First, he quotes Isaiah 8:11, sandwiched between "the virgin will be with child" and "unto us a child is born" chapters. Second, he quotes Luke 9:55, which, in the King James Bible Chambers used, has this additional phrase: "Ye know not what manner of spirit ye are of." Third, he mentions 1 Corinthians 13, the "love chapter." Finally, he quotes Psalm 40:8, which Hebrews 10 reveals to be Jesus' words.

As you read these four passages, think about how each relates to today's lesson. What was Isaiah tempted to follow? How did James and John (the "sons of thunder") want to serve

God? What from the "love chapter" is missing in you and in the Christians you know? What exactly was God's will that Jesus delighted to do? (See Hebrews 10:9.)

WHAT'S THE DEVOTIONAL SAYING?
What does Chambers mean by *ignorance*? Does he mean that we lack information? Is that why we want to serve God in our own way? While Chambers hated "intellectual slovenliness, disguised by a seemingly true regard for the spiritual interests," in today's devotional he's not speaking against mental sloth. The target of his criticism might be highly trained Christian workers who have labored intellectually to build up their "own convictions." The problem is that these convictions are their own, not God's. Chambers says that God destroys our trust in our convictions by putting our mind "under arrest," as it were, using carefully engineered circumstances. God is the master at showing us how little we actually know!

What are your circumstances right now? Are you letting God speak through them about your absolute cluelessness? Have you been overconfident that you're serving God (merely because you're doing something unpleasant)? Do people see 1 Corinthians 13 in you? Decide today to lose your ignorance!

APPLICATION
Is there some way in which you are hurting Jesus? How so?
What is God saying to you through your circumstances?
Finish this prayer: "Lord, my greatest aim is . . ."

JANUARY 30
THE DILEMMA OF OBEDIENCE

Circumstances are warning lights. Their flashing sends us to the Great Mechanic.

BACKGROUND The phrase "amateur providences" is a recurring theme in *Utmost*. We first saw this concept on January 1. There Oswald Chambers warned us not to worry about how giving our all to God affects others. He told us that this worry is just a smokescreen we use to avoid giving God our all. Today (and also in March, August, and November), Chambers warns us against this smokescreen and against shielding our loved ones from God's words, which is how we fail the test of obedience.

SCRIPTURAL CONTEXT Although today's devotional features young Samuel, Chambers also brings in four other verses to make his points. First, he quotes Isaiah 8:11 again (see January 29, *Companion*) to show that God speaks through circumstances. Second, he gives us his "life verse" (Luke 11:13) and a related one (1 Thessalonians 5:23) as examples of what we can call to mind when hearing God's voice in our circumstances. Third, he quotes from Matthew 5 to warn us not to let the pain that comes from obeying God's truths deter us from sharing those truths with others. Finally, he cites the example of Galatians 1:16, where Paul avoided getting earthly advice for something that he really needed to figure out from God alone.

WHAT'S THE DEVOTIONAL SAYING? Today Chambers gives us a four-part lesson. First, God speaks to us in every circumstance. "Nothing touches our lives but it is God Himself speaking," is how the Classic Edition puts it. Second, we must cultivate the habit of listening to God's voice in everything that happens to us, especially in times of "chastening." Third, Chambers reminds us that listening to God is dangerous: It may cause hurt to the best people we know. The decision to tell others about what God has shown you, no matter how it hurts them, is the "Dilemma of Obedience." Finally, Chambers warns against the temptation to seek other people's advice when we face the "dilemma," since God wants us to make this decision alone.

If we didn't already know Chambers and then came across today's reading, we might think he was the leader of an insidious cult. It's as if he wants to cut us off from friends and make us soothsayers of God's will, who read the tea leaves of circumstances. But Chambers wants us to avoid friends' *advice* only when God wants us to make the decision alone. Also, we aren't told to use circumstances to find God's will for our careers, spouses, and so forth. The role of circumstances is to drive us to listen to God to learn where we are not yet close to Him.

APPLICATION

Why doesn't God make himself perfectly clear when He speaks?

Have you sought human advice or prevented suffering? Did God want you to?

Finish this prayer: "Through my circumstances, God, I'm hearing you say . . ."

JANUARY 31
DO YOU SEE YOUR CALLING?

Will you get dirty for God in humanity's filth?
Christ did by becoming a servant.

➤

BACKGROUND It has become vogue in Christian circles to write books and preach sermons about how everything in life must hinge on the gospel. This is an excellent trend, but it's good to remember that many, including Oswald Chambers, have been down this road before. Not only did Chambers preach on this topic, as we read today, but he also lived a life that matched this kind of preaching. Indeed, the last days of his forty-three years on earth were spent pouring out his life and sharing the gospel to World War I soldiers on their way to bloody Middle Eastern battlefields.

SCRIPTURAL CONTEXT Today's main verse is from Paul's greeting to the Roman church. Right from the first sentence of his letter, Paul made it clear that his most vital need—what he was set apart to spread around the world—was the gospel of God. One week ago, on January 25, we saw how Chambers used Paul's words in Galatians 1:15 to emphasize God's prerogative and perfect timing as He shows up in our lives. Today Chambers uses the same verse to point out that it is not us but *God* who sets us apart for the gospel and sanctifies us. The third verse we see today is Romans 9:3,

where Paul says he would be willing to be cut off from Christ if it would help his people accept the gospel. For Paul to have this view of his life showed that the gospel had "begun to touch" him.

WHAT'S THE DEVOTIONAL SAYING? Chambers splits the lesson into two parts today. First, he stresses the gospel's priority over all else. Second, he warns us not to be so caught up in our own holiness that we avoid the "rugged reality of Redemption."

In putting the good news about God's redemption above personal holiness, Chambers neutralizes a danger in groups like the League of Prayer that emphasized scriptural holiness (see January 10, *Companion*). It was the balance that he struck—between an intense struggle against sin and an unflinching conviction that God alone can change the human heart through the gospel—that gave Chambers a lasting impact on other people to this very day. This gave Chambers a lasting impact on other people, an impact that continues to this day. Do you strive for that same balance? Do you put the gospel first, while still fighting tooth and nail against sin?

APPLICATION
Have you gotten beyond concentrating on your own goodness?
How do you feel about coming into contact with redemption and the filth of humanity?
Finish this prayer: "Today I'll begin my walk in reckless abandon to you, God, by . . ."

☙ FEBRUARY 1 ☙
THE CALL OF GOD

*Get the big picture of the gospel: God will deliver **all** things, not just you.*

◄ ►

BACKGROUND Oswald Chambers' biography *Abandoned to God* sheds light on the background to the readings in *Utmost*. And the reverse is also true. For example, today's reading gives insight into Chambers' four years of darkness that we can read about in *Abandoned to God*. Today we learn that Chambers considered his fixation on holiness during those four years as misguided. He would have urged his younger self just as he urges us in today's devotional: Don't constantly ask for deliverance from bad habits; focus instead on the reality of the gospel!

SCRIPTURAL CONTEXT The first part of today's lesson is a commentary on 1 Corinthians 1:17. In this verse, Paul contrasts his calling of preaching the gospel with another possible calling—baptizing. In the second part of today's lesson, Chambers refers to John 12:32 and extends Paul's contrast to other callings, such as the call to preach sanctification and salvation. How is the image of lifting up Jesus in John 3:14 and 8:28 (see Numbers 21:8) a good antidote for our temptation to lift up other things?

Often the *Utmost* readings imply a passage in the Bible without ever mentioning it by verse. Today we see Chambers referring to two such passages. The first is Romans 8:18–27 and the second is 2 Corinthians 4:8–10. Read these verses and find where they appear in the reading.

WHAT'S THE DEVOTIONAL SAYING? Today we continue with yesterday's theme of our calling (in other words, God's call), which is to preach the gospel and the gospel alone. Yesterday we saw the danger of worrying about our own holiness and how that can block us from getting dirty for God. Today we see the danger of preaching holiness and how it competes for the only thing we ought to be preaching: the good news of redemption.

Not only is it dangerous to preach holiness, but it is also dangerous to worry about our own holiness. This worry gets in the way of "devotion to the gospel of God." It's also unnecessary. As soon as we touch the "reality of the gospel of God," we will find that our "personal holiness is an effect" of redemption, not the cause of redemption (see January 31, *Companion*).

APPLICATION

What does it mean to "touch the underlying foundation of the reality of the gospel" (Updated Edition)?

What heartbreak have you experienced? How has it refocused you from self to God?

Finish this prayer: "Father, I want to begin lifting up Jesus Christ by . . ."

wed

THE COMPELLING FORCE OF THE CALL

God calls twice: salvation, then service. The second call breaks us until we heed.

BACKGROUND Today's devotional draws directly from Oswald Chambers' four years of darkness. The details of his struggle are instructive. In February 1897, Chambers gave up his artist's life in Edinburgh (see January 5, *Companion*) and began theological training in Dunoon, eighty miles to the west. At some point that year he heard a preacher speak about the Holy Spirit. Afterward, Chambers "asked God . . . for the baptism of the Holy Spirit." In 1901 at a prayer meeting (see January 10, *Companion*), Chambers realized that he "had been wanting power in [his] own hand . . . that [he] might say—'Look what I have by putting my all on the altar.' "

So when Chambers says in today's devotional that God's call induces a suffering "worthy of the name," he speaks from his own painful experience. And when he says that the gospel is more important than our own goodness and holiness (see February 1, *Companion*), he is recalling the lesson he learned: The Holy Spirit's power is not meant for our own hands or to improve our "whiteness."

SCRIPTURAL CONTEXT In his letters to Corinth, Paul reveals insights into his life. For example, today's theme verse tells us that Paul felt he had no choice but to preach the gospel. Perhaps Paul, like Chambers, experienced darkness and was shown that he had no choice but to preach. Chambers quotes Isaiah 45:22 and Romans 1:1 again (see January 22 and 31, *Utmost*) and also Luke 14:26. Read Luke 14:25–35. How is building a tower or going to war like God's call to service?

WHAT'S THE DEVOTIONAL SAYING?

Chambers teaches us that salvation is the easy part of a Christian's life. The hard part is being set apart unto the gospel. Would Chambers say that those called to preach the gospel have a higher status than those who are merely saved? Undoubtedly, Chambers would abhor that notion. We are *all* called to preach and are just at different places in our willingness to submit to God's call. Why was Moses a shepherd for forty years? Because thirty-nine years wasn't enough time for him to be ready for his next job!

Chambers separated salvation from being set apart so his audience wouldn't wrestle with the full cost of discipleship when they first heard the gospel. Think back on how you were saved. Did you know the full extent of your sin? Probably not! Nor does it seem that the twelve apostles realized this fact until much later. But in God's mercy, He first saves us then slowly chips away at the idols that compete for our hearts. He is relentless! We have no rest until we find *all* our rest in Him.

APPLICATION

If you hear the call and choose to follow it, what other decisions must you make?

Have you heeded God's call? Why is it important to be reminded that you have?

Finish this prayer: "God, one area in my life that continues to compete with your call is . . ."

⇜ FEBRUARY 3 ⇝
BECOMING THE "FILTH OF THE WORLD"

Would you die for the gospel?
If you knew how deep it goes, you'd go all out for sinners.

◄

BACKGROUND When Oswald Chambers fell ill in Egypt, was he wrong to push through his pain until it was too late for an uncomplicated appendectomy? Did he die because of stubbornness, or did he die the way he lived—as a selfless servant of the gospel?

We don't know all that was in Chambers' heart, and we certainly don't know what God had in mind by taking him from Biddy and their young daughter. But as Chambers had told Biddy a few months before his death, "I don't care what God *does*. It's what God *is* that I care about."

SCRIPTURAL CONTEXT Chambers uses two verses he has already quoted before (Romans 1:1 and Galatians 1:16) and three we see for the first time (1 Corinthians 4:13; Colossians 1:24; and 1 Peter 4:12). As you read these three verses and their contexts, what do you learn about the effects of God's relentless call? What happened to Paul for the sake of the Corinthians and the Colossians? Why did Peter tell the saints in Pontus, Galatia, Cappadocia, Asia, and Bithynia to rejoice (1 Peter 1:1)?

WHAT'S THE DEVOTIONAL SAYING? Today's title in the Classic Edition is a bit cryptic: *The Recognized Ban of Relationship*. As you read today's text, what do you think this means? The word *desires* (sentence 2) in the Updated Edition was originally *affinities*. What relationships or affinities are keeping you from the "filth of human life" (see January 31, *Utmost*)?

Chambers' main point today is that we have a choice: We can either be saved by the skin of our teeth or we can enter into all that God has in mind for us, which includes being made as the filth of the world. He calls this second option being "set apart unto the gospel," and he distinguishes it from merely being saved (see February 2, *Utmost*) and from being sanctified.

Nowadays we use the word *sanctification* to describe the second option, which makes Chambers' devotionals a bit confusing. But Chambers often used the phrase "set apart unto the gospel" (the Updated Edition adds "consecrated" to further help us) when he meant "God's work" in a believer's life, and he used the term *sanctified* when he was talking about "*our* decision to live holy and set apart to God." Are you letting God do His work in your life today? Or are you resisting Him by not banning certain relationships and affinities?

APPLICATION

When was the last time you felt like refuse for the cause of Christ?

Are you turned off by sinners, or do you see their need for salvation? How so?

Finish this prayer: "Lord, my last encounter with a nonbeliever revealed all of my . . ."

ᘍᘓᔈᘔᘓ FEBRUARY 4 ᘍᘓᔈᘔᘓ
THE COMPELLING MAJESTY OF HIS POWER

Has God cornered you?
If so, nothing matters but telling others about Him.

BACKGROUND For the past two days we saw that Oswald Chambers made a distinction between being merely saved and being "set apart unto the gospel." Today we will see him differentiate "born again" from the baptism of the Holy Spirit—when the Spirit's power comes upon a believer (Acts 1:8).

There is a debate today about whether every believer should have a point in their lives, usually after being saved, when they experience the Spirit's baptism. One way to resolve this debate is to say, "Salvation and the Spirit's infilling *should* occur at the same moment in time, but since many 'saved' people *don't* know about the Holy Spirit's power, we should tell them about it!"

SCRIPTURAL CONTEXT A key verse in this debate, and for today's devotional, is Acts 1:8. Skim Acts 1 and 2 to see what Jesus said and how the Holy Spirit filled the disciples. Now read 2 Corinthians 5:11–21. What did people say about Paul (verse 13)? How does Paul describe being born again (verse 17)? What did Paul beg the Christians in Corinth to do (verse 20)?

In 2 Corinthians 5, Paul talks about one conversion, not two. Yet he also urges people who already call themselves Christians to be "reconciled to God."

WHAT'S THE DEVOTIONAL SAYING? Chambers' first point is that the love of God is the only thing that matters. This is the same point he made at the League of Prayer's annual convention in 1906 as he described the darkness he experienced from 1897 to 1901: "Love is the beginning, love is the middle, and love is the end."

The second point Chambers makes is that we should be witnesses for *Christ*, not for what He does. If we are *Christ's* witnesses, we won't worry if people think we are good or bad, since all their feelings about us are really their feelings about Jesus.

Chambers' final point is that our surrender to Christ's love is the only thing that matters and the only thing that bears fruit in our lives. If we surrender like this, others will see God's holiness, not our own.

So where does this leave us with the baptism of the Holy Spirit? It's safe to say that our goal should be to put all the focus on God. If our experience of a "second conversion" puts the focus on us, we're doing something wrong. Let all glory be to Him.

APPLICATION

Do you take everything that people say to you, good or bad, as if it were said to Jesus?

What is one area where you realize you are gripped by God's love?

Finish this prayer: "Lord, I want to confess how I draw attention to my personal holiness by . . ."

ᥬᥫ FEBRUARY 5 ᥬᥫ
ARE YOU READY TO BE POURED OUT AS AN OFFERING?

Want glamorous martyrdom?
Get over your ego and find ways to serve others.

➤

BACKGROUND Mention to your Christian friends that you are reading *My Utmost for His Highest,* and most will smile with recognition. Even the name "Oswald Chambers" rings a bell for most churchgoers. But in his lifetime very few people knew him. Outside of one small Christian group (the League of Prayer), one tiny school (the Bible Training College), and one YMCA hut northeast of Cairo (El-Zaytoun), his name was practically unknown. Today's devotional reminds us that serving as an unknown might be exactly what God wants for us.

SCRIPTURAL CONTEXT For five days we have learned about God's call from Romans 1:1, parts of Paul's letters to the Corinthians, and various supporting verses. Today we look at Philippians and a very concrete lesson about serving others. Read the whole book of Philippians if you can, or at least chapters 2 and 4. What was the Philippians' main problem, and what did Paul say to help them?

WHAT'S THE DEVOTIONAL SAYING?
Today's lesson is very simple and clear: Don't expect people to notice you as you serve others. If you wait for that, you will never start serving. Though it's a simple message, it's very hard to put in practice. Chambers has a few choice words that may help us. Chambers was known for using humor to help his audiences understand spiritual truths, and we see some of that in the following list (taken from the Classic Edition) summarizing today's lesson:

Don't "choose the scenery of your sacrifice." Be willing to be "hopelessly insignificant," and to be "not so much as a drop in the bucket" but "a doormat under other people's feet."

This sounds depressing, but it's better to know what we are getting ourselves into before we launch into serving others. If not, we run the risk of giving up before God has even started to have His way in our hearts.

APPLICATION

Does God really want you to be a doormat? If so, are you willing to be one?

Why do you need to be humbled before you can be exalted by God (Luke 14:11)?

Finish this prayer: "I know it would bless your heart, Lord, if I humbled myself and . . ."

FEBRUARY 6
ARE YOU READY TO BE POURED OUT AS AN OFFERING?

Will you burn for God?
When we're on His altar, we forget our petty worries.

BACKGROUND Today's lesson continues yesterday's theme. In fact, Oswald Chambers is returning to the same lesson he taught us on January 1. We need to be constantly reminded of these truths and challenged to actively turn our whole lives over to God.

SCRIPTURAL CONTEXT Paul's last recorded words are found in his second letter to Timothy. Today's theme verse is from the last chapter of this letter. It is from this verse that we learn that Paul knew he was going to die soon. But what does the "already" in this verse mean? Is being poured out only something you do when you are a martyr?

One of the delightful aspects of *Utmost* is how Chambers pulls together such different parts of Scripture. Today is no exception. He quotes from an obscure part of Psalm 118, which also contains the well-known verse: "The stone the builders rejected has become the cornerstone." Read this psalm, and if you have Internet access (or the right book!), read Matthew Henry's commentary for 118:27. Chambers could have easily read this same commentary. Do you find similarities in thought?

WHAT'S THE DEVOTIONAL SAYING?
If things are troubling, oppressing, or depressing you, today's lesson has your solution. Chambers says that when we *tell* God we are ready to be offered as His sacrifice, we are at that moment letting God burn up all of the things that hold us to this world, which takes away all our troubles and depression.

Does that sound too easy? Chambers warns that when we do not deal with God at the level of our will, we won't get any freedom from our troubles. In fact, when troubles come, we will be trapped in self-pity. Are you already trapped like this? Go back to the drawing board and *tell* God you're ready to be poured out for Him—and mean what you say!

APPLICATION
Have you ever submitted your will to the will of God? Did He take you seriously?

Do you nurture self-pity? How can you recognize it in your life?

Finish this prayer: "Lord, I have desires and affections in my life that are not directed toward you, so . . ."

SPIRITUAL DEJECTION

Don't grab God's blessings. Grab the tasks at hand,
and you'll find you're holding on to Him!

BACKGROUND Imagine being eight days into a biblical theology class, and you're given the following test:

1. What do you understand by biblical theology?
2. Define *science*.
3. What do you mean by Bible facts being revelation facts?
4. Show the difference between common sense and the common people.
5. Define agnosticism, theory, and hypothesis.
6. Give scriptural proof that God created both the material and Bible worlds.
7. What do you understand by *insanity*?
8. What is biblical criticism? What is higher criticism?

It's interesting that Oswald Chambers, a former art student and then Bible professor, would include questions about science, facts, theory, hypothesis, creation, and even insanity. It's as if a science buff inserted questions 2 through 7 into a two-question biblical theology exam. Today's devotional begins with an astute observation about humans (whether they are scientists, theologians, or disciples on their way to Emmaus): People interpret the same facts differently. Chambers clearly understood the difference between unchangeable facts and easily biased interpretations.

SCRIPTURAL CONTEXT Chambers refers to only one verse. Read Luke 24, paying special attention to verse 21 and the mood of Cleopas and his friend. Can you remember an unanswered prayer that made you feel this way?

WHAT'S THE DEVOTIONAL SAYING?
The main point of today's lesson is that spiritual dejection comes when we want our prayers answered more than we want God. The antidote for lusting after answered prayer is to do the task that, due to God's engineering of our circumstances, is what lies closest to us. It's not that we shouldn't pray and expect miracles, but that we should remember that very often our prayers won't be answered the way we hope.

Today begins a series of lessons sprinkled throughout *Utmost* (Classic Edition). They are titled "The Discipline of ___," on such fill-in-the-blank topics as Dejection, Dismay, Disillusionment, and Difficulty. How do you feel about the idea that God uses unpleasant things to help us draw near to Him?

APPLICATION
Do you seek God's answers to prayer? Why do you need to seek Him instead?
What would it be like to "get ahold of God" (Updated Edition) in your life today?
Finish this prayer: "There are everyday tasks I need to start doing. Father, please help me . . ."

FEBRUARY 8
THE COST OF SANCTIFICATION

Be narrow-minded: focus on being made one with Jesus.
That's sanctification!

BACKGROUND Were you confused by the lesson on February 3? Was the difference between being "separated unto the gospel" and being "sanctified" perplexing? If so, today's study may clarify things. Here we see that "separation" is the first step in our sanctification process. It's something only God can do (see January 31, *Companion*). Once God's work of setting us apart is finished, we begin the long process of being sanctified.

God's separating work often happens at the same time as our decision of will—our "white funeral" in Oswald Chambers' poetic language. But we must remember that just as we were saved by God's power, we are separated by God's power, not by anything we can do. That is why Chambers calls sanctification, which begins when God separates us, the "second mighty work of grace" (see January 10, *Utmost*). In the final analysis, it is all by God's grace, not by our will.

SCRIPTURAL CONTEXT On January 9, we saw the second half of today's theme verse (1 Thessalonians 5:23). Read the context again and also 1 Thessalonians 4:3. What did *sanctify* mean to Paul? Chambers quotes from John 17. Read that chapter. What did *sanctify* mean to Jesus?

WHAT'S THE DEVOTIONAL SAYING? Chambers' audience must have been praying for "sanctification" when he delivered this message. Maybe God had at some point given them today's theme verse and was using circumstances to help them recall it (see January 30, *Companion*). But Chambers was telling them they didn't really understand sanctification. Nor do we!

Chambers tells us that *sanctification* means that "every useful aspect of our bodies, souls, and spirits will be enslaved to God." And we know that we are enslaved like this when we start to be one with and act like Jesus, who obeyed God even unto death!

APPLICATION

What narrowing or restriction of concerns is God prodding you to make?

In what way do you want to be a person with God's point of view?

Finish this prayer: "Lord Jesus, I want the Holy Spirit to dwell in me so I resemble you as I . . ."

༄ FEBRUARY 9 ༄
ARE YOU EXHAUSTED SPIRITUALLY?

Do people drain your energy?
No fear: God's got unlimited refills!

➤

BACKGROUND Oswald Chambers was an incredibly hard worker. He often rose before the crack of dawn to pray for other people, which he considered the *real* work. His motto was: "Get out of bed first and think about it later." He felt his job was to let God make him broken bread and poured-out wine for others through intercessory prayer and whatever else God had him do. Today Chambers tells us why we get exhausted spiritually and how God protects us from utter exhaustion or complaining.

SCRIPTURAL CONTEXT One of the great joys of reading *Utmost* is that it points us to encouraging Scriptures. Read Isaiah 40:27–31. Have you been feeling beaten down and poured out for others? Are you a hamster running endlessly on a wheel? These verses, and today's lesson, will remind you that your troubles are not hidden from God. Moreover, He has limitless power to fill up all that you have poured out.

The other verses today are from John 21 and Psalm 87. Read these two chapters and imagine yourself on the shores of Galilee or standing at the ancient walls of Jerusalem. Would you have leaped into the water and swum to Jesus?

Would you, assuming you had not been born in the City of David, want to change your birth certificate to say that you had been? Peter and the psalmist were people filled with love and energy for God and His kingdom. What gave them their energy?

WHAT'S THE DEVOTIONAL SAYING?
Two days ago, we read how spiritual *dejection* is always our fault and that it comes from the sin of lusting after answered prayer. Today we learn that spiritual *exhaustion* is not from sin but a natural result of serving others. This "why" of spiritual exhaustion is Chambers' first point. Are you willing for other people to drain you to the last drop until they learn to get strength straight from God?

Chambers' second point is on how to protect yourself from being "utterly exhausted." Our "supply" comes from the foundation of Christ's redemption and not from our own sympathy for lost souls or the pain in people's lives. Chambers warns us that we are apt to start complaining about our exhaustion. The solution to this is to go to God for a refill of living water!

APPLICATION

In what way are you getting exhausted? What can replenish you?

What does 1 Corinthians 13 tell you about how to relate to others?

Finish this prayer: "Father, I invite you now to flow through me so that I can pour myself out for . . ."

Imagination. part of our thinking that reasons + visualizes. Look to G and not idols —
How do we turn from Idols to G? Look to nature

⟋⟋⟋ FEBRUARY 10 ⟋⟋⟋
IS YOUR ABILITY TO SEE GOD BLINDED?

Idle in prayer? Idolizing work?
Spend time outside. Nature connects your mind to God.

◄ ►

BACKGROUND When James Reimann (editor of the Updated Edition of *Utmost*) thought of how to rewrite the word "imagination" from the original *Utmost*, he often chose phrases such as "mind" and "thought processes" (see January 9, February 11, September 14, November 18, November 24, and December 5, *Utmost*). Reimann did well to change this word, because now when we think of *imagination* we think of children's make-believe.

Today's lesson, however, still has the word *imagination*. (If you read the Updated Edition online, you might not see it, but it's still in the print and ebook versions.) In order to better understand Oswald Chambers' use of this word, you can go to utmost.org/classic and search for the term *imagination*. Chambers takes this word from the King James Version rendering of 2 Corinthians; the word is translated "arguments" in modern versions. It seems Chambers used the word *imagination* to indicate the part of our thinking that reasons and visualizes. Today's lesson says that we starve this part of our mind by our idols.

SCRIPTURAL CONTEXT The only verse today is Isaiah 40:26. But it must be understood in the context of Isaiah 26:3 (tomorrow's verse)

and 2 Corinthians 10:5. Read all three verses now, and think about what part of your thought life this past week Chambers would have considered your *imagination*.

WHAT'S THE DEVOTIONAL SAYING? It's easy to understand how we starve our body, our hearing, our sight, or even our taste buds. But how can we starve our imagination? How do we starve the part of our thinking that does all of our reasoning? According to Chambers, we starve this essential part of our mind when we look to idols instead of God.

Chambers' advice for how to turn from idols to God is interesting. He says we should look at nature and see each piece as God's handiwork. He also lists the most common idols (ourselves, our work, our ideals of Christian work, our particular brand of salvation and sanctification) so we will be on guard. Finally, he motivates us not to starve our imagination by reminding us of its power to aid our prayers.

How are you praying for others today? Do you use the reasoning and visualizing part of your mind as you set them before God and ask Him—who calls each star by name—to meet their needs?

APPLICATION

How have you observed nature reflecting God's glory?

What are some idols in your life? How do they steal your energy, especially for prayer?

Finish this prayer: "As I pray now for people who need you, please give me the power to visualize . . ."

IS YOUR MIND STAYED ON GOD?

Are we empty, weak, tired?
Nip bad habits in the bud; envision God, not worries!

BACKGROUND Today is the third day in a series of questions—questions that ask us about our level of exhaustion, our ability to see and imagine God, and our focus on God and His hope. These questions are important for us to ask ourselves and each other, especially when we feel tired of doing God's work.

We noticed yesterday that Oswald Chambers liked to use the word *imagination*. He uses it again today, and he says that instead of letting our imagination be *starved* (yesterday's lesson) we should keep it *stayed* on God.

SCRIPTURAL CONTEXT We see two of the same verses we saw yesterday (Isaiah 26:3 and 2 Corinthians 10:5), an old favorite (Isaiah 45:22), and one from Psalm 106. Read this whole psalm now. What were some of the many things God's people forgot? What have you forgotten? Will you prod your memory with a knife, or stiletto (as Chambers put it in the Classic Edition), so you don't continue to sin with your "fathers"?

WHAT'S THE DEVOTIONAL SAYING? We began this three-day lesson series with Chambers telling us that our spiritual exhaustion was not from sin but from service. It has become obvious, however, that we can easily block our ability to be replenished as we sin with our idols. Not only will our replenishment be in danger, but one of our "greatest assets" will be as well. This asset, according to Chambers, is our imagination, which is our ability to mentally bring each thought into captivity to Christ.

It's hard to overstate the importance of keeping our imagination stayed on God. When the center of our reasoning and visualizing power is devoted 100 percent to God, our faith and the Holy Spirit can work together in our lives. But when we starve our imagination, God's gift of faith, though not taken away from us, is hindered from working properly with God's Spirit. The end result is total exhaustion. If you are feeling exhausted, feed your mind with creation!

APPLICATION

What trials have you gone through lately? Did your mind work for you or against you?

How can you make a habit of associating God's creation (sunsets and other wonders) with worthy thinking?

Finish this prayer: "Father, it's rare that I use my mind to place myself in your presence, but I'll do it now by . . ."

FEBRUARY 12
ARE YOU LISTENING TO GOD?

Saying, "I can't hear God" isn't open rebellion, but it's our shame, once God speaks.

➤

BACKGROUND Imagine praying for the Holy Spirit to fill you up and then having to wait four years until He filled you. That is what happened to Oswald Chambers. What was the problem? Chambers said that when he first asked God to give him His Holy Spirit, he had been asking so that he could have power in his own hand (see February 2, *Companion*).

In today's lesson, Chambers says that we disrespect God by not listening to Him and that when He finally breaks through to us, the disrespect and shame comes back to us. Chambers' joy in receiving the Holy Spirit was tempered by his shame in being obstinate, wanting power in his own hand and his friends' esteem more than he wanted God.

SCRIPTURAL CONTEXT The story of Moses at Sinai is fascinating. Skim Exodus 19–20, 24, and 32 to get a sense for what happened. How does today's theme verse fit into the story? How would *you* feel camped at the foot of Sinai?

Now turn to John 14. Chambers loved this chapter and quoted from it in at least twenty of the devotionals. Does it seem strange that Jesus introduces the topic of the Spirit's immi-

nent coming by saying, "Keep my commands"? How do God's commands and His Spirit relate to one another?

WHAT'S THE DEVOTIONAL SAYING? Today we begin a three-part series on hearing God. Chambers starts with a lesson that cuts like a sharp knife: God has given us commands, but we don't pay attention to them. If that sentence doesn't prick our conscience, nothing will! So often we pretend to want to hear God, but we really only want to hear from His servants. (That's why it's so important to read *Utmost* with Bible in hand. We don't need to hear Oswald Chambers; we need to hear God!)

The reason we prefer to hear God's servants is that we feel better about picking and choosing which things to obey. That's our favorite way of "obeying," and we instinctively know we can't get away with that when we read the Bible. So put down *Utmost* and this *Daily Companion* and pick up the Bible. See what God has been trying to tell you. You may feel ashamed when you finally hear (and obey) His voice, but it will be worth the shame to hear it. He is the only one who knows our deepest needs.

APPLICATION

Are you afraid of what God will ask of you if you listen to Him? How so?

Have you ever tried to misunderstand God's will to avoid obeying Him?

Finish this prayer: "Lord, I want to hear your voice right now, even if you tell me to . . ."

FEBRUARY 13
THE DEVOTION OF HEARING

It's not enough to hear God just once; you need to hear him as a friend.

BACKGROUND A potential pitfall in this three-day series on hearing God is that we forget that to hear means to obey. So when Oswald Chambers talks about listening (yesterday), hearing (today), and heeding (tomorrow—rephrased as "hearing" in the Updated Edition), we need to translate all of those words into "obeying" in order to really grasp what they mean.

Today, for example, we read that we must always *hear* God. In other words, we must always *obey* God. Interestingly, the Bible is not the only place where Chambers says we hear God.

SCRIPTURAL CONTEXT Although Chambers cites nature as another place we can hear God, God speaks only the same things He has already said in the Bible. With that in mind, look up today's verses (1 Samuel 3:10; John 11:41; 15:14). We've looked at the context before with the exception of John 11, so read that chapter now. Imagine standing at Lazarus' tomb and hearing Jesus say that God always hears Him. Would you believe Him when He first said that? Would you after Lazarus walked out of the tomb?

WHAT'S THE DEVOTIONAL SAYING? If you have close friends, you know how important it is to communicate. If you don't know what your friends like, how can you do the things that bless them most? In the same way, Chambers says we need to communicate with God—especially the *hearing* part of communication—so we know how to bless Him.

The biggest obstacle to communication is our preoccupation with other things. Just as in a marriage where one spouse has all kinds of other things going on, our friendship with God suffers when we fill our lives with things, service, and even convictions. Anything that's not a simple childlike love of spending time with our heavenly Father will break our relationship with Him. Is it time to drop your plans and romp on the floor with God?

APPLICATION

Have you developed a friendship with God? How do you know His heart?

How do you plan to get past the habit of ignoring God's voice?

Finish this prayer: "Lord Jesus, you know I *want* to hear your voice, but things get in my way, such as . . ."

᧡ FEBRUARY 14 ᧡
THE DISCIPLINE OF HEARING

To sing God's salvation, you need darkness so that your message will be His.

◄

BACKGROUND The only two holidays referred to in *Utmost* are Christmas and New Year's Eve. All the other holidays have whatever devotional Biddy Chambers chose for that day. Yet it is fitting that on this day, when many celebrate romantic love, we come to the end of our three-day series on listening to God (and becoming better friends with Him).

SCRIPTURAL CONTEXT When Jesus spoke the words of today's theme verse, He was telling His disciples not to fear the Pharisees, who were hypocrites and whose duplicity would soon be exposed. And Oswald Chambers, for whom darkness was an important motif in his spiritual growth (see January 3, *Utmost*), sees added significance in this verse. Read this chapter and imagine you are one of the Twelve hearing Jesus' words. Would they make sense?

The second quoted verse is Isaiah 49:2. Can you think of other times when God hid one of His servants in a shadowy place? Why does God do that? Have you ever been put in darkness like that?

WHAT'S THE DEVOTIONAL SAYING? To make his main point, Chambers refers to songbirds. Did you know that one hundred years ago (and perhaps still today) you could buy a canary that had been taught to sing beautiful songs by listening to musical recordings in a completely dark room? It sounds strange, and so is the idea that God teaches us to heed His voice and make "music" as we preach His Word by putting us in the dark.

The importance of darkness is that it cuts us off from distractions such as those we read about yesterday. If you are in a time of darkness, Chambers counsels you to avoid talking about or reading books about why you are going through it. Simply listen for God's voice. When you finally hear and obey God's voice, what beautiful music you will make!

APPLICATION
Are you going through a time of darkness? If so, what is it like? Why is it important to listen to God?
Why would Chambers say we shouldn't read books that explain our darkness or talk on and on with others about our darkness? Do you agree?
Finish this prayer: "God, the last time you put me in darkness, the way I responded and what I learned was . . ."

◌∽ FEBRUARY 15 ∽◌
"AM I MY BROTHER'S KEEPER?"

Tired of trying?
Just remember, what you do affects everyone.

BACKGROUND Oswald Chambers loved learning. When he taught from January until June 1907 in Cincinnati (see January 25, *Companion*), he wrote the following to his sister on April 7: "I have been having a reveling few days. My box has at last arrived. My books! . . . I do thank God for my books with every fibre of my being."

Chambers also hated intellectual laziness (see the quote on January 29, *Companion*). In his last year of life, while working near Cairo, Egypt, he wrote, "A grave defect in much work of today is that men do not follow Solomon's admonition, 'Whatsoever thy hand findeth to do, do it with thy might.' The tendency is to argue, 'It's only for so short a time, why trouble?' If it is only for five minutes, let it be well done." Many of his thoughts about learning and laziness come through clearly in today's devotional.

SCRIPTURAL CONTEXT One of Chambers' main points today is that we must give all our mental energy for Jesus. We can do this by working hard to understand the Bible. To that end, Chambers peppers us with no less than seven Scripture references. As you look up each one (Romans 14:7; Ephesians 2:6; 1 Corinthians 9:27 and 12:26; 2 Corinthians 3:5; Acts 1:8; Jeremiah 6:30), see if you can answer the fol- lowing questions: Which verse best captures the essence of today's study? Do we sit in heaven with Christ, with each other, or both? How can we be sitting in heaven right now? How do Romans 14 and 1 Corinthians 12 differ? How are they the same? Were the Corinthians asking Paul to live up to a high standard? And about what do we witness? What made the Jews "rep- robate silver" (the Updated Edition says "set . . . aside"), and how are we the same? Where does today's title come from?

WHAT'S THE DEVOTIONAL SAYING? Many teachers (Christian or not) tell us to avoid laziness and work hard. But today, Chambers gives us the reason for hard work: to better "dis- ciple men and women to the Lord Jesus Christ" and to thank God for saving us. If that weren't reason enough to spend our all for God, Cham- bers reminds us that God might set us aside as a refiner throws out the dross from silver and as God did to the Jews of Jeremiah's day.

How are you doing in the laziness depart- ment? Are you spending every ounce of your mental, moral, and spiritual energy for Jesus? Probably not! In that case, you will take great comfort in 2 Corinthians 3:5, "Our sufficiency comes from God."

APPLICATION
"Selfishness, carelessness, insensitivity, hardness." Which word describes you most? Why? What are you doing to become a better witness for God? What is your long-term plan? Finish this prayer: "Father, my actions affect the souls of people around me, so I . . ."

FEBRUARY 16
THE INSPIRATION OF SPIRITUAL INITIATIVE

Are your dreams crushed?
God revives them as you receive His inspiration.

➢

BACKGROUND When Oswald Chambers claimed the Holy Spirit's infilling power "in dogged committal on Luke 11:13," his four years of darkness were ended. But he said that he was "as dry and empty as ever" and had "no power or realization of God, no witness of the Holy Spirit." Two days later, however, he spoke at a meeting, and God poured out power on the audience through Chambers' words: Forty people came to the front at the altar call.

Today's lesson says that when we step forward to do what God wants us to do, He will give us power—but not before! In Chambers' time of darkness, God wanted him to claim the gift of the Holy Spirit on the authority of Jesus and the promise of Luke 11:13. When he did, God gave him divine power to preach the gospel and witness the power of redemption.

SCRIPTURAL CONTEXT Read Ephesians 4:17–5:20. What kind of life does Paul urge the church to stop living? What does the new life look like? How should you "arise from the dead" with respect to old ways of living?

Chambers illustrates how to "arise" with the story of Jesus healing a man's withered hand. Read this account in Matthew 12. In what other stories did Jesus command a person to do something before getting healed? How would it feel to be one of those people?

WHAT'S THE DEVOTIONAL SAYING? First, Chambers warns that not all of our first steps are preludes to God's power. We know it's from God when, after taking that step, God gives us power.

Second, Chambers points out that we need these first steps after we realize that we have no power to accomplish our dreams. Chambers had to realize this when he, for four years, sought the Spirit's infilling. Once he realized it, God could finally tell him to "arise from the dead." How about you? Are you dreaming about being controlled by the Spirit instead of your bad motives? The sooner you realize that you can't accomplish this goal yourself, the sooner God can help you awaken from your sleep and shine Christ's light on you.

APPLICATION

What dreams did you have when you were younger? What happened to them?

When will God give you the life and power to realize your dreams? Is it time now?

Finish this prayer: "Lord Jesus, thank you for inspiring me to get up and get going. I'll respond by . . ."

FEBRUARY 17
TAKING THE INITIATIVE AGAINST DEPRESSION

Are you masking depression in fun?
It'll only get worse. God's joy melts sorrow.

◄ ►

BACKGROUND Yesterday we learned that initiative can come either from God or from other sources, but only God's initiative gives us the power to really get up and go. Today and for the next three days, we will see different ways God's initiative can help us arise from depression, despair, drudgery, and dreaming (the kind of dreams that distract us from the real dreams God has for us).

Do you face these four obstacles? Oswald Chambers did. He constantly battled depression, and he knew it was a natural part of being human. If you are facing the same battle, be of good cheer! Today's message is just for you.

SCRIPTURAL CONTEXT Read the story of Elijah running for his life in 1 Kings 19. What was the first thing the angel told him to do? How was he able to obey? What was the outcome? Now read Acts 27:33. Can you find any other verses where people are urged to do simple things as in these two passages? What simple thing might you need to do today?

WHAT'S THE DEVOTIONAL SAYING?
When Chambers visited the United States, he took his hosts, Meredith and Bessie Standley, on a sleigh ride. Later, Mr. Standley said the sleighing vacation with Chambers was "exactly what we needed." With a legal battle on the horizon, the simple joy of a two-horse open sleigh ride gave the Standleys a short respite from their spiritual depression.

Chambers' main point today is that God will inspire us to do simple things, which will protect us from depression. If we try to do something to fight off depression (overeating, thrill-seeking, sexual intimacy, for example) we will make our depression worse. But God's inspiration is a proactive initiative that is perfectly effective against depression.

A sub-point is that everyone gets depressed at some time. If we forget this, we greatly overestimate ourselves. Are you turned off from the everyday "things of God's creation"? If so, you are probably depressed and need to listen to God's inspiration to hear what simple thing He wants you to do.

APPLICATION
How does depression affect your life? What does it cause you to focus on?
How does the Holy Spirit lift you out of depression? What does He help you focus on?
Finish this prayer: "Lord, depression is bound to come, but I trust you to . . ."

⌒⌒ FEBRUARY 18 ⌒⌒
TAKING THE INITIATIVE AGAINST DESPAIR

Have you ever blown it?
Let it go and move on with God's holy hug.

BACKGROUND Today's lesson is yesterday's—with a twist. Instead of depression, Oswald Chambers analyzes despair, the most intense form of depression, which is usually brought on by our spectacular failures.

What did Chambers know about despair? His four years of darkness were fraught with the despair of his missed opportunity to receive the Holy Spirit. Also during this time, he was falsely accused by a young woman of misconduct with her. Even though an investigation cleared his name, the townsfolk still talked behind his back. This exacerbated Oswald's despair and made him painfully aware that the sin he was accused of was something he *could* have done.

SCRIPTURAL CONTEXT Read the passion narrative in Matthew 26. How does Jesus treat His sleepy disciples? Does He seem to speak to you in the same way when you've failed? What was the "next thing" Jesus called His disciples to do?

WHAT'S THE DEVOTIONAL SAYING?
If you feel hopeless over a missed opportunity or terrible mistake, today's lesson reminds you that despair is "a very ordinary human experience." The solution to despair is to put the past in Jesus' redemptive hands and move on to what He wants you to do next.

If you're the type who reads the last page of a mystery, go ahead and turn to December 31 right now. You will find a devotional similar to today's lesson, along with added insight into how God uses the failures of our past to help us be more careful in the future as we do the next thing. We don't want to be caught sleeping again!

You can also flip forward to October 10, another time Chambers uses the term "next thing," a favorite expression of his that meant, "whatever God wants you to do next." What is your "next thing" today?

APPLICATION
Have you ever missed a great opportunity? Did you despair? What happened?
What is the best way to "arise and do the next thing" when you are despairing?
Finish this prayer: "Precious Jesus, I give all of my missed opportunities to you.
   Help me to let go of . . ."

59

FEBRUARY 19
TAKING THE INITIATIVE AGAINST DRUDGERY

In the same old, same old?
Christ can make old things new as you step out in faith.

◄ ►

BACKGROUND Depression and despair are par for the course of life, and so is drudgery. Oswald Chambers calls drudgery one of life's "finest touchstones" ("tests" in the Updated Edition).

A touchstone, usually a piece of slate, is an object on which you rub gold to test its purity. Slate and gold are as different as can be—just as drudgery is far removed from "ideal" work. And just as the black dullness of slate is the perfect background for examining the color of gold rubbings, so also the boring nature of drudgery is a perfect backdrop for our character. What does your character look like as it's rubbed against the blandness of boring tasks? Does it shine like pure gold?

SCRIPTURAL CONTEXT Isaiah 60 and 61 have some of the most hope-filled passages in the entire Bible. If you are stuck in drudgery, you probably have feelings similar to those of the Jews in Babylon, for whom Isaiah's prophecies were written long before they were exiled from their native land. As you read these two chapters, what images come to mind? In what ways does Isaiah use light to describe things?

Chambers also wants us to read John 13. What do you notice from verses 1, 2, 4, and 5 about the "who" and the "how" of Jesus' "drudgery"? Why does John include verse 3?

WHAT'S THE DEVOTIONAL SAYING? Chambers tells all of us who experience drudgery that when we "arise and shine" three things happen: We find God, our drudgery becomes a divine task, and other people see that we do our job in a holy way. Have you ever met someone who can do a menial job in a way that shines with God's light?

If you are struggling with drudgery, Chambers' advice is again to "take the first step." Whatever you have in front of you, do it, then look for God to show up. Never mind that your task is "far removed" from your ideals of Christian work; God will bless you as you do the next thing He has for you.

APPLICATION

What are your "duties of drudgery"? How do you respond to them?

Have you, or someone you know, made drudgery holy? How?

Finish this prayer: "Today, Lord, I want to transform my tasks into something holy, starting with . . ."

TAKING THE INITIATIVE AGAINST DAYDREAMING

Dreaming your life away?
Trust God to make it so, and join in His adventure!

◄

BACKGROUND The love story of Oswald Chambers and his Beloved Disciple (B.D.), or "Biddy," was fast-paced. They fell in love in early June on a ten-day voyage across the Atlantic, and by August Oswald wrote to Biddy about their "blended" lives. By November they were engaged. Oswald's love for Biddy was all-permeating. Whatever love he had felt for Chrissie Brain ten years earlier was nothing compared to this. Before his engagement to Biddy, he wrote to his parents, "I am in love and it is quite such a new experience that . . . I do not know quite how to put it." In today's lesson, romantic love is our example for how we ought to treat God. Through it we learn the relationship between love and action.

SCRIPTURAL CONTEXT Our readings have quoted Scripture from the Passion Week. Today's verse is John 14:31, which links what Jesus said in the upper room to what he said en route to Gethsemane. Chambers says Jesus' Upper Room Discourse is full of "wonderful things" and speculates that the disciples might have thought they should go away to meditate over His words. Is that how you feel as you read John 14?

Now read Mark 6:7–34. How might Jesus feel to hear the Twelve's report and then to hear about His cousin's death? Have you ever been so tied up with other people's needs, as Jesus was in Mark 6:31, that you haven't been able to share a meal or get some rest with your close friends? How long did the Twelve have for "meditation" in a solitary place before Jesus had them "do something for Him"?

WHAT'S THE DEVOTIONAL SAYING? We come to the end of five lessons on "spiritual initiative." Do you find it strange that Chambers groups daydreaming with the other "*D*s" (despair, drudgery, etc.)? When are you tempted to daydream? Isn't it often when you are dealing with the other *D*s? How you react as you face the other *D*s is a reflection of how you seek God's will. If you turn drudgery into divine deeds, move from despair to the "next thing," and face depression by embracing it, you'll seek God's will for the sake of knowing what to do. But if you fail to handle the other *D*s, then you'll "seek God's will" even when He's already told you what to do.

But what does romantic love have to do with all of this? Chambers says, paraphrasing, "When a man is in love with a woman, he knows instinctively not to sit around thinking about her if there's an opportunity to instead do something for her." So also we shouldn't daydream about God or His will for our futures, but instead we should take action.

APPLICATION
Have you ever known what God wanted but daydreamed instead of doing it? How so?
When is it right to daydream or meditate?
Finish this prayer: "Father, there are things that you have told me to do, such as . . ."

FEBRUARY 21
DO YOU REALLY LOVE HIM?

We're of no use to God, but we're of great value! He loves our little gifts.

BACKGROUND When Oswald Chambers gave a drunkard his last half crown (the equivalent of a $20 bill), he said, "My Master tells me to give to everyone that asks." His hostess, however, greatly disapproved of this foolish gift. Today, we read how acts of "foolishness" are the small tokens of our surrender to God.

SCRIPTURAL CONTEXT A fascinating story featuring Mary of Bethany is found in Mark 14 (and in Matthew 26 and John 12). Read all of these accounts and think about why Mary, Martha, and Lazarus were at Simon the leper's house. Also, how do you think Judas used the money he stole from the disciples' moneybag?

Now read 1 John 4:7–21. How do we know we are born again? What is the source of love? Of fear? How do we show we really love God?

WHAT'S THE DEVOTIONAL SAYING? The lesson for today is clear: We can satisfy God (see January 2, 18, and 21, *Companion*) as we love in simple human ways, just as Mary loved Jesus at Bethany. Chambers outlines five ways our simple gifts of love can be short-circuited. First, if we are cautious and sensible, we will never be carried away by love the way Mary was when she "wasted" more than a year's wages. Second, if we restrict ourselves to "useful" things, we'll never really love. Third, if we meditate on God's "amazingness" at the expense of loving actions, we will never have time to love. Fourth, if we worry about our holiness, we will be too afraid to do bold acts of love. Fifth, if we focus on what we *do* for God, we will never realize how valuable we *are* to Him and thus will never respond with the same outrageous acts of love that He showers on us.

After his hostess voiced her disapproval about his gift to the drunkard, Chambers replied, "I believe beggars are sent to test our faith." He may as well have added that they are sent to test our love. How is your love for God today? Are you willing to look foolish for a chance to satisfy God's heart?

APPLICATION
Have you ever been carried away by your love for Jesus? What did you do? Was God happy? Are you focused on doing the morally right things or on abandoning yourself to God? Finish this prayer: "Lord God, today I want to give you a small gift of surrender by . . ."

⌘ FEBRUARY 22 ⌘
THE DISCIPLINE OF SPIRITUAL PERSEVERANCE

Is Jesus your faithful hero?
He'll always win, so don't be afraid to trust Him.

➤

BACKGROUND Oswald Chambers stopped in Japan on his round-the-world journey. There he met a missionary who was "mildly apologetic . . . with clasped hands and a sweet inoffensive smile." Have you been around people like that? Are *you* ever apologetic about the gospel?

Today's devotional deals with our fear that we are on the losing side. If you've ever felt that being a Christian is tantamount to being a social outcast, a loser, or a dork, you can find great comfort in the truths Chambers gives us today.

SCRIPTURAL CONTEXT Read about the power and majesty of God as described in Psalm 46. How does verse 10 fit into the rest of the psalm? How does this verse help us when we need perseverance and tenacity?

Chambers also quotes from Revelation 3. Read the letter to the Philadelphians. Why did the colonists name their city Philadelphia and not Laodicea? In verse 8 God praises the church for keeping His word; and in verse 10 He rewards them for keeping the word of His endurance. What do you think "word of My endurance" means?

WHAT'S THE DEVOTIONAL SAYING? Today we begin a four-part series on serving others. The main point of today's lesson is that we shouldn't just keep going out of a fear of change, but that we should keep going out of confidence that God will win. "Keep going" applies to many things we do for God. In the context of the next three lessons, it applies to how we tenaciously serve others. When do you serve others? Do you do it out of habit—out of mere "hanging on"? Chambers tells us to find our motivation in the heroic certainty of our Savior.

What have you hoped for? Have your hopes been disappointed? Chambers says this means your hopes are being purified. Will you believe that to be true? Jesus, our hero, is no will-o'-the-wisp. He's not a disappearing light over a bog, which tricks us weary travelers to think we are near our home. He is our true friend who will never leave or forsake us.

APPLICATION

In what way are you worried that Jesus won't win (in other words, the world will defeat His cause)?

For what cause are you persevering? What makes it hard to keep holding on?

Finish this prayer: "Lord Jesus, I know you will triumph, but things around me seem so bad. Please . . ."

THE DETERMINATION TO SERVE

Sick of serving?
God's love for you gives you power to serve ungrateful people.

◁   ▷

BACKGROUND Oswald Chambers loved animals. So did his daughter, Kathleen. A few months before he died, Chambers devoted several paragraphs in his journal to the description of the animals in his family's life. Regarding a dog they were keeping, Chambers wrote, "he is . . . lavishly fond of Kathleen" and "fills in Tweed's place like no other dog I ever had." (Tweed was his dog during his four years of "darkness," see January 3, *Companion*). So when Chambers says in the Classic Edition that we will be confronted by more ingratitude from people than from a dog, he speaks from the experience of a longtime dog lover.

SCRIPTURAL CONTEXT As we continue in this four-part series on service, Chambers draws three lessons from Paul's life. Today's lesson about Paul comes from 2 Corinthians 4:5 and Philippians 4:12. Read these verses and compare them to the theme verse and Luke 22:27. Do you see the parallel that Chambers points out? Chambers also ties Paul's motivation for serving to 1 Timothy 1:13. What haunts *you* about your past? Does it motivate you to love people who spite you?

WHAT'S THE DEVOTIONAL SAYING? In the first eight sentences, Chambers describes the depth of Paul's determination to serve. He spends the rest of the study explaining the motivation to serve: our love for Christ and the debt we owe Him. If serving others exhausts you, chances are you don't really appreciate the debt you owe Christ.

Are you disheartened by the ingratitude of people you are trying to help? Do you feel that a dog would be more grateful than those people? If so, think about today's lesson and the verses you read. Pray that God will give you eyes to see how you too are a blasphemer and a persecutor and a violent person who is saved by grace.

APPLICATION

Do you see yourself as a "doormat servant"? What motivates this kind of service?

What were you like before you gave in to the love of Christ?

Finish this prayer: "God, I know how badly I treated your Son. When I'm treated badly for your sake, help me . . ."

THE DELIGHT OF SACRIFICE

Are you a closet Christian?
Get out of there! People need the Christ in you.

BACKGROUND To get from the USA to Japan in 1907, Oswald Chambers sailed on the RMS *Empress of Japan*. Seven Yale graduates were on board, and Chambers said they would "study their Bibles constantly." He was also impressed by how they were "men of the world," which inspired him to write in his journal the following entry: "I am sure we cannot understand any 'set' but our own, hence the need for the servant of God to be like Paul and have humanity as his 'set.'" Today's lesson helps us avoid two extremes: being "of the world" but not having any Christ in us, and being so "*out of the world*" that no one can see Christ in us.

SCRIPTURAL CONTEXT Once again, Paul's life sets the stage for today's message. Read 2 Corinthians 12:11–21, 1 Corinthians 9:19–23, and Romans 9:1–5. What is Paul's tone in each passage? If Paul was martyred, as tradition suggests, what do you think he felt as he faced execution? Scared? Triumphant? Now read John 15:9–25. How is love connected to suffering, persecution, and martyrdom? Are you willing to lay down your physical life, or any part of your life, for Jesus?

WHAT'S THE DEVOTIONAL SAYING? What "Christian things" do you do? What motivates you to do them? Could any of the things be considered a "cause"? Is part of your motivation to point people to yourself? Today, Chambers lays out three threats to the "Delight of Sacrifice." First, we are tempted to sacrifice for a cause, not other people. Second, we often point people to ourselves, not to Jesus. Third, we focus more on our personal holiness than on what would be of use to others.

These three things are what Chambers calls "our own ends" ("goals" in the Updated Edition). They keep us from being a doormat for others and from letting Christ help himself to our lives. If we truly love Jesus with the true love of the best love story, we will be even willing to be "accursed from Christ" in order to bring our brothers and our sisters to Him.

APPLICATION
What are your interests? What are Jesus' interests?
Are you isolating yourself from people in any way? How so?
Finish this prayer: "Jesus, I know I won't waste my life if I throw it away for you.
  Help me today to . . ."

\sim FEBRUARY 25 \sim
THE DESTITUTION OF SERVICE

Wondering what's ahead?
Dive in to God's plan, and He'll watch over you.

◄

BACKGROUND Chambers appendicitis began October 17, 1917. He didn't go to the hospital until October 29. Five days after surgery, a blood clot went to his lung, and, though he recovered for a while, ten days later he began bleeding from his lung. In two days, he was dead.

In the February 3 entry, we considered whether Chambers was right to wait twelve days to go to the hospital (to avoid taking a bed needed by a wounded soldier). Today, consider the ramifications of his death. Biddy and Kathleen were left behind without the head of their household, and though perhaps not destitute, they were in a poor financial situation. On the other hand, they and all who knew Chambers (including us) were left with the spiritual legacy of a man who did not just proclaim the gospel, he became "broken bread and poured-out wine" for the sake of others, even in his death.

SCRIPTURAL CONTEXT Second Corinthians is a letter like no other. In it, Paul pours out his heart to his friends—and detractors! If you have time to read the whole letter, do so right now. Otherwise, read 12:11–21 again and chapter 8. The New Living Translation renders 12:15 as "it seems that the more I love you, the less you love me." Have you experienced this as you serve others? Now read Matthew 23. Why was it so hard for the disciples (or the Pharisees, for that matter) to understand Jesus' way of serving?

WHAT'S THE DEVOTIONAL SAYING Here, in the climax of our four-day study on service, Chambers paints a vivid picture of a true servant's life. First, true servants work without expecting anything in return. Second, true servants are extravagant and joyful with their love—no matter what the personal cost. Third, they serve man knowing they are actually serving God. Fourth, they do the most menial tasks. Fifth, they don't think along the lines of common sense ("What is the salary?" for instance). Finally, they do not hold back anything in reserve.

If he had lived that long, perhaps Chambers would have enjoyed the 1997 film *Gattaca*. In it, the hero overcomes his inferior genes, even besting his genetically engineered brother in a swimming duel. He does it by not ever holding anything in reserve. If the hero of a Hollywood plot held nothing back to achieve his dream of being an astronaut, will you hold anything back as you serve God by serving others?

APPLICATION

How do you feel about being a "servant to all" even when people are ungrateful?

What are your priorities (finances, comfort, security, pleasing God)?

Finish this prayer: "Father God, it's my intention and desire to serve you without reservation by . . ."

FEBRUARY 26
OUR MISGIVINGS ABOUT JESUS

Afraid God is out of touch with reality?
He is! But God is so much bigger than our reality.

➤

BACKGROUND Reading Oswald Chambers' biographies might leave you with the impression that he never struggled with trusting God, at least not after his four years of darkness (see January 3, *Companion*). But today he teaches us how to trust God, and we know that he tried to follow a line from Henry Alford's poem (see January 28, *Companion*) whenever he taught:

What thou hast not by suffering bought,
presume thou not to teach.
("Be Just and Fear Not," 1863)

So we are on safe ground to assume that Chambers suffered with the struggle to trust God, like we all do. Today's lesson will help us learn to trust Him more.

SCRIPTURAL CONTEXT The only verse for today's study is from John 4. Read that chapter and put yourself in the woman's shoes and then in the disciples'. When would you move from not trusting Jesus' authority to trusting (if ever)? Now imagine you are one of the townspeople. Would you have trusted when the woman spoke, when Jesus spoke, or neither?

WHAT'S THE DEVOTIONAL SAYING?
Chambers tells us that our lack of trust in God comes from two sources. First, it's from people asking us what Chambers calls "commonsense" questions about such things as money, housing, and medical insurance. Second, it comes from our own commonsense questions. Either way, we buy into the idea that God is out of touch with reality and can't be trusted.

Are you at a point where you don't trust God about something? Chambers urges you to confess to God your lack of trust in Him. Paraphrasing the final few sentences of today's devotional, you could try this prayer: "Lord, I've doubted your power. I rely on my ability to figure things out, but I don't trust you and the secret plans you have for me. You have infinite wisdom and power. I have a finite brain. I'm sorry for always wanting you to explain things to me before I trust you." Remember, God is merciful; He will forgive!

APPLICATION
When it really comes down to it, what do you believe about God's "lofty ideals"?
What happens when you trust God and He makes you depend on Him for provision?
Finish this prayer: "Lord, I'm suspicious about your ability to take care of me, especially concerning . . ."

FEBRUARY 27
THE IMPOVERISHED MINISTRY OF JESUS

Feeling worthless inside?
You are! But God can fill you with the Almighty.

◄

BACKGROUND Yesterday's title is "Inferior Misgivings About Jesus" (in the Classic Edition), and the main point is that we have misgivings, or lack of trust, in God due to our inferior understanding. Today we look at "The Impoverished Ministry of Jesus," how we impoverish God's work in our lives by impoverishing ourselves when we forget how *all-mighty* God really is.

Do you have a deep pit of trouble inside your heart? The temptation is to think that somehow you'll have to "draw water" out of that pit by yourself. The good news is that Almighty God will provide "water" from above, if you just let Him.

SCRIPTURAL CONTEXT We find our two verses in John 4 and 14. Read the verses and remind yourself of what else is said in those chapters. What trouble was in the woman's heart? How about the disciples in the upper room? How does that compare to your trouble today?

WHAT'S THE DEVOTIONAL SAYING? There are many dangers that threaten our relationship with Jesus. When we have no hardships, we often neglect our friendship with Christ. But when we face adversity, our relationship with Him can also suffer, since we start to despair and think God can't handle it. We think He can't help us to follow His command: "Do not let your hearts be troubled."

Where are you today? Does today's main point—that we need to stop limiting God to only what we've experienced of Him—speak to you? Or are you blissfully unaware that it is impossible to "draw" anything good from the "well" of your human heart? If the latter, spend some time thinking about how far you fall short. Then, once God makes you aware of the depths of your sin, follow Oswald Chambers' advice in today's lesson: Come to God as the Almighty; He is able to fill you with holiness from above.

APPLICATION
Have you blocked God's work in your soul by not believing in His almightiness? How?
What does your soul need most today (joy, peace, love, forgiveness, fulfillment)?
Finish this prayer: "Lord Jesus, I'm empty inside because I don't see you as you really are.
    Please . . ."

FEBRUARY 28
"DO YOU NOW BELIEVE?"

Forging ahead on your own while asking God for a blessing is a recipe for disaster.

➤

BACKGROUND In the final year of Oswald Chambers' life, he taught British soldiers from the book of Job. His main point was that God uses suffering to free us from our preconceived notions about Him and how we should serve Him. Today, Chambers tells us that our preconceived notions are in direct competition with our relationship with Jesus, and only through our relationship with Him can we hope to have His blessings.

SCRIPTURAL CONTEXT The upper room marks a key moment in the disciples' lives. They were coasting along for three years with only a minor hiccup here and there—such as when they couldn't help the epileptic boy or when Jesus had to rebuke them for their lack of faith. But on *this* night, the night Jesus was betrayed, everything fell apart. The disciples' world came crashing down. Chambers loves to quote verses from *this* night, since they speak to us in our moments of crisis.

Read John 16:17–33, and put yourself in the disciples' shoes. What would make a bigger impact on you: when Jesus said that you would be scattered, or when He said, "I have told you these things, so that in me you may have peace"? Now read Proverbs 3:5–6 and 1 John 1. How will you avoid leaning on your own understanding today? How will you walk in the light (see January 9, *Companion*)?

WHAT'S THE DEVOTIONAL SAYING? Do you serve God based out of a sense of duty, based on the needs you see around you, or based on something else? The only basis for our service, according to Chambers, is Jesus' resurrection life working intimately inside of us.

One way we know we are living in intimate contact with Jesus' resurrection life is that our actions don't make sense to some people. This is not proof that we walk in the light. There are plenty of people whose actions don't make sense and who are far from walking in God's light! But other people's responses do give us a test of our reasons for serving God: If everyone compliments us on our wise plans, we probably are basing our service on duty or needs, not on Christ.

APPLICATION

By trying to obey God these past two months, have you been ridiculed/misunderstood?

Are there ways in which you are still serving Jesus Christ out of a sense of duty?

Finish this prayer: "Lord, I want to walk in your light, not in my own sense of duty, so please help me to . . ."

ᘒᘖ FEBRUARY 29 ᘒᘖ
WHAT DO YOU WANT THE LORD TO DO FOR YOU?

Struggling with "it" again?
Don't put it past God to deliver you completely.

◄

BACKGROUND If you are reading today's lesson, it's probably because this year is a leap year. And even if it's not a leap year, enjoy the lesson anyway. This article fits well with February 28's lesson.

Do you find yourself getting rid of your old way of living? In today's study, Oswald Chambers says that doing this and completely identifying with Jesus is a miracle like the healing of a blind man.

SCRIPTURAL CONTEXT In Luke 18, we read the story of blind Bartimaeus (and his blind friend, as Matthew 20:29–34 records). As you read about this healing and the "disturbance" the blind men cause, can you think of anything you need that might lead you to cause this kind of disturbance?

WHAT'S THE DEVOTIONAL SAYING? Do you "deify" common sense? God loves wisdom. But the first rule of wisdom is "fear the Lord," which means we have to look to God first and foremost, and only as a distant second to the principles collected in Proverbs, Ecclesiastes, and elsewhere.

Today's lesson teaches us that a good indication we are seeking God is that our desire for identification with Jesus causes a disturbance for others. Again, this is not proof that we are properly seeking God, but it helps us know when we are *not* seeking Him. Do you live your life without making waves? Then you are either very blessed to have been close to God all your life, or perhaps you have never earnestly sought Him. Throw yourself on Him today and see if He doesn't come through for you!

APPLICATION

What is your biggest "disturbance"? How are you going to deal with it?

Are you a disturbance to people around you? How does this relate to your "disturbance"?

Finish this prayer: "Jesus, I've been using common sense to overcome my disturbance, but only you can . . ."

ᑜᓑ MARCH 1 ᑜᓑ
THE PIERCING QUESTION

Are you numbed by sin?
Let Jesus question you—and cut you to the core!

➤

BACKGROUND Today we begin a three-day study that introduces us to the concept of "natural individuality." Oswald Chambers will refer to this concept more than fifty times in *Utmost*. He contrasts *individuality* with *personality*, which today in the Updated Edition is reworded as "inner spiritual self" (skip to December 11 and 12 for a more thorough treatment).

Do you find yourself making promises to God and to others that you don't keep? Today's lesson helps us understand why this happens and how simple questions from God's Word can help us to stop doing that.

SCRIPTURAL CONTEXT We have seen Jesus' loving talk with Peter already (January 5 and February 9, *Utmost*). But today and for the next two days we'll look more closely at their conversation on the shore of Galilee. Read Matthew 26:31–35 and John 21. Think about how Peter must have felt the night he denied Jesus, and then consider what he felt when Jesus reinstated him as a "sheep feeder."

Now read Luke 12:1–12 and Hebrews 4. What is the difference between professing ("declaring" in the Updated Edition) and confessing? How does God's Word help us be confessors instead of professors?

WHAT'S THE DEVOTIONAL SAYING? Chambers discussed Peter's bold profession of his natural love as well as the end of his natural sufficiency (see January 4 and 5, *Utmost*). Today we see how Peter made the transition from professing to confessing: It was thanks to the unswerving, penetrating question of his Lord.

Has God's Word ever been as sharp as a two-edged sword to you? How so? Was it just when you read it, or did someone have to deliver His Word to you in the form of a piercing question? If you have experienced this hurt, you know it doesn't feel good. But perhaps you at least could recognize it as your Father's hurt and not just someone being preachy. Ask God to show you *His* hand in any past, present, or future hurt that He has sent or will send your way.

APPLICATION

What part of the Bible hurts you the most? Why? Is it a personal hurt?

Do you love Jesus? How do you know?

Finish this prayer: "Jesus, sin has dulled my senses for so long, but your question sensitizes me and . . ."

MARCH 2
HAVE YOU FELT THE PAIN
INFLICTED BY THE LORD?

Been through the wringer?
God presses you like wine so your true flavor ripens.

◄ ►

BACKGROUND Has a loved one ever said to you, "You don't really love me"? If so, how did you deal with that pain? Did you say, "Look at this or that" to prove your love? What about the times when that person asked, "Do you love me?"

Today we read about how Peter dealt with similar questions from his friend and master. We learn that we can expect Jesus to pin us down with the same kind of questions at least once in our lives. How will we respond?

SCRIPTURAL CONTEXT If John 21 is not still fresh in your mind from yesterday, read it again. Think about how Peter felt the third time Jesus asked the same question.

When you come to the end of your sufficiency and can't imagine how you will ever keep going, will you say with Peter, "Lord, you know all things" (verse 17)?

WHAT'S THE DEVOTIONAL SAYING?
The main point today is that Jesus' well-aimed question (see March 1, *Companion*) will produce exquisite pain in our hearts. But this pain is just what we need to get rid of our delusion and deception, which made us think we could do something or passionately *feel* something for Jesus.

Isn't it hard to know if we really love God? It's hard enough to know whether or not we love a certain person, and God is invisible! Today's lesson tells us that the once-in-a-lifetime painful questions of Jesus are our best way to see the love we have for God. Has Jesus asked you something that goes to your very soul? If not, be ready for when He does.

APPLICATION

What have you learned from Jesus' patient questioning? Were His questions effective?

Is there a way in which you will "never be deceived again"? What gives you that confidence?

Finish this prayer: "Lord Jesus, I know you have touched me with some of your questions
   because . . ."

⟨⟩ MARCH 3 ⟨⟩
HIS COMMISSION TO US

Trouble loving others?
Don't try it alone. Let God form His love in you.

◄

BACKGROUND Did you ever work as a shepherd? Oswald Chambers did! During his four years of darkness (see January 3, *Companion*), he helped his friend John Cameron pasture sheep on the slopes of Britain's highest mountain. Today's lesson reminds us that sheep are often dirty, awkward creatures, and that when Jesus tells us, "Feed My sheep," we will need supernatural love to do the job right.

SCRIPTURAL CONTEXT In addition to the passage we've been studying for three days, Chambers also quotes John 20:21. Read John 20:19–23 and think about how the disciples felt on Sunday evening in that locked room when Jesus appeared. He probably spoke to them in Aramaic. So when He breathed on them and said, "Receive the Holy Spirit," they would have heard it also as "Receive the Holy Breath" since *spirit, breath,* and *wind* are all the same Aramaic word.

What if the risen Christ were to show up in your living room and breathe His own breath on you? If He told you that He was sending you the way He had been sent by God, how would you feel? Would it help that He said, "Receive the Holy Spirit"? Read John 14:26 and Luke 3:16, 11:13, and 12:10–12 to see what the disciples had already learned about the Holy Spirit.

WHAT'S THE DEVOTIONAL SAYING? As a finale to this three-day series, Chambers tells us why our "natural individuality" must be eclipsed by "personality"—so we can pour ourselves out for God's sheep. When we discover, through Jesus' painful questions, that we love Him and have His love in our heart, we can love others with real love. Fake love will result in people blaspheming God's love, since people will think our fake love is what God's love looks like.

Do you want to be one with God as Jesus was? The sign that you do is when you spend yourself like Jesus did. Who are the "sheep" around you? You may be more awkward and "dirty" than they are, but they still need you, just as you need them. Give freely of all the gifts God has given you. Love the sheep extravagantly, with the true love of God. Don't worry about your love wearing out. If it's from God, it won't!

APPLICATION

What is God's ultimate goal for you? How will you know if He's achieved it?
How would natural human sympathies cause you to blaspheme God's true love?
Finish this prayer: "Today, Lord, I will feed your sheep by . . ."

⚬⚬ MARCH 4 ⚬⚬
IS THIS TRUE OF ME?

Is your faith a fraud?
Or do God's desires burn in you, driving you to Christ?

➤

BACKGROUND Reading today's devotional might give you the impression that Oswald Chambers never had any fun—that all his time was taken up with fulfilling the ministry God gave him. But we saw on February 17 how he convinced his American hosts to take a sleighing vacation with him, so we know that his efforts to follow single-mindedly after his God-given ministry did not preclude fun. In fact, his "next thing" (see February 18, *Companion*) was often something that the world would consider a frivolous waste of time, but since it flowed from his intimate relationship with God, it was part and parcel of the ministry God gave him. Today's lesson urges us to avoid the prosperity, success, and leisure time that comes from serving God from our common sense. We should instead serve Him from His calling on our lives.

SCRIPTURAL CONTEXT Paul's return to Jerusalem is a fascinating drama. Read Acts 20–21. How did the Ephesian elders and those who gathered at Paul's house respond to what Paul said? Did they think Paul had an unhealthy death wish? Now read 1 Corinthians 6:19–20. Paul wrote this about sexual sins, but how is it applicable in any situation? Does it fit your situation today?

WHAT'S THE DEVOTIONAL SAYING? Where do you think you are most useful to God? We saw on February 21 that doing "useful" things can keep us from loving God in extravagant ways. Today we find out more details about why focusing on the "useful" is so dangerous. First, when dressed up with the emotions you'd expect from a Christian (love, joy, friendliness, and so on), usefulness can masquerade as a call from God and keep us from our true calling. Second, usefulness tempts us with prosperity, success, and leisure time, which also can keep us from God's call. Third, when we focus on being "useful," we end up resenting the time we "waste" on serving God—similar to the way Judas resented Mary's "waste" of perfume (John 12:5). Finally, it will keep God from being our guide.

Have you focused too much on the "useful" things you can do for God? Have you ever spent time serving God in a way that would seem like a "waste" to people like Judas? Or are you trying to be so useful that your life, and all your time, seems "dear" to you? Look in today's lesson for the ways Chambers contrasts a life focused on being "useful" as opposed to a life burning with God's desires. Which of these lives do you want today?

APPLICATION

What will it cost you to receive God's commission?

How "dear" do you consider your time given to God, your acts of service, and your life?

Finish this prayer: "Father, although I usually decide what to do with my life by considering . . ."

⟳ MARCH 5 ⟳
IS HE REALLY MY LORD?

Be faithful to what you hear God say in the times you are closest to Him.

◄

BACKGROUND As World War I broke out, Oswald Chambers saw obvious needs. Soldiers, doctors, nurses, and supporting personnel needed spiritual guidance, manpower was needed in troop staging areas such as Egypt, and the country's morale needed everyone to have an "all hands on deck" mentality. How could he stay at the Bible Training College while there were clear needs for him to meet elsewhere?

In today's lesson, Chambers tells us that needs are not God's call; they are merely opportunities. Chambers did not immediately rush to Egypt or another troop staging area. Instead, he drew even closer to God and listened for His call. Today's devotional encourages us to do the same.

SCRIPTURAL CONTEXT In addition to the second half of yesterday's theme verse, Chambers quotes from John 20:21 (as we saw on March 3), Matthew 25:21, Acts 9:16, and John 21:17 (which we looked at on March 1). He also uses the phrase "companied with Jesus" (Classic Edition), which he took from Acts 1:21 in the King James Version. Read all of these verses now and think about the following questions: What would make your Master say to you, "Well done"? Why did Jesus tell Ananias, and not Saul, that Saul would suffer? How have you "companied" with Jesus and His disciples?

WHAT'S THE DEVOTIONAL SAYING? Besides continuing yesterday's theme about the priority of our God-given ministry, today's lesson teaches many things. First, it tells us that true joy comes from more than just success in one isolated job, but from how that task fits in with our calling—why God made us and re-made us. Second, finding our calling and ministry is the spiritual equivalent of finding our "niche" in life. Third, we can't find this calling until we know Jesus as more than just our Savior—we must know Him as a close friend. Fourth, our call doesn't start with the needs we see—they are important, but not the source—but instead with what we hear and feel when we are closest to Jesus. Finally, Chambers warns that what we hear when we are closest to Jesus doesn't always point us to specific jobs, but it does always point us away from things that would conflict with the whole reason God created us.

APPLICATION

What gives you joy? What gave Jesus joy?

Why should we ignore demands for service in certain areas?

Finish this prayer: "God, when I'm in close fellowship with you, I feel you calling me to the ministry of . . ."

TAKING THE NEXT STEP

Is the daily grind wearing you down?
That's when you need God's grace big-time!

➤

BACKGROUND David McCasland, one of Oswald Chambers' recent biographers, said that Chambers worked hard on projects that might be scrapped in a few months. For example, he continually made improvements on the YMCA hut in El-Zaytoun (see February 5, *Companion*) even though he hoped to move his operations to Palestine. He lamented that "men do not follow Solomon's admonition, 'Whatsoever thy hand findeth to do, do it with thy might' (Ecclesiastes 9:10 KJV). The tendency is to argue, 'It's only for so short a time, why trouble?' If it is only for five minutes, let it be well done."

Are you having trouble doing the daily grind with all your might? Today's devotional will encourage you "Amid a Crowd of Paltry Things" (Classic Edition title).

SCRIPTURAL CONTEXT Chambers gives us two Scripture passages today that at first don't seem related. Second Corinthians 6:4 is the first verse in a seven-verse list of Paul's hardships. John 13 is a chapter about Jesus washing the disciples' feet. Tomorrow Chambers mentions the "everyday" and "terrible" experiences of life (Updated Edition). Does the list in 2 Corinthians 6 sound more terrible or everyday?

Chambers tells us that our need to consciously draw on God and His grace is even greater when we take the next step in our mundane duties than when we preach the gospel. Is that your experience? Why did Jesus wash the disciples' feet on the last night before His crucifixion?

WHAT'S THE DEVOTIONAL SAYING? Today's lesson is one of the shortest, yet by no means the easiest to apply. How do you respond to the daily grind of life? Do you try to drum up spectators? People who will notice what you're doing and give you a pat on the back for all your hard work? Or do you soldier on, unseen by any eyes, as your heart is increasingly crushed by the meaningless of it all?

Chambers tells us that there is a third way. He implies that God will lead us to that third way by thwarting our efforts to attract an audience. He also points us to John 13, perhaps with a particular focus on verse 3, so we can know that God has put all things under our power through Christ. No matter how much we lack vision, spectators, and encouragement, we can be certain that the Spirit in us comes from God and is taking us back to Him. Nothing can crush us or discourage us as we look to God and the power He has made available to us in Christ!

APPLICATION
When was the last time you felt like giving up in the face of everyday life?
Were you crushed? How did the grace of Almighty God affect you?
Finish this prayer: "Jesus, I live your incarnation by taking the next step in . . ."

⌖ MARCH 7 ⌖
THE SOURCE OF ABUNDANT JOY

Is your faith shaken?
God's love is not. He'll turn trials into reasons to rejoice!

◄

BACKGROUND Self-taught Hebrew scholar Robert Young died in Edinburgh seven years before a twenty-one-year-old Oswald Chambers arrived there to study art. We don't know if Chambers used Young's analytical concordance or his literal version of the Bible. But we can read Romans 8:35 in Young's Literal Translation (YLT) and compare it to yesterday's verse. Two words ("tribulation" and "distress") appear in both. These words highlight the connection between today and yesterday, while the rest of the words (for example, "patience" and "persecution") underscore the differences.

Do you need both patience for the daily grind and strength in persecution? Today's devotional will remind you of God's love—no matter what you face.

SCRIPTURAL CONTEXT If you don't have access, Internet or otherwise, to the YLT, you can still use your own Bible to compare Romans 8:35 to yesterday's theme verse and try to spot the similarities and differences. How do "these things" that Paul faced compare to the things that can't separate us from God's love? How are we super-conquerers "in all these things"? Turn also to 2 Corinthians 7:4. How is this verse a fitting end to what Paul said in chapter 6?

WHAT'S THE DEVOTIONAL SAYING? Do you like swimming? How would you like to swim in pounding, fifty-foot swells? Talk about a fear factor! Yet some surfers joyfully crisscross the globe looking for fifty-foot waves. Today Chambers tells us that the trials we face can produce fear or joy, depending on whether we believe that nothing can separate us from God's love.

Do you take joy in your trials, both the "terrible" and "monotonous" (Classic Edition) kind? If not, take time to meditate on the limitless miracle, the fathomless marvel of God's love at Calvary. With God's love at work, your trials will actually *fuel* your joy.

APPLICATION

When has a trial given you joy? Why?

Do you have a source of abundant joy? How do you display an attitude of joy?

Finish this prayer: "Thank you, Father, that nothing can separate me from your limitless love. Help me . . ."

⤜∞⤛ MARCH 8 ⤜∞⤛
THE SURRENDERED LIFE

Does your ugly pride keep you from God?
Let go of pretense and cling to Him.

BACKGROUND We know that Oswald Chambers thought highly of himself before his four years of darkness (see January 3, *Companion*) ended. Otherwise, why would he feel such dread when he stood up and admitted, "Either Christianity is a downright fraud, or I have not got hold of the right end of the stick." As we saw on January 16 (*Companion*), Chambers didn't want to "be a fool," and he valued the esteem of his friends more than the blessing of God (see February 12, *Companion*). So today's lesson is based on his own struggle with coming to grips with his pride. Do you struggle with pride? If so, today's teaching is for you!

SCRIPTURAL CONTEXT Paul's letter to the Galatians is an antidote to pride. Read as much of it as you can right now, and see how today's theme verse fits into the larger context of the Judaizers' spiritual pride. How was Paul like the Judaizers in his past life? How did Peter and Barnabas fall into the same sin?

Have you been crucified with Christ? In what practical ways? Paul said, "I no longer live, but Christ lives in me" (Galatians 2:20 NIV). Can you say this too?

WHAT'S THE DEVOTIONAL SAYING? The key word today is "relinquish" or "surrender" (Updated Edition). Chambers uses this word ten times in today's lesson. He says we have to relinquish not only our sins but also our pretense. In fact, if we *really* surrender our sins, seeing all our trash the way God sees it, we won't have any room left for pretense.

It's the hardest thing to see your pride as God sees it. Chambers calls it "painful disillusionment." Have you had the shame, horror, and desperate conviction that Chambers describes? If not, just wait!

APPLICATION

What pretense is God asking you to surrender? How does His request make you feel? Why do we have to let go before grasping God? What will He do if we resist surrender? Finish this prayer: "Lord, I'm reluctant to surrender, but I know that if I do, you will equip me to . . ."

TURNING BACK OR WALKING WITH JESUS?

Are you walking with Jesus, even in uncertainty?
Besides being our Savior, He's also our travel guide!

BACKGROUND Meredith and Bessie Standley, whom Oswald Chambers took sleighing (see February 17, *Companion*), had a three-year-old daughter named Dorothea, Chamber's "irresistible companion." He wrote about the time she made him split with laughter: "She lifted her baby brother and put him on his feet; he flopped on the floor and began yelling, and Dorothea said, 'Oh, he ain't sankified yet!' "

Today's lesson says that after we are sanctified, life is about being one with Jesus. Interestingly even a three-year-old picked up the lingo of "sanctification." When does God call you a yokefellow and give you a "clear" realization of what He wants? Is it immediately when you are saved, or is it after you have asked for His gift of the Holy Spirit?

SCRIPTURAL CONTEXT Chambers walks us through the end of John 6. Read that chapter from the viewpoint of someone who stopped following Jesus. How would Jesus' discussion make you feel? Now think of it from Peter's perspective. How would you feel when everyone walked away?

Notice to whom Jesus asked, "Do you want to go away?" Was it to people who knew Jesus? Do you think you know Jesus? How might He surprise you?

What's the Devotional Saying?
The message today is that we must walk with Jesus into all uncertainties, allowing Him to surprise us as our travel guide. Peter knew Jesus—as God's Holy One—but didn't fully realize that Jesus had chosen him to be a fellow laborer. Jesus supplied Peter with what he lacked in knowledge by reminding him that he *was* chosen as a "yoke-fellow" (see the Classic Edition). Will you be yoked to Jesus and His surprises today?

Application
Do you have an adventurous attitude toward God? How so? Are you too impulsive?

Why is it essential to maintain intimate oneness with Jesus while serving Him?

Finish this prayer: "Precious Jesus, I only have absolute devotion to offer you. Please help me stay . . ."

BEING AN EXAMPLE OF HIS MESSAGE

When you talk about God, is your life "exhibit A"?
Let God mold and shape you.

BACKGROUND Is your heart crumpled into the purpose of God? In other words, has He, through things that have happened, taken your emotions and put them in the blender?

Today, in the Classic Edition, we read a line from Alfred, Lord Tennyson's poem *In Memoriam A.H.H.*: "batter'd . . . to shape and use." Oswald Chambers quotes this line three times in *Utmost* (also July 6 and October 4). If your heart feels battered, today's devotional is for you!

SCRIPTURAL CONTEXT Yesterday we read from John 6. Today we see more of John 6 (verse 63), as well as 2 Timothy 4:2 and Acts 1:8. Read these verses and their contexts. When Jesus gave words that were "spirit and life," what happened? How much of 2 Timothy is the "how-to" of preaching, and how much talks about how to live as an example? What happened at Pentecost that made the disciples the incarnation of what they preached?

WHAT'S THE DEVOTIONAL SAYING? Today's message is for people who preach sermons. But even if you never plan to preach one, the point Chambers makes is applicable: We are not merely the wire in God's telephone conversation with the world; we are part of His message. Chambers backs up this point with three thoughts. First, we are called sons and daughters of God (2 Corinthians 6:18), so the best way we can "speak" God's message is to have a family resemblance with Him. Second, Jesus didn't just tell God's message, His words were His spirit and His life. Third, God clearly shapes our hearts through suffering, which would be unnecessary if all He wanted was for us to parrot His words.

Chambers' analogy that preachers are living sacrifices set on fire (as in 1 Kings 18) is fitting for all Christians. Will you be a fiery offering today?

APPLICATION

Have you been molded and shaped by God for His purpose? How did He do that?

Why must liberation be real in us before we can liberate other people?

Finish this prayer: "Lord, please continue to break, baptize, and crush me into submission, so I can be . . ."

OBEDIENCE TO THE "HEAVENLY VISION"

Got a vision but missed its fulfillment?
Set aside busywork; let God carry it out.

BACKGROUND Today's lesson has only the second instance of the phrase "utmost for God's highest" in the famous devotional with that title. We will encounter these words three more times (July 7, September 15, and December 27). Each time, we should pay close attention to what Oswald Chambers is saying. For example, today he is telling us that keeping God's vision is essential, and the only way to do that is to live our utmost for God's glory.

What is God's heavenly vision? In Chambers' mind, the "vision" is God letting us see himself and *why* He made us. We were all created for God and His special purpose for us. Our hearts resonate with that purpose (see January 16–17, *Companion*).

Why do you think God made you? If you don't know yet, you can still benefit from today's lesson by allowing it to apply to the general "vision" of sharing God's love.

SCRIPTURAL CONTEXT Today's theme verse is from Acts 26. We looked at this chapter on January 10, 24, 28, and 29. In verse 19, Paul says he obeyed the vision. Why did God create Paul?

Now turn to Habakkuk 2. What was Habakkuk's vision? How long do you think he had to wait in order to see his vision fulfilled? Finally, consider the phrases "bring forth fruit" and "in the light." What verses come to mind? Ask God to help you walk in the light of the vision He's given you so you can bear fruit!

WHAT'S THE DEVOTIONAL SAYING? The lesson today is full of the same messages we've read all year: Work out the lofty spiritual ideals in day-to-day living, but don't get so caught up in daily duties that you lose sight of God. Chambers' word pictures are superb—can you picture yourself a seedpod, spinning in a whirlwind? Is that how God's way of sending you sometimes feels?

If you're like a lot of people, you find it easier to work on a well-defined project than to work at whatever is the "next thing" while you wait for God's vision to "accomplish itself." We like to know exactly how the vision will be accomplished, and we have a hard time giving our utmost to God when we don't know how it all is supposed to happen. Are you having that trouble right now? Chambers' advice is to walk in God's light second-by-second and minute-by-minute, which we do by focusing on God's vision.

APPLICATION

Why will the vision never be fulfilled if we don't apply God's truth in everyday things?

What storms of God have you been through? Did you end up "planted" in a new spot?

Finish this prayer: "God, I want to give my utmost for your highest so I can live true to the vision and . . ."

MARCH 12
TOTAL SURRENDER

Family and job make you lukewarm?
Get red-hot for God! He'll care for everything else.

➢

BACKGROUND Oswald Chambers was likely given his "vision" (see March 11, *Utmost*) of surrender the day his four years of darkness ended. Everything he did after that moment was the working out of this vision in his day-to-day activities. So why did he have to wait so long for this vision? We saw on February 2 that his problem was that he had wanted the Spirit's power in his *own* hand. This "commercial" (see the Classic Edition) attitude is what he warns us against today.

SCRIPTURAL CONTEXT Jesus cautioned His disciples about following Him for the wrong reasons or without counting the costs. Read Mark 10:17–34, Luke 9:57–62, and 14:26–33. How do we know that the blessings Jesus promises are secondary to His sake and the gospel's sake? Have you thought about what it would cost to give your utmost to His highest? Are you prepared to pay the whole cost? Who or what is still holding you back?

WHAT'S THE DEVOTIONAL SAYING? What is a "personal sovereign preference for Jesus Christ Himself"? It's a decision of will saying we want Jesus. When we get so sick of how our sin separates us from Jesus, we decide, in the deepest place of our free will, that we *must* have Jesus above all else. Theologians will tell us that we are powerless to have faith in Christ or to repent without God. Chambers agreed. Yet God does allow our will to play a role. Perhaps it is after He puts a new heart in us, but our will-power definitely comes into play at some point. So Chambers urges us to get our will to the place where it has a preference for Jesus above anything else.

What keeps you from wanting Jesus more than anything? Ironically, it may be His blessings that you most appreciate. Chambers assures us: God takes care of any blessings that we sacrifice on the altar of total surrender. Will you trust that this is true today?

APPLICATION

What motivates you to want to surrender yourself to God?

What keeps you from surrender (family, comfort, ambition)? What does Jesus say about surrender?

Finish this prayer: "God, I'm responding now to your call. Help me go beyond my natural devotion . . ."

MARCH 13
GOD'S TOTAL SURRENDER TO US

What is total surrender?
It's giving yourself to God as Christ gave himself to us.

◄

BACKGROUND Yesterday Oswald Chambers encouraged us to surrender in total abandonment to God. Today he tells us that our abandonment to God is completely empowered by God's abandonment to us. Nothing in our abandonment makes us think about our surrender. Throwing ourselves in reckless abandon at God thrills our thoughts with God's "infinitely greater" abandonment to us.

Chambers and the League of Prayer (see January 10, *Companion*) preached holiness and sanctification. But today he reminds us that God's abandonment to us is far more important than our holiness. Thus, proclaiming Jesus, whose cross demonstrates God's great abandon, is our foremost preaching job. And getting caught up in God's abandonment is the best thing we can do with our life.

SCRIPTURAL CONTEXT The only verse that Chambers quotes today is John 3:16. What does this well-known verse really mean? According to Chambers, it means that God gave himself absolutely to us.

What a profound mystery! How could the creator of the universe give himself in reckless abandon to creatures like us? Meditate on this truth. Chambers said we shouldn't talk about surrendering to God until we have grasped John 3:16.

WHAT'S THE DEVOTIONAL SAYING? When did you "get saved"? From *what* were you saved? Chambers tells us that salvation is being rescued out of our self and into union with God. We notice that we are saved because we watch our pathological addiction to self be completely broken. But freedom from our sin-complex is just an effect of being submerged in the powerful flood of God's abandon.

If you were a sponge saturated with God's reckless abandon, would it be hard to pour yourself out for others, no matter how ungrateful they were? No! God's abandon is the most over-the-top outpouring of goodness to the undeserving. So even having a little of His abandon in you will allow you to throw yourself in reckless abandon to Him and to those He wants you to serve. Don't think about what you are sacrificing, just give, give, and give still more!

APPLICATION

How are we "completely delivered from [self] and . . . placed in perfect union with Him"?

What are we called to proclaim? How does our message relate to John 3:16?

Finish this prayer: "Holy Spirit, you have brought me into intimate contact with God to show me that . . ."

In bondage to a bad habit?
Admit that you can't stop, and let Christ set you free.

➤

BACKGROUND For the last two and a half years of his life, Oswald Chambers was surrounded by soldiers. Many of his soldier friends were undoubtedly plagued with the same bad habits that we all face. And everyone, Chambers included, is prone to bad habits of the mind. So how do we break these bad habits?

Chambers recommends we first acknowledge that *we* are to blame for being enslaved to bad habits. He then says that we can become "enslaved" to God. Is our power to say "yes" to a bad habit the same as our ability to say "yes" to God? Chambers implies that it is, but before we impeach him for preaching a do-it-yourself theology, read what he says in the second paragraph: "There is no power within the human soul itself that is capable of breaking the bondage of the nature created by yielding [to a bad habit]."

SCRIPTURAL CONTEXT We haven't looked at Romans 6 since January 15, but what a great chapter it is! Read it now and think about the difference between verses 1–14 and 15–23. Which passage motivates you more to live free from bad habits? What is the motivation behind verses 15–18 compared to 19–23?

Now turn to Luke 4. Do you think the synagogue members considered themselves captives? Did they think Jesus could help them? Why or why not?

WHAT'S THE DEVOTIONAL SAYING? Today's lesson on "Obedience" is summed up by the Updated Edition's title: "Yielding." What's the difference between yielding and obedience? Nothing really. It's just that we think of obedience as good and yielding as bad (don't *yield* to temptation!). Chambers uses "yield" ten times today and "obey" only once. He uses "yield" more than "obey" so that we understand that giving in to either God or a bad habit can be a very passive thing, like a driver who yields to the car with the right-of-way. Have you passively yielded to your selfishness? *All* our lusts are selfish, because our lusts don't wait for God's timing—only our own.

The good news is that yielding to God can be a very passive thing too. The only required ingredient is "utter humiliation." We must humbly acknowledge that God has the right-of-way in *everything* that happens to us. Confess that to Him right now and begin the good habit of yielding to Him in all things.

APPLICATION
What controls and dominates you lately? Is it the sinful nature or the Spirit (Galatians 5)?
How did a particular bondage begin in your life and how can (did) you break free?
Finish this prayer: "Lord Jesus Christ, you alone, by your redemption power, can set me free from . . ."

MARCH 15
THE DISCIPLINE OF DISMAY

Is Jesus too otherworldly?
Let Him be far off for now; to follow will be pure joy.

◄

BACKGROUND Why didn't Biddy Chambers group the "Discipline of D..." lessons (February 7, 14, 22, March 15, July 30, and August 2) into a series the way she did with other interrelated devotionals? Perhaps she felt it would be hard to digest all six in one week! Whatever the reason, let us steel ourselves for today's truths, no matter how difficult they are for us to understand and apply.

SCRIPTURAL CONTEXT For today's lesson, Oswald Chambers quotes from Mark 10:32 and Luke 9:51. When did these verses occur in Jesus' three-year earthly ministry? Most scholars put Luke 9:51 after Jesus' autumn visit to Jerusalem for the Festival of Booths and Mark 10:32 after His winter visit to Jerusalem for Chanukah. But Mark's gospel "fast-forwards" from the transfiguration to the Judean ministry that ended with Jesus' crucifixion. It's as if for Mark—and Peter, who influenced Mark's gospel—Jesus had already "set his face like flint" (Vulgate translation of Luke 9:51, see also Isaiah 50:7) to die in Jerusalem.

How do you think Peter and the other disciples felt when Jesus predicted His suffering right before He was transfigured and again just afterward? The very next Passover would feature their friend and master as the sacrificial lamb. Is it any wonder that Peter had Mark skip Jesus' two trips to Jerusalem, the Perean ministry, and the raising of Lazarus? Jesus had suddenly changed from the rabbi they knew into someone completely different!

WHAT'S THE DEVOTIONAL SAYING?
Today is another *clouds and darkness* kind of lesson (see January 3, *Utmost*). If you are struggling with situations from God that seem totally out of character with the loving Savior you thought you knew, this reading is for you! Chambers gives us reasons Jesus is sometimes so otherworldly—for example, he had to "fathom" (as if He took depth readings of) our sin and sorrow, which would make anyone otherworldly! But the main thing Chambers does is to encourage us to endure our darkness and not to bolster our enthusiasm by our own burnt offerings, as the people in Isaiah 1 were criticized for doing.

Are you in darkness? You're not alone! Jesus seems to be looking straight ahead, but whenever you're not looking, He lovingly checks on you.

APPLICATION

Have you ever felt distant from God? Did you feel at the time that He had a strange point of view?

When does Jesus, the Man of Sorrows, sometimes make you feel as if you don't recognize Him?

Finish this prayer: "Jesus, when I'm in times of dismay, feeling like I don't know you, I will . . ."

MARCH 16
THE MASTER WILL JUDGE

Are you judging others?
A smug heart will judge itself by becoming callous.

BACKGROUND Some of Oswald Chambers' devotionals in the Classic Edition are crystal clear. Others, like today's, require more careful reading—and a quick glance at the Updated Edition certainly doesn't hurt!

Today Chambers tells us to live our lives in light of final judgment. It sounds like a rather depressing way to live, but he says that if we do, then the final judgment will bring us "delight" as we see God's work in us.

SCRIPTURAL CONTEXT We looked at 2 Corinthians 5 on February 4. Today, we see that Paul was compelled not only by "Christ's love" but also because he knew what it was like to "fear the Lord." It seems a bit depressing to live in fear of God's judgment, but Paul's knowledge of that judgment is what allowed Christ's love to so richly compel him.

We have also looked at 1 John 1:7 many times. As you reread this chapter today, think about how John tried to help his readers avoid hypocrisy. In what ways are you a spiritual hypocrite?

WHAT'S THE DEVOTIONAL SAYING? The beauty of *Utmost* is that it takes a hard line against sin while avoiding the other extreme of being self-righteous. We are prone to either give up the fight against sin or rewrite the rules and declare ourselves victorious (and everyone else a bunch of losers!). But today's devotional finds the third way: walking in the light. We've seen this concept before (January 9, February 28, and March 11), but today we get more insight into how it works: We bring our bad attitudes and non-Christ-centered judgments to God *quickly* and admit our guilt *fully* for the dangerous thing it is.

Are you dogged by your own sour attitudes and mean-spirited, judgmental heart? Your only hope is the Spirit's power. His power comes as we bring our hazardous, toxic attitudes and judgments to Him.

APPLICATION

How can we avoid shame on judgment day? Have you been tolerating wrong attitudes? Has sin taken its toll in you? How? Who can prevent sin's inherent consequences?

Finish this prayer: "Holy Spirit, I'm in danger of being numb to sin and unconsciously living a lie, so please . . ."

MARCH 17
THE SERVANT'S PRIMARY GOAL

The hardest thing to do is to keep your focus on performing only for God.

BACKGROUND Oswald Chambers was an excellent musician. Both at the Bible Training College in London and the YMCA meetings in Cairo, he led music on a small organ. So when we read today about a musician who ignores the audience if he can catch a look from his master, we know that Chambers felt the tension of having to choose whose approval he would seek.

How do you handle the tension of wanting God's approval and not the world's? Today's lesson will encourage you to keep fighting the temptation to play for the audience.

SCRIPTURAL CONTEXT The theme verse today is a prequel to yesterday's verse. Paul talks about his efforts to seek God's approval in the context of the final judgment. Reread this chapter and answer the questions: Why does Paul want to please God? What is he longing to be?

Now flip to 2 Timothy 2:15. In the King James Version, the wording is "approved unto God," which emphasizes *who* approves us—God and God only. Next, turn to Hebrews 12:1–2. What's the point of "facing the Lord Jesus," as the Classic Edition reads? What motivates us to throw off our besetting sins? Finally, read 1 Corinthians 9:24–27. Chambers quotes the KJV word "castaway," which in modern versions is "disqualified." Then he paraphrases verse 27, highlighting the way our body can lead us down the wrong path if we don't constantly watch it.

WHAT'S THE DEVOTIONAL SAYING? The point today is that it's hard work to keep the main thing the main thing. And what is the main thing? To be accepted by God!

Reading this devotional might make you think that it's up to *you* to do the hard work of focusing on the main thing. Isn't our spiritual life God's responsibility? Are we completely incapable of doing anything without Him? Chambers would probably say, "Yes, apart from God, we can do nothing, but don't use that as an excuse for laziness! The Spirit of God is *already* in you, if you've claimed Luke 11:13." So take hold of your life by both horns, and root out any ambition that is not focused on the main thing of pleasing God. Follow Chambers' advice to "once a week at least" see if you are up to God's standards. Fix your eyes on Jesus, and consider the terrible "castaway" consequences that will result if your noble goals lead you off the path of pleasing God.

APPLICATION

What is your greatest ambition? From whom do you seek approval? Why?

How can the wrong first priority (win souls, plant churches, for instance) disqualify you for the race?

Finish this prayer: "God, as I examine my priorities this week, I realize that . . ."

WILL I BRING MYSELF UP TO THIS LEVEL?

God promises to be our Dad so we can know (and act like!) we are His family.

BACKGROUND Oswald and Biddy Chambers banked on God's promises. For example, they made a pact never to use the excuse, "We can't afford it" when presented with an opportunity. They relied completely on God as their loving Father and lived accordingly, so much so that many people who knew the Chambers family assumed they had some other source of income, since they never seemed to lack anything. But they also lived out the weighty responsibility of these promises, as today's lesson discusses.

SCRIPTURAL CONTEXT In today's lesson, Chambers examines what Paul told the Corinthians. Read 2 Corinthians 6:14–7:1. What are the "promises" Paul mentions? Why does Paul (and Chambers) consider them a privilege *and* a responsibility?

The other verses Chambers quotes are 1 Corinthians 6:19 and Galatians 1:16 (with reference to how Jesus is "formed" in us, as in Galatians 4:19, and the "mind of Christ," as in 1 Corinthians 2:16 or Philippians 2:5). Read these verses and compare the first one to 2 Corinthians 6:16 and the second one to Matthew 16:17. Do you treat your body as if it were God's temple? Are you tempted to get your spiritual direction only from "flesh and blood"? If you have time, look at the other references for today and think about what you can do to facilitate God's process of forming Christ and Christ's mind in you.

WHAT'S THE DEVOTIONAL SAYING? The point today is that God's great promises demand great responsibility on our part—a responsibility to listen to God as he instructs us down to the smallest scruples in life. Have you felt Him "begin to check" or "bring you conviction of sin"? Chambers would urge you to cleanse yourself at once, without waiting to get advice on the issue from "flesh and blood."

In today's devotional, we see again what Chambers meant by "sanctification." He said that in sanctification, Christ is formed in us. So we might think he meant what we mean today: the process of becoming more like Christ. But right after discussing sanctification, he said, "then I have to transform my natural life into a spiritual life by obedience to Him." So he meant that sanctification happens first and becoming more Christlike follows. In other words, sanctification for Chambers is when the Holy Spirit starts to empower a person's life. Have you asked the Holy Spirit to empower you? If not, don't wait! Ask the Spirit to fill and empower you today.

APPLICATION

Do you have some habit in your body or mind that is against God? If so, what is it?

How can you deal with that particular habit or with bad habits in general?

Finish this prayer: "Holy Spirit, I'll keep my spirit in agreement with you so Jesus can . . ."

ABRAHAM'S LIFE OF FAITH

Want to be close to God?
Stay far from unholiness and your faith will grow.

➤

BACKGROUND On January 2, we had the same theme verse as today, but a different focus. Back then we looked at "going without knowing." Today we see how our going requires mental and moral separation from friends and family who do not yet have a "personal relationship with God."

Oswald separated from his father, Rev. Clarence Chambers, over issues such as money (see January 11, *Companion*) and what career he should pursue. His mental and moral separation from his father, who was a Christian, demonstrates that Chambers applied today's main point even to those who *do* have a "personal relationship with God." Are you so eager for a relationship with God that you are willing to separate even from your closest friends?

SCRIPTURAL CONTEXT Read Hebrews 11:8, Luke 14:26, Isaiah 40:31, and Romans 4:3. Each of these verses captures aspects of the "life of faith." First, Hebrews 11:8 shows how the life of faith obeys the Master even when it doesn't know the final outcome. Second, Luke 14:26 describes how the life of faith embraces discipleship at the expense of all other relationships. Third, in Isaiah 40:31 the life of faith does not just soar through mountaintop experiences with God. Instead, it walks without fainting, which Chambers says is the most difficult and the best evidence of the true life of faith. Finally, Romans 4:3 points to Abraham as the premier example of the life of faith.

The context for these four verses is instructive. For example, read Romans 4:18–25 to find out why righteousness "was credited" to Abraham. What insights can you glean from the context of the other three verses?

WHAT'S THE DEVOTIONAL SAYING?
Through the verses Chambers quotes, we saw four aspects of the life of faith. The overarching theme is that we need a personal relationship with God. Only with this close friendship can we do the following: go without knowing, leave our "kith and kin" (our friends and family), walk without fainting, and believe God as Abraham did.

Do you have a personal relationship with God? Chambers says we have "passing transfigurations"—brief glimpses—of godly character but that real character is attained by walking without fainting through many tests. Only by the power of the real, true God do we pass those tests and receive godly character, which is the hallmark of the life of faith.

APPLICATION
Why is it a trap to think that God will give us success in the world?
In what area have I been put to the test yet kept walking without fainting?
Finish this prayer: "God, I want to go beyond being holy and obtain character. Please use my everyday . . ."

MARCH 20
FRIENDSHIP WITH GOD

Is God your friend or your vending machine?
Let your prayer requests lead you to know Him deeply.

BACKGROUND Today we continue the theme of the "life of faith," again using Abraham as our example. From an early age, Oswald Chambers had a close friendship with God. Once, he wanted two guinea pigs, so he asked God for them and every morning ran outside to see if they had arrived. When they finally did (thanks to his family), he never questioned God's involvement and just thanked God for sending them.

Yet it took him four years of constantly asking God for the Holy Spirit before he felt the Spirit's presence (see January 3, *Companion*). Why did his prayers go unanswered for so long? Today Chambers asks us to consider our most recent prayer time: Were we "determined to get some gift of the Spirit or to get at God?" He had come to understand that his trouble in prayer during those four years was due to his desire to have the Spirit's power in his own hands. His lesson today will help us avoid the same mistake.

SCRIPTURAL CONTEXT Genesis 18 has two important stories: the foretelling of Isaac's birth and Abraham's bargaining with God over Sodom. If you and your friend were having the conversation that Abraham was having with God and the three visitors, would you consider your friend a good friend or just an acquaintance? Why?

Now read the other verses that Chambers quotes (John 17:22, Matthew 6:8, and Psalm 37:4). Will these verses change the way you pray? Who was the audience for these verses?

WHAT'S THE DEVOTIONAL SAYING?
We love to give God our requests. But Chambers finds two faults in how we ask. First, we stop asking before God grants our desire—even Abraham was guilty of this! Second, we focus on our requests, rather than on being better friends with God.

Do you want the delights of friendship with God? Do you want all of your common-sense decisions to be in line with His will and the sense of restraint He gives you when they aren't? If so, "keep praying" with a "perfect understanding of God Himself" as your goal. Chambers described the result as "you *are* God's will" not "you *do* God's will."

APPLICATION
In the life of faith, what stage have you reached? How well do you know God's will?

Has God ever produced in you a sense of restraint about something? What happened?

Finish this prayer: "Lord, I have desires in my heart, but I've always stopped short of asking you for . . ."

IDENTIFIED OR SIMPLY INTERESTED?

Has God killed your right to yourself?
Let it die so God can live in you!

BACKGROUND Have you ever turned the knob of a wind-up toy? When you turned the knob, you twisted its mainspring, which powers all its cogs and gears. Today, we read (in the Classic Edition) about how our "mainspring" gets radically altered when we are crucified with Christ.

SCRIPTURAL CONTEXT Are you someone who does the things you don't want to do? So was Paul! (He freely admits this in Romans 7.) Our old "mainspring" causes us to do the things we don't want to do. But according to Oswald Chambers, we get a brand-new one when we are crucified with Christ.

Read Galatians 2:20. In three steps, Chambers walks us through this verse. Read the devotional and think about the following questions: What part of "I" gets crucified and what part still lives? Whose faith allows us to live the part of "I" that doesn't get crucified? How does the King James Version translation for this verse differ from other Bible translations? As Chambers walks us through Galatians 2:20, he leaves out

"yet not I, but Christ liveth in me" and "who loved me, and gave himself for me." If you were asked to add two more paragraphs to today's devotional that focused on these missing pieces, what Chambers-like insights would you have?

WHAT'S THE DEVOTIONAL SAYING? In his book *Baffled to Fight Better*, Chambers wrote, "The only reality in life is moral reality, not intellectual or aesthetic." So we know that for him "moral" was a category in the same vein as "intellectual." This helps us as we try to understand today's devotional and the "moral verdict" Chambers urges us to have against sin's nature. He is urging us to use the center of our will—not our intellect, but our *will*—to make a decision against sin.

Have you let God kill your right to yourself? This "right" is the essence of sin. It must be pronounced dead before the Spirit can make us like Jesus. Until we are more Christlike, with His faith in us and not our own, those around us won't see any difference between our life "in the flesh" and everyone else's.

APPLICATION

Have you given up your right to yourself and been "crucified" with Christ? When?
Have you allowed the Holy Spirit to grant you Christ's holiness? Did you see a change?
Finish this prayer: "God, I'm tired of longing to live the life of faith, I want to live it *now*!
Please help me . . ."

MARCH 22
THE BURNING HEART

Tired of "bleeding-heart" Christians?
*God wants us to have **more** emotions (and better ones), not less.*

BACKGROUND Oswald Chambers' *Complete Works* quotes Matthew Arnold's poem "Morality" seven times. As in today's lesson, Chambers often quotes just the first stanza. The next four stanzas continue the theme: Our will (morality) must accomplish in "hours of gloom" the tasks we are given in "hours of insight." The final stanza says that human will is not from human nature but from God.

Chambers agreed with Arnold that our will is from God, and Chambers added that morality is the *only* reality (see March 21, *Companion*). But he sharply disagreed with Arnold's statement in 1876 that "the [gospel] story is not true." As with today's poem, Chambers often redeemed the works of scholars who rejected the gospel. He saw how "sordid actualities" created the "right arena" for God's reality. Let's follow his example and redeem the things of our day!

SCRIPTURAL CONTEXT Chambers relates today's lesson to two stories. The first is from Luke 24, which we read on February 7. What is the focus today compared to the last time we read it?

The second story is from Mark 9 (or Matthew 17 or Luke 9). What "business" did the disciples want to transact after seeing Jesus transfigured? What did God instruct them to do instead? Did they live faithful to what they were told to do in their "hours of insight"?

WHAT'S THE DEVOTIONAL SAYING? We've all felt our hearts burn for something. Today Chambers gives us the secret to keeping our heart burning for God even during our hours of gloom. The secret is "abiding in Jesus"—a difficult secret of its own!

But more than reminding us to abide in Christ, today's lesson tells us how people become bleeding-heart Christians, full of sentimentalism and out of touch with the world around them: God inspired them, but they didn't obey Him during the mundane times. Do you gush with fake emotions about how God is so great? God doesn't want that! He wants you to abide in His Son in daily life and to make commitments that are based on what He shows you on the mountaintop—commitments you keep, no matter how mundane life gets.

APPLICATION
Has God given you a vision for your life? Has it been smothered in daily cares? How?
What emotions are ruling your life right now? Will they have a good end result?
Finish this prayer: "Lord, 'in hours of gloom,' I want to do what you showed me 'in hours of insight,' especially when . . ."

AM I CARNALLY MINDED?

Trying to fix your wrongs?
Owning it is the first step toward making it right.

BACKGROUND On January 11, we saw how, during his four years of darkness (see January 3, *Companion*), Oswald Chambers resisted his father's request for "money help" because to send money home to his family, Chambers would have needed to get a higher paying job, which was not what he felt God was calling him to do. But on March 4 we saw that being "useful" is not God's goal for us. Chambers might have written his father differently after his "darkness," when he experienced the Spirit's filling in a new way. He might have even described his reply to his father as "carnal" in the sense of today's devotional.

Are you tempted to defend your actions against other people's criticisms? Chambers says you should admit your defensiveness to the Holy Spirit. Then the Spirit himself can make you less defensive and can fix the problems that He points out in your heart.

SCRIPTURAL CONTEXT Paul pulled no punches when he wrote to the churches in Corinth and Galatia! Read 1 Corinthians 3 and Galatians 5:13–25. What was the cause of the Corinthian's "strife"? Do you think it was over important issues or over trifles and small things?

How were the Galatians "biting and devouring" each other? What was Paul's advice to them?

When we look at the list of sins in Galatians 5:19–21, our eyes gravitate to the ones we are least likely to exhibit. But what about jealousy, selfish ambition, envy, and impurity: Are any of those evident in your life?

WHAT'S THE DEVOTIONAL SAYING?
How we love to make excuses! Have your shortcomings ever been pointed out and you *haven't* had the urge to lash out or make an excuse? Today Chambers tells us that we know sanctification (i.e., the Spirit's presence) is being worked out in our lives when we are no longer carnal. And we know that we aren't carnal anymore if, whenever someone points out something we've done wrong, we don't have the spirit of resentment.

Have you felt the "most real thing," the feeling of no resentment when you *know* you would have been resentful just a few years or months earlier? If not, pray for that feeling, so you will have confidence that the Spirit who lives in you is working out His sanctifying presence in your life.

APPLICATION
Since becoming a Christian, have you noticed more "warring" against sin? How so?
Has the Bible stirred up resentment in you? How did you respond? How about now?
Finish this prayer: "Father, I want to see how you've taken away my carnality by passing your test of . . ."

MARCH 24
DECREASING FOR HIS PURPOSE

Want to be center stage?
Let people see God, and you'll be filled with joy!

➤

BACKGROUND Today we revisit the theme of "amateur providence" (trying to be for others what only God can be; see January 30, *Companion*). Interestingly, on February 9 Oswald Chambers encouraged us to let others feed on our "broken bread and poured-out wine" lives until they learn to feed on God. So there is a balance: We must let some people come to us for godly nourishment but never let ourselves "increase" and God "decrease."

Are you tempted to be an amateur providence, or do you avoid people who feed off you? Today, we learn how to resist the first temptation, especially if the person we are helping has learned to feed on God.

SCRIPTURAL CONTEXT We haven't yet examined John 3:22–36. Read that passage now. Does John the Baptist resolve the dispute between his disciples and the Jews? Who is speaking in verses 31–36, and what do these verses tell us about why we must decrease?

At the end of the devotional, Chambers calls our attention to Matthew 10:34. How does this apply to our friends who have learned to feed on God?

WHAT'S THE DEVOTIONAL SAYING?
On January 30, we learned not to be an amateur providence to our spiritual leaders, as Samuel was tempted to be to Eli. Chambers urges us today to avoid playing God to those who, like John's disciples, are learning from us. Our motivation in either case should be the same: We should desire God's unbroken relationship for ourselves and also for whomever it is we are trying to "shield" by being an amateur providence.

The temptation to play God is strong. Whether we are dealing with our spiritual leaders or with students, we love to have influence over other people and hate to "decrease." Where are you being tempted to increase today?

APPLICATION

Has your sympathy gotten in the way of godly growth in someone's life? How?

Is there a way in which you can step aside and let God do His work now?

Finish this prayer: "Lord Jesus, you are the bridegroom and I am your friend, help me to rejoice as you . . ."

MAINTAINING THE PROPER RELATIONSHIP

Don't be a "beautiful saint" if being one distracts people from God's beauty.

◄

BACKGROUND The term "amateur providence" occurs more than thirty times in Oswald Chambers' *Complete Works*. He clearly wanted his students and friends to avoid this trap! We continue today in the same passage of Scripture with the same theme but a new emphasis: Friendship is better than obedience. Friendship is especially helpful when it comes to avoiding the trap of being an amateur providence!

SCRIPTURAL CONTEXT Since we just read John 3:22–36 yesterday, take some time today to put yourself in the shoes of John the baptizer's disciples. How would you feel about Jesus' ministry and about your fellow disciples, like John the gospel writer and Andrew, who had left John the baptizer to follow Jesus? How would you feel about the Jew who was asking questions about baptism? How would you feel when John talked about being a "friend of the bridegroom"?

WHAT'S THE DEVOTIONAL SAYING? The original title today is "The Most Delicate Mission on Earth." What mission does Chambers mean? Is it our mission to be Jesus' friends—or something else? It's actually our mission to point people to God and not ourselves.

Yesterday we saw that there is a balance between letting people "feed" on us and letting them learn to feed on God. Balancing our relationships with others and with God is a delicate job. It can only be done by prioritizing our "moral and vital" relationship to Jesus. And what does "moral and vital" mean? *Moral* means that we "make constant decisions of will to forsake all but Jesus." *Vital* means that we "allow the Spirit to give us His vitality in our daily lives."

We make big decisions only a few times in our lives. But hourly we face decisions of will for or against God. What will you decide right now?

APPLICATION

What has Christ done for you? Do you talk about it? How will you present Jesus instead? When was your last "crisis" of obedience? How do you stay close to Jesus between crises? Finish this prayer: "Jesus, your weapons are powerful, but I don't want to use them to work against you as I . . ."

SPIRITUAL VISION THROUGH PERSONAL PURITY

We are flowers: our roots are most vital; our petals tell us if trouble lies ahead.

➤

BACKGROUND Biddy Chambers is as much the author of *Utmost* as her husband. True, practically all the words were spoken by Oswald at some point during their seven years of marriage, but Biddy had to collect, edit, combine, and organize them into 366 readings. And if she had not lived out what *Utmost* describes, it's hard to imagine how she would have been able to do what she did!

Today's reading tells us to maintain unblemished purity. How did Biddy do that as she came into contact with people whose actions and points of view were "apt to sully"? One story illustrates how she practiced what she and her husband preached. Two years after her return from Egypt, she and her daughter, Kathleen, moved into a primitive cottage located on a manor whose inhabitant was an ailing lady prone to drunken rages. During her rages, the lady sometimes called for Biddy, who would listen patiently and then, after an hour or so when the rage had subsided, would kiss the lady's forehead and say, "God bless you. Sleep well." What an example of the kind of purity we read about today!

SCRIPTURAL CONTEXT The Beatitudes capture the essence of our faith. Read them now. How do the first four differ from the second four? How does today's theme verse fit in the progression? Why is there a connection between purity and seeing God? Is seeing God the same as what Chambers calls "vision"?

WHAT'S THE DEVOTIONAL SAYING? Today's message couldn't be clearer: Get purity and you will get the all-important "vision," a word we see nearly one hundred times in *Utmost*. We know we want vision, since it allows us to see *why* God created us (see March 11, *Companion*) and keeps us going during our "hours of gloom" (see March 22, *Companion*). But how do we get purity? Chambers' final paragraph explains how. If you have trouble understanding his advice in the Classic Edition, the Updated Edition spells it out for you.

Using two analogies, Chambers explains the difference between inner and outer purity. In the first analogy, our inner purity is the root of a flower and our outer purity is the blossom. In the second, the two kinds of purity are like the inner and outer courts of the temple. The point with both analogies is that we can more easily see how our outer purity is doing. This is how God protects our inner purity: We fix our outer problems before they reach our core.

APPLICATION
What is the difference between purity and innocence? Which describes you best? Why?

Is there something that God is asking you not to do or to think? Do other people do it?

Finish this prayer: "God, I know that I get off track when I'm around certain people. Help me to see them . . ."

MARCH 27
SPIRITUAL VISION
THROUGH PERSONAL CHARACTER

Has God showed you a truth?
Follow it now! Or you might miss His next step for you.

◄

BACKGROUND Yesterday we read that vision comes through purity, which Oswald Chambers said is the same as our character. Today we look deeper into how character opens the door to clearer vision for what God has done and plans to do.

Chambers needed a clearer vision for where God wanted him during World War I. Was his place still at the Bible Training College? He asked God, "Is this Thy place for me?" and added, "Hold me steady doing Thy will." This prayer is the essence of our lesson today: As we steadily do what we know God's will is, God shows us more of what He wants for us.

SCRIPTURAL CONTEXT On March 20, we read Genesis 18:17. Today Chambers uses it to complement the theme verse, Revelation 4:1. Who tells John the apostle, "Come up"? How is John like Abraham? What did John learn? (You may want to skim other chapters in Revelation.) What did Abraham learn?

Today's message is that God gives us more vision as we go higher in our character. Do any other Bible stories demonstrate this principle? How have you seen this truth at work in your life?

WHAT'S THE DEVOTIONAL SAYING? In our January 12 reading, Chambers introduced an important concept that we return to today: We don't get more of what God wants to show us until we, in the external, day-to-day aspects of our lives, live up to the highest He's already shown us. To this main point, Chambers adds four lessons that correspond to the four paragraphs of the Updated Edition.

First, he compares how God takes us higher (as we embrace each new truth) with the way Satan tempts us (as we embrace each new temptation, including the temptation to a super-human view of holiness). Second, he advises us to take stock of our spiritual growth by looking one year into the past. Third, he encourages us backsliders that turning back to God can give us spiritual insight as we hear Him calling us to something better. Finally, he explains that a lot of truth is hidden from us until we have grown spiritually.

Do you have a super-human view of holiness? Are you afraid that one wrong move will ruin your purity? God's higher level of holiness is a spacious place. Pray for that kind of holy freedom today.

APPLICATION

Both God and Satan invite us to "go higher." How has this principle worked in you?

Where were you spiritually at this time last year? (Check last year's entry, if possible.)

Finish this prayer: "Father, I don't rejoice in merely staying a Christian; I want to go higher in my walk with you and know . . ."

ISN'T THERE SOME MISUNDERSTANDING?

Flip-flopping on what to do?
Act on what God has already told you; He'll make your way clear.

BACKGROUND We saw yesterday how Oswald Chambers prayed for God to show him what to do during World War I. In early 1915, he made the decision to "work with the Forces." But even after this decision, he wrote, "how unrelieved my mind has been about the future."

Chambers' mind was usually at peace with the future, even on his round-the-world trip when he didn't have a clue about how he would pay for his next meal (see January 22, *Companion*). But it is encouraging to know that at least once he had to struggle to trust God with his future, particularly as we read today's lesson.

SCRIPTURAL CONTEXT Doubting Thomas earned his nickname by saying that he needed to see and feel Jesus' wounds before he would believe the resurrection took place. Today's theme verse occurs at another poignant moment in Thomas' life. Read John 11:1–16. Why is Thomas the only disciple named? How does his statement sum up how the others felt?

Two other passages drive home the main point about trusting God. First, Matthew 14:22–36 tells the story of Peter walking on water (for a little while) to Jesus. John 2:1–12 describes how the wedding servants did what Jesus said, even though it sounded strange! If you were Peter or the servants, how would you have felt?

WHAT'S THE DEVOTIONAL SAYING? Have you ever had an idea but then decided it was too risky? Were you worried you would fail and people would mock you and mock God, who takes care of you? Today's study says that the only way for God to be mocked is when we don't act on the ideas He gives us. Not every idea comes from God, but some of the riskiest ideas do. Can you think of some ideas He's given you that you haven't acted on? If so, take action!

An even more fundamental point today is that we must serve God, not our ideas about God. Our fear of doing something risky is a sign that we are putting our ideas about God above God himself.

APPLICATION

What is the next step of faith you must take? Might it shame Jesus if you take it? How?
What is good and bad about "weighing the pros and cons" before making a decision?
Finish this prayer: "Jesus, please help me to follow your lead this week without stopping to worry about . . ."

OUR LORD'S SURPRISE VISITS

Proud of practicality?
Good! But don't miss Jesus' subtle arrivals.

BACKGROUND The Bible Training College had many illustrious visitors. For example, the rich and famous cricket-player-turned-missionary C. T. Studd gave a guest lecture shortly before Oswald Chambers left for Egypt. Clearly Chambers saw the value of having respected religious leaders teach him and his students. But today's lesson reminds us not to put anyone, no matter how famous or godly, above Jesus in our lives. One way to ensure this is by looking for Jesus where He is least expected—in other words, *not* in our Christian work.

Where could Jesus appear in your life today? Are there some particularly difficult people or situations where you would never expect to see Him? Look for Jesus there as you go through your week!

SCRIPTURAL CONTEXT Jesus used vivid word pictures to help His followers understand old truths about God in a new, clearer way. Read Luke 12:35–48. What would modern versions of these parables be? Did Jesus answer Peter's question?

Turn to Hebrews 12:1–3 and read these inspiring verses. "Looking to Jesus" takes the central location, right between three human actions (remembering witnesses, renouncing sin, and running the race) and three of Christ's actions (enduring the cross, sitting with God, and enduring opposition). Is "looking to Jesus" the central theme of your life?

WHAT'S THE DEVOTIONAL SAYING? What does it mean to be, as the Classic Edition puts it, "facing our belief, or our creed, or the question whether we are of any use"? How does that compare to facing Jesus? Chambers says facing Jesus is ultimately our "one great need." Are you facing Jesus today? In other words, do you have your mind tuned to Him in whatever else you are doing?

On March 20 and 27, we looked at Genesis 18. In the first verse of that chapter, Abraham is sitting at the entrance of his tent in "the heat of the day." Today, Chambers uses that same phrase to point out *when* we should be ready for Jesus to appear—right during the hottest part of the day—which is exactly when Abraham was ready! What will be the hottest part of your day or week? Will you be ready?

APPLICATION

What were you doing yesterday afternoon? How would you have felt if Jesus had appeared to you then?

Has Jesus ever "appeared" to you in a certain situation? How did you know it was Him?

Finish this prayer: "Lord, I want to stop idolizing being religious and start being spiritually real. Help me . . ."

MARCH 30
HOLINESS OR HARDNESS TOWARD GOD?

Looking for a job?
Be an intercessor! It's the only work that is snare-free.

➤

BACKGROUND Three times in *Utmost*—today, June 7 and December 13—Oswald Chambers tells us that there is only one thing we can do that has no "snare." What is that one thing? *Intercession.* Chambers says it is getting "the mind of Christ" about the people for whom we pray.

There are many good things, according to Chambers, that have snares: preaching the gospel, quiet days with God (see January 6, *Utmost*), and rare moments of inspiration (which we will look at on May 1). So when we find something that has no snare at all, we really need to pay attention!

SCRIPTURAL CONTEXT Read Isaiah 59. What New Testament passages come from this chapter? In the NKJV, verse 16 contains the word *intercessor*. How does the version of the Bible you read translate this word? Is it surprising to you that there was "no intercessor"? How can God expect us to be intercessors yet be amazed when we aren't?

The Updated Edition cites Philippians 2:5. But as we saw on March 18, it's probably more likely that Chambers was quoting from 1 Corinthians 2:16. Read both of those verses. What would it be like to get "the mind of Christ" about the people for whom you pray?

WHAT'S THE DEVOTIONAL SAYING? Today's title contrasts holiness and hardness. The first paragraph says that our hardness toward God is related to our ineffective, emotional interest in prayer. We see in the second paragraph that worship is the key to prayer and the antidote to a hard, dogmatic attitude toward God and others. The third paragraph points out the difference between a hard, dogmatic relationship and one that is holy. Finally, the last paragraph is where we learn that intercessory prayer has no snare to it.

Do you ever wonder what to do with your free time, or whether the things you do are the best way for you to spend your life? Take some time today to pray for others. Chambers used the word *rouse* to describe how, as we pray, we must lift our hearts up to a new level that is closer to God. Rouse yourself today to the throne room of the heavenly Father!

APPLICATION

On a scale of 1 to 10, how is your prayer life? What discourages/motivates you to pray?

On the same scale, how is your worship? Do you feel as if you dispute God—or embrace Him?

Finish this prayer: "God, you are holy above all others. I want to live in holiness with you, interceding . . ."

HEEDFULNESS OR HYPOCRISY IN OURSELVES?

Tempted to criticize?
Intercede for the faults that God helps you see!

◄ ►

BACKGROUND Today's lesson continues a three-day series that examines intercession in three different relationships: in our relationship with God, with ourselves, and with others. Yesterday we saw our need to be holy, not hard, toward God. Tomorrow we will learn to be helpful, not heartless, in our relationship with others. And today we look at how an attitude of heeding God's insight about other people, not fostering judgmental hypocrisy toward them, is the key to our intercession.

Did you try interceding in prayer for someone yesterday? Did it go as well as it usually goes when you try to pray for someone? What stops you from "wholeheartedly" interceding as Oswald Chambers would like you to be doing? If the problem is that you spend your time unproductively mulling over the issues God reveals to you about the people for whom you intercede, then today's lesson is just what you need!

SCRIPTURAL CONTEXT We have read 1 John 1 and 4 (see January 9 and February 21, *Companion*), but today read chapter 5. How does the theme verse for today (verse 16) fit into this chapter? What does the chapter mainly discuss? Why is our relationship with God so important to our prayers for others?

WHAT'S THE DEVOTIONAL SAYING?

For this series on prayer, Chambers picked verses from three different writers. Today's verse from John underscores our responsibility to others as we ask God to give them life in place of the sin we see in them. What is our responsibility? To rightly handle our insight about others' sin. How do we handle it rightly? By realizing that it's not *our* insight but God's. Otherwise, we will ridicule others for their sin, which makes us hypocrites, since we do the same things!

Think of a sin in someone else's life. Now thank the Holy Spirit for giving you that insight, and ask Him to help you intercede wholeheartedly for that person.

APPLICATION

Can you see where someone is failing? What does that person need the most? Do you pray for him or her?

By worshiping Jesus, do you better identify with Him? How is your intercession helped?

Finish this prayer: "Jesus, your soul suffers for all of us who are failing. Help me to support my peers by . . ."

ᕼᕼᕼᕼ APRIL 1 ᕼᕼᕼᕼ
HELPFUL OR HEARTLESS TOWARD OTHERS?

Mad at others?
Stress does that if you don't worship God. Simplify and pray!

◄

BACKGROUND Are you stressed? Do daily worries, combined with fears about the economy, crime, and global uncertainties, get you down? Oswald Chambers had all the same reasons to be stressed, and more. His point about "the present crisis" (see the Classic Edition) referred to World War I, no less!

Today's lesson gives us more reasons to wholeheartedly devote ourselves to intercessory prayer. Two days ago, we saw that intercession has no snare. Yesterday we learned that "our" insight into other people's sin is actually from God and thus a responsibility that motivates us to intercede. Today we see that Jesus and the Holy Spirit are intercessors, which means we should be intercessors too.

SCRIPTURAL CONTEXT The three sections of Romans 8 are all extremely powerful. We looked at the final section (verses 31–39) on March 7. Today we will look at a connection between the second and third sections—a connection that has to do with intercession. Read verses 27 and 34. How do these verses relate to each other and to their respective sections?

Verse 27 is in the context of how the Spirit helps us pray as we hold on to our future hope of glory, whereas verse 34 talks about how Jesus helps defend us against accusations before God. Both kinds of help are "intercessory." Which kind do you need more today? How can you intercede in those ways for others?

WHAT'S THE DEVOTIONAL SAYING? Today Chambers pleads with us to intercede for others as Jesus and the Holy Spirit intercede for all of us. That's a tall order! But if we don't set our sights this high, we will give up interceding as we feel the stress of life. We will become heartless instead of hearty or helpful. People will show up in our lives, and we will turn them away with just a quick one-two punch of Scripture. We won't have any reserves for them!

Look again at Romans 8:27. How many persons are involved in this verse? It actually helps to think about all three persons of the Trinity in this verse: God the Spirit becomes intimately acquainted with us as He intercedes for us; God the Son searches our hearts and knows us intimately because He knows everything that's in the Spirit's mind; and God the Father sets the plan for everything, including all the details of our lives, so that all the Spirit's interceding and all the Son's pleading work out for our good!

APPLICATION

What crises do you face? Do they hurt your worship? How can you stop being distracted?

Are you so burdened by your activities that you can't intercede or help people? How so?

Finish this prayer: "Holy Spirit, I want to intercede for the saints as you do. Please help me put aside . . ."

APRIL 2
THE GLORY THAT'S UNSURPASSED

Received a blessing?
You're seeing Jesus! Live for Him alone.

BACKGROUND Today's title in the Classic Edition is "The Glory That Excels." We find this phrase in 1 Corinthians 3:10. In that verse Paul contrasts the glory of the covenant God made through Moses with the new covenant that comes through Jesus. In today's lesson, Oswald Chambers contrasts the glory of "other things," whatever they may be, with the glory that excels, which is Christ's glory and nothing else.

Has God blessed you? He blessed Paul by healing him of his blindness. Today's lesson tells us that, along with physical blessings, God gives the spiritual insight of seeing more of Christ's glory. Once you see this glory, nothing but Christ matters to you!

SCRIPTURAL CONTEXT Can you imagine being Ananias of Damascus (Acts 9:10)? If a murderous man were hunting you down, how would you feel when God said to go heal his eyes? As you read Acts 9:10–19, are you amazed that Ananias didn't put up more resistance to God's command to visit Paul? How can you say "Yes, Lord" today?

Although Chambers uses Acts 9 as the backdrop to today's lesson, the key passage is 1 Corinthians 1:18–2:16. How does verse 2 (in chapter 2) fit into this section? How does this section fit into the whole book? Do you want to be a person after God's own heart?

WHAT'S THE DEVOTIONAL SAYING? Oswald Chambers was only nine years old when Mary D. James, who wrote the hymn quoted in today's lesson, died in New York City. Both she and Chambers participated in the "holiness movement," which lasted several generations and which focused on the empowering work of the Holy Spirit. Today's lesson is summed up by these words from "All for Jesus," which Mary James penned in 1871, "Since mine eyes have looked on Jesus, I've lost sight of all beside."

Have you grown sick of everything in the world besides Jesus? It's hard to say that about the blessings God gives us. We can't imagine losing or ever getting sick of a blessing such as our sense of sight. But Chambers says that once we see God's glory, nothing will have a hold on us compared to Him. How can you see Jesus in this way? Can you look at one of your blessings and see who's behind it?

APPLICATION

Have you received something from God? Did it give you insight into Jesus? How?
Can you live up to the insights God has revealed and that explain His purposes? How so?
Finish this prayer: "God, there is so much distracting me from Jesus. Help me cut out my
fascination with . . ."

"IF YOU HAD KNOWN!"

Missed God's best?
Let that sadness sink in and produce fruit.

BACKGROUND Do you feel the tragedy of the moment? Jesus, the long-awaited Messiah, is sitting on the ancient equivalent of a presidential limousine, right in front of the very walls of Jerusalem. Yet the powers within those walls have poisoned the minds of the people with the false god of religious pride. Not one of them can recognize their King—He who could give them their precious *shalom*.

In today's lesson, Oswald Chambers unpacks this story and applies it to our own lives. Are you haunted by what "might have been"? The opportunities you missed as you clung to your false gods? Today's devotional will give your heart peace!

SCRIPTURAL CONTEXT Read Luke 19:28–44. What jumps out at you? Where were Jesus' followers as He wept over Jerusalem? Would you have been inside or outside the walls at that moment? Might Jesus be now weeping over *you* for something?

Jesus wept over Jerusalem because He foresaw what travesty would come to her as a result of her inability to recognize Him for who He was. Read Matthew 23 to see what traits caused Jerusalem to miss His arrival. Can you find any of those traits in your own life?

WHAT'S THE DEVOTIONAL SAYING? In a rare autobiographical passage, Chambers reveals his own struggle with the strange god of religious pride. Although he gave this devotional long after his four years of darkness (see January 3, *Companion*), we see that when he broke free of a wrong and prideful version of Christianity, he continued to find himself "in the possession of" and "still under the control of" the strange god. Like all of us, Chambers was blind to the things that could give him peace.

What helped Chambers battle the "disposition" and the "unholy nature" that ruled his life? It was when God haunted him with what "might have been"! Chambers encourages us in today's lesson not to be afraid of those ghosts from the past. They are God's ministers to help us turn our might-have-beens into the seeds of beautiful growth.

APPLICATION

Has your pride (even in being set apart for God) hidden God's peace from you? How?

Do you look down on, judge, or try to impress others? What does this reveal about you?

Finish this prayer: "Lord, I'm broken when I remember doors that, by my choices, were shut. For example . . ."

⚭ APRIL 4 ⚭
THE WAY TO PERMANENT FAITH

Is your faith primed and ready for real life?
God fortifies our faith by letting us despair.

BACKGROUND The theme of darkness, which we first saw on January 3, appears again today and many times in *Utmost* (though we haven't seen it since March 15 and won't see it again until July 16). This theme flows from Oswald Chambers' own struggle with four years of God-given darkness, which was the key instrument in helping him put God first in his life in a new, more profound way.

Today Chambers adds two more metaphors to the metaphor of darkness: scattering and "internal death." Are you prepared to face darkness, scattering, and death—all at the hand of God? He does it for your good, but it takes "spiritual grit" to make it through!

SCRIPTURAL CONTEXT On February 28, we looked at John 16:17–33 and came to a similar conclusion as with today's lesson: Many things scatter our love for Jesus, which shows us that we need a deeper level of love for Him. Read this passage again. What did Jesus say that suddenly made the disciples think they understood Him clearly and could believe He came from God? Did they really believe?

Notice how this passage ends. Are you an overcomer? What will it take for you to have this kind of "spiritual grit"?

WHAT'S THE DEVOTIONAL SAYING? In the first paragraph, Chambers tells us that our faith is often supported by flimsy feelings. We need to be scattered into desolation as the disciples were. Then our faith will withstand anything.

The second half of the devotional expands on the point that *God* is the one who sends circumstances of darkness into our lives. Chambers again points us to God's goal for us: faith that is permanent. God makes our faith permanent by separating us from outward, conscious blessings. But Chambers tells us that our sense of God's blessings is fundamental ("elemental," Classic Edition) to our new life in Christ. So even if God cuts off our conscious sense of blessing, we will still have a deeper sense of how He loves and blesses us. It's this deeper sense of blessing that makes up permanent faith and is the "spiritual grit" Chambers says we need.

APPLICATION

Have you ever despaired at your life's emptiness? How did it affect your faith?

What goals are you serving? Are they your own or God's?

Finish this prayer: "Lord, I want to have spiritual grit and to be able to praise you in all circumstances, so . . ."

HIS AGONY AND OUR ACCESS

Jesus made our way simple by taking the hardest road—the one to Calvary.

➤

BACKGROUND In 1922, Biddy Chambers published her first book after returning from Egypt. At 147 pages, *The Psychology of Redemption* was also the longest one, up to that point, she had compiled without Oswald's help. Her verbatim notes came from Oswald's talks on psychology at the Bible Training College (1915) and in Egypt (1916). One of the twelve chapters of this book shares today's title (Classic Edition): *His Agony and Our Fellowship*. Biddy took snippets of this 15-page chapter to create today's half-page reading.

Do you wonder what happened in Gethsemane? According to Oswald, it was where Jesus feared He would not be able to endure the cross as both God *and* man. If He hadn't, we wouldn't be saved. Thankfully, with the help of an angel, He triumphed, and His worst fear did not come true. Today's lesson helps us to soak in the drama of that evening and to live reverently in the simplicity of our faith.

SCRIPTURAL CONTEXT Notice which words Biddy takes from Matthew 26 for this shortened version of her husband's talk. They point us to an application of today's lesson: *We must stay and watch Jesus' agony in order to understand the simplicity of our salvation.*

Read the context Oswald used for his original talk (Matthew 26:36–46 and Luke 22:40–46). What changes do you see in Jesus' heart as He prayed? Do you experience these changes when you pray?

WHAT'S THE DEVOTIONAL SAYING? Today's devotional is clear in its meaning: Jesus suffered in Gethsemane to bring His human nature in line with His divine nature. The application for today's lesson is a bit less clear. For starters, we can avoid the misunderstanding that Jesus didn't want to die. He was ready to die all along. What concerned Him was that His human nature might not get through the struggle without His divine nature doing all the work.

Chambers says that the "veil" is pulled away as we study what happened in Gethsemane. Meditate on the Scripture that reveals what it cost Jesus to fight for our salvation—to fight to keep His human nature an equal part in the crucifixion. Let the agony of His sweat mixed with blood remind you today to live in a simple, reverent way.

APPLICATION
How are Gethsemane and Calvary the gateway into life for you?

What did Jesus agonize over when He came face-to-face with death?

Finish this prayer: "Jesus, if you hadn't fulfilled your destiny as Savior, I'd be lost. Thank you for . . ."

THE COLLISION OF GOD AND SIN

Crashed into God?
When we merge into His lane, He absorbs sin's impact.

◄

BACKGROUND Yesterday's lesson came from chapter eight of Oswald Chambers' book *The Psychology of Redemption.* Today we look at parts of chapter nine and finish a two-day series.

What was Jesus' cross? It was two pieces of wood at right angles to each other. But what *else* was His cross? It was the intersection of holy God with sinful man. Yesterday we studied Gethsemane and saw how our knowledge of it can help us live simple, holy lives. Today we will study the cross in order to live gratefully and wisely.

SCRIPTURAL CONTEXT Besides the theme verse from Peter's writings, Chambers quotes John (Revelation 13:8) and Paul (1 Timothy 3:16 and 2 Corinthians 5:21). Read all four verses. Have you died to sin, and are you living to righteousness? How do you know? Was Jesus really slain from before creation? How else could you interpret Revelation 13:8? Which part of 1 Timothy 3:16 is the biggest mystery? Why does this early Christian creed not mention the cross? How could God make Jesus to be sin?

These four verses are filled with weighty, hard-to-understand truths—just like today's lesson! As you work through the lesson, ask the Holy Spirit to reveal the things you need to understand and obey.

WHAT'S THE DEVOTIONAL SAYING? The four paragraphs of today's lesson teach us four truths about the cross. First, the cross is the central reality of human life. To be human now means to have the possibility of friendship with God. Second, the cross is the reason for the incarnation. God became flesh so He could become sin and give us His righteousness. Third, the cross is where we live as Christians. We don't just go through the experience of Jesus' cross; we live lives that are a part of it. Finally, the cross is the collision between a holy God and man's sin. We have easy access to God's friendship because of the costly pain Jesus endured.

This two-day series teaches us *how* God won our salvation. The staggering costs He paid at Gethsemane and at Calvary should lead us to live more humbly and thankfully. Our misconceptions about the cross—that Jesus feared it or was martyred on it—are unhelpful because they lead us to feel sorry for Jesus rather than feel proud of His victory. How do *you* think God saved you? Meditate on these truths today!

APPLICATION

List the truths you just learned about the cross of Christ. Can you think of any others?

How does the cross answer the questions and problems you face about time/eternity?

Finish this prayer: "Jesus, you made me able to have fellowship with God, and I specifically appreciate . . ."

APRIL 7
WHY WE LACK UNDERSTANDING

Don't understand God?
You'll get it if you live it. Let the Spirit purify you!

BACKGROUND On March 27 we saw that we have to be living up to the "highest" God revealed to us before He shows us even more. Today Oswald Chambers turns that truth around and tells us that we know we've started living up to the resurrection life in us when we begin to understand new things in the Bible.

The past two days of *Utmost* have featured more theological concepts than usual. Have you been able to understand what you read? If so, be encouraged. The resurrection life of Jesus is living in you!

SCRIPTURAL CONTEXT When Jesus told Peter, James, and John not to tell anyone about the transfiguration until "the Son of Man had risen" (Mark 9:9), did they know what He meant? When He told His disciples that He had many things to say to them, did He ever get to say them? When? These are just a few questions to ponder as you read the two verses Chambers quotes today and their contexts.

Does the Bible teach that we don't get more understanding until we get right in our hearts?

Where else might you find this teaching? How does this affect the way you study the Bible? Ask God to take away your obstinate nature and form Christ in you.

WHAT'S THE DEVOTIONAL SAYING? Do you have strong opinions? In the Classic Edition of *Utmost,* we read, "If we have our minds made up about a doctrine, the light of God will come no more to us on that line." Have you made up your mind about certain doctrines? Do your headstrong opinions keep God from showing you more?

The main point in today's lesson is that we need to have Christ's risen life at work in us before we understand spiritual truths. The last paragraph of today's lesson shows us that having Christ's life in us means that we live according to the mountaintop visions we have seen. Have you been on the mountaintop with God? Does your life match that vision? If not, God won't give you any new insight. Ask Him for the humility to let Him have His way in your heart today.

APPLICATION

How dominated are you by Christ? Do you connect what you preach and how you live? How have you cultivated a heart that can understand God's Word? Can you do more? Finish this prayer: "Holy Spirit, I need you at work in me so God can reveal His truth. Please help me . . ."

∽ APRIL 8 ∽
HIS RESURRECTION DESTINY

Do you have Christ's life?
The Spirit will give it to you if you ask and obey.

BACKGROUND Today we return to *The Psychology of Redemption* and look at parts of chapter ten. Two days ago we saw that the cross was the gateway to our union with God. Today we see that this union flows from the life and power of Jesus, which can be our life and power too as we obey the Spirit.

Oswald Chambers, though an artist and preacher, was foremost a teacher. As he taught *The Psychology of Redemption* to the students at the Bible Training College (and later to soldiers in Egypt), he used a chalkboard to diagram his carefully organized points. Read today's lesson looking for what points Chambers is making about Christ's resurrection.

SCRIPTURAL CONTEXT We have seen the context of today's theme verse twice before (February 7 and March 22). These words are from Jesus himself, and they underscore Chambers' point that Jesus knew His destiny was to suffer and be resurrected. What else do you think Jesus may have taught Cleopas and his friend on the road to Emmaus?

The other verses for today come from John 3:3 ("born from above"—a marginal note in the Revised Version), Hebrews 2:10, Romans 6:4, Philippians 3:10, and John 17:2. Look up all of these verses. How is being born from above different from being born again? Since there is no difference in Greek between these two, which one do you think John had in mind?

WHAT'S THE DEVOTIONAL SAYING? Did you find some of Chambers' points? Here are a few of the more important ones. First, the cross allows us to be born again, which means we have Jesus' life in us. Second, the resurrection makes us children of God, not an "only begotten," but still part of God's family. Third, we don't yet have Jesus' kind of glorified body, but we can still experience a new life right now because of His resurrection. Finally, when the Bible talks about receiving eternal life, it's talking about receiving the Holy Spirit. This is because, as Chambers put it in *The Psychology of Redemption*, "The only thing that makes eternal life actual [i.e., real] is the entrance of the Holy Spirit." So when we receive the Holy Spirit, we receive eternal life. In the very last sentence, Chambers urges us to thank God for how His Holy Spirit can work Jesus' nature into us. Can you picture the Holy Spirit working Jesus into you as a baker works the yeast into dough? It takes a lot of kneading, pushing, and prodding! Thank God now for this process, even though it is often painful.

APPLICATION

What is the evidence in your life that you have a "relation of sonship" with God?

How are you walking "in newness of life" and experiencing Christ's atoning power?

Finish this prayer: "Thank you, Holy Spirit, for working Jesus into my life! I'll . . ."

HAVE YOU SEEN JESUS?

If you've seen Jesus, go tell everyone! (Though at first they probably won't see.)

BACKGROUND Frederic W. H. Myers had been dead for six years when Oswald Chambers wrote to his sister in 1907: "I could have cried for excess of joy when I got hold of [my books] again. I see them all just at my elbow now—Plato, Wordsworth, Myers . . ." Chambers goes on to list other authors whose writing he treasured.

Today, Chambers quotes the ninety-seventh stanza of Myers' book-length poem *Saint Paul* to summarize the main point: We will have a burning desire to tell others when we have seen Jesus, but we must tell them knowing that they won't understand until *Jesus* shows himself to them.

The first stanza of *Saint Paul* is also a fitting summary of Chambers' life:

> *Christ! I am Christ's! and let the name*
> *suffice you,*
> *Ay, for me too He greatly hath sufficed;*
> *Lo with no winning words I would entice*
> *you,*
> *Paul has no honour and no friend but*
> *Christ.*

SCRIPTURAL CONTEXT Today's theme verse is a recap of what happened on the road to Emmaus, which we read about yesterday. Chambers also quotes the next verse (Mark 16:13) to show that people don't always believe when you tell them you've seen Jesus.

Have you "seen" Jesus? If so, your faith will be put into action. Read Hebrews 11:23–28. What did Moses *do* as a result of seeing the invisible God? What did the man born blind *do* as a result of seeing Jesus (read John 9)? Do you have similar evidence of "seeing" Jesus?

WHAT'S THE DEVOTIONAL SAYING?

Once again, Chambers seems to describe two classes of Christians: those who are merely saved and those who have seen Jesus. Do you think there are these two classes? Did the man born blind become a Christian only when he said, "Lord, I believe" (John 9:38)?

Chambers would probably be the first to correct wrongheaded ideas about "ordinary" and "superstar" Christians. Clearly, we are partakers in God's grace (see Philippians 1:7 ESV) from the moment we are called and continue to be throughout eternity. There are many points where we gain new understanding of that grace; and today Chambers is reminding us that we must have the experience of "seeing" Jesus, not just what He does for us. Have *you* seen Jesus?

APPLICATION
What does it mean to see Jesus? Have you ever seen Him in that way? When?

How big is your God? Do you base His "bigness" on what He's *done* or on who He *is*?

Finish this prayer: "Father, to see Jesus for who He is, not just for what He does, is essential. Please help me . . ."

<small>∽</small> APRIL 10 <small>∽</small>
COMPLETE AND EFFECTIVE DECISION ABOUT SIN

How do you deal with sin? Don't mollify it; mortify it!

➤

BACKGROUND For the next three days we will look at "complete and effective" decision, divinity, and dominion. In the Classic Edition, "complete and effective" is written as "moral," which for Oswald Chambers (as we saw on March 21) was a broad category like "intellectual" and was the greatest of any such category. To be a person of good morals meant that one made good decisions, not just in the intellectual manner of weighing pros and cons, but in the "complete and effective" manner, which is why the Updated Edition's title is so helpful.

Have you decided, in the deepest center of your will, that sin needs to leave your life once and for all? Or are you harboring an illicit, on-again-off-again love affair with some of your more "respectable" sins? Today's lesson may give you just the kick in the pants that you need to make the right moral decision.

SCRIPTURAL CONTEXT Whenever we look at Romans 6, as we did on January 15 and March 14, we are challenged to make a clean break with sin and follow wholeheartedly after Jesus. Today is no exception. Read this chapter again and find all the reasons we should break with sin. Which ones are the most convincing?

What would it be like to completely die to sin? To answer that question, Chambers quotes Galatians 2:20. What is left of our old selves when we die to sin? Are you reluctant to lose part of who you are? How will *you* know when Christ lives in you more than He already does? How will others?

WHAT'S THE DEVOTIONAL SAYING? Chambers makes four points in his four paragraphs, and each helps us make the moral decision to die to sin. First, don't think that suppressing sin is the same as dying to sin. Second, get time alone with God to make this important decision. Third, ask the Holy Spirit to search your heart to show you the ways that your sin wars against God. Finally, don't settle until only Christ's life, not your own, is alive in your body.

All this talk of "decision" might make some people uncomfortable. Do we have power to *decide* to die to sin? Isn't human will incapable of choosing anything good? Remember, God regenerates our will at our conversion, and He expects us to use it!

APPLICATION

Have you tried to restrain, suppress, or counteract sin? What should you do instead?

What keeps you from deciding to radically deal with sin? What in your life struggles against God?

Finish this prayer: "Lord, I'm alone with you now to make this complete and effective decision to . . ."

COMPLETE AND EFFECTIVE DIVINITY

Are you really a Christian?
Check the Spirit's mirror for a Christ look-alike.

BACKGROUND As we continue our three-day series, we move from crucifixion to resurrection (tomorrow: eternal life). Resurrection is meaningless without death. Likewise, today's lesson makes no sense without yesterday's lesson.

Yesterday we learned that dying to sin is the first step to Christ living in us. Today we look more closely at what the invasion of Christ's resurrection life does to us. But don't forget, Christ can't live in us until we die to sin!

SCRIPTURAL CONTEXT Romans 6 is again our focus, both for the theme verse and the verse quoted in the lesson. This chapter has two sections. The first (verses 1–14) tells us that we shouldn't keep sinning, because we were freed from sin. How were we freed? Through death!

How do the two verses quoted today support Paul's reason for not living in sin? How do they help Oswald Chambers make his point?

What is the difference between the first and second sections of Romans 6? Which one is more helpful to you?

WHAT'S THE DEVOTIONAL SAYING? Today's summary makes it seem as if we must look like mini-Christs in order to be Christians. But taken out of context, this might give you a wrong idea of what the lesson says. The lesson says that the Spirit reveals to us all that we must obey as we "walk in the light." If we are really Christians, we will find that Jesus' life and holiness are in us, making it easy to obey the Spirit and make all our decisions as if we are completely dead to sin.

If you could look at your soul in a mirror, would you see the life and holiness of Jesus? Is there anything distinctively Jesus-like about what you do? There should be a resemblance to Jesus in all that you do as the Spirit reveals ways you can walk in the light.

APPLICATION
What recent evidence do you have that Jesus lives in you?
What "rooms in your house" still need to be invaded by the Holy Spirit?
Finish this prayer: "Father, today I want to walk in the light and obey what the Spirit says.
In particular, . . ."

❧ APRIL 12 ❧
COMPLETE AND EFFECTIVE DOMINION

Eternal life isn't just about living forever.
It's Christ permeating everything we do.

◀

BACKGROUND What does "let go and let God" mean to you? What must you let go? Are there things you shouldn't let go? Today Oswald Chambers tells us that only when we "let go" of our own efforts can God's life fully invade us.

Is "letting go" consistent with past lessons? On March 18 (and anytime the Classic Edition uses the word *rouse*), Chambers speaks boldly about our responsibility to put aside sin and live holy lives. So which is it? Are we to "let go and let God"? Or must we rouse ourselves to holy living? Obviously the answer is both. We must let go of the illusion that we can do anything good apart from Christ. But we must also strive with all our might to obey everything the Holy Spirit reveals to us, knowing that "our" might is really the might that God puts in us.

SCRIPTURAL CONTEXT As we end this three-day series, we again focus on Romans 6:1–14. What reasons for not sinning do today's theme verses give us? How would you describe the life that Jesus now lives? How does it compare to the life you live?

Chambers also references Acts 1:8, Ephesians 3:19, and Acts 4:13. Do you think of the Spirit as *a* gift from God or *the* gift *of* God? What else does Paul pray in Ephesians 3:16–21? Why did the Sanhedrin take "knowledge of [the apostles], that they had been with Jesus"? Would anyone notice that about you?

WHAT'S THE DEVOTIONAL SAYING? Do you ever feel like the weakest saint? Or are there always other Christians that you feel are needier than you are? The sad truth is that we rarely get to the end of our rope. God orchestrates our circumstances to show us how lost and sinful we are. But we still manage to see ourselves in the best possible light. We need to let go! The least little thread that connects us to our own power is high treason against God. Our power is worthless, *and* it blocks God's life from invading our hearts.

Do any of these lessons about decision, divinity, and dominion connect with you? Has God worn you down yet with what He reveals about your sinful heart? When will you finally make the moral decision, the "complete and effective" verdict of the reborn will that God entrusted to you? When will you let go of your useless efforts to curb sin and die with Christ?

APPLICATION

What role does God gives us in receiving eternal life? How have you fulfilled that role?

What do you "hang on" to? What helps you to "let go"?

Finish this prayer: "Holy Spirit, *you're* the power I need to live Christ's life. I want Christ's life to penetrate . . ."

WHAT TO DO WHEN YOUR BURDEN IS OVERWHELMING

Stuck under a load?
God might take it away or want you to give it to Him.

➤

BACKGROUND Many things weighed heavily on Oswald Chambers when he arrived in Egypt on October 26, 1915: the burden of war, the burden of ministering to soldiers on their way to deadly battlefields, and the burden of a wife and child who lived thousands of miles away. Today he passes on to us the wisdom he learned as he faced hardships. Biddy, who edited this lesson, also blesses us with her wisdom: the wisdom that eased her burdens of poverty, no husband, and a four-year-old daughter. What will you learn from these precious words today?

SCRIPTURAL CONTEXT When the burdens pile up, what better book to read than the Psalms? Read Psalms 37 and 55. Do you ever want to fly away from your troubles like a dove? Do you envy the wicked for how successful they are? What are the concluding verses of each chapter? How does the Amplified Bible translate Psalm 37:5? How does that help you apply this verse?

Chambers (almost tongue-in-cheek) quotes from Isaiah 9:6 and hints at Matthew 11:29. What would it be like to share a yoke with the God of the universe?

WHAT'S THE DEVOTIONAL SAYING? Chambers uses the marginal reading of Psalm 55 in the Revised Version to make the point that God *gives* us our burdens. Do you think that's true? Are you willing to believe that the hardest burdens you face right now are from God and that He gave them to you so you can learn to roll your burdens back to Him?

The very last sentence of today's reading reminds us that although God wants us to share our burden with him, we shouldn't try to escape it. When David recalled how he wanted to fly away like a dove, he was already trusting in God and had come to grips with his burden. He was not trying to avoid it. In the same way, we must come to grips with our burdens, accept them as our own, and share them with God.

APPLICATION

What burdens does God want to "lift off" you and which does He want you to "roll off" to Him?

Have you seen Christians burn out under their burdens? Could this happen to you?

Finish this prayer: "Jesus, you ask me to take *your* yoke, the one you're still carrying. Don't let me carry . . ."

God brews you like tea to release your true flavors. Are you bitter or fragrant?

◄

BACKGROUND The verse Oswald Chambers hinted at yesterday is our theme verse today. In the first day of this series, we saw that God offers his shoulders to share our burdens and that He even gives us the burdens in the first place so we can have the joy of sharing with Him. Today we see how burden sharing gives us a deep well of strength.

On January 28, we saw the line of a poem Chambers liked to quote: "What thou hast not by suffering bought, presume thou not to teach." This must have been a favorite line for Biddy too. All of the hard work she did to organize, splice together, and edit her husband's words amounted to a form of teaching; and she "by suffering bought" all of the lessons in *Utmost*, especially the one today!

SCRIPTURAL CONTEXT In addition to the theme verse, which we looked at yesterday, Chambers picks three verses to lead us through the first three paragraphs. Hebrews 12:6 reminds us that our burdens are part of God's love, so to complain about them is missing the point. Isaiah 40:29 says we must realize we have "no might," so God can give us strength. Finally, Nehemiah 8 shows that joy is from God's strength.

Read the context of each of these three verses. What "chastening" did the Hebrews experience? What in Isaiah 40 most connects with you? Why did Nehemiah tell people that God's joy was their strength?

WHAT'S THE DEVOTIONAL SAYING? In each paragraph, Chambers connects the three verses he quotes to his main point about how we receive "invincibility" as we accept our burdens. For example, in the second paragraph he says that accepting the yoke of our burdens is the only path to God's strength. Why is this? It's because God's strength comes to people who "have no might." And who better grasps the reality of "no might" than those who take up their yoke?

In the third paragraph, Chambers compares the way God gives us invincibility with the way wine is made. First, the grapes are squeezed by a burden (pressure), and only then does the precious wine come out. Chambers returns to this analogy again later in *Utmost* (See September 30 and Decembr 15). We can also think about the way tea is made: First, the leaves are placed in hot water; then, the tea is ready. In either case (wine or tea) the true nature of the plant is revealed. Are you sweet grapes and fragrant leaves? Or are you sour and bitter? God's chastening will bring out your true flavor!

APPLICATION

Find these pairs: yoke/learn, love/chasten, joy/strength, and no-might/increased-strength. Do you whine if God's hand is on you? How will you kick complaining out of your life? Finish this prayer: "God, to have inner invincibility I need your help. Today your hand is . . ."

THE FAILURE TO PAY CLOSE ATTENTION

What bugs you?
Details people forget? God also is grieved by our "little" sins.

BACKGROUND George MacDonald was, according to G. K. Chesterton, one of the three or four greatest men of the nineteenth century. He died in November 1905, a year and a half before Oswald Chambers preached about him in Cincinnati (see February 15, *Companion*). Chambers told those gathered, "It is a striking indication of the . . . shallowness of the modern reading public that George MacDonald's books have been so neglected." In his diary later that year, Chambers wrote, "MacDonald appeals to my bias; I love that writer." Indeed, Chambers' *Complete Works* refers to MacDonald more than twenty times. Today's lesson ends on a line from MacDonald's first publication: a book-length poem called *Within and Without*. Chambers uses this quote to remind us that today's message about concentration cannot be achieved by only a few minutes of effort.

SCRIPTURAL CONTEXT The theme verse for today comes from an obscure passage in 2 Chronicles 15. Read that chapter and notice all that Asa did. How can a king's heart be loyal to God yet not be willing to destroy what God had clearly said to destroy (see Numbers 33:50–52)? Did any other king before Asa have this kind of divided heart (see 1 Kings 3:3)?

The Bible contains several examples of people who were doing well but who later failed to maintain their focus on God. How about you? In what ways are you doing well? Where have you turned a blind eye to the "high places" that should have been destroyed?

WHAT'S THE DEVOTIONAL SAYING? One of Chambers' points today is that we must yield to God's lessons about *every* detail, no matter how small. Chambers asks a piercing question: How long will we keep God waiting while He teaches us the same lesson over and over? Does that describe your life? Is God patiently teaching you the same "small" thing again and again? If so, let go of your tendency to think you are already right with God!

The second paragraph focuses on our tendency to give up and take a break on obeying what God shows us. This is where MacDonald's quote is so helpful. We follow God in short bursts and expect to "clear the numberless" hills and mountains in one wild leap of effort. But Chambers reminds us that having a heart that is 100 percent right with God (not 99.9 percent) takes a tremendous amount of time and constant vigilance. Are you willing to put in the time and effort today and the rest of your life?

APPLICATION

What trips you up most: lying, lusting, craving, or something else?

How have you been physically or intellectually lazy? What can you do about it?

Finish this prayer: "Lord, when I take my eyes off you, I'm in real trouble. Today I want to ensure . . ."

CAN YOU COME DOWN FROM THE MOUNTAIN?

Are you a porcelain saint, painted—and then shelved?
Blend God's glorious art into your daily routine!

BACKGROUND As we learned on March 26, Oswald Chambers mentions "vision" nearly one hundred times in *Utmost* (and about four hundred times in the rest of his *Complete Works*)! Clearly, this word plays a key role in Chambers' teaching. Today we see that our mountaintop experiences are where we get our vision, but our valleys are where we work our vision into reality.

On March 12, Chambers ended the lesson by saying, "Most of us know abandonment in vision only," which, in the Updated Edition, was rendered, "Most of us have only a vision of what this really means, but have never truly experienced it." Today we learn how to go from vision to true experience.

SCRIPTURAL CONTEXT The story of the Greeks who wanted to see Jesus is sandwiched between Palm Sunday and Maundy Thursday. Read all of John 12. Who does Jesus address in each paragraph? Was the crowd (verse 34) full of disciples or skeptics? How does their experience of "the light" compare to your experiences? How can you become more of a child of the light?

WHAT'S THE DEVOTIONAL SAYING? Although Chambers doesn't use the word *vision* today, he discusses the same concept we have seen many times before (for example, March 11). At key points, God reveals to us why He created us, and we must live in light of this vision even in the hours of gloom (see March 22, *Companion*). How can we live in light of this vision? As we saw on March 22 and see again today, it's by burning bridges and making as many things inevitable as possible *while* you are still on the mountaintop. That way you will be forced to live with the decisions you made when you most clearly saw God's vision, even if you don't want to!

Even in mundane things, Chambers preached against a "do it tomorrow" attitude. For example, he told his students, "Never *intend* to look up a word; *do it now.*" Chambers was always urging people to fight against intellectual laziness. Today's lesson reminds us that craving another mountaintop experience is a sure sign of laziness. The point of the mountaintop is to show us how to live in the ordinary "gray" days. Did you burn your bridges while on the mountaintop? If not, do that today!

APPLICATION

What has God shown you on the mountaintop? What did you do about it?

Have you given up living to a higher standard? How can you go after it again—today?

Finish this prayer: "Father, I need to pick myself up by the scruff of my neck and, today, start . . ."

⚭ APRIL 17 ⚭
ALL OR NOTHING?

Know what it costs to live for God?
Peter didn't just dip a toe. He took the plunge!

BACKGROUND Today's title in the Classic Edition is "Neck or Nothing." Have you risked it all—nothing less than your own neck—for God? Probably not! But even if you haven't had the opportunity to risk your life, have you at least risked your whole reputation as a reasonable, normal man or woman? Today is the day Oswald Chambers will challenge you to do so!

Thankfully, Chambers has gone before us on this point. For example, he pursued an art education instead of the more stable engraver apprenticeship that his father had chosen for him. He decided against trying to make more money as a teacher despite his father's urging (see January 11, *Companion*). He took a round-the-world voyage with no idea how God would provide for his needs. He married without having an income. He decided to work with the soldiers in Egypt not knowing for sure if his wife and baby would be able to join him. In general, he lived hand-to-mouth without fear of what others would say.

SCRIPTURAL CONTEXT Twice Peter got wet for Jesus. Once it was for his lack of faith (see March 28, *Companion*), and once it was for his great joy (today's verse). Read John 21. If you had recently denied Jesus, would you have swum to Him as Peter did? Do you think Peter had second thoughts when he got closer to shore? If so, what might have kept him going?

WHAT'S THE DEVOTIONAL SAYING?
In three short paragraphs, Chambers makes his points. First, abandon yourself to God, not by giving up some external thing, but by making an inner decision. Second, abandon yourself with your inner will, not your inner emotions. Third, trying to maintain your consistency (or what you think others see as your consistency) will block your abandonment to God, but focusing on your relationship with Him will help you abandon yourself.

What blocks you from abandoning to God? Did you try giving up an external thing but realized that you are actually in bondage? Is your emotional desire to abandon stopping you from making a transaction of your will? Is the sacred cow of one of your precious convictions stopping you? Whatever it is, throw it aside and leap into the water!

APPLICATION
What was your greatest crisis? Did it make you more abandoned to God? Why or why not? How do your emotions and external things get in the way of abandoning yourself to God? Finish this prayer: "Jesus, I hear you calling me and I want to come. Already I see that I need to surrender . . ."

READINESS

Do you protest if called to a drudgery?
Or are you ready to spring into action?

BACKGROUND Oswald Chambers was quick to respond to God's call. When World War I broke out, he and Biddy committed themselves to doing God's will and to be where He wanted them to be. When, as a result of his prayer time, Chambers felt the call to work with the armed forces, he prayed to God, "Guide me in each particular."

Being ready for God's work doesn't mean we are always single-minded once He calls us. Even Chambers had doubts after deciding to go to Egypt (see March 28, *Companion*). But it *does* mean that we will waste less time telling God where we want to go and what we want to do, since that only makes it harder to hear Him!

SCRIPTURAL CONTEXT The burning bush serves as our guiding symbol for today. Just as an ordinary bush became remarkable because it was ablaze with God's presence, so our ready lives will be visibly engulfed with God's power as we await our next job. Read Exodus 3 from the *bush's* perspective. How long had the bush been growing in that spot before God had a job for it? How long had it been burning before Moses noticed? If you had been the bush, would you have grown impatient as you tried to be ready for God's work?

Now read John 17, particularly verses 11 and 22. Does our oneness with other Christians look like the apostles' oneness? Have you ever done a menial job for someone else? If so, did you feel one with that person? How so?

WHAT'S THE DEVOTIONAL SAYING? Have you read something in *Utmost* that didn't seem to apply to your current situation? For example, do you feel as if you've never really had the kind of "call" or "vision" Chambers discusses? Today's lesson helps us see how to apply *any* of the lessons in *Utmost* to *whatever* we are experiencing. It tells us that God's call can be to the largest or to the smallest, most menial task. This means that all of us will hear God's call and see God's vision each day!

Unfortunately, we often miss God's call to small tasks because we are looking for the big things. Chambers says, "We wait with the idea of some great opportunity, something sensational." But this kind of waiting is counterproductive. Will you wait instead for God's call, no matter how menial?

APPLICATION

When have you heard God's call? How did you answer? How should you answer?

What does "readiness" mean for you? Do you know "where you are" right now?

Finish this prayer: "God, there are a lot of obscure duties on my plate. Please help me today to . . ."

BEWARE OF THE LEAST LIKELY TEMPTATION

The most insidious tests look innocuous. But don't relax your grip on God!

BACKGROUND Shortly after his four years of darkness (see January 3, *Companion*), Oswald Chambers had a discussion with an acquaintance about Emmanuel Swedenborg, the Swedish intellectual. Thereafter, Chambers got *all* of Swedenborg's books. Chambers' knack for reading whole collections and analyzing their arguments led him to present an entire paper on the subject of Swedenborg!

Chambers also liked many of the works of Londoner J. J. Garth Wilkinson, the editor of Swedenborg's books. For instance, in today's devotional (Classic Edition) he quotes the phrase "retired sphere of the leasts" out of Wilkinson's 1890 book *The Soul Is Form and Doth the Body Make*. Chambers was a man in tune with deep thoughts, like Swedenborg's and Wilkinson's, and also with the least likely things. Today he urges us to watch out for things in the "sphere of the leasts" that trip us even more than big temptations.

SCRIPTURAL CONTEXT Today's lesson is easy to remember, possibly because the theme verse is one that we don't read often and yet is part of a sad and memorable story. Read 1 Kings 1–2. Why did Joab support Adonijah (see 1:6)? But if that's the reason, why *didn't* he support Absalom? How are some of your bigger and smaller temptations related? Which ones are more dangerous?

Chambers also refers us to 1 Corinthians 10:13. Read this familiar verse and also 1 Peter 1:3–5. What temptations do you face? Do you know anyone else who has experienced the same temptations? In the midst of temptations, how has God used your faith in Him to protect you?

WHAT'S THE DEVOTIONAL SAYING? The message today is loud and clear: Don't let smaller temptations trick you into letting down your guard. Chambers warns those who have triumphed in a supreme crisis, perhaps their own "white funeral" (see January 15, *Utmost*), not to think that they won't therefore be tempted to turn their back on God in a smaller crisis. That is foolishness! He says that any temptation, as long as it can trip up one person, can trip up anyone, which is an interesting interpretation of 1 Corinthians 10:13!

Where are your strengths? Chambers said that people in the Bible fell to temptation in their areas of strength. Do you think this is true? Is it true for you?

APPLICATION
What was the biggest temptation or trial you overcame? Have you stumbled since then?
What is your area of strength? Are you guarding it against "least likely" temptations?
Finish this prayer: "Lord, I don't want to end my life in shame like Joab did. Please keep me from . . ."

♠ APRIL 20 ♠
CAN A SAINT FALSELY ACCUSE GOD?

What keeps you from God's best?
The Holy Spirit is the only key to success.

BACKGROUND When Oswald and Biddy Chambers got married, they committed to never say, "We cannot afford it." Oswald explained his reason for this by saying that he didn't want his "intercourse with God rudely corrupted by the perpetual plaint of chronic impecuniousness." In other words, he didn't ever want to hurt his closeness with God by complaining about not having enough money.

Do you bellyache about not having enough money? Or, as today's lesson warns against, do you complain about not having enough power to overcome a situation that God gave you? Chambers' exposition of Matthew 25 cuts to the heart. Will you be a wicked servant who raises petty objections to try and justify yourself to your Lord? Or will you invest your God-given spiritual talents and be the best you can be by the power of the Spirit?

SCRIPTURAL CONTEXT Today's theme verse says it all: We can bank on everything God promised because of Jesus. Read the context (1 Corinthians 1:15–24). Why did Paul have to remind his friends that all God's promises are "yes" and "so be it"? What might they have thought about Paul's ability to do what he had planned to do? Do you complain to God about your own insufficient power *and* about how other people let you down?

We've looked at the encouraging theme verse. Are you ready now for the conviction of Matthew 25:14–30? Read with two different scenarios in mind: one in which the wicked servant *didn't* know what the other two had done, and one where he did. How do the scenarios change your view of how he tries to pin the blame on his master? Do you ever accuse God in this way? Now read Matthew 6:19–30. How is worrying connected to money?

WHAT'S THE DEVOTIONAL SAYING? Oh, if we could just read *Utmost* and then do what it says! But there is nothing stopping us from making *today* the day when we make a true breakthrough. Chambers passionately reminds us that we don't have to be spiritual paupers and beggars. Vast resources are at our disposal if we only stop making excuses for our failures.

Do you think *any* of your lame excuses are valid? What was your most recent failure? How did you try to downplay it to keep yourself from feeling like a loser? Tell God *right now* that you are sorry for spinning a tale to minimize your shame, and thank Him for not just minimizing but *erasing* all of your shame at Calvary.

APPLICATION

When have you tried justifying your inabilities to God? Were you also worrying? How?

What is the true basis of our abilities? Is it hard to believe that day-to-day? Why?

Finish this prayer: "Father, please forgive me for being critical and for worrying. I want to start fresh by . . ."

◦◦◦ APRIL 21 ◦◦◦
DON'T HURT THE LORD

Want God's presence?
If you have childlike trust, You already have it.

BACKGROUND Today's 279-word lesson, an average length for *Utmost*, comes from a sermon that was almost three times longer. Biddy Chambers carefully boiled down this sermon to provide us with its essence. But some of it is now so concentrated that it forces us to think deeply. For example, what does it mean to want to "be conscious of God," and why is this morbid (see the Classic Edition)?

In the book *God's Workmanship,* we find the longer sermon that Biddy condensed into today's reading. It says that our desire to "be conscious of God" includes asking God to show you His presence, asking Him to explain something to you, and even asking Him to show His face. Have you ever asked God for these seemingly good things? Today's lesson tells us why this is wrong.

SCRIPTURAL CONTEXT It seems like all of today's Scripture comes from John 14. But the original sermon was actually structured around John 1:43–44, and 46. These three verses and John 14:8–9 show a contrast between Philip's strengths and weaknesses. What do you think Philip did well? Where did he fail?

As you read through John 1 and 14, imagine the disciples before and after their three years with Jesus. How was your relationship with Christ three years ago? How has it changed?

WHAT'S THE DEVOTIONAL SAYING?
The two paragraphs in today's lesson both warn against hurting Jesus. The first tells us we can hurt Him by asking Him to show us what He already has shown us (God, for example), or by expecting something amazing that isn't the amazing thing we already have: a relationship with God. Our expectations cause the biggest problems, since any time we expect, we rely on our own notions and opinions instead of believing God with childlike trust.

The second paragraph warns against hurting Jesus by worrying about the future. Do you worry? Oswald Chambers' advice is to take everything, even the most worrisome things, "as it comes from Him"!

APPLICATION
What opinions do you have about how God works? Have you been questioning Him?
Are you looking for God to exhibit himself and asking to be conscious of His work?
Finish this prayer: "God, I know you exhibit yourself *in* me and not *to* me. Please help me to set aside . . ."

APRIL 22
THE LIGHT THAT NEVER FAILS

Fixated on your spiritual ups and downs?
Fix your eyes on Jesus instead!

BACKGROUND In November 1908, Oswald Chambers asked Biddy Hobbs to marry him. In March 1909, more than a year before the two finally were married, Oswald's mentor and friend, Reader Harris, died suddenly of a stroke. On his way to Harris' funeral, Oswald wrote the following short poem: *I war alone, I shall not see his face; But I shall strive more gladly in the sun, More bravely in the shadow for this grace, He fought his fight and won.*

Today's devotional reminds us that we must not base our faith on lights that can fail. As Oswald and Biddy started life together, God took away Oswald's key advisor. Was God being cruel? Or was his engagement to Biddy when Oswald *most* needed to learn the lesson that he shares with us today?

SCRIPTURAL CONTEXT What is the connection between 2 Corinthians 3:18 and today's theme? Perhaps an easier place to start is 2 Timothy 4:16–17. How does Paul's attitude at his defense embody Chambers' message to us today?

Read Exodus 34:29–35. How is today's second paragraph a picture of Moses' ministry? How are the Israelites described in Exodus 34 similar to the Jews of 2 Corinthians 3?

WHAT'S THE DEVOTIONAL SAYING? Today's three paragraphs each teach a different truth about our walk of faith. First, we learn that our faith must not be based on "big" or "important" people. Second, we must have God's glory in our lives (though we should not notice when we have it). We get His glory by looking into the face of God, which means we open every part of our lives to Him with complete readiness to change what He wants us to change. Third, we must not fixate on our every high and low. Chambers says we must instead be "in tune with God all the time."

How will you keep in tune with God today? Are there people or ideas you are clinging to that prevent you from staying in sync with God alone? What will you cast aside even before God removes it from you? Today look to Him alone!

APPLICATION

Have you ever been disappointed by other Christians? Did you end up standing alone?

How are we supposed to preach the good news? Have you ever told others the gospel in this way?

Finish this prayer: "Jesus, when no one else stands with me, you still will. Thank you for helping me . . ."

DO YOU WORSHIP THE WORK?

Does work get you down?
Don't focus on what you do but on who you do it for.

➤

BACKGROUND At many points, Oswald Chambers looked like a man consumed by Christian work. Before he married, he criss-crossed England and preached so frequently that he didn't see his fiancée, Biddy, for months. After he married, he threw himself into the Bible Training College and all of the extension classes he taught, plus grading the mountains of final papers from correspondence students. In Egypt, Chambers' intense efforts to share the good news weakened his body to the point where he never recovered from an emergency appendectomy.

But was he really "consumed" by work? Today's lesson shows us that Chambers knew the dangers of worshiping work instead of God. Are you in danger of worshiping what you do, what you stand for, or anything besides God? If so, today's lesson will give you a much-needed corrective.

SCRIPTURAL CONTEXT Today's theme verse in the Amplified Bible reads: "For we are fellow workmen (joint promoters, laborers together) with *and* for God." What does "with *and* for" mean in Christian work? And what is *Christian* work, anyway? Does today's lesson

also apply to work that isn't called "Christian work"? Does the theme verse? Read the whole third chapter of 1 Corinthians and try to answer that question.

Chambers also quotes from Ecclesiastes 9. As you read that chapter, think about how working "with your might" (verse 10) is related to the second half of that verse and the rest of the chapter. Do you skimp on "might" when you go about the activities that God put in your hand?

WHAT'S THE DEVOTIONAL SAYING? Today Chambers makes the same point he makes in one of his favorite sayings: "Do your work; don't let your work cling to you. The latter impedes you while the former expresses you." He says that when we do our work without letting it cling to us, we receive the freedom of a child.

In the last paragraph, Chambers tells us that it is not our place to question the "where's" and "what's" in our lives. Are you happy with where you are and what you are doing? It may not always be fun. But Chambers, always the "apostle of the haphazard," reminds us that God engineers everything!

APPLICATION

Looking at the phrases "God's fellow worker" and "work worshiper," which fits you? Are you changing?

Right now, where has God put you? Knowing yourself as you do, why aren't you wholehearted to God?

Finish this prayer: "I want to stay in touch with you, God. Nothing but you will . . ."

THE WARNING AGAINST DESIRING SPIRITUAL SUCCESS

Led others to Christ?
Your job isn't done until they are sold out for God.

◄

BACKGROUND As you may have already noticed, Oswald Chambers was master of alliteration. Today's lesson, "The Warning Against Wantoning," follows yesterday's "The Worship of the Work" (Classic Edition) and both are directed at those in full-time Christian ministry. But like yesterday's lesson, there is plenty of insight for anyone who loves God, no matter how they earn their living.

What will be your legacy? What will people remember about you, and what lasting good do you think you will leave behind on earth? Today's lesson says that our job is to leave behind people who are wholly devoted to God. And there's no way we can do that until we ourselves are 100 percent yielded to Him!

SCRIPTURAL CONTEXT What is the context of today's theme verse, Luke 10:20? What would it be like to be one of the 72? How long do you think they were away from Jesus? What did He want them to learn?

Now turn to Hebrews 13:13. Those who originally read this letter were tempted to abandon Christianity and return to Judaism. What would verse 13 have meant to them? What does it mean for you?

Finally, can you find any times when Jesus says "if" to His disciples? What would He have said if He were being an "irritating dictator"?

WHAT'S THE DEVOTIONAL SAYING?

As we first dive into today's reading, it seems as if Chambers is going to tell us that counting up our Christian ministry victories is wrongheaded. But instead he shifts our focus. He tells us that our job is <u>not to win converts but to make disciples</u>. By doing this, he avoids the easy excuse for not working hard in Christian ministry ("We can't look at any results; it's all up to God!"), and he points us to where we ought to put all our energy.

What does Chambers mean by "reproducing that standard in others"? The final paragraph sheds some light. This is where Chambers discusses how Jesus invites rather than dictates. This is a "standard" that God's grace puts in us and that we can reproduce in others. Are you experiencing the grace of Jesus' invitations? Are you extending the same grace to others? Today pray that you will speak more about "if" and less about "you must."

APPLICATION

When have you gone "outside the camp" of what is acceptable in order to be with Jesus?
Have you been a dictator instead of a discipler? How can you avoid that tendency?
Finish this prayer: "Lord, your grace allows me to live a higher standard. Please help me reproduce that . . ."

Your best days are not the norm! Learn to obey God even on the ho-hum days.

BACKGROUND Today we read a terrifying truth: God ensures we won't always act as well as we do when we are full of inspiration. As Oswald Chambers put it in the Classic Edition: "God will take care that you are not."

Why would God prevent us from consistently being at our best? According to Chambers, it's so that we learn to do the duties that are right in front of our faces.

Are you struggling to do the menial jobs that you know you should do? Today's lesson will give you energy for those times you feel "out of season."

SCRIPTURAL CONTEXT How many different translations of today's theme verse can you find? Chambers quotes from the King James Version, which says, "be instant," instead of "be ready" (NKJV). No matter what version you read, it gives the same message: You need to prepare in order to do a great job preaching the Word. How can you apply this truth to your life?

Chambers applies this verse to all of us. Whether we preach as Timothy did in Ephesus, or whether we preach by living our lives, we all are tempted to make a fetish of and be obsessed with our best, "out of season" days. Fight this temptation! Be "unflagging and inexhaustible" (Amplified Bible) *in* season, not just on our rare, out-of-season days.

WHAT'S THE DEVOTIONAL SAYING? Chambers points out our tendency to be ready only for *out*-of-season days. Once we understand that such days are our *best* days, today's lesson becomes simple. Are you making an idol out of your best days? God will topple that idol by ensuring you never have another "best" day. Scary thought!

Have you ever considered the possibility that you might be an "intolerable" burden on God? Chambers says we become a drag on God when we say we will only have "best days." Put aside that pipe dream! Ho-hum days are the norm, so decide today to obey God even when you are not feeling inspired.

APPLICATION

When has God inspired you? Did you become dependent on more inspiration? How so?

Are you ready in season, in other words, in your daily routine? What tasks do you have to do today?

Finish this prayer: "Father, I'm sorry for making a god out of my best moments; I want to be obedient to . . ."

APRIL 26
THE SUPREME CLIMB

God fixed Abraham's bad beliefs at Mount Moriah. Where's He taking you?

BACKGROUND On January 4, we read about Peter's brave declaration. Then on March 1, we saw how Peter's declarations ended under Jesus' probing questions. Today we will see how Abraham avoided the faith rollercoaster by simply obeying God. As a result, God was able to free Abraham from wrong thinking about what He meant when He said to offer Isaac.

Have you ever misunderstood God? How did He help correct your thinking? Today you will see how simple obedience takes you on "The Supreme Climb" where God can perform surgery on your misconceptions about who He is.

SCRIPTURAL CONTEXT We haven't studied Genesis 22 since January 8. Read this chapter again. Do you agree with Chambers that Abraham misunderstood what God wanted him to do? Does verse 12 support Oswald Chambers' view?

Chambers references two verses from Psalm 18. How do they fit into the psalm and into this lesson? What in Abraham's character caused him to interpret God's command the way he did?

WHAT'S THE DEVOTIONAL SAYING? Two days ago we read that our job is discipling others, and God's job is saving and sanctifying souls. Today we see how God is also in the business of discipling! He goes to any length to break us of our wrong thinking so we can know Him better and follow Him with reckless abandon.

Another thing we see today is the difference between faith and fanaticism. Abraham exemplifies faith. He did not cling to his preconceived notions about God. Instead, he continued to obey God even when God's instructions ("Do not lay a hand on the boy") went against his earlier understanding of God's will. Let us strive for this kind of obedience and faith!

APPLICATION
What traditional belief about God have you left behind? How did God help you do that?
Have you, like Peter, declared great things? How was Abraham's attitude different?
Finish this prayer: "God, I know that I still have wrong views about you. Please help me as you lead me . . ."

WHAT DO YOU WANT?

Which is better: God or things? It's your choice!

➤

BACKGROUND All good things are from God, as James 1:17 teaches. But what about "great things"? Today, Oswald Chambers distinguishes what God gives us from what we think of as "great things." He says, "A great thing is accidental," whereas "God never gives us anything accidental" (Classic Edition). Is that true? Do the "great things" in life just come and go? We assume that great things come through careful planning. But when we list things we consider "great" (worldwide fame, international power and influence), we see that they are the accidental outcome of being in the right place at the right time.

Thankfully, today's devotional isn't trying to persuade us to rely on chance rather than on wise planning. Instead, it urges us to seek God instead of "great things." Do you have the power of the Holy Spirit in your life? If not, today's lesson points to the reason: You are seeking things and not God himself.

SCRIPTURAL CONTEXT In today's theme verse, God speaks to Jeremiah's scribe, Baruch. Read the whole message. What was Baruch's complaint? (See chapter 36.) How did God's reply address his complaint? What was God's promise? Did it come true?

Chambers also quotes from Matthew 6:8, 7:7, and John 17:22. According to Chambers, what is the relationship between prayer and being one with God? Is it true that we ask God for fewer things as we grow closer to Him?

WHAT'S THE DEVOTIONAL SAYING?
Who *doesn't* want great things for themselves? By nature, we humans are greedy. Even in spiritual matters, we desire more and more. If you've been following *Utmost*, you have probably asked God to empower you more and more with the Holy Spirit. What was the result? Did you feel rest and peace? Chambers says that if we asked for the Spirit's power in order to get rest and peace, then that is the very reason we *didn't* receive the Spirit's power. The Spirit wants us to seek *Him* when we ask for His power, not any of the things His power brings into our lives.

The other reason, according to Chambers, that we don't receive the Spirit's power is that there is something we are not willing to do. Does it seem counterproductive for God to withhold His Spirit's power? Wouldn't His power help us overcome our unwillingness? But by holding back the full release of the Spirit's power in our lives, God is "working out His ultimate perfection" in us. Can you trust in God enough to go through a time of darkness in order to be made perfect in the end? Keep asking for the Spirit's power until God makes your heart ready to receive it!

APPLICATION
What great thing do you want? Why? How does it compare to a relationship with God?
Have you asked for the Spirit's power? Do you know if He empowered you? How so?
Finish this prayer: "Lord, I have many things to ask of you, most importantly . . ."

WHAT YOU WILL GET

What's life?
All we want! We miss it if we aren't simple and don't obey.

◅

BACKGROUND Today's lesson continues yesterday's theme: We need to stop seeking great things so we can seek what is really important. Yesterday Oswald Chambers told us to seek God rather than His gifts. But today he reminds us of the one gift we should seek—our life!

Do you have a life that is hidden with Christ? If you have received the gift of your life from God, in the way Chambers describes, you will be "the most surprised and delighted" person around! Today's lesson reveals what stops you from receiving your life in this new, delightful way.

SCRIPTURAL CONTEXT As we saw yesterday, God promised Baruch his life as a spoil of war. The Amplified Bible adds (perhaps because "prize" is singular) that this prize was the *only* thing God promised him. What else can you learn about verse 5 by reading it in different Bible versions?

The other key to today's lesson is in Colossians 3. How does that whole chapter describe a life that is "hidden with Christ in God"? How are we hidden "with Christ" and "in God"? What things in chapter 3 would you like to see in your life today?

WHAT'S THE DEVOTIONAL SAYING? In addition to his main point about our need to receive our life from God, Chambers warns us against asking God questions. Normally it's good to ask questions. How else can we learn? But Chambers is talking about when we question God's wisdom and His plans by asking Him, "But what about this issue? Have you considered it in your plan?" Are you guilty of this kind of questioning? How will you abandon yourself to God today?

Chambers' final point is that sometimes we don't abandon to God either because we are disobedient or because we aren't willing to be "simple" enough. Which of these reasons trips you up most often? What can you do today to counteract one of these problems? Learn to be a simple fool for God! Obey Him no matter what!

APPLICATION

Do you get tired of life? What's the antidote for that kind of thinking? Has it worked? Why would we be surprised when we get the life that "is hidden with Christ"? Are you? Finish this prayer: "Father, I show off your blessings but miss out on true life in Christ. Please help me . . ."

GRACIOUS UNCERTAINTY

Are you calculating your future?
Relax! Your job is to trust Jesus. He will surprise you daily!

➢

BACKGROUND What do you believe about God? Do you believe He loves you, sent His Son to die for you, and will welcome you into His eternal presence if you accept His free gift of salvation? Those are all great beliefs. But today Oswald Chambers warns us about believing in our beliefs rather than in Jesus. Can you spot the difference between those two in your own life?

Today we are also introduced to the phrase "ban of finality" (Classic Edition). This is Chambers' way of describing how being "complete and settled" (see Updated Edition) in our views and beliefs can "ban" us from the freedom God wants us to have. Have you made up your mind about certain things? Let today's lesson help you reconsider!

SCRIPTURAL CONTEXT The whole first letter of John is full of deep truths. Chambers picks out an interesting verse from chapter 3. What is its context? There are a lot of ideas whizzing around in this chapter (and the last two verses of chapter 2). But the main theme is that we are God's children. This means the world can't understand us—we can't even understand ourselves or what God does in us. This uncertainty about God's work is exactly Chambers' point.

Chambers also quotes from Matthew 18 and John 14. Read these verses and reflect on today's main point. How are children different from adults? How does believing in Jesus differ from believing things about Him? How will you believe *in* Him like a child today?

WHAT'S THE DEVOTIONAL SAYING? In today's first paragraph, Chambers warns against strategizing a future that we think will be good. He reminds us that it's foolish to be so sure a certain condition or circumstance will be better for us than another one.

In the second paragraph, he makes his main point about how uncertainty is the norm, not something to be avoided. In fact, it's more than just the norm. When we get right with God, it's what makes life fun!

In the final paragraph, Chambers reminds us to believe in Jesus and loyally wait for Him to arrive in unexpected ways in our life. Jesus will surprise you!

APPLICATION
How do you feel about uncertainty? In what ways is your future uncertain?
What predetermined goal are you striving for? Do you self-righteously defend a belief?
Finish this prayer: "Jesus, I want to believe in you, not certain things about you, so I can have joy in . . . "

ᗋᗍᎧ APRIL 30 ᗋᗍᎧ
SPONTANEOUS LOVE

Trying to love God more?
Let the Spirit invade you, pouring out love for God as He takes total control.

◄

BACKGROUND On October 15, 1916, Oswald Chambers gave today's lesson (and yesterday's) to British troops gathered for Sunday morning communion. This was only Chambers' third Sunday back in El-Zaytoun (see February 5, *Companion*) after being away at the Suez Canal for several months.

The situation in El-Zaytoun (or Zeitoun, its name in 1916) had changed in the intervening months. Instead of housing a normal army unit, the camp was used by the Imperial School of Instruction. Therefore, the soldiers who heard this lesson the first time were officers and others who had come to learn how to operate new weapons and signaling devices with the utmost precision. How might they have reacted to yesterday's lesson about how uncertainty is good? What about today's lesson?

SCRIPTURAL CONTEXT First Corinthians 13 is an oft-quoted chapter at weddings. The "meat" of this chapter is verses 4–8, which list love's qualities. What from this list best describes spontaneous love? Why do you think Biddy picked out just the first part of verse 4 as the theme verse?

Romans 5:5 and John 17:26 also are key verses for today's lesson. What does each one say about love? According to Chambers, how are we supposed to love God? Why are *we* able to feel the love that God has for Jesus?

WHAT'S THE DEVOTIONAL SAYING? Yesterday's lesson helped Chambers' original audience of army officers see uncertainty in a better light. Today's lesson cut right to their (and our) hearts.

In the original sermon, Chambers said, "If I try to engineer ways to show I love my wife, it is a certain sign I am beginning *not* to love her." He added, "If we try to show how much we love God, it is a sure sign we do *not* love Him." Picture a husband who is concocting schemes to show he loves his wife. His elaborate romantic plans are touching only as long as they flow from his spontaneous love. Similarly, our efforts to prove to others that we love God are meaningful only if they aren't really "efforts" but just the outpouring of our spontaneous love for Him.

APPLICATION

Has your love for God ever burst forth spontaneously? Looking back, what do you see? Why can't we prove or take credit for our love for God? What role do emotions play? Finish this prayer: "Holy Spirit, the love I have in me has been poured out by you. Thank you for giving me . . ."

∾ MAY 1 ∾
FAITH—NOT EMOTION

Looking for the limelight?
When you accept your duty, you'll find God's light instead.

BACKGROUND After Oswald Chambers' death, Biddy wrote, "Through all the days of the illness, . . . the word which held me was, 'This sickness is not unto death, but for the glory of God,' [John 11:4] and there were times when it seemed that the promise was to have a literal fulfillment. But . . . God had a fuller meaning."

The "fuller meaning" was that Chambers' sickness didn't end in the death of his ministry, even though it did result in his bodily death. And how true "but for the glory of God" proved to be! Today's lesson reminds us that God has no obligation to bring *us* glory as we serve Him. All glory goes to Him: "whether we live or die, we are the Lord's" (Romans 14:8).

SCRIPTURAL CONTEXT In 2 Corinthians 4 and 5, Paul compares bodily life on earth with the resurrection life we will receive in heaven. In that context, 2 Corinthians 5:7 means we walk through our lives guided by our faith in future glory, not by anything we see on earth. How does this verse relate to today's lesson?

Chambers quotes this verse from Moffatt (see January 1, *Companion*): "I have to lead my life in faith, without seeing Him," instead of from the King James: "For we walk by faith, not by sight." What is the difference? How does Moffatt's version better fit with Chambers' point today?

WHAT'S THE DEVOTIONAL SAYING? Today's title is "Insight Not Emotion" (Classic Edition). Chambers' point is that we need insight into God's plan for us—to be hidden, obscure people. We don't need emotion. God sends us times of passionate emotion by giving us moments of inspiration. But if we rely on those moments and the emotions they give us, we will be "unfit for daily life."

Are you fit for your daily life? Do you overcome daily tests, or do they overcome you? Chambers' advice is to remember that we have infinitely greater power at work in us and that we need to "get up" *before* we feel inspired. Do you have something today that you know you need to do? Get started on that duty right now. God will be there as you do!

APPLICATION

Has God "sealed up heaven"? What was your response? Why is our work our standard? Why is a hidden saint of more value than a self-assured one? Do you seek to be needed? Finish this prayer: "Lord, you've given me infinite power. Help me 'get up,' without inspiration, and see . . ."

MAY 2
THE PASSION OF PATIENCE

Be impatiently patient: hungry for more of God, yet enduring His silences.

BACKGROUND While at Dunoon (see February 2, *Companion*), Oswald Chambers started a society dedicated to Robert Browning, his favorite poet. Today we read how our "reach must exceed our grasp." This line is from Browning's 1855 poem "Andrea del Sarto," a work named after a contemporary of Michelangelo. Artist del Sarto was praised as a flawless painter, but he was also criticized for having no inspiring "reach."

What have you reached for that exceeded your grasp? Chambers says when we reach for more than we can grasp of God, it's proof that we have the God-given *vision* of God. Today we will see how that vision is the key to being patient.

SCRIPTURAL CONTEXT On March 11, we looked closely at what Chambers means by "vision." We also read today's theme verse from Habakkuk 2. Reread chapters 1 and 2. What was Habakkuk's question? How does God answer? How does this vision differ from the vision Chambers describes?

Chambers also quotes from Hebrews 11:27, Psalm 116:12-13, and Philippians 3:12. What did Moses do that required endurance? Is this referring to the first or second time he left Egypt? Do you think it's ironic that we "render" as we "take"? How was Paul perfect? How was he not?

WHAT'S THE DEVOTIONAL SAYING?

Do you need more patience? Today Chambers says that vision is the key to patience because it gives us "moral inspiration" (Classic Edition). When we look back at the lessons on March 21 and 22, we see that when Chambers says "moral" he often means "from the center of our will." When we gain a clear vision of God, we are inspired at the center of our will to make right decisions. How often we lose patience just because we lack the will to decide to wait!

Sometimes we seem patient, but we are actually just passively indifferent. Chambers wants us to have "passion" and immense strength as we are patient. He wants us to be like the Rock of Gibraltar that he passed on his way to Egypt.

In the last paragraph, Chambers quotes Browning to give us the litmus test for whether we have the vision. If we continually thirst for God, we have the vision. Once we lose our thirst for Him, we try to slake our thirst from our own cisterns (Jeremiah 2:13). Are *you* thirsty for God?

APPLICATION

What causes/issues inspire you? How is that different from being devoted to God?

Have you been through a "wilderness" time? Did it cause you to reach out for more?

Finish this prayer: "Father, I want the vitality your vision gives. Please help me to keep your vision in . . ."

MAY 3
VITAL INTERCESSION

Do you pray powerfully?
If you're too sympathetic, it will limit your strength.

➤

BACKGROUND Today begins a two-day series on intercession. We saw on March 30 through April 1 that intercession is the one job we can do that doesn't have a snare. Today we see the key to intercession: identifying with God. We also see an obstacle to intercession: sympathy exceeding our identification with God.

It's strange that our sympathy for others can block intercession, but Oswald Chambers says that even *sin* is less likely to break our identification with God. Do you find that to be true? Does your sin drive you closer to God, while your own understanding of what God should do drives you further from Him?

SCRIPTURAL CONTEXT Today's theme verse follows the memorable passage about our spiritual armor. It's as if Paul wants the Ephesians to remember that all our powerful defenses (and one weapon) are for one purpose: intercessory prayer. Read this chapter and see what prayers Paul asks the Ephesians to pray. Whose armor is it? Ours or God's? Where in the Bible can you find descriptions of God wearing His armor?

WHAT'S THE DEVOTIONAL SAYING? In four paragraphs, Chambers dissects the obstacles to intercession. In the first two paragraphs, he says that sympathy with others breaks our identification with God and blocks intercession. The key is complete trust in God and His plan; otherwise, we will trust our own views about what is best for others.

Do you often throw yourself a pity party when you're trying to intercede? In the second paragraph, we see that when we fully identify with God we don't even have to try to stop thinking about ourselves.

The last paragraph is short and sweet (so short that the Updated Edition tacks it on to the third paragraph). Do you have discernment into other people's faults? Why do you think God opened your eyes to their problems? Pray for them right now!

APPLICATION

How do we rebuke God as our sympathy undercuts our intercession? Do you do that?

For whom do you intercede? What discernment has God given you about them?

Finish this prayer: "God, right now I want to identify with your interest and concern for . . ."

VICARIOUS INTERCESSION

Where are your strengths?
Pray for that! It might be what God wants to change.

◄

BACKGROUND Yesterday's devotional taught us the importance of a vital, living connection with God. Today we see the reason our connection is even possible: the "vicarious identification of our Lord with sin." Moreover, as Christ identified so completely with our sin that He *became* sin, we should completely identify with His interests and plans in others.

When you hear a sad story, does it move you to pray for those involved? While that is a natural and good reaction, Oswald Chambers warns against thinking that this is what intercession means. Instead, as we saw yesterday, intercession is about embracing *God's* plan for others.

SCRIPTURAL CONTEXT Hebrews 10 doesn't usually spring to mind when we think of intercession. As you read this chapter, what verses do you recognize? How might they relate to identifying with God's plan for others?

The point of quoting verse 19 is to emphasize Jesus' role in our intercession. When priests approached God, they needed blood to pay for their sins. The blood they used only symbolized the blood of Jesus, which would eventually pay for everyone's sins. Likewise, when we come before God to intercede for others, we need the blood of Jesus. Do you ever think about this when you pray? Try to do so today!

WHAT'S THE DEVOTIONAL SAYING? The main obstacle to intercession, as we saw yesterday, is sympathy for others. Today we learn that it's the prideful attitude behind our sympathy that is the real obstacle. We also learn that it is in Christ's vicarious death that we gain access to true intercession. This is because His blood cleanses our sin and lets us into God's holy presence, and also because His vicarious substitution for our sins makes it possible for us to substitute God's plan for our human sympathy.

God's plan is not always pleasant. Are you willing to go with His plan and forsake all of your great ideas about what is best? Trust in Him today!

APPLICATION

List what is and isn't intercession. Are you interceding well? How can you improve?

In what areas of your life do you think you need no atoning? Does this affect your prayer?

Finish this prayer: "Lord, I'm willing to give up my own sympathies and substitute your interests in . . ."

JUDGMENT AND THE LOVE OF GOD

Does your God-talk fall on deaf ears?
Have no fear! God will help them to hear.

➤

BACKGROUND Classes at the Bible Training College were open to visitors, with the exception of the weekly devotional hour (see January 1, *Companion*) and sermon class. Many of the lessons in *Utmost* come from the weekly devotional hour, but today we start a two-part series that comes from sermon class.

Can you picture the twenty-five resident students? Some were terrified of sermon preparation and delivery. Others enjoyed it. But Oswald Chambers reminded them all that giving a sermon is serious: "The element of judgment must always come out; it is the sign of God's love."

Does God's loving judgment against sin and evil shine through in what you say? Today's lesson gives us motivation to be winsome and bold as we talk about God.

SCRIPTURAL CONTEXT It's tricky to find the connection between today's theme verse, its context, and the lesson. The verse connects to the lesson, since both are about God's judgment. The second half of today's verse connects it to its context, which is about how we should praise God when persecuted for being a Christian. But the context does not seem to directly connect to the lesson until we realize that the context helps us know *how* to preach judgment. We need to preach judgment both to non-Christians *and* Christians. To Christians, we preach that God uses suffering and persecution to purify us from our flaws.

What are your flaws? Are your "inabilities" an excuse for not obeying God's commands? How might God purify you? Be open to His judgment as you preach it to others.

WHAT'S THE DEVOTIONAL SAYING?
Today's lesson opens with a profound truth: Salvation is bigger than our experience of salvation. How did you experience salvation? Did coming to Christ give you peace? If you tell people Jesus will give them peace, you are missing the point. Chambers says we must preach the "great thought of God" behind our experience of salvation; the rest of the lesson (800 words in his original lecture) describes this "great thought."

God's great thought is an "unfathomable abyss" (Classic Edition). If we are to preach it, we need to "be sure of the abysses of God," which is the title of his original lecture. Chambers lists four abysses—love, the cross, the atonement, and the gospel—and shows how these relate to judgment, conscience, morality, and liberty. In today's lesson we see the interplay between God's love and His judgment. How do those concepts relate in your life? Ask God to show you His love in His judgment today.

APPLICATION
How would you summarize the good news? What is the "great thought of God" in it?
How is judgment the sign of God's love? Have you ever brought someone to judgment?
Finish this prayer: "Jesus, you only command things I can do by your power; help me . . ."

LIBERTY AND THE STANDARDS OF JESUS

To set others free, let God reign over you.
What you feel will spread to others.

◄

BACKGROUND The concepts in yesterday's lesson were so deep that it's a good thing we have another day to look at them! Yesterday Oswald Chambers showed us how God's love and judgment are related. Today he compares liberty and the gospel (Classic Edition). Specifically, he compares liberty to the standards that the gospel places on our lives.

Love and judgment seem like opposites. So also liberty and high standards appear to be at odds. Doesn't liberty mean that we are free from any standards? Not at all! Chambers tells us to preach *Christ's* standards. This will free our listeners from lesser standards, which are often ones *we* inadvertently placed on them.

SCRIPTURAL CONTEXT Chambers uses three passages for today's lesson. First, we see Galatians 5:1, which beautifully summarizes Galatians *and* today's lesson. In the NIV, this verse reads, "It is for freedom that Christ has set us free." How does this compare to the "where-with" in the KJV that Chambers quotes? Do you think both meanings are true?

The second passage is John 5:39–40. What were the Jewish leaders missing? Are you missing the same thing?

Finally, read the Great Commission in Matthew 28. What is the difference between a disciple and a convert to an opinion? How did Jesus ensure He made disciples? How will He help you do the same?

WHAT'S THE DEVOTIONAL SAYING? If you've spent time around Christians who try to squeeze you into their mold, you will appreciate today's lesson. It's also a great warning to us, since we all secretly like to have a set of human standards to follow, and we all like to make converts to our own opinions. It's nice to have friends who think like we do!

Chambers is saying that we follow, and hold up to others, only one set of standards: Christ's. What are His standards? They certainly are not a list of dos and don'ts. In a part of his lecture that didn't make it into *Utmost*, Chambers gives a good way to think about God's standards of holiness: "It means every part of the life under the scrutiny of God, knowing that the grace of God is sufficient for every detail." Is that how you live? When we let God reign over us, we experience a freedom that is contagious!

APPLICATION

List the comparisons that Chambers uses in today's lesson. Which ones can relate to you? Are you impatient—burdening yourself or others under a yoke that isn't Christ's? How? Finish this prayer: "Lord, you want me to stop forcing people to think like I do, but I'm stubborn. Please . . ."

᪶ MAY 7 ᪶
BUILDING FOR ETERNITY

Christ is the mason; we are the bricks—formed and baked by Christ himself.

BACKGROUND Oswald Chambers was no stonemason. But he was the foreman for the construction of his living quarters, meeting hall, and study hut while in Egypt. He ordered materials, hired workers, and inspected the work. In today's lesson, he talks about how God inspects our work to determine whether we are building things according to His plan or according to our own ideas.

Jesus paid the full price to lay a proper foundation. What are you building on it? If you are using your own bricks and therefore building according to your own plans, your work will be consumed by fire on the day of judgment. If, however, the brick you use is your own life, and you let God be the bricklayer, the building will turn out according to His perfect plan. Be a brick today!

SCRIPTURAL CONTEXT Today's Scripture is from Luke 14:25–33 and 1 Corinthians 3:10–15. Both passages compare spiritual work to a building project. In these verses, who is building what? What are you building? How does today's lesson change your view of Luke 14? As you build, what must you keep in mind?

WHAT'S THE DEVOTIONAL SAYING? Do you like the tasks God has given you? Today's lesson reminds us that "no one has any right to demand where he will be put to work" (Updated Edition). Why? We don't work for God; He takes us over and uses us for His plans. As you think of a building project, think of yourself as one of the bricks, not one of the hired carpenters or stonemasons. There is only one builder, and He uses any brick who loves Him "personally, passionately and devotedly," "in whom He has done everything."

Did God do everything in you? Have you given Him permission to do everything? Or are there ties on earth that pull you away from the heart surgery He wants to perform in you? Yield fully to Him today!

APPLICATION

What difference does it make whether the "cost" is something we pay or Christ has paid?
What has Christ done in you? How do you love Him? Do you demand where to work?
Finish this prayer: "Jesus, you are coming back to judge my works. I want them built on you, not me. So . . ."

THE FAITH TO PERSEVERE

Faith isn't whiny, nor is patience desperate. They show God's power.

BACKGROUND In the Classic Edition, the opening sentence on May 2 was "Patience is not indifference." Today it is "Patience is more than endurance." The Updated Edition uses "perseverance" instead of "patience" in order to convey the larger sense that Oswald Chambers gives this word. But it might have been better, as was done in some of Chambers' other transcribed talks, to capitalize it. For example, the first sentence of one of his lectures at the League of Prayer (see January 10, *Companion*) was written: "The subject of Patience is so largely dealt with in the Bible that it ought to have a much larger place in our Bible studies and talks."

In the same lecture, Chambers said, "Patience is the result of well-centered strength." Do you have strength that is centered on God? Chambers told his students, "Patience is not the same as endurance because the heart of endurance is frequently stoical, whereas the heart of Patience is a blazing love." Today's devotional will help you develop well-centered faith, which bears fruit of blazing Patience.

SCRIPTURAL CONTEXT The church in Philadelphia slips by without any rebukes. The same cannot be said for most of the other seven churches mentioned in Revelation! Read 3:7–13. What did they do well (see February 22, *Companion*)? What *does* "the word of My patience" mean?

The next quote is from Job. Chambers talks about Job more than any other Bible character with the exception of Paul. Like Job, do you feel as if God has slayed you? Do you still trust Him? How do you know?

Last, Chambers brings in the definition of eternal life from John 17. What else does Jesus say in this chapter that relates to today's lesson?

WHAT'S THE DEVOTIONAL SAYING?

The main point today is that we need passionate patience (see May 2, *Utmost*). In *The Message* (MSG) Bible, Revelation 3:10 begins: "Because you kept my Word in passionate patience . . ." Do you passionately trust God and His goodness as you wait to see what He's doing?

Chambers' bow-and-arrow analogy helps us during times when God stretches and bends us. When we truly know God, we know His goodness and are able to wait with fiery passion. Will you venture your all on God? Ask Him to help you have dynamic patience today.

APPLICATION

Are you stretched to the breaking point? Can you maintain your intimacy with Jesus? Is your life a great romance? How are you being disciplined to throw yourself on God? Finish this prayer: "God, my life's big effort should be to abandon myself to you. Today please help me . . ."

MAY 9
REACHING BEYOND OUR GRASP

Are you on a downward spiral?
When what you do matches His plan, you'll rise in joy.

BACKGROUND Today we return to the theme of vision. This time, Oswald Chambers contrasts vision with ideals. On February 16 and March 17, these concepts were equivalent, but today Chambers points out an important difference. Vision, as we saw on May 2, gives us moral inspiration. This is why people with vision are inspired to *do* things, while people with ideals are not.

Are you somewhat depressed? Maybe not desperately so, but are you counting the days and wishing the time would pass? Chambers challenges us to live with the expectation that God will do greater things than He ever did before. Chambers' nickname for the BTC (Bible Training College) was "Better to Come." Let that be your motto today!

SCRIPTURAL CONTEXT Today is the only time the theme verse comes from Proverbs. What is the second half of this verse? How is wisdom personified in Proverbs? Could she equally well have been called "vision"?

Jonah is only mentioned once in *Utmost*. The Updated Edition helps us find where (see 4:2). Jonah inappropriately used a correct ideal about God to get out of actually *doing* something. When did he make this argument? What did he try to get out of doing? Do you do the same?

WHAT'S THE DEVOTIONAL SAYING? Today Chambers tells us that if we do what matches *our* plan, only what we can grasp, we get on a downward spiral. The opposite is also true. When we do God's plan and reach beyond our grasp, we will rise ever higher in God's joy.

Chambers tells you to examine and take stock of yourself. Do you have vision, or only ideals? Are you fighting hard to restrain evil, or are you lulled to ruin? Ask for more of a vision of God today, and the Holy Spirit will give it to you!

APPLICATION
Do you have a vision from God or only idealistic principles about Him? In what ways?
How is your prayer life? Have you cast off restraints or done things on your own?
Finish this prayer: "Today, Lord, I will regain freshness and vitality in my spiritual outlook by . . ."

ᗛ MAY 10 ᗛ
TAKE THE INITIATIVE

Do you want to make a conflict right?
Stop reading this and do it now!

➤

BACKGROUND In late 1914, as all Europe grappled with the first months of World War I, Oswald Chambers gave the expanded version of today's lesson to his students. In the full version, he made three points: Stop hesitating; start hearkening; and stand heroically. In today's lesson, we see the same points in a more condensed format.

What have you been meaning to do? What keeps you from acting? We fall into the trap of thinking God has to do things for us that He actually wants us to do ourselves. Or we keep asking God what to do when we already know what we should do. Sometimes, we think we would act boldly if we were in a different situation. But that is just another excuse. Which of these excuses are you using? Let today's lesson help you take action!

SCRIPTURAL CONTEXT Second Peter 1:5 was also the theme verse for Chambers' original 1914 lecture. He quotes both the King James and the Moffatt ("Furnish your faith with resolution") versions of this verse. What are the differences? How does 2 Peter 1:1–11 help you know how to take the initiative to form better habits?

Chambers also refers to Philippians 2:12–13. What do these verses teach us about our responsibility and God's?

WHAT'S THE DEVOTIONAL SAYING?
The three paragraphs in today's lesson give us three common excuses for not taking action. First, we wait for God to do the things that God wants *us* to do. Second, we ask God for guidance, which is just a smokescreen for our fear of taking action (see January 2, *Companion*). Third, we think that when a *big* crisis comes, we will take initiative. But in doing so, we miss out on all the *small* ways God wants us to take action.

What is on your to-do list? Will you keep putting it off, or will you start forming the habit of obeying God right away? Let God work in you as He wills, and act according to the good purpose He has shown you.

APPLICATION
What *won't* God do for you (that you have expected Him to do)? What should *you* do?
How can you know if you have the habit of listening to God? Do you have it yet?
Finish this prayer: "God, I know you want me to get things started without looking back, so today I will . . ."

"LOVE ONE ANOTHER"

Do people irk you?
Think how God feels! Yet He still loves you.

◄   ►

BACKGROUND Today we continue a seven-part series that Biddy Chambers took from weekly lectures her husband Oswald gave to his students in 1914. The subject of these lectures was "Christian habits." Biddy sent the full lecture transcripts to the League of Prayer (see January 10, *Companion*) for its monthly magazine. They appeared from 1926 to 1928, around the same time she was writing *Utmost*, which was published in 1927. As you read today's lesson, think about Biddy in 1926, taking care of her 13-year-old daughter and four Oxford students. The fact that she edited *Utmost* and published full lecture transcripts while running a boarding house as a single mom is a tribute to God's power and grace!

Today's title, "You Won't Reach It on Tiptoe" (Classic Edition), describes how it's impossible to love God or others using our own strength. It would be like trying to stand on your tiptoes for a whole week! Today's lesson points you in a better direction; love with the love that *God* put in your heart!

SCRIPTURAL CONTEXT All the theme verses for Chambers' seven-part lecture series in 1914 came from one of Peter's letters. All but one came from 2 Peter 1:5–11 (the other, which we will study on May 13, came from 1 Peter 3:16). We looked at these verses yesterday, but read them again to see how love fits into Peter's list.

Besides 2 Peter 1:7, Chambers references four other verses: Luke 14:26, Romans 5:5, John 15:12, and 2 Peter 3:9. What do these verses say about love?

WHAT'S THE DEVOTIONAL SAYING? Chambers walks a good line between telling us to do it all ourselves and giving us the impression that God will do it all for us. In today's lesson, for example, he gives us a practical way to love "unlovable" people. He reminds us that the only way we can do that is with God's love. But he also urges us to actively remember how much God loves us and to allow that thought to send us forth into love for the unlovable world.

Who do you have trouble loving? What irritating person has God put in your life? Thank God for that person! As today's final sentence says, "Love is spontaneous, but it has to be maintained through discipline." The unlovable people in our lives will help us maintain God's divine love in our hearts.

APPLICATION

Has God removed insincerity, pride, and vanity from you? Do you feel lovable or loved?
Are there people you can't respect? How do you treat them? How does God treat you?
Finish this prayer: "God, you love me, though I've been so disagreeable with you. Help me to love . . ."

THE HABIT OF HAVING NO HABITS

Do you enjoy your Bible study, or do you enjoy hearing from God?
There's a difference!

BACKGROUND Of Oswald Chambers' seven lectures on Christian habits, only the last five mention "habit" in their titles. Since today's lesson comes from the first of these five lectures, it's appropriate that it teaches us the most important truth about Christian habits: Habits can become our idols if we're not careful!

Are you in the habit of doing something "Christian"? If you have been reading *Utmost* every day, you at least have one such habit! Do any of your habits encroach on what God really wants you to do? Today's lesson will help you make good habits your goal while remaining free from worshipping them.

SCRIPTURAL CONTEXT At the end of the list of godly qualities, Peter tells us, "For as these qualities exist and increase with you, they render you active and fruitful in the knowledge of our Lord Jesus Christ" (2 Peter 1:8 Moffatt). How fruitful and active are you? Does focusing on the various qualities prevent you from being fruitful?

Chambers' original three points follow the three parts of this verse. "For as these qualities exist and increase" goes with the point that we should exercise habits and qualities until they are so much a part of us that we don't even notice them. The next part, "render you active and fruitful," goes with the point that our well-exercised, now-unnoticed habits will allow us to be more fruitful than our earlier, more conscious habits. The third part, "in the knowledge of our Lord Jesus Christ," goes with the point that, though we must strive to know God, knowledge must be eventually swallowed up by the greatness of God's actual presence. When that happens, we will live the "simple life of a child."

WHAT'S THE DEVOTIONAL SAYING?

How can we make a habit of having no habits? That seems paradoxical! But the clear point of today's lesson is that any good habit can become harmful if it takes the place of God in our lives.

After we have disciplined ourselves and have added to our faith all the things listed in 2 Peter, those qualities will become so much a part of the life of God in us that we won't even notice them. Are there other things you need to add to your faith? If you are conscious of being holy, that's proof that you still need to add to your faith. Let God show you what you still need to add, and work at it until it is second nature.

APPLICATION

What are your spiritual habits? Have they become your "gods," restricting you at times?

In what area(s) do you still lack and aren't at home with God? How can you add these?

Finish this prayer: "Lord, I want to live the simple life of the child, but I self-examine too much. Help me . . ."

THE HABIT OF KEEPING A CLEAR CONSCIENCE

Your highest ideal will direct you toward God's law—or away from it!

◄ ►

BACKGROUND Here at the halfway point of our seven-day series, it's good to take stock of where we've been and where we're headed. First, Oswald Chambers told us to furnish our faith with resolution by avoiding three common excuses. Second, he reminded us that we can't love with our own love, only with God's. Third, he warned us against making habits into idols. Tomorrow, we will see how to enjoy adversity. The next day we will hear how to rise to the level of what God sends our way. Finally, we will look at how to handle money. Today's lesson returns us to the same theme as the first of the seven lectures and gets us in the right frame of mind for the next two lessons. If you have been dragging your feet when you already know what God wants, today's message is for you!

SCRIPTURAL CONTEXT Chambers' lectures often had three sections that were given alliterative titles (see April 24, *Companion*). The titles he used for the lecture "The Habit of a Good Conscience" were the following: Sensitive Conscience, Seared Conscience, and Saintly Conscience. Biddy took his thoughts from the first of these three sections to use in today's devotional. The theme verse is Acts 24:16. How did Paul "strive" for a clear conscience? The Amplified Bible says he would "always exercise and discipline myself [mortifying my body, deadening my carnal affections, bodily appetites, and worldly desires, endeavoring in all respects] to have a clear [unshaken, blameless] conscience" and so on. Is all that really necessary? Do you do any of those things?

What other verses does Chambers quote? How do they relate to our conscience? How do we "make out" (Moffatt) the nature of God's will?

WHAT'S THE DEVOTIONAL SAYING? Based on the title, we might think that today's lesson would tell us to follow high moral standards so our consciences won't feel guilty for the bad things we do. Instead, Chambers tells us to develop *sensitive* consciences, which in turn help us listen to God and do the right thing. Can you see the difference between these two approaches? To develop a sensitive conscience, we must know what a conscience is. In the original lecture, Chambers says that conscience is *not* the voice of God in our hearts. Instead, it is "the eye of the soul." Just as our eyes want to fix themselves on the most beautiful thing they see, so also our conscience fixes itself on the highest thing it sees, and it informs the rest of our soul how to respond. How will you respond to what your soul "sees" in Jesus? Will you see Him as He truly is? If so, your life won't be the same!

APPLICATION

Has your love for God ever burst forth spontaneously? Looking back, what do you see? Why can't we prove or take credit for our love for God? What role do emotions play? Finish this prayer: "Holy Spirit, the love I have is yours. Thank you for giving me . . ."

⌒᷉ᴗ᷉⌒ MAY 14 ⌒᷉ᴗ᷉⌒
THE HABIT OF ENJOYING ADVERSITY

What's irritating you?
It might be just what helps you reflect God's glory!

BACKGROUND Do you think Biddy Chambers enjoyed the hard task of selecting which parts of her husband's talks she should use to write this seven-part series on Christian habits? The original lectures were six times too long to use as *Utmost* devotionals. So Biddy had to pick and choose what to use and what to save for when she published Oswald's full lectures (see May 11, *Companion*).

As she sliced and diced her verbatim shorthand notes, she often combined paragraphs from two lectures into a single devotional. For example, yesterday's devotional lesson opened with a paragraph from Oswald's lecture, "The Habit of Enjoying the Disagreeable," which is the topic of today's lesson. In the same way, today's lesson ends with a paragraph from a different lecture ("Make a Habit of Having No Habits," which is also the source material for May 12). Understanding Biddy's method of mixing of paragraphs helps us tie together Chambers' main points, especially for all-encompassing themes such as "Christian habits."

SCRIPTURAL CONTEXT The theme verse is one that Chambers references at least ten times in his *Complete Works*. Interestingly, however, he didn't mention this verse in his original lecture, so we can conclude that Biddy considered it a perfect verse to summarize the devotional. How does 2 Corinthians 4:10 relate to today's main point? What other verses might Chambers have been thinking about as he spoke the words that ended up in today's lesson?

WHAT'S THE DEVOTIONAL SAYING? Is getting saved by Jesus just "fire insurance"? Do we ask Him to take control of our life and forgive our sins only to avoid hell? Obviously not! God has much more in store for those He saves. Today's lesson reminds us that the main thing He wants us to do is to show signs of *Jesus'* life in *our* lives.

How can you allow Jesus' life to shine out of your own? By enjoying disagreeable things. And you will enjoy them only if you are *extremely* hungry for His life to be manifest in your life. When you must do an unpleasant thing, do you ever think about how that thing might help you shine Christ's life through yours? Try to think about that today and embrace all unpleasantness!

APPLICATION

Describe a time you experienced adversity. What was your response? Were you ready?

How can you keep your soul ready to manifest Christ this week?

Finish this prayer: "Father, you engineer my life to make your Son's glory evident. Help me today to . . ."

THE HABIT OF RISING TO THE OCCASION

God won't put us in a museum. He displays His glory in our living flesh.

BACKGROUND Oswald Chambers probably gave his second-to-last lecture on Christian habits on December 3, 1914. He divided the lecture into three sections, and today's lesson comes primarily from the second section, "The Habit of Realizing Your Exercises." In this section, he urged his students to embrace difficult situations so they could manifest Christ's life in their own lives.

What is it you need to just get up and do? Are you putting off something unpleasant? Rise to the occasion as you read today's devotional!

SCRIPTURAL CONTEXT Today's theme verse comes from the lecture's first section, "The Habit of Ratifying Your Election." Chambers used Ephesians 1:18 to show how much God has given us and how blasphemous it is for us to say we can't be made into saints, even though that kind of talk sounds humble to others.

Read the context of this verse and list what God has given us. What do the other verses Chambers quotes say about God's provision? Do you ever catch yourself being so "humble" that you blaspheme God's power to make you a saint?

WHAT'S THE DEVOTIONAL SAYING? The four paragraphs today lead us through four interrelated points. First, Chambers reminds us

that the reason we are saved is so Christ's life can shine through our own (see May 14, *Utmost*). Second, he distinguishes between our responsibility and God's: God saves us and we "work out" the salvation He worked in us. Third, he urges us again to embrace difficulties, since they help reveal Christ in us. Finally, he encourages us to exercise as disciplined athletes do as we prepare our lives for Jesus' life to shine in them. He also warns us that our goal in Christian habits is not to become trophies in some museum for holiness.

In Chambers' commentary on Genesis 25:1–10, he makes the same point about trophies and says, "You can often find better [trophies] in the world than in the Church," since God gives Christians crises that nonbelievers don't have to face. If God wanted to display *human* goodness, would He give you crises that break, irritate, and upset you? No. But God wants to display *His* goodness and glory. That's why the "net result of your life is not admiration for you but a longing after God." Isn't this true of Oswald and Biddy? The net result of their lives has been millions of people longing after God. (Most of those people don't know who they were, so admiration for Oswald and Biddy has never been an issue.) Is that true of you?

APPLICATION

What wall is God placing in your life? How are you planning to jump over it?

How have (or haven't) you worked out your salvation in speech, thinking, and emotions?

Finish this prayer: "Lord Jesus, you never demanded your rights. Please help me to do the same as I face . . ."

THE HABIT OF RECOGNIZING GOD'S PROVISION

Who wants to be a millionaire?
God has more buying power than that!

◄

BACKGROUND On December 17, 1914, Oswald Chambers told his students that they should "be going about like multimillionaires." This was despite their lack of basic necessities because of World War I. He reminded them that even though they didn't have a dime to their names, spiritually they "have all the grace of God to spend on others."

Biddy carefully edited this nearly 2,000-word lecture on wealth to create today's short devotional. She picked out the essence of what we need to know about God's provision. Are you willing to learn about this today?

SCRIPTURAL CONTEXT The theme verse for the lecture was 2 Peter 1:11, but Biddy picked verse 4 for the devotional. What do these verses have in common? How do these verses relate to the "add to your . . . " verses that are sandwiched between them?

Chambers also references Psalm 87:7, which he finds in *The Book of Common Prayer of the Church of England* ("all my fresh springs are in thee"). How does the word "fresh" emphasize his point? Why does Chambers quote 2 Corinthians 9:8? How is this point a great way to end the devotional?

WHAT'S THE DEVOTIONAL SAYING? Our final lesson in this seven-part series teaches us about the first habit to form as we "work out" the salvation that God worked in us. How do you handle "The Habit of Wealth" (Classic Edition)? Are you working out the awareness of God's provision, which He put in you when He saved you? Or are you still saying, "Oh, I can't afford it"?

The second paragraph makes the additional point that God dries up every other spring of wealth so we know all our fresh springs are in Him. Are you going through a drying-up experience? Thank God that He is breaking your confidence in your own powers. Don't forget to drink deeply of His reserves!

APPLICATION

What is your "so-called wealth" (money, education)? Has God ever taken it away?

Where are you tempted to say, "I can't afford it"? How might God provide for you?

Finish this prayer: "Father, you own the cattle on a thousand hills (Psalm 50:10). Today I commit to trusting . . ."

HIS ASCENSION AND OUR ACCESS

Jesus gave up His power to be like us. He regained it to make us like Him.

BACKGROUND On April 5, 6, and 8, we read lessons excerpted from Oswald Chambers' twelve-lecture series on psychology. Today's first paragraph recaps the seventh through tenth lectures in this series. In these four lectures, Chambers told how the transfiguration, Gethsemane, the cross, and the resurrection affect our study of psychology.

Do you often think about these four other-worldly events or about the fifth one—Christ's ascension? Do you ever think about your psychology and what makes you tick? Today's lesson will show you how the deep-thinking Chambers linked Christ's ascension with our psyche.

SCRIPTURAL CONTEXT As was typical of Chambers, he referenced dozens of verses in his lecture on Christ's ascension. The main passages were Luke 24:50–51 and Acts 1:9–10. How do these verses connect the two books Luke wrote?

Other verses Chambers referred to were John 17:5, Acts 2:33, Matthew 28:18 (with Matthew 11:27), John 14:13, Acts 7:56, and John 17:23. Can you see how these verses relate to the ascension? For example, what does John 17:23 say is the reason Jesus stands at the Father's right hand (Acts 7:56)?

WHAT'S THE DEVOTIONAL SAYING? In the first paragraph, Chambers refers to his previous four lectures. He briefly explains the main point of the previous two: "His cross is the door . . . into the life of God" and "by His resurrection He has the right to give eternal life." In the same paragraph, Chambers summarizes today's lesson: "by His ascension our Lord enters heaven and keeps the door open for humanity."

It's as if Christ opened an airlock to heaven. First, through the cross, He opened the door on earth. Then, through His resurrection, He earned the right to let people through the airlock. Finally, through His ascension, He opened the door into heaven.

Of course there's not really an airlock to get into heaven. But imagining two doors, one on earth and one in heaven, helps us make sense of the cross and the ascension. Part of Jesus' job was to be on earth as the Son of Man, to reopen the door that was shut at the fall. But His job wasn't finished until He went back to heaven and held open the door for us there too.

Take time today to thank Jesus for going back to heaven. If He hadn't done that, your psyche would be forever trapped in the old earthly patterns!

APPLICATION

How do you think the disciples thought of Jesus before and after the transfiguration?

What did Jesus' cross, resurrection, and ascension do for us, and how did they do it?

Finish this prayer: "Jesus, I praise you for being willing to lay down your glory and give us access into . . ."

LIVING SIMPLY—YET FOCUSED

Want to be useful?
Just be who Christ made you to be.

BACKGROUND At noon in Perth, Scotland, on July 19, 1911, Oswald Chambers gave the third lecture in his five-part Sermon on the Mount series. Four years later, he and Biddy sent the modified transcripts to a publisher in Cincinnati (see February 15, *Companion*). From this *Studies in the Sermon on the Mount*, Biddy extracted today's lesson: "Careful Unreasonableness" (Classic Edition).

At Chambers' funeral, his good friend David Lambert said that Chambers' life was "the finest commentary on the Sermon on the Mount" that he knew. How does your life compare? How does it compare to the part about "Do not worry"? Are you "unreasonable" in how carefully you guard your relationship with God? Today's lesson gives us a fresh look at this part of Jesus' most famous sermon.

SCRIPTURAL CONTEXT On January 26 and 27, we looked at this part of the Sermon on the Mount. If you made notes from those days, look back at them as you read the whole Sermon on the Mount. How did the "do not worry" section affect you earlier? How is it the climax of Jesus' sermon? Why do you think He used more words in this section than in any of the other nineteen sections of His sermon?

Chambers also quotes John 7:38. Why is it so important to believe in Jesus as we live simple lives? How does God exert influence on others through our simple lives?

WHAT'S THE DEVOTIONAL SAYING? Have you felt guilty for not "buttonholing" an acquaintance to talk with him or her about God? Christians have at times put an unnatural emphasis on the need to verbally share our faith with others at the expense of what Chambers is teaching us in today's lesson. He urges us to focus on our relationship with God and to approach everything else the way a lily approaches life.

Looking to a lily for life advice seems strange from a non-Christian perspective. As Chambers put it in his 1911 lecture, "It seems unreasonable to expect a man to consider the lilies, yet that is the only way he can grow in grace." You will definitely be seen as unreasonable if you are so careful about your union with God that all else falls by the wayside. But that is the only way you can grow in grace!

APPLICATION
How should your life be like a lily's? Do you know someone who lives like this? Who? Where are you trying to be useful? Which circumstances have your focus right now? Finish this prayer: "God, I want to be useful to you, but it can only happen as I focus on Jesus. Help me . . ."

⌒ MAY 19 ⌒
OUT OF THE WRECK I RISE

Getting bugged? Want a change?
Pesky problems lead to victory through Jesus.

BACKGROUND Do you ever feel like a total wreck? How can you make today's title true and rise out of your wreck? Oswald Chambers gave a sermon with this same title to World War I soldiers. Some may have caught the reference to Browning's poem "Ixion." But others probably just imagined rising up out of their own wreck of a situation.

Why are you a wreck? Is it because of tribulation? Anguish? Whatever helps you realize the wrecked state of your life is actually a blessing. As today's lesson teaches us, it is right in the midst of troubles that we receive God's victory.

SCRIPTURAL CONTEXT The foreword to the 1959 book that included Chambers' "Out of the Wreck I Rise" said it was a "remarkable exposition of the closing verses of Romans 8." Read these final three verses. What does Paul list as things that can't separate us from God's love? Which ones did Biddy include in today's lesson? Why do you think she picked these?

Chambers also quotes Psalm 91:15. How does this Psalm help you know that God will be with you *in* the very things that make you feel like a wreck?

WHAT'S THE DEVOTIONAL SAYING? Have you ever met someone whose life is full of troubles but who still holds on to the love of God? Are there any signs or wonders that better prove God's love?

Isn't it odd that we don't become super-victors through our courage? Our Hollywood-soaked culture adores courageous victors and abhors wrecks. But God loves wrecks like us and loves to wreck us until we learn to rise out of our wreck by *His* power.

APPLICATION

What do you wish *wasn't* in your circumstances? Has it made you Christ's super-victor?

What can you do to remember that God loves you despite tribulation, distress, and famine?

Finish this prayer: "Jesus, I know you haven't deceived us. I want to hold on to your love despite what I . . ."

MAY 20
TAKING POSSESSION OF OUR OWN SOUL

Moody? Tried praying?
God tells us to kick bad moods by taking action!

BACKGROUND For today's devotional, it seems that Biddy Chambers took two paragraphs from different talks and combined them. Today's second paragraph comes from a talk on "Attention" that Oswald Chambers gave to his Bible Training College students. The complete version of this talk is preserved in a book published nine years after *Utmost*. We don't know where today's first paragraph came from, but it rings with expressions that Chambers used elsewhere.

Are you struggling to give more attention to the real, spiritual world? Are you distracted by the realm of the unreal—the things that steal our attention from the spiritual? Today's lesson helps you put away your excuses and get "roused," or awakened, to God's reality.

SCRIPTURAL CONTEXT In some translations of the Bible, Luke 21:19 is a promise that we will stay alive during the hardships Jesus describes. But the King James Version, which Chambers quotes, commands us to possess our souls. Do you think Chambers uses this verse out of context? How does patient acquisition of the "mind of Christ" relate to our surviving the end times that are discussed in Luke 21?

WHAT'S THE DEVOTIONAL SAYING? What a convicting message today! In response to today's lesson, a person blogged, "I've tried praying away my blues, but instead of dispersing them, my moods only seem to increase with the increased attention."

Is that your experience as well? Take stock of what it is you say you can't do, and rouse yourself to do those things. God doesn't want you to sit around praying about it. He wants you to use the Holy Spirit's power that is already in you and to take the first step toward making it happen!

APPLICATION

When you became a Christian or got serious about God, did you feel a setback in focus? How can you take possession of your new life? In what ways have you done that?

Finish this prayer: "Father, the life you gave me is so precious! I commit to shaking myself out of my . . ."

᳽ MAY 21 ᳽
HAVING GOD'S "UNREASONABLE" FAITH

We think we know what's important. But God's the one who made the rules.

BACKGROUND We return again to the topic of our May 18 study: being careful to live an "unreasonable" life. Oswald Chambers uses the phrase "carefully careless" in today's study (Classic Edition) and more than twenty times in his *Complete Works*, often to sum up the main point of the Sermon on the Mount. What do you think this phrase means? How are you careful to live carelessly about everything except your relationship with God?

SCRIPTURAL CONTEXT Read again Matthew 5–7. In his *Complete Works*, Chambers quotes these three chapters more than three hundred times and recommended we read them whenever we want to see just how dull and slow we are in following the teachings of our Savior.

What parts of the "do not worry . . ." section are you still not obeying?

WHAT'S THE DEVOTIONAL SAYING? Chambers was not a man who dressed sloppily or put off improvements to his house, garden, and place of work (see March 6, *Companion*). He used the term "Bohemian" to describe people who refused to put adequate effort into doing quality work. So when he says we should take great care to put our relationship with God first, the implication is that the "great care" we take in our heavenly relationship insures that we are also responsible for our earthly affairs. The key is to keep these earthly affairs in clear subordination to God and our relationship with Him.

APPLICATION

How many hours a day do you spend making money, eating, relating to God, and so forth?

Where should you reprioritize? Why is it so difficult to harmonize with the verses in Matthew 5–7?

Finish this prayer: "Jesus, I don't want to be lazy with my responsibilities, but on the other hand I need to . . ."

MAY 22
THE EXPLANATION FOR OUR DIFFICULTIES

Prayer is not God giving us more stuff. It's us learning what's on our Lord's heart.

BACKGROUND Imagine Biddy Chambers digging out her old shorthand notes for Oswald's talk "Now This Explains It." He said in this talk that God's purpose "is not to answer our prayers." Oh, how she had prayed that Oswald would recover! Then to read these words! Few of us can relate to her deep loss and the way these words must have affected her.

Which of your prayers has God decided not to grant the way you were hoping? Has this made you sweeter, better, and more noble, or more insistent on your own way? Let today's study prepare you for the next time God doesn't answer your prayer.

SCRIPTURAL CONTEXT In his *Complete Works*, Chambers quotes from John 17 more than one hundred times. The only chapter he references more frequently is Matthew 5 (see May 21, *Companion*). Indeed, Jesus' high priestly prayer and His Sermon on the Mount were the two lynchpins of Chambers' whole view of Scripture.

Read through Jesus' prayer in John 17. What parts stand out to you? How many times does He talk about "oneness"?

WHAT'S THE DEVOTIONAL SAYING? Have you ever wondered why you have to go through difficulties? Many of our troubles are self-inflicted, but we still can be left wondering why God didn't keep us from those bad choices. Plus, there are many troubles that are not our fault at all.

Today's lesson explains that God wants oneness with us. All our troubles are toward that end. It's comforting to know that this is true even of our self-inflicted troubles. So in the midst of troubles, will you say to God, "Your will be done"? If not, troubles will only make you bitter because you are not getting your own way.

APPLICATION

What does it mean to be one with God? How do you feel about being that close to Him?

What difficulty are you facing? Is it making you sweeter or more critical?

Finish this prayer: "Jesus, thank you for praying to the Father that I become one with Him. I commit to . . ."

⚬⚬⚬ MAY 23 ⚬⚬⚬
OUR CAREFUL UNBELIEF

Are you worrying?
It's not just useless; it's the sin of unbelief!

BACKGROUND Today's lesson is the third in a three-part series that began May 18 and continued on May 21. Oswald Chambers saw Matthew 5–7 as central to Jesus' teaching, and he considered the lesson of "careful carelessness" from chapter 6 the essence of the whole sermon.

Have you ever thought of worry as a sin? What about common sense? Is it really "infidelity" as Chambers says (Classic Edition)? Today's lesson pulls no punches as it warns us against commonsense carefulness!

SCRIPTURAL CONTEXT Instead of reading Matthew 5–7 for the third time in five days, just focus on 6:19–34. Try to read it in a few different versions. What new ideas come to mind?

The truth is we will spend the rest of our lives trying to live out these verses. We can try with all our might to be "carefully careless" about everything except our relationship with God, and we will still miss the mark. Only with the Holy Spirit's power will our concerted efforts make any headway in the "Realm of the Real" (May 20). Ask the Spirit to fill you with trust and "careful carelessness" today.

WHAT'S THE DEVOTIONAL SAYING? Chambers gives us three examples of where we show our infidelity to God: relationships, vacations, and books. Obviously, these are only examples, but they are at least a place to start. List some of your plans in the first two areas. Is the Holy Spirit pointing to where you haven't put God first in these areas? How do you choose what books you will read? In what other areas of your life is the Spirit calling for fidelity?

The full "Careful Infidelity" sermon elaborates on "abandon," Jesus' "great word" to His disciples. Chambers says we must learn to abandon the way our bodies learn to do things physically, by practicing over and over. What can you do this week that will further your practice of abandonment to God? What step is the Holy Spirit asking you to take next?

APPLICATION

What worries or confuses you? Do you always put Christ first? If not, what is first?

Do you see worry as unbelief? How do you view common sense and carefulness?

Finish this prayer: "Lord, I want to abandon myself to you. Right now, the place where I need to obey is . . ."

⟳ MAY 24 ⟳
THE DELIGHT OF DESPAIR

Until we've fallen down and been raised up by God, we don't have real peace.

BACKGROUND Back on February 24, we learned about "The Delight of Sacrifice"—the joy of being a "doormat." Today's lesson, "The Delight of Despair," teaches us that we will experience great delight when we finally know that, in our flesh, there is not a single good thing.

Have you ever felt despair? Have you wanted to fall down and not get up? Often our despair is from unholy sources that take away all hope and give no delight. Oswald Chambers is referring to holy despair that helps us realize our need to fall prostrate before God. Have you ever felt that kind of holy despair? Today's lesson will prepare your heart for it, whether you have felt it yet or not.

SCRIPTURAL CONTEXT Do you find it hard to relate to John's vision in Revelation 1? God rarely manifests himself like this. Chambers often said that though we look for God to manifest himself *to* us, "God only manifests himself *in* His children" (see April 21, *Utmost*). Yet there are many ways that God's presence

and our sin become so clear that we feel like falling down as if we were dead.

How does the rest of the theme verse comfort you? What about Deuteronomy 33:27? What else in that chapter is comforting? How did Paul respond to the realization that he had nothing good inside his old, human flesh (Romans 7:18)? How do you respond?

WHAT'S THE DEVOTIONAL SAYING? First, Chambers describes the experience of holy despair. He talks about how Jesus will seem completely different from who we thought He was (see March 15, *Utmost*). Second, Chambers says that God will lift us out of this holy despair with His "ineffably sweet" tenderness. Third, Chambers warns against unholy despair and draws the connection between holy despair and our realization that nothing in our old selves is good.

Have you come to grips with the lack of anything good in you, in your old self? The proof will be that you have experienced God's sweetness. Ask Him for that sweetness today!

APPLICATION

Have you felt despair? Was it because God revealed himself? How did you react?

Do you see your natural self as basically good or do you see it as totally bad—in dire need of God?

Finish this prayer: "God, if you appear to me, my whole being falls prostrate, since I am so unworthy . . ."

MAY 25
THE GOOD OR THE BEST?
(BIDDY AND OSWALD'S ANNIVERSARY)

Stuck in a spiritual rut?
Yield up your rights to "golden opportunities."

BACKGROUND As 1915 got underway and Britain prepared for the second year of World War I, Oswald Chambers began a four-month series on the life of Abraham. By the end of this series, Chambers decided to leave London's comforts to serve with soldiers (see March 28, *Companion*). In today's study, Abraham makes a similar choice by giving up his rights to the well-watered land. Chambers says that when we give up our rights to good things, we grow spiritually.

SCRIPTURAL CONTEXT Chambers quotes from two parts of Abraham's life. Genesis 13:9 is from an early time, when Abraham was still Abram and was sharing land with his nephew, Lot. Read this chapter and see how God rewards the way Abraham gives up his rights.

In the second quotation, Abraham is 99 years old. Read Genesis 17. Why did God change Abram's name to Abraham? Did Abraham follow God's command (see Genesis 24:40)? How do *you* walk before God?

WHAT'S THE DEVOTIONAL SAYING? When you first started following God, did "fascinating" prospects open up before you? Did you face golden opportunities? Chambers says this is bound to happen, since God uses them to help us grow. Surprisingly, it is in giving up our right to them that we grow spiritually.

Related to this, Chambers says that the good is the enemy of the best. We must avoid a perspective that puts our rights ahead of God's best for us. Let God make the decision, as Abraham did when he let Lot choose first. What right can you relinquish today? Don't shirk your responsibility to choose wisely, but when you are faced with a golden opportunity, let God make the final choice. You'll grow as a result!

APPLICATION

What good things could you choose right now? Does God want you to yield your rights?

How much have you grown spiritually this year? Have you chosen "good" over "best"?

Finish this prayer: "Lord, I want to live a higher standard, one focused on you. Specifically, I commit to . . ."

MAY 26
THINKING OF PRAYER AS JESUS TAUGHT

Prayed but didn't receive?
Disillusioned with God? He answers best—always!

BACKGROUND On May 22, we saw that the only prayer God always answers is Jesus' prayer for our oneness with Him. Today Oswald Chambers tells us that God always answers *every* prayer. Is this a contradiction? Chambers says the answer might not be immediate, "in the domain in which we want it" (Classic Edition). So the lesson on May 22 was that Jesus' prayer for our oneness is the only prayer that God immediately answers in the exact way Jesus prayed it.

Think about your prayers that were unanswered. Can you see how God answered them "in the best way," as today's lesson says? Don't give up on your childlike certainty that God *will* answer prayer!

SCRIPTURAL CONTEXT First Thessalonians 5 ends with a rapid-fire list of instructions. How does verse 17 fit into this list? What kind of prayers could you pray continually? How can life be prayer and prayer be "the life"?

Chambers also quotes from Luke 11:10 (identical to Matthew 7:8). Do you believe that when you ask you receive? How does that fit in with Luke 11:13, the verse that changed Chambers' life?

WHAT'S THE DEVOTIONAL SAYING?
Today's lesson makes two points. First, prayer should be unceasing. It should not merely be an exercise, but it should constantly be a part of our lives.

Second, prayers *will* be answered. We remember times when an answer was not immediately evident "in the domain in which we want it," so we think we've misunderstood verses like Luke 11:10 that promise an answer to all prayers. Take Jesus at His word, and pray without ceasing!

APPLICATION

List truths about prayer described in today's devotional. Is this how you've been thinking about prayer?

How has your view been shaped by common sense? Have you had unanswered prayers?

Finish this prayer: "Holy Spirit, I know that you can help me pray as I ought. Please give me continual . . ."

MAY 27
THE LIFE THAT REALLY LIVES

The disciples waited for the Spirit, but we receive the gift of Christ's power now!

BACKGROUND Before he left for Egypt, Oswald Chambers organized Bible correspondence courses. Chambers used material from these courses as he taught soldiers in El-Zaytoun (see April 30, *Companion*). Biddy published one of these courses, *The Making of a Christian*, while she was still in Egypt a year after Chambers died. Today's lesson comes from the final chapters of this little booklet.

Do you understand Pentecost and how it relates to the Holy Spirit in you? Today's lesson gives us valuable insight into both topics.

SCRIPTURAL CONTEXT The theme verse and the first two verses Chambers quotes (Acts 2:33 and John 7:39) outline the Holy Spirit's grand entrance to our planet. First, we learn that Jesus was the one who sent the Holy Spirit to earth. In the second verse we see that He didn't send the Spirit until He was "exalted" to God's right hand. Finally, we learn that the Spirit's coming happened after Jesus was "glorified."

Does any of this matter to us? Chambers thinks it does! He says we often separate the Spirit's infilling power from the power of our risen Lord. Instead, we must see the Spirit's baptism as the evidence of Jesus' glorified life in our lives. This truth is highlighted by the fact that the Spirit wasn't even *here* on earth before Jesus had risen, ascended, and been glorified.

WHAT'S THE DEVOTIONAL SAYING? The final verse Chambers quotes points us to the take-home lesson. We must know God. Period. The experience of the Spirit's baptism serves to help us know God. Although it's important to understand the timing of the Spirit's appearance at Pentecost, our experience of Him should be here-and-now, since God wants us to know Him right *now*.

In *The Making of a Christian*, a sentence Biddy used in today's lesson: "The reception of the Holy Spirit is the maintained attitude of the believer" (Classic Edition) is followed by another intriguing sentence: "The way of His entrance into us is the knowledge of our own poverty." What does this mean?

This intriguing sentence means that the Holy Spirit's power can't fully be expressed in your life until you know that you are "poor in spirit" and realize how much you need Him. Do you know your own poverty? Let God show it to you today, so you can continually welcome the Holy Spirit's entrance into your daily life. Then you will truly experience "The Life That Lives"!

APPLICATION

What's the importance of the Holy Spirit's coming *after* Christ was glorified?

How could "reviving life" help you really live? How can you receive the Holy Spirit?

Finish this prayer: "Spirit of Jesus, I welcome you into my life today and every day. Please empower me to . . ."

UNQUESTIONED REVELATION

Are you just asking for things you want?
Or are you asking in Jesus' name?

BACKGROUND Do you ever wish God would level with you? Do you feel as if it would be a lot easier if He just spelled things out clearly once in a while? In a sermon titled "Why Are We Not Told Plainly?" Oswald Chambers spoke about this feeling. His threefold conclusion was that God doesn't tell us plainly because we can't bear it; we can't believe it; and we don't need to know it once we know Him. Today's lesson comes from the third point.

Are you experiencing something "dark to your understanding" (Classic Edition)? Do you ask God *nothing* about it and trust that He will work things out "in accordance with His will"? That's hard to do! But today's study will help you in your times of darkness.

SCRIPTURAL CONTEXT Read John 16:16–33. How does today's theme verse contribute to the change in the disciples' attitude? How does it relate to verse 25?

Chambers says that John 14:1 will become a reality in our hearts once we know God well enough to stop questioning Him. Is your heart troubled? Or do you trust in God?

WHAT'S THE DEVOTIONAL SAYING? On May 26 we saw that when we ask, we receive. But we also learned on May 22 that the only prayer God *must* answer is Jesus' prayer for our oneness with Him. The question is this: Are we asking for what Jesus would ask for—in His name—or are we just asking for what *we* want?

When our prayer coincides with Jesus' prayer and we have oneness and perfect contact with God and His purpose, Chambers says our questions will cease. Does that mean we won't ask for anything? Absolutely not! Two days ago we were told, in the Updated Edition, to "maintain the childlike habit of offering up prayer in your heart to God all the time." When we do, our prayers will be less about questioning God for what He is doing and more about communicating with Him as our Father and our best friend.

APPLICATION

What questions have you asked Jesus? Are they separating you from Him? How so?

Compare mind vs. spirit and asking Jesus vs. asking God in Jesus' name (John 16:23, 26).

Finish this prayer: "Jesus, I'm willing to submit to your life—relying completely on your resurrection . . ."

MAY 29
UNTROUBLED RELATIONSHIP

Do you ask in Jesus' name?
Get with God and you will!

BACKGROUND On a Wednesday evening in November 1912, Oswald Chambers left his home at Number 45 North Side, Clapham Common, to speak at the annual League of Prayer meeting in Caxton Hall.

Was Oswald Chambers nervous as he made the three-mile trip through London to give the address? We can't know for sure. But we are blessed to have the talk he gave preserved in the book *If Ye Shall Ask* and to read a condensed version of this talk in today's lesson.

SCRIPTURAL CONTEXT On February 28 we noted how the upper room (and from there to Gethsemane) marked a turning point in the disciples' lives. How does John 16 fit into their transition from "smooth sailing" to "world crashing down"? How does Jesus' prayer in John 17 complete the transition?

WHAT'S THE DEVOTIONAL SAYING? Yesterday, we focused on those times when we ask God about things dark to our understanding. Today we look at how the same closeness that keeps us from questioning God's plan will allow us to pray in Jesus' name and will allow us to receive from God whatever we ask.

Do you use "in Jesus' name" as magic words to make your prayers official? Or are you so intimate with God that you really pray for the things that are part of God's mind and plan? Ask God today for the closeness that will protect your heart from being troubled and allow you to pray in Jesus' name, which is a guarantee that you will receive your requests!

APPLICATION
How should/shouldn't we pray in Jesus' name? How is Jesus' character proved?
What is the point of God's love—if not to keep us free from difficulties?
Finish this prayer: "Father, I want to live in an undisturbed relationship with you today and every day . . ."

"YES—BUT . . . !"

Christians take risks in order to do big things.
What do you risk for God?

BACKGROUND "Sometimes your whole life boils down to one insane move" is a line from the 2009 film *Avatar*. Though *Avatar* is by no means a Christian film, we can appreciate the spiritual truth in that quote, especially after we read today's devotional.

Today's lesson teaches us that the more we practice stepping out of our comfort zone to do things that defy common sense, the better we will be at following God. Conversely, the more we say, "Yes—But . . . !" the harder it will be to do what He asks. Are you willing to take a leap for God today?

SCRIPTURAL CONTEXT The source material for today's lesson is from the same part of *Studies in the Sermon on the Mount* that we saw on May 23 (Matthew 6:30–32). But Biddy, when she edited the source material into this devotional, chose Luke 9:61 as the theme verse. Read verses 57–62. Can you identify with any of these excuses? How are you saying "Yes—But . . . !" to God?

WHAT'S THE DEVOTIONAL SAYING? What kind of "reckless, sporting" ("unrestrained, adventurous," Updated Edition) spirit does a natural man exhibit? In his original sermon, Oswald Chambers explains this cryptic phrase with an example from track and field. When a hurdler starts to balk at a hurdle, he will continue to turn back each time until he breaks his fearful habit with a reckless sporting spirit.

Have you made a habit of balking at what God wants you to do? Will you throw yourself today in reckless abandon at whatever barrier He puts in your way? If you are going to do anything worthwhile, you will have to risk everything on your leap. Ask Him for wisdom to know what risky actions *He* wants you to take and what things are your own ideas. Remember, God will give you wisdom as you read His Word and compare it to your situation. Will you be that one out of a hundred who will bank it all on God's faithful character?

APPLICATION

Has God asked you to do something contrary to common sense? How did you respond?

Search the New Testament for "mad" statements made by Jesus. Have you proven them true?

Finish this prayer: "Lord, I want to be that one person willing to invest my faith in your character, so I'll . . ."

⟅⟆ MAY 31 ⟅⟆
PUT GOD FIRST

Who is first in your life?
God, or someone else?

BACKGROUND We learned on January 1 that much of the source material Biddy Chambers used to create *Utmost* came from a weekly devotional hour at the Bible Training College, which was closed to everyone except full-time students (see May 5, *Companion*). Today's lesson most likely comes from one of these devotional hours. Oswald Chambers speaks intimately with his students about the believer's need to put God first in every area, and he tells them that the whole "purpose of this College is to get us rightly related to the needs of God" (see Classic Edition).

SCRIPTURAL CONTEXT Chambers uses three verses to walk us through three aspects of putting God first. He first quotes John 2:24–25 to show how we put God, not humans, first in our trust. Second, he uses Hebrews 10:9 to remind us that we put God's needs in *us* first, then His needs elsewhere. As we learned in kindergarten, "Just worry about yourself." When we try to meet God's needs in other people before we meet His needs in us, we are in danger of seeing the speck in our brother's eye and not the log in our own!

The final verse for today is Matthew 18:5. This verse highlights how God has given us a precious trust. Have you ever babysat for someone else's child? It's a weighty responsibility! God says that we must receive Jesus in the way we receive a little child. We must be very careful to provide a nurturing environment for His life, so that His life will grow up to maturity inside us and be evident to all around us.

WHAT'S THE DEVOTIONAL SAYING?
Do you put God first in anything? What evidence is there that you do? Where are you *not* putting Him first? Do you trust human beings first? Have you been burned? Do you focus on God's needs elsewhere more than His needs right inside your own heart? Do you value, first and foremost, the way God entrusted His Son's life to you?

We fall short in so many ways. Let us take today to renew our efforts to put God *first*.

APPLICATION
Who has let you down? How are you going to get better at trusting God first?
Why might we temporarily set aside others' needs? What are God's "needs" in you?
Finish this prayer: "God, I want my life to be a Bethlehem. Although it might take a while, I want to start by . . ."

⌒ JUNE 1 ⌒
THE STAGGERING QUESTION

Are you working with God, or just for Him?

BACKGROUND Today Oswald Chambers says that when God's Spirit reveals your sinful heart, "you know there is no criminal who is half so bad in actuality as you know yourself to be in possibility." This echoes a painful chapter of his life that revealed to him the horrors of what he was capable of doing (see February 18, *Companion*).

Have you seen the blackness of your heart? How does seeing your own "grave" relate to not despairing of anyone, no matter how far away from God's grace they seem?

SCRIPTURAL CONTEXT Ezekiel 37 is a funny chapter. Imagine seeing a whole valley full of bones that are rattling around and joining together to form human skeletons. It would either be very scary or somewhat comical!

As you read this chapter, do you see how Ezekiel avoided religious common sense when he answered God? Do you see a connection between Ezekiel 37:12 and Romans 7:18? How

has God taken *you* up from your "grave" and put His Spirit in you?

WHAT'S THE DEVOTIONAL SAYING? The two parts of today's lesson teach us an important truth about Christian ministry. In the first two paragraphs, Chambers warns against "religious common sense," which begins with overconfidence but ends with hopeless despair over the depravity of human nature apart from God. In the third paragraph, he explains how God can show us human depravity—by revealing it in *our* hearts first.

Together, these three paragraphs help those of us who want to bring God's light to a broken world. We shouldn't try to guess how God will heal the brokenness around us. We simply need to remember how He healed our own broken hearts and then continue to let Him heal us. From the experience of His power in *us*, we can go to the world without despair.

APPLICATION

Have you forged ahead by common sense? What happened? Did you feel hopeless?

What has God shown you about your human nature? Has it changed your view of God?

Finish this prayer: "Lord, you know the skeletons in my closet. Please show them to me so I can see . . ."

JUNE 2
ARE YOU OBSESSED BY SOMETHING?

God is obsessed with you. Are you equally obsessed and haunted by Him?

➤

BACKGROUND Ever the poet, Oswald Chambers uses the poetic language of Psalms 25 and 46 and Acts 17 to show us how to keep our lives focused on God. Do you fear God? Are you haunted by His continual presence? Is your mind obsessed with Him? Today's lesson will show you how the life focused on God is really the same as the life that is haunted and obsessed by Him.

SCRIPTURAL CONTEXT Read Psalms 25 and 46. What phrases are familiar? How do these psalms describe a person who trusts in God?

Now read how Paul quotes Epimenides in Acts 17:28. Is Paul's use of secular poetry similar to how Chambers quotes non-Christians (see March 22, *Utmost*)?

WHAT'S THE DEVOTIONAL SAYING? The key sentence for today's lesson is this: "The abiding consciousness of the life is to be God, not thinking about Him." In the Updated Edition, this sentence reads: "The abiding awareness of the Christian life is to be God Himself, not just thoughts about Him." How do you experience God? Do you merely think about Him, or are you "haunted by" and "absorbed in" Him the way young children are completely wrapped up in their mothers?

It's impossible to fake being obsessed. Either you are obsessed by something—forever wrapped up in it—or you aren't. It's obvious when a child is mother-obsessed. Whenever there's trouble, the child will run to Mommy. Are you like that with God? Is He the first place you run to when trouble strikes? Make it your goal to turn to God in every situation. Ask the Holy Spirit to fill you with His presence so you can be surrounded by His shelter.

APPLICATION

What obsesses you? Why is it best to be obsessed with God? Can you be *too* obsessed? Why does Jesus emphasize the sin of worrying? What worries are controlling you now? Finish this prayer: " Jesus, even if I'm 100 percent obsessed with you, I know it's not too much. Thank you that . . ."

JUNE 3
"THE SECRET OF THE LORD"

Do you share your joys with others?
God wants that closeness with you.

BACKGROUND Yesterday Psalm 25 showed that we are God's "mother-haunted" children—constantly aware of His saving presence should trouble come our way. Today the same psalm shows us we are also God's friends, sharing in His secret joys.

What are God's joys? Has He ever showed you a sunset that delighted His heart, or a child's compassion toward another child that filled Him with joy? Let today's lesson remind you to listen for God's secret joys. This will be the "last mark of intimacy" in your friendship with Him.

SCRIPTURAL CONTEXT The theme yesterday was protection. Today it is direction. What fraction of Psalm 25 is devoted to these two themes? How are they related?

Oswald Chambers also quotes Matthew 6:10. Where in Psalm 25 is this same attitude of trust expressed? How is this a different attitude than when *we* make sure that we aren't put to shame and that our enemies don't triumph over us? How would that look in your own life today?

WHAT'S THE DEVOTIONAL SAYING?
The first paragraph in today's lesson tells us to leave room and time for God to talk to us about *His* secret joys. The second paragraph focuses on God's direction for our lives.

Do you want to know God's will for your life? We spend a lot of time wondering what job He wants us to take, where He wants us to live, and so forth. In the beginning of our Christian life, God may guide us in ways we consciously see: signs, particular Bible verses, others. But Chambers says that eventually all the decisions we make for our life will be so in tune with God's will that we won't consciously see how He guides us.

A caveat to this is that the Holy Spirit still can "check" our course of action (Classic Edition), which means He can give us an internal sense that something is not right. Chambers warns us that when this happens we should immediately stop what we were going to do. Where are you in your walk with God? Do you consciously see how He's guiding you? Are you sensitive to the ways He "checks"? Ask God for more intimacy, more of His secret joys, so you can be even more in tune with His will.

APPLICATION
Has God ever included you in on His secret joys? Have you noticed what delights Him? Do you feel a need to be aware of God guiding you? Do you ignore Him when He does? Finish this prayer: "Holy Spirit, I don't want to resist you when you prompt me, and I also want to be so . . ."

JUNE 4
THE NEVER-FORSAKING GOD

What keeps you going?
Let God's unwavering faithfulness uphold you!

➤

BACKGROUND The way Oswald Chambers uses the phrase "say-so" is loaded with meaning. Remember Chambers' victory over his clouds and darkness (see January 3, *Companion*)? Years later, as he recalled that pivotal day, he told his listeners, "I knew emphatically my time had come, and I rose to my feet. I had no vision of God, only a sheer dogged determination to take God at His word and to prove this thing to myself, and I stood up and said so." Chambers' "said-so" was key to the change God wanted him to make in his life.

Have you voiced your "say-so" about something? Did it make that something more real than before you voiced it? Imagine a wedding without the bride and groom saying, "I do"! Today and tomorrow, we will look at the power of our "say-so" and how it must be linked to the ultimate, never-failing "say-so" of God.

SCRIPTURAL CONTEXT Hebrews 13 exhorts and gives us promises like few other chapters. Which promises and exhortations connect with you most? Chambers focuses on the promise in verses 5 and 6. Does God's promised "say-so" hold true no matter what?

WHAT'S THE DEVOTIONAL SAYING? The Updated Edition translates "say-so" into "assurance." If you usually only read one edition or the other, today would be a good day to compare the two. How does what God says in the Bible give us assurance? Are you able to really *hear* what He says and respond as in verse 6?

Three things keep us from believing that God will never forsake us: our fears, our sins, and drudgery. Chambers tackles each of these in turn. (He spends two paragraphs on drudgery!) Which one trips you the most? Ask God to speak His "say-so" to you today!

APPLICATION

Lately, have you worried more than focused on what God says? Have you heard Him?

Has God's "never-forsakingness" assured you when you've strayed? During drudgery?

Finish this prayer: "Father, you will never leave me, and I need that assurance behind me today so that I . . ."

JUNE 5
GOD'S ASSURANCE

Haunted by worry?
Learn God's promise by heart: "I will never . . . forsake you."

◄

BACKGROUND "My 'say-so' is to be built on God's 'say-so.'" So begins today's devotional. Yesterday we saw that Oswald Chambers gave his "say-so" and gained victory over his "clouds and darkness." But his "say-so" only had power because it was built on God's ultimate say-so.

What do you fear? Are you like Chambers was, afraid that others will see your sins (see January 16, *Companion*)? Let today's lesson remind you of God's promised "say-so"!

SCRIPTURAL CONTEXT Although Chambers uses the same theme verse as yesterday, his emphasis is different: *He* said, so *we* may say. Read Hebrews 13 again, but this time after each promise, respond with your own words back to God. Which of these responses will help you in the fears you face?

WHAT'S THE DEVOTIONAL SAYING? The last line of yesterday's lesson was "we learn to sing in the ordinary days and ways." Today we see that we learn to sing "after hearing God's keynote." Did you have trouble singing during the drudgeries you faced these past 24 hours? Do you think you can do better today? If you listen to the keynote of God's promises, your mind won't dwell on your fears but will turn to your friend and Savior.

Three things keep us from building on God's "say-so": worries, dread, and frailty. When it comes to worries, Chambers urges us to "buck up," like a child whose father has asked him to do something brave. If we remember that our heavenly Father is watching as we fight our worries and apprehensions, we will stand tall.

Our dread is even more paralyzing than our worries, but Chambers encourages us to listen to God's promises and then respond with our own "say-so," just as you may have done when you read through Hebrews 13 today.

Finally, our frailty keeps us from making God's "say-so" our "say-so." Are you feeling weak and frail? Chambers, quoting from the Revised Version, points us to one promise in particular, "I will in no wise fail you." Although our human flesh is frail and fails us all the time, God is unfailing. He *will* honor His "say-so"!

APPLICATION

Are you experiencing any fear, temptations, or apprehensions? What can you do?

How can saying something before knowing God's Word get us in trouble? Are you in His Word?

Finish this prayer: "Lord, I feel so feeble, and you seem so far from my difficulties. But I remember now . . ."

JUNE 6
"WORK OUT" WHAT GOD "WORKS IN" YOU

God's will shapes our will and trumps sin every time.

BACKGROUND Sometimes the *Utmost* devotions are packed with urgent exhortations. Other times, like today, they are full of deep insights. What Oswald Chambers says today about our conscience, our will, and our sin is simple, yet profound. Conscience is the part of us that sees the highest thing we can know (God) and tells us what that requires. Our will is the most essential thing in us, and after we are born again, God's power flows into our will and shapes it. The problem is that our sin blocks our will from doing what our conscience says is required. Only by obeying the Holy Spirit can we overcome this blockade.

Does this description of your conscience, will, and sin ring true? Ask the Spirit to give you a clear understanding of what happens in your heart as you live the Christian life, and obey Him today!

SCRIPTURAL CONTEXT In the past month, we have seen Philippians 2:12–13 twice (May 10 and 15). We will see it two more times (July 7 and December 5), since it is one of Chambers' favorite passages. How do these verses link the two halves of chapter 2? How are you working out your own salvation?

WHAT'S THE DEVOTIONAL SAYING?
Are there things you do even though you know you shouldn't? Do you fail to do the things you know you should? Why is it that *knowing* what to do is not enough? Chambers explains all of this today and concludes that the only way we can overcome this situation is by "obedience to the Holy Spirit." He also asks us if we believe that God is the source of our will, since He knows how important it is that we believe the truth. Once we give in to the lie that says, "My will is not in agreement with God," we lose the battle to work out our salvation.

Picture your conscience as a secretary, receiving memos from the CEO and handing them to the manager, Ms. Will, who is newly appointed by the CEO and perfectly capable of accomplishing all the CEO's instructions. Now imagine the old manager, the no-good Mr. Sin, who comes by to check on Ms. Will's progress, telling her that she will never be able to get anything done. What can poor Ms. Will do? Stick to the memos, of course! Nothing short of obedience to the CEO will rid her of the pesky Mr. Sin and keep her on the right track. Remember this picture today as you listen to sin's discouraging lies!

APPLICATION
List truths about our will and our flesh. What misconceptions did you have about them? Where could you use some "dynamite"? How will you obey the Holy Spirit in that area?
Finish this prayer: "Holy Spirit, you are working in my life, so I'll will and act according to your purpose as I . . ."

JUNE 7
DON'T SLACK OFF

Be Ministers of the Interior by abiding in Christ and interceding by His power.

➤

BACKGROUND "Pull Yourself Together" and "Don't Slack Off" are titles for two of Oswald Chambers' hard-hitting talks. Today's lesson, pared down from both talks, packs no less of a punch. It also kicks off a nine-day series on Christian experience.

Do you fritter away your spiritual life? Are you wasting Christ's atonement and the oneness with God that He bought for us? Today's devotional will inspire you to pull yourself together and keep yourself from slacking off.

SCRIPTURAL CONTEXT Our Scripture for today is again from Jesus' Upper Room Discourse (see May 29, *Companion*). What was the disciples' response to these amazing promises? Did they intercede for others? Where is the evidence?

How many times does Jesus say, "abide" in John 15? What does this word mean? Chambers says we *abide* when we continuously "act and think and work from that center." The center, of course, is Jesus and His atonement, whereby He reconciled us to God.

WHAT'S THE DEVOTIONAL SAYING? The action item from today's lesson is to "take time to realize what the central point of power is." Chambers asks if we are willing to take fifteen minutes a day to concentrate on the atonement. Are you? Will you take the next fifteen minutes of your life to look up more information about the atonement and think about how it affects your "ministry of the interior" (your prayers for other people)?

A second action item is to limit and concentrate our "affinities." What are your affinities? Who and what things hold your attention? Can you limit those things to only what keeps you focused on the atonement? Ask God to help you do that today.

APPLICATION

How much do you intercede? Has your spiritual life been wasted? How do you "abide"?

What exerts the most power over you? Can you let the atonement control you more?

Finish this prayer: "Jesus, through your great sacrifice I find power to constantly intercede. Right now I . . ."

WHAT'S NEXT?

Are you feeling distracted?
It may be that you knew God's will but didn't do it.

◁   ▷

BACKGROUND From now until June 15 we continue our nine-day series that comes from Oswald Chambers' talks on Christian experience that he began on April 30, 1914. Starting with today's lesson, each devotional comes with a subtitle that answers a question. For example, today's subtitle, "Determine to Know More Than Others" answers the question, "What's Next?"

Are you determined to know more than others? This subtitle sounds a bit prideful. But Chambers explains that to "know more" requires *doing* what you already know.

SCRIPTURAL CONTEXT In John 13:17, what are "these things"? Are the menial assignments the hardest to obey? What was Saul's assignment in 1 Samuel 15? Why was that hard for him?

Now turn to Romans 12. What is the relationship between sacrifice and obedience? Why do we need to focus more on obedience?

What is the context for John 7:17? How does this verse connect to John 7:38? Will you *do* what God has already shown you?

WHAT'S THE DEVOTIONAL SAYING?
The three paragraphs in today's lesson each have a point to make. The first one tells us to launch out into the next thing that God wants us to do. When we ignore His will and don't live up to the highest He has already shown us, it prevents God from giving us further instructions (see March 27, *Utmost*). The final paragraph teaches that obedience is better than bold sacrifices. This last point helps us understand the first one. When we launch into God's will, it won't look like bold sacrifice but like simple obedience, even though it may terrify us. Can you think of something similar that God might be asking you to do?

Has God's storm driven you away from your safe harbor? Thank Him for His mercy in keeping you from spiritual stagnation!

APPLICATION

What storms has God used to send you out to sea? Have you begun to discern His will? How?

Have you ever done or not done something you knew you should do? What happened?

Finish this prayer: "Father, I want to discern your will instead of just zealously sacrificing myself. Today . . ."

JUNE 9
WHAT'S THE NEXT THING?

Have you hit rock bottom yet?
Until you do, you won't actually ask God.

◄ ►

BACKGROUND Oswald Chambers gives advice today to those of us who are not "spiritually real." He says, "The next best thing to do if you are not spiritually real is to ask God for the Holy Spirit on the word of Jesus Christ (see Luke 11:13)." As we saw on January 3, Chambers' victory over "clouds and darkness" began when he realized that Luke 11:13 meant he could claim the gift of the Spirit on the authority of Jesus, not based on his own worthiness.

Are you spiritually real? Or do you feel, as Chambers did during his time of darkness, that you "have not got hold of the right end of the stick" (see March 8, *Companion*). No matter where you are spiritually, today's lesson will help you *ask* for what you need.

SCRIPTURAL CONTEXT Chambers quotes three different New Testament authors today. First, he references Luke 11:10 and 11:13. What do verses 5–13 say about how God sees our asking?

Chambers uses our asking for wisdom as an example of asking. Second, what does James 1:5 say about this? Why must we really know that we lack wisdom before we ask for it?

Third, look at Matthew 5. Which of the Beatitudes show our neediness? Why is this so good? Isn't it also interesting how we still get things even if we don't ask for them (see Matthew 5:45)? What a mercy! But God wants us to ask so we can receive with the full knowledge of the One who granted our requests.

WHAT'S THE DEVOTIONAL SAYING?
The main point today is that it is hard to truly ask, but we must do it if we are going to know God more intimately. So how can we truly ask? Only by realizing our complete spiritual poverty.

It makes sense, right? We know that if we were starving, we would ask for food with only one thing on our mind—food! If we realized we were starving spiritually, our requests to God for spiritual gifts would be about one thing— God's Spirit. Have you asked like that before? Try it now. There's no way to conjure up the feeling of spiritual poverty, but God could be ready to show you your poverty right now.

APPLICATION

Why is asking difficult? Have you been confronted by spiritual reality? To what effect? What has brought you to the limit of desperation? Did you try to act reasonable? How? Finish this prayer: "Holy Spirit, I'm lacking spiritual reality and need you to make Jesus' work real in my life . . ."

AND AFTER THAT WHAT'S NEXT TO DO?

Want the God experience? Or God himself?
You'll find Him only if you are desperate!

BACKGROUND Today's lesson builds on yesterday's point that we don't realize our spiritual poverty, so we don't ask God for help. Today's final paragraph explains how the process of knocking on a closed door shows us our spiritual poverty. It shows us how dirty our hands are as we knock and how powerless we are to make the door open. If you have even a shred of spiritual smugness left in you, let today's study drive it straight out of your heart.

SCRIPTURAL CONTEXT In fewer than three hundred words, Oswald Chambers uses more than ten Bible quotes—one quote per twenty-eight words! Look up as many of the quotes as you can (using the Updated Edition will help). Which ones help you best see the depraved state of your heart?

WHAT'S THE DEVOTIONAL SAYING?
Today's lesson is part of Chambers' series on Christian experience (see June 7, *Companion*).

Not surprisingly, he warns us against building our faith on experience. If you are blessed with a rich Christian experience, filled with answered prayers and transformed lives, you will be tempted to be "so satisfied with your experience that you want nothing more of God." One consequence of this is that you won't draw anyone to God. You will talk about your experience but live a life apart from God, which will pale in comparison to the talk you talk. Is this true of you? Are you living so close to God that it makes other people homesick for Him? Or do you merely talk about how great the Christian experience is?

The antidote to a faith built on experience is to actually seek, ask, and knock. Read today's final paragraph. Can you see yourself going through those six stages? Will you persevere until you make it to Luke 11:10? Seek, concentrate, and you will find!

APPLICATION

How do you seek fulfillment? Do your prayers reflect this? Can you seek God more?

What's been morally painful for you? How did you respond? Were you wholehearted?

Finish this prayer: "God, I'm knocking at your door, aware of what kind of person I really am. Please let . . ."

JUNE 11
GETTING THERE (PART 1)

Can't get out of bed?
God gives true rest that invigorates us for action.

◄   ►

BACKGROUND Within the nine-day series that we began on June 7, there is a shorter three-day series that begins today. It's focused on Jesus' use of the word *come*. If you have the Classic Edition, note the progression from "Come unto Me" to "Come with Me" to "Come after Me." We need to come in all of these ways: *to* Jesus (when we feel sorrows), *with* Him (though our self-interest tries to stop us), and *after* Him (with no mind for our natural affinities).

Have you felt sorrow? Oswald Chambers said, in his full "Getting There" lecture, that when we realize "that longings and ideals are not being worked out . . . there is an encroachment of sorrow." Is this your experience? Have your longings and ideals not worked out? Jesus says, "Come." He will make your sorrow cease.

SCRIPTURAL CONTEXT Read Matthew 11:25–30. Who are the "little children" in verse 25? How does this relate to verse 28?

We can find today's theme verse on refrigerator magnets and embroidered wall hangings. It's so familiar, yet do we ever do what it says? We saw on June 9 how it is hard to ask God. It is equally difficult to come to God. As you read today's context verses, ask God to help you come to Him.

WHAT'S THE DEVOTIONAL SAYING? Where is "There" in the title of this three-part mini-series? The subtitle for each day tells us. Today, "There" is "Where the Sin and Sorrow Cease and the Song and the Saint Commence." Do you want to get there? Do you want your sin and sorrow to cease and God's song and your sainthood to start? Aren't you weary of all your longings and ideals not working out?

So how do we get there? Chambers says, "Be stupid enough to come" (Classic Edition). Will you be that foolish? Will you "commit yourself to what He says"? If you will, God will give you restful vitality!

APPLICATION
What are you asking God? How can the answer be "Come to me" and not "Do this or that"?

Why is it hard for you to "come to Jesus"? How is "coming" a test of your genuineness?

Finish this prayer: "Jesus, I want to be a fool for you. I come to you earnestly and commit to what you say . . ."

∾ JUNE 12 ∾
GETTING THERE (PART 2)

We crave godhood, yet we "humbly" reject God's offer of sainthood!

‹ ›

BACKGROUND Today's subtitle (Classic Edition) contrasts self-interest with real interest. What is "real" interest? Oswald Chambers explains, in his *Getting There* lecture, that real interest "identifies you with Jesus."

Are you interested in identifying with God, or are you only interested in yourself? What does it mean to identify with Jesus? Chambers tells us, "Let Jesus do everything." Biddy edited this for *Utmost* as "let Jesus *be* everything." Will you let Jesus *do* and *be* everything in your life, placing no conditions on Him?

SCRIPTURAL CONTEXT We remember John 1 for the words: "In the beginning was the Word." But it's also the chapter that tells us how five of the disciples began to follow Jesus. Read John 1:35–51. Who were the five disciples? How long did they "abide" with Jesus at this encounter (verse 39)? How did abiding with Jesus characterize the rest of their lives? How does it characterize your life?

Chambers also quotes John 14:23 and the story of the Pharisee and the tax collector from Luke 18. Read both of these passages. Why is it wrong to want God to take you straight to heaven? Why is it wrong to say, "Oh, I'm no saint"?

WHAT'S THE DEVOTIONAL SAYING?
Do you think God can make your sin cease (see June 11, *Utmost*) and turn you into a saint? At the heart of our refusal of sainthood is pride and our desire to be like God. We must come *with* Jesus and learn to stay with Him for longer than just one day. Only by persistent abiding will Jesus erase pride from every area of our lives and give us new names.

APPLICATION
When have you abided with Christ? Did your abiding end? How? Was mood a factor?
Do you have spiritual measles? What can you do to let Jesus be everything to you?
Finish this prayer: "Lord, I'm guilty of not wanting sainthood or believing you can grant it.
    Please help . . ."

Is there a dedication on your "Bill of Rights"?
To whom did you dedicate them? Or are you still holding on to them?

◄ ➤

BACKGROUND Today is the final day of the three-part mini-series on "Getting There." Where are we heading in this lesson? To "Where the Selective Affinity Dies and the Sanctified Abandon Lives," as the subtitle in the Classic Edition says. Oswald Chambers explains that natural affinities and temperament keep us from coming to Jesus.

What are your natural affinities and temperament—your outlook on life? If you have an affinity for the outdoors, does that mean you can't work in the inner city? Does having a somber temperament mean you can't do children's ministry? Chambers says that God pays no attention to our affinities and temperament. Why? Because our temperament was shaped by our "disposition of sin" (see March 21, *Utmost*) and is changing now that we are saved. Our affinities depend on where we are—they will change as God engineers us to be right where He wants us.

SCRIPTURAL CONTEXT Today is the last day in our mini-series on coming to, with, and after Jesus. The first "come" was for all who are weary, the second was for John and Andrew the first time they came to learn from Jesus, and today's is for Peter and Andrew, when they left their careers to be full-time students under Jesus' teaching.

How does Romans 12:1 fit into these three times when Jesus invited people to come to Him? How is it about our rights? Will you offer God all of your rights to yourself? How will you do this?

WHAT'S THE DEVOTIONAL SAYING? The theme in this mini-series is getting there—getting to sainthood. Saints are simply born-again Christians. But since we wrongly think we are "born-again" if we merely believe certain things, the old-fashioned word *saint* is a more useful term. Do you want to be a saint? Give your rights to God, and you'll be one!

How will you know if you are a saint? Chambers says you will have "moral originality" (Classic Edition). This is one of Chambers' unique phrases that can only be defined by looking at how he uses it: to describe Spirit-led anti-commonsense actions. Do you do spontaneous things that show crazy love for Jesus? If so, you are definitely "getting there."

APPLICATION

What are your natural desires and gifts? Are they yours? Do you dedicate them to God?

Why are saints so creative? Have you seen a creative well in you? When?

Finish this prayer: "Father, I want to call others to you and to let you be creative in them just as you have . . ."

～ JUNE 14 ～
GET MOVING! (PART 1)

Not abiding in Christ? Blaming circumstances?
We can abide anywhere!

◄ ►

BACKGROUND Only two more days left of hard-hitting lessons. You can make it! By now, you might be accustomed to the forceful nature of *Utmost*. But even so, this past week has been extra hard. And today is no exception!

Was it just a coincidence that Oswald Chambers started these convicting talks on Christian experience three months before World War I began? Clearly, God knew that his students needed to be prepared for the radically different circumstances they would face. What about you? Will you learn today's lesson in preparation for what difficulties might lay ahead?

SCRIPTURAL CONTEXT Although the main verse for the original "Get a Move On!" lecture was 2 Peter 1:5, the three subsections of the lecture took their verses from the Upper Room Discourse. Today's devotional comes from the second subsection, which has as its theme verse John 15:4. If you haven't yet underlined every instance of the word *abide* in this chapter, do so now. What new things can you learn about abiding?

Chambers also references 2 Corinthians 10:5 and Colossians 3:3. What thoughts have you taken captive? What characterizes the life "hidden with Christ"? How has your mind been set on earthly things lately?

WHAT'S THE DEVOTIONAL SAYING?
What did Jesus do during his first thirty years of life on earth? In the original lecture, Chambers says, "Think of the amazing leisure of our Lord's life! For thirty years He did nothing" (meaning that Jesus wasn't worried about doing public ministry until it was God's time for Him).

Are you anxious to do something spectacular for God? Do you long to be in a different situation so you can really live for Jesus? Don't be anxious! Abide in Him wherever you are and in whatever you are doing.

It takes a long time and much patience for God to help us think as Jesus does. Let Him keep working on your thinking today, and don't fret for the future.

APPLICATION

What is "abiding in Christ"? Do you think circumstances keep you from abiding? How?

Is your pace feverish and distracted? What can you do to have God's hidden serenity?

Finish this prayer: "Lord Jesus, I've let things keep me from abiding in you. Today I'll make the effort to . . ."

GET MOVING! (PART 2)

Are you a Super-Christian? Or a work of our Super God?
The details will decide it.

◄

BACKGROUND At last—the final day in our nine-part series. What a fitting end! We learn that the way God makes us saints who naturally think the way Jesus thinks is through drudgery. We would love for Him to make us saints through "big things" and to take us "to heaven on flowery beds of ease." But drudgery is the exact opposite. It is neither big nor easy.

What's your drudgery? Will you concentrate on forming good habits in the midst of your drudgery? Let today's lesson help you make up your mind to embrace your drudgery.

SCRIPTURAL CONTEXT Oswald Chambers used 2 Peter 1:5 as the main verse for his "Get a Move On!" lecture, and in each subsection he illustrated the concept of "adding" with verses from Jesus' Upper Room Discourse. For example, he used John 13:1–17 to show how Jesus embraced drudgery. As a result, Jesus formed good character. As you read this passage, how do you think Jesus "learned obedience" (Hebrews 5:8) and added virtues to form character? How will you form character today?

WHAT'S THE DEVOTIONAL SAYING? On May 15, we read that "God never has museums" (Classic Edition). Today Chambers tells us that God also doesn't want "illuminated versions" (or "perfect, bright-shining examples" as the Updated Edition reads). He doesn't give the spiritual version of Esther's yearlong beauty treatment (Esther 2:12). He gives us drudgery. Are you willing to learn to live joyfully in the domain of drudgery by the power of God?

APPLICATION

What habits are you forming now? How is drudgery a test of character? Do you pass?

When was a time of inspiration for you? Was it followed by drudgery? Was this "God's way of saving" you?

Finish this prayer: "God, I know that your grace will be mine if I simply obey. Please help me today to . . ."

ᐧᐧᐧᐧ JUNE 16 ᐧᐧᐧᐧ
"WILL YOU LAY DOWN YOUR LIFE?"

Yielding by the Spirit or by willpower?
It's hard already—don't make it impossible!

BACKGROUND As hot desert air stifled the YMCA hut on May 7, 1916, Oswald Chambers addressed the crowd of soldiers on the topic of friendship with Jesus. Biddy took one paragraph from this talk and combined it with other material to create today's devotional. Although the audience was different, Chambers gave the same message he gave in his Christian experience lectures (see June 7–15, *Utmost*): Thoughtfully lay down your life in ordinary, day-to-day things.

Are you Jesus' friend? Will you be loyal to Him while everything around you pushes you to be unfaithful? This is the essence of friendship. It's the subject of great stories of friendships—like that of Jonathan and David. Will you be Christ's friend today?

SCRIPTURAL CONTEXT All of today's references, except the mention of the transfiguration, come from John's writings. What is the common theme of these four verses? Why is it

hard to lay down one's life? How does this truth give us the key to today's lesson?

Do you think the transfiguration was Jesus' *only* "brilliant moment"? Why doesn't Luke 3:22 qualify? What are your bright-shining moments? How can you walk in the light of them?

WHAT'S THE DEVOTIONAL SAYING?
What do you make of the news that Jesus called us His friends? Will you respond with heroic boldness, as did Peter? That's a good start. But Chambers reminds us again that it is in the ordinary things that we prove our friendship to Jesus.

What pushes you to be disloyal to Jesus? The world around us wants our loyalty. Will you give loyalty to your email, your friends, your image, yourself? Or will you take up your daily tasks with a sense of the high calling of God?

APPLICATION

Has God asked you to lay down your life (interests, hobbies, activities)? Did you? Why is that heroic?

What is difficult about "exhibiting salvation"? How can you do that better?

Finish this prayer: "Lord, you laid down your life for me. Please help me to lay down my life today by . . ."

⁓ JUNE 17 ⁓
BEWARE OF CRITICIZING OTHERS

Bad-talking someone?
God will show how bad you'd be without Him.

BACKGROUND We have looked at Oswald Chambers' *Studies in the Sermon on the Mount* several times (for instance, May 18 and 30). Today's devotional is taken from the same source. Matthew 7:1–12 takes up an entire section of Chambers' five-part commentary, and he spends more time on the first verse than any of the others.

Why is Matthew 7:1 so crucial? In the source material for today's lesson, Chambers says, "The average Christian is the most penetratingly critical individual; there is nothing of the likeness of Jesus Christ about him." Each of us is "the average Christian," and we *all* need help being less critical.

SCRIPTURAL CONTEXT Read Matthew 7:1–12. Can you see why Chambers ended this section at verse 12? Why, out of all the elements in the Sermon on the Mount, did Chambers call this section "Character and Conduct"? How do these verses compare to Romans 2:17–24? List some reasons to not judge others.

WHAT'S THE DEVOTIONAL SAYING? Today's point is clear: Don't criticize others. There is no wiggle room. If we consult the source material Biddy used for today's devotional, we won't find any wiggle room there either. Chambers acknowledges that God allows for "discernment and discrimination." But Chambers clearly says that God doesn't allow criticism in the spiritual domain.

So why does God give us discernment? On May 3 we learned that discernment is given to us only so we can pray for others. Do not criticize them out loud or in your mind! "There is always one fact more in every man's case about which we know nothing."

APPLICATION

Who have you criticized recently? What happens to them (and you) when you criticize?

Have you ever not known the whole story when you criticized? Is that always the case?

Finish this prayer: "God, I can't enter into fellowship with you when I'm critical, so please help me to . . ."

❦ JUNE 18 ❦
KEEP RECOGNIZING JESUS

Afraid of your problems?
Spend time with Jesus, and He'll take care of them.

BACKGROUND Today's 240-word devotional came from a 900-word talk by the same title. As she edited the talk, Biddy Chambers captured the essential point: When we look at our situation more than at Jesus, we go down in flames. The opposite is also true. When we practice listening to God's voice even in little things, we rise up on eagles' wings.

How does God speak to you? Does He pinprick your mind when you are about to feel sorry for yourself? Does He speak to you with your own voice? Have you thought of doing something sacrificial for others that you never thought you would be willing to do? Next time that happens, throw yourself in reckless abandon to what you hear God saying.

SCRIPTURAL CONTEXT Matthew 14:22–33 is a familiar story, but as you reread it, see what stands out in a fresh way. Was it that Jesus didn't need the disciples' help in dismissing the crowd? Was it that the disciples believed in ghosts (see 1 Samuel 28:13)? How does what you see in this story relate to today's lesson?

For fun, read Psalm 107. Do any of the people in that psalm peacefully trust God in the midst of their trouble? What do you do when trouble strikes?

WHAT'S THE DEVOTIONAL SAYING? What does "keep recognizing Jesus" mean? It means to factor in Jesus, His power and desires, first and only. This is hard to do! But as we spend more time with Jesus—reading about Him, talking to Him, and thinking about Him, it becomes easier.

Do you have problems that make you anxious, fearful, and worried? Are you starting to sink? Cry out to Jesus. Like Peter and the people in Psalm 107, you may have already stopped recognizing your Lord. But He can lift you up and help you "give thanks to the Lord for His unfailing love."

APPLICATION

What are the "waves" in your life? Can you overcome them without focusing on them?

Have you ever heard God speak, even faintly? Did you obey His leading with abandon?

Finish this prayer: "Father, I focus on my problems and sink even though you can help me stand. Please . . ."

SERVICE OF PASSIONATE DEVOTION

Are you tired before even trying to help others?
Let Jesus be your lifeblood!

BACKGROUND One hundred years ago, Christian denominations were booming. Each had its creeds on baptism, speaking in tongues, predestination, and a host of other issues. Today, many of those denominations are declining, and people focus less on creeds. Does that mean today's devotional is less relevant? Not at all! We still put lots of things above nourishing God's sheep and being devoted to Jesus. Worship music, church programs, celebrity Christians, and more can distract us from passionate devotion to Jesus. We need today's lesson more than ever!

SCRIPTURAL CONTEXT We've seen the context of John 21:16 and Luke 14:26 before (February 2 and 9). But John 12:24 is a new one for us. Read John 12:23–26. What did Jesus say would happen to Him? How did He generalize this to all His followers?

Are you willing to hate everything compared to Jesus and to die to yourself, even if you're doing it for smelly sheep that don't even notice your "amazing" sacrifice? This willingness comes from God's power. But He expects us to use our own wills with His.

WHAT'S THE DEVOTIONAL SAYING? What is your cause? (Check your answers to the questions on February 22 and May 2.) Do you think of Jesus as your comrade in that cause? Or are you letting Him be your friend in all areas of your life, so much so that He is your all in all?

If you embark on a cause, even one as noble as saving souls, you will get tired. Jesus asks us to feed His sheep, but the only way we can do it without getting exhausted is by complete, 100 percent devotion to Jesus. Will you give Him your devotion today?

APPLICATION
How do you serve God? What's the source of your devotion to Jesus?
Do your beliefs substitute for your devotion to Jesus? Why do you serve humanity?
Finish this prayer: "Jesus, I want to serve people with the energy that stems from my love for you. So . . ."

⌘ JUNE 20 ⌘
HAVE YOU COME TO "WHEN" YET?

Want 10,000 percent returns?
When we pray for others, God gives a hundredfold.

BACKGROUND Today's theme connects to tomorrow's message—stop worrying about whether you're good enough, and start praying for others! We've seen many times how important Oswald Chambers considered intercessory prayer to be (see March 30, *Utmost*). But now Chambers tells us we must first give up the idea that we can be good, and then we can start to pray for our friends.

Have you been following along in *Utmost*? If so, have you tried to intercede more? How is your intercession this week compared to four months ago? Today's lesson will give your prayers for others a much-needed boost.

SCRIPTURAL CONTEXT We learned on February 28 that Chambers preached on the book of Job in 1917. The story of Job is a story of a saint who sees God, is humbled by Him, and prays for his friends. Today's theme verse comes from the final chapter in this epic story. Read as much of Job as you can and think about whether Job thought he could be "good" after he saw God. What happened to Job's friends?

Chambers also quotes Mark 10:30 (or Matthew 19:29). What was the context of this promise of a 10,000 percent return on the disciples' investment?

WHAT'S THE DEVOTIONAL SAYING? Have you asked God to help you be "good"? We all sin and do bad things, so isn't it a good idea to ask God to help us "walk rightly"? No! Chambers explains that asking God to help us purify our hearts misses the point. God *already* purified us through the atonement. We don't need to pray for more of His help. We need to accept the gift of the atonement.

If the frequency and duration of your intercession haven't increased over these past months, and if God hasn't answered your prayers more than before, and if you still pray that God will help you be "good," it could be a sign you need to change your belief about the atonement. Do you think the atonement is complete? Do you think it, and it alone, has already made you perfect? Once you simply accept the fact that the atonement is finished and has put you right with God—and you accept it as a gift—then you can live freely as God's child. Stop worrying about yourself and start living!

APPLICATION
What's wrong with telling God, "I'll be able to fix up my life if you help me do it"?
Have you ever made this "deal"? What happened? Have you now accepted the atonement?
Finish this prayer: "Lord, I'm not receiving or getting insight like I should. Starting now I'll intercede for . . ."

THE MINISTRY OF THE INNER LIFE

Like priests, we have God's atonement so we can pray for it in others' lives.

BACKGROUND Today we read that "We must get sick unto death of ourselves, until there is no longer any surprise at anything God can tell us about ourselves" (Classic Edition). Are you truly sick of the patterns of sin in your life? Or are you shocked and defensive every time God tries to tell you about yourself?

Today's lesson is again about intercession. It tells us that we don't intercede because our minds focus on whether we are good enough for God to hear us. The good news, as we saw yesterday, is that we can *never* be good enough on our own but that we are *already* good enough—thanks to the atonement.

SCRIPTURAL CONTEXT First Peter is a book for suffering Christians. Read the first two chapters. What is the first thing Peter commands us to do? What is the reason we should do it (see 1:18)? After his list of commands and the reasons we can and should obey them, Peter calls us a holy (2:5) and royal (2:9) priesthood. In what ways are you holy and royal? How do you fill your role as a priest?

WHAT'S THE DEVOTIONAL SAYING? Yesterday Oswald Chambers warned us against praying, "I'll be good if you help." Today he warns us against praying, "I've been good, so answer my intercessory prayers." We know that the second prayer is foolish (we can't bargain with God!). And we saw how the first prayer is also foolish. Yet we often pray both kinds of foolish prayers, and the root of these prayers is focusing too much on our own "goodness." The sooner we realize that we aren't good on our own but are completely good based on the redemption, the sooner we will be able to pray effectively for others.

Are you so sick of yourself that there is no question in your mind that your only goodness comes from God? You'll know whether you're heading in the right direction the next time God engineers your circumstances to tell you something unpleasant about yourself. If you respond with surprise, you still have a long way to go, which is how it is for most of us!

APPLICATION
How do you feel when comparing yourself to God's standards? How productive is that?
Are you sick of yourself? What has God shown you about yourself? Were you surprised?
Finish this prayer: "God, I'm not obsessing about myself anymore. Instead I'm continuing to intercede for . . ."

JUNE 22
THE UNCHANGING LAW OF JUDGMENT

Surrounded by hypocrites?
It takes one to know one.

BACKGROUND Today's lesson has its roots in two lectures. The first was his 1911 Sermon on the Mount series (see May 18, *Companion*). The other was a talk Oswald Chambers gave in 1916 to soldiers in Egypt. It appears that Biddy took the structure of today's lesson from the 1911 talk and filled it in with particular sentences from the 1916 lecture. As always, Biddy captures the essence of what Chambers was saying. Today he tells us that God has an undeviating, unchanging law that returns to each person what he or she has given others. In this way it is a "test" of how we judge. Are you prepared for God to apply this test to you?

SCRIPTURAL CONTEXT Chambers cites three passages that deal with judgment. The first is Matthew 7:1–2. According to these verses, why shouldn't we judge others? Second up is Psalm 18:25–26. Is it strange that God would be shrewd? Does God's character change depending on the circumstances? Last is Romans 2. The first verse explains the "undeviating test."

How does this test work to condemn people? In what ways might it condemn you?

WHAT'S THE DEVOTIONAL SAYING? In his 1916 lecture on the topic of forgiving others, Chambers ends by saying, "We are to have the same relationship to our fellow men that God has to us." Do you forgive others the way God has forgiven you? If not, you are beating your head against the undeviating test that will find you sorely wanting.

What do you dislike most in the people around you? God gives you a discerning eye to see these faults so you can intercede for them. This is a good thing! But as soon as you are "shrewd in finding out" these faults, you have crossed the line. When you move from *knowing* faults to *criticizing* them, even in your own mind, you have activated the "eternal law of God" that makes you guilty of the same things. If you don't think you could be guilty of those faults, look out! Be careful that you don't succumb to the same sin.

APPLICATION

What sins annoy you in others? Why? Do you believe in the eternal law of retribution?
How would God judge you as you judge others? If not for God's grace where would you be?
Finish this prayer: "Lord, I want to stop being judgmental. Your law of retribution is a good motivator—I . . ."

JUNE 23
"ACQUAINTED WITH GRIEF"

Our reason is irrational because it doesn't account for sin being a real force.

➤

BACKGROUND Today and for the next two days, our lessons come from a talk Oswald Chambers gave in Egypt on June 10, 1917. He taught the soldiers in his audience that sorrow and grief are the keys to receiving our very selves from God.

Do you have sorrows? Today Chambers teaches us the source of sorrows: not taking sin into account. Tomorrow he expands on that topic; and on June 25, he explains what good can come from sorrows. Get ready to see sin and sorrow in a new light!

SCRIPTURAL CONTEXT If you don't understand who Jesus is, Isaiah 53 is confusing. It mystified the Ethiopian eunuch in Acts 8 until Philip set him straight. Read this chapter now, and imagine trying to understand the "Man of Sorrows" as Isaiah or the people of Israel had to do. How does Jesus fulfill this prophecy far more completely than Israel ever did?

The point of Isaiah 53 is that God took on our sin, sorrow, suffering, and grief. He became so intimate with it that he *became* sin. Chambers' point today is that we need to become more acquainted with grief and sin so we don't forget to take them into account, as we are often prone to do.

WHAT'S THE DEVOTIONAL SAYING? What is sin? Is it missing the mark, the way an archer might miss the bull's-eye? That's a good way to understand how everything that's not perfect is considered sin. But it's a bad way to understand that sin is blatant "red-handed mutiny against God." An archer can, with careful practice, learn to hit the bull's-eye. But we can't do that with sin. God has to help us kill sin—otherwise sin, which crouches at our door (Genesis 4:7), will kill us.

Do you put stock in a rational, reasonable view of life? Don't! Every time you forget to take sin into account, you risk huge disasters.

APPLICATION

What grief have you endured? Is intimacy with grief hard? Is being rational easier?

What things kill sin in your life? Will you do those things? What happens if you don't?

Finish this prayer: "Jesus, you're intimate with grief because you came to kill sin, and sin breeds grief. I . . ."

JUNE 24
RECONCILING YOURSELF TO THE FACT OF SIN

Are you pure, or merely innocent?
Remember not to underestimate sin!

◁ ▷

BACKGROUND The source of today's lesson (a 1917 sermon—see June 23, *Companion*) ends with the words: "The man who accepts salvation from Jesus Christ recognizes the fact of sin; he does not ignore it. Thereafter he will not demand too much of human beings." Today's devotional teaches us not to ignore sin. This doesn't spell the end of our human friendships. Once we deal with the fact of sin, we won't "demand too much of human beings" and will be true friends.

SCRIPTURAL CONTEXT The theme verse for today is the same as the theme verse for the original sermon. Throughout the sermon, Oswald Chambers refers back to this verse and the "hour" it describes. Read Luke 22 and think about Jesus' "hour." How would you have felt in His shoes?

WHAT'S THE DEVOTIONAL SAYING? Does it confuse you when Chambers says, "Yes, I see what that would mean" (Classic Edition)? Chamber's original sermon includes more of the context about this enigmatic statement: "Do we reconcile ourselves to the fact that there is sin? If not, we will be caught round the next corner of the high road and begin to compromise with it. If we recognize that sin is there, we will not make that mistake. 'Yes, I see what that means and where it would lead me.'"

Have you compromised with sin? Chambers says that if we start with the assumption that there is sin, then when we approach the next "corner" of our lives, we will realize at once that sin is dangerously lurking just around it. We will say, "Aha! I know what that corner means. It means I'm about to be faced with a temptation to compromise with sin, which will lead me to ruin."

Take Chambers' advice—reconcile yourself to the fact of sin. Don't be caught off-guard. Don't go through life merely innocent. Go through life pure!

APPLICATION

Have you ever failed to take sin into account and then had a disaster? What happened?

Who have you naively trusted? Are you becoming more cynical? What can you do?

Finish this prayer: "Jesus, you balanced trust and realism because you understood sin. Please help me as I . . ."

RECEIVING YOURSELF IN THE FIRES OF SORROW

Are you avoiding sorrow?
Embrace it! You will find who God made you to be.

◄

BACKGROUND Sin produces sorrow. For the past two days we've been looking at the reality of sin. Today we see how the sorrow that inevitably flows from sin helps us receive the gift of our true selves.

Since sin leads to sorrow, which leads to a precious gift, does that mean sin is good? Obviously not! Oswald Chambers says it well in the original sermon (see June 23, *Companion*): "Because God overrules a thing and brings good out of it does not mean that in itself that thing is a good thing." We thank God that He brings good out of sin and sorrow. We also remember that sin and sorrow are not in themselves good things.

SCRIPTURAL CONTEXT On April 16, we saw the story of the Greeks who wanted to see Jesus. Read John 12 again. Why did Jesus tell Andrew and Philip about His death? Why did He tell them in such a roundabout way? Who did Jesus have in mind when He said, "What shall I say?" Did they immediately figure out what Jesus was trying to teach them, or did it take them a long time?

What is Jesus trying to teach you today? Is it something too difficult for you to understand immediately? Ask Him to help you learn what He is teaching you.

WHAT'S THE DEVOTIONAL SAYING? The key to today's lesson is the term "receiving one's self." What does this mean? Chambers explains that sorrow burns up shallowness and is the only way to "find" one's self. The person who has found himself, according to Chambers, is one who has "ample leisure for you" when you are in trouble.

Sorrow is the *only* way we find the self that God created us to be. But Chambers says sorrow doesn't *always* have that effect. Sometimes sorrow destroys us. Do you know anyone who has been destroyed by sorrow? Ask God today to preserve your true self as you go through sorrows.

APPLICATION

Has someone in the fire of sorrow come to you? Did you make time for them? Why?

What fires of sorrow have you experienced? Have they helped you find yourself? How?

Finish this prayer: "Father, I don't want to be shallow, but I don't want to lose the *self* you made. Please . . ."

DRAWING ON THE GRACE OF GOD—NOW

Why wait to ask God for grace?
It's what every one of us needs right now!

BACKGROUND Biddy Chambers took her husband's 1,500-word sermon "Always Now" and trimmed it to today's 300-word lesson. In the original sermon and in today's lesson, Oswald Chambers' message to us is that we must draw on God's grace immediately and not just pray about the troubles we face.

Do you know how to draw on God's grace? Chambers says that the last place we learn how to do this is in our prayers. When we pray, we draw on everything *but* God's grace. We draw on our past experiences, our present desires, but rarely on God's grace. Will you pray today in the midst of every trial? Will you draw on God's grace and nothing else?

SCRIPTURAL CONTEXT Second Corinthians 5:18–6:10 tells how God reconciled us to himself, and how He gave us the job of reconciling others to God. These verses also list the things Paul experienced, which proved he was doing the job of reconciliation that God gave him to do. How do you think the Corinthians responded to this letter? How might they have felt when Paul listed his experiences? How do you respond? Do you see this list as applying to your experiences too?

WHAT'S THE DEVOTIONAL SAYING? The theme verse for the original sermon was "Behold, now is the accepted time; behold, now is the day of salvation" (2 Corinthians 6:2). If you look in the NIV, you'll notice that "accepted time" is translated as "time of God's favor." Chambers reminds us that *grace* is a synonym for *overflowing favor*. Paul says to the Corinthians, "Now is the time of God's grace."

Do you believe that *right now* God's grace could overflow to you? What about in the midst of each trial you face? Is God's overflowing favor available then? The structure of today's lesson is built on three sections of 2 Corinthians 6. First, drawing on God's grace gives us patience. Second, God's grace protects us from external tumults. Third, God's grace makes us generous. Draw on His grace right now. You will marvel at yourself—as will others!

APPLICATION

Have you been humiliated? What did you do? What would God's grace have done?

Where are you in need of God's grace? What can you do to receive it *now*?

Finish this prayer: "God, I need your grace so badly, but I cling to my own strength instead of emptying . . ."

THE OVERSHADOWING OF GOD'S PERSONAL DELIVERANCE

Street smarts don't keep you safe—God does.

BACKGROUND No one likes being a doormat. Is it even right for a Christian to be one? Oswald Chambers often urges us to be doormats. He typically calls it "broken bread and poured-out wine."

Today's lesson is about how God preserves our lives and souls, but not necessarily anything else. As a result, we must be doormats, since God may intend for people to walk all over us. We must not try to use our street smarts to preserve our things or our rights. God wants us to hold on to them loosely.

SCRIPTURAL CONTEXT Jeremiah was Judah's doormat. People ridiculed him, imprisoned him, and threw him into a mud pit to let him die. But from the beginning, God promised to deliver him, and He confirmed this promise throughout his life. Read Jeremiah 1 and 39. What other promises did God make?

Chambers mentions the Sermon on the Mount and a well-known passage in Proverbs. Do you lean on your own understanding? Do you turn your other cheek? What else can you find in Proverbs 3 or Matthew 5–7 that relates to this theme?

WHAT'S THE DEVOTIONAL SAYING? What caused you "panic, heartache, and distress"? Most likely, it was a situation involving your things or your rights. Today's lesson urges us to hold those things loosely. That's hard to do! But if we focus our inward being on how God completely delivers us personally, it will be easier to let go of them.

What injustice have you suffered recently? Where have you failed to give someone justice? Let go of your quest for justice, but strive to grant justice to everyone God puts in your life.

APPLICATION

Whose mission are you on: yours or God's? What is it? Does it alter how you see justice? When did you worry about your life or possessions? Did it keep you from trusting God? Finish this prayer: "Lord, you will take care of me no matter what, yet I doubt so often. Help me to keep . . ."

JUNE 28
HELD BY THE GRIP OF GOD

Why push ahead to be a spokesman for God?
He'll know when you're ready.

BACKGROUND As we saw on May 5, Oswald Chambers made sure only full-time students were allowed to attend the sermon preparation classes at the Bible Training College. Today's devotional comes from one of these classes. Even if you do not feel the agonizing grip of God on your life to preach sermons, today's lesson can still help you. If nothing else, it can remind you that someday God may grip you in this way. When He does, woe to you if you do not preach!

SCRIPTURAL CONTEXT In Philippians 3, Paul gives his assessment of his previous life as a Pharisee. He also powerfully describes the right way to live the Christian life: forgetting what is behind and pressing toward what is ahead. As you read this chapter, what do you think would be especially meaningful to people who are called to preach? What is particularly meaningful to you?

Chambers' words are filled with expressions from the Bible. Today, for example, he says, "Woe be to you if you turn to the right hand or to the left," which combines language from many parts of the Bible. The Updated Edition gives us Deuteronomy 5:32 as a starting point. In this verse, who was Moses warning not to "turn to the right hand or to the left"? How might Moses' warning be related to Chambers' lecture about the call to preach?

WHAT'S THE DEVOTIONAL SAYING? Today's lesson teaches us two things. First, we must preach when we are called, and not before. Second, when we preach, we must not water down God's Word. Most of us have not received the call (see January 14, *Utmost*), but there is one thing that today's lesson can teach all of us. Chambers ends by quoting Philippians 3:13, emphasizing, "this one thing I do." What is the "one thing"? It is to press on until we apprehend and have in our own grip the prize God has for us. What is the prize? It's the "high calling of God," which is a call that all of us have on our lives.

Have you made it your goal to strive for the prize? If you don't have this as your conscious goal, how will you ever attain it? Think about how you can actively make this the goal of your life, and take steps toward that today.

APPLICATION

Why shouldn't we choose to be a worker (see James 3:1)? Has God called you to work?

Do you water down the word or give only your testimony? How about in personal issues?

Finish this prayer: "Father God, your grip is on me as I preach about you. My one job is to keep my soul . . ."

JUNE 29
THE STRICTEST DISCIPLINE

All things are permissible, but not all are profitable. Are you drawing the line?

➤

BACKGROUND In *Studies in the Sermon on the Mount* (see May 18, *Companion*), Oswald Chambers took Jesus' hard-hitting statements head on. Today's devotional tackles the part about cutting off our right hand and gouging out our right eye. Gruesome? Maybe. But as Chambers points out, God is more interested in making us lovely in His sight than lovely in man's eyes.

Have you given up some things you used to do because of God? Do you still give those things up, or have you started doing them again? Today's lesson teaches us that there ought to be things we give up when we start drawing close to God. Later, it might be appropriate to do them again, but only in God's perfect time.

SCRIPTURAL CONTEXT Where else in the Bible can you find these harsh words? What is the difference in the contexts? What does this say about how God sees marriage and children? How are believers like "little ones"?

WHAT'S THE DEVOTIONAL SAYING? The main point today, though challenging, is simple: The Spirit restrains or "checks" us (see June 3, *Utmost*) from doing things when He starts changing our lives, but later God may allow us to do them again.

What is so challenging about today's lesson? It's the fact that God can ask us to give up *anything*, even our hand or eye! What has He asked you to give up? Did you give it up? Did people think you were going to extremes? If God hasn't asked you to give anything up, it may be a sign that He hasn't started changing your life as part of the regeneration process. Ask Him to start today!

APPLICATION

After your regeneration, were parts of you "maimed"? Is that a contradiction? How so?

If you avoid something that causes sin, do people ridicule you? How do you respond?

Finish this prayer: "Lord, there are things that I can't do because they cause me to sin. But please help me . . ."

DO IT NOW!

Want to avoid agony?
Don't put off what is right!

◀ ▶

[handwritten: wanted to sin + light will expose sin + ultimately feared punishment]

BACKGROUND Today's devotional picks up where yesterday's left off. Yesterday we saw that God asks us to stop doing things in order for us to be lovely in His sight. Today we see that He asks us to pay what we "owe" so we can be as white as driven snow.

What do you "owe" to those around you? Oswald Chambers reminds us not to think about what others owe us. If there is any anger in your heart about a relationship, go and make it right. Don't wait, as today's title reminds us, *do it now!*

SCRIPTURAL CONTEXT Chambers has a knack for finding new meanings in familiar passages. Today he takes the passage on "Do not murder" from Matthew 5 and applies it to all our relationships. What can you find in this passage that relates to your life? Are you angry? Have you called anyone a fool? Does anyone have anything against you?

The law of "do it now" that Chambers describes applies even beyond our relationships. Any moral matter that we don't obey immediately will initiate the inexorable process of pain, *[handwritten: impossible to prevent]*

agony, and distress. Not only that, but John 3:19–21 reminds us that the more we disobey, the more we will hide from the light. Be sure to obey even little things today so this process doesn't start in your life!

WHAT'S THE DEVOTIONAL SAYING? There are four paragraphs today, and each one teaches a different facet of today's study. First, there is an unchangeable law that begins as soon as we don't do something God wants us to do. Second, we pay our debts to others, which is something God wants us to do—regardless of whether they pay their debts to us. Third, if we insist we don't need to do something, it is a sign that we are likely disobeying God. Finally, if we have anger about a person, we must confess our anger to God and reconcile with that person right away.

Do you agree that "it does not matter whether I am defrauded or not; what does matter is that I do not defraud"? Is that how you live your life? Let go of the thoughts about how you've been mistreated and focus earnestly on where you have mistreated others.

APPLICATION

With whom are you angry right now? What should you do? What happens if you don't?
In what ways are you hoping to be proved right? Does it indicate "disobedience" in you?
Finish this prayer: "Holy Spirit, you are at work to help me stay in the light. To do that, I
need to first . . ."

THE INEVITABLE PENALTY

God locks us up so we'll see the debt of love we owe Him and those around us—
and He'll tax the universe to help us pay it.

◄

BACKGROUND What does *disposition* mean when Oswald Chambers says, "The moment you are willing that God should alter your disposition, His re-creating forces will begin to work"? On March 21, we saw that he compared our disposition to the mainspring of a wind-up device, like a clock or a wind-up toy. Everything about us flows from our disposition. If we are willing to let God alter our disposition (the Updated Edition calls this our "nature"), God can re-create us into a new creature.

The problem with our old disposition is not that it made us immoral. Some people, like Pharisees, are very moral. The problem is that because of our old disposition, we don't want to give up our right to control our own lives. Do you manifest an old disposition? Let today's lesson free you from it!

SCRIPTURAL CONTEXT Today ends a three-day series from Matthew 5. If you've been following *Utmost*, you should be familiar with the whole Sermon on the Mount. How does today's verse fit in? Does Chambers apply it in the way you expected? Is there anything from Matthew 5 that your head disputes? Why does this blunt the text's appeal to your heart?

WHAT'S THE DEVOTIONAL SAYING?
Today's lesson is extremely important. It's unlikely that many of us have been "thrown into prison" literally. But most of us have experienced a time when we didn't "come to judgment" after the Holy Spirit convicted us of something. As a result of not coming to judgment immediately, God gives "the inevitable penalty" to help us become spotless. At that point, the question is this: Are we willing to let God change our disposition or not?

If you can't remember giving God the right to change your sinful disposition into Jesus' disposition, give Him that right today. Make a note of this day. From now on, God will tax the universe to help you be rightly related to Him and to those around you.

APPLICATION
Have you brought the "fire of hell" into your heavenly life? How? What did God do?
Are you growing spiritually? What things will you do someday that you could do now?
Finish this prayer: "Holy Spirit, you'll hound me until I'm spotless. I want you to change
  my nature . . ."

༄ JULY 2 ༄
THE CONDITIONS OF DISCIPLESHIP

Compare your devotion to your family with your love for Jesus. Which is deeper?

BACKGROUND Today's lesson, like many we've seen, has its roots in Oswald Chambers' *Studies in the Sermon on the Mount* (see May 18, *Companion*). Biddy extracted for us parts of Chambers' discussion of Matthew 5:11–12 and 38–39. The "conditions" for following Jesus include personal, passionate devotion and "moral originality" (see June 13, *Utmost*). We can't muster devotion to Jesus or crazy, spontaneous love for Him. Only the Holy Spirit gives us these two conditions of discipleship.

Do you want to follow Jesus for real? Ask the Spirit to give you personal devotion and moral originality and to help you lose your fascination for creeds and causes.

SCRIPTURAL CONTEXT The first sentence connects today's theme verse with the lesson. Interestingly, Biddy took this sentence from *The Psychology of Redemption* (see April 5, *Companion*), in which Chambers tells us that Luke 14:26–27 and 33 give the conditions of discipleship. Do these verses mention personal devotion and moral originality? How do they relate?

What does it mean to hate family? How does this reconcile with Colossians 3:19 and Ephesians 5:25? How will you carry your cross today?

WHAT'S THE DEVOTIONAL SAYING? The main two points today are the following: We can't love God like a true disciple unless the Spirit helps us; and we must devote ourselves to Jesus the person, not Jesus the cause. Which of these points hit home with you? Are you trying to love God by mustering up reverence and admiration for Him? Are you throwing yourself into a human cause or a set of beliefs?

Everything in life competes with your devotion to Jesus. Only after you throw yourself at Jesus as His devoted servant will you be able to enjoy or love other things. What is keeping you from Him today?

APPLICATION

Who are your closest friends? Do they make you conflict with Jesus? What can you do?

Has your life been creative and "inconsistent"? What preconceived ideas do you have?

Finish this prayer: "Holy Spirit, I need you to pour God's love into my heart so I can love Jesus. Please . . ."

THE CONCENTRATION OF PERSONAL SIN

God's conviction is always razor sharp and pinpoint precise.

BACKGROUND Do you ever wonder if Oswald Chambers ever struggled with sin? Sure, we know he went through "clouds and darkness" (see January 3, *Companion*), but after he got through that, did the Holy Spirit fill him so thoroughly that he never battled with sin?

Today's lesson teaches us that God convicts us, not in a general way, but of *specific* sins, and this "is true in the greatest and the least of saints." So we know that Chambers felt God's conviction and that all Christians will too. Take comfort: No one is fully perfected in God's eyes. And be warned: No true Christian should stop at "I'm a sinner." God will constantly show us our *specific* sin if we are truly saved.

SCRIPTURAL CONTEXT We first looked at Isaiah 6 on January 14. Why were "unclean lips" Isaiah's specific sin? What are your specific sins?

Today's lesson reminds us that God convicts us of what we *are* ("I am this or that or the other," see the Classic Edition) not what we have *done*. Was this true for Isaiah?

WHAT'S THE DEVOTIONAL SAYING? Besides teaching us how God's conviction operates—specifically, not generally—today's lesson makes two additional points. First, our "experience of the concentration of sin" begins with the realization that God's conviction is specific, and we must wait for it. Second, we experience God's cleansing at the very point where our sin is concentrated.

In what ways *are* you sinful? Are you selfish? In what specific ways? How can you yield to God's conviction in that area? If you yield, you will start to see your full "disposition of sin" (see March 21, *Utmost*).

APPLICATION

What area of sin has God recently exposed in your life? How did He do it? How did you respond?

Has submitting to conviction led to insight into your vast underlying sin nature? How?

Finish this prayer: "Lord, I'm sinful at such a basic level, but to really see it I need you to convict me of . . ."

☞ JULY 4 ☞
ONE OF GOD'S GREAT "DON'TS"

God's command "don't worry" always works, since it's based on Him alone.

➤

BACKGROUND Today begins a two-day series taken from a short, 800-word sermon. The sermon's three points are preserved in tomorrow's devotional, and the main idea ("don't worry") is in today's study.

In terms of God's command, "Do not worry," do you walk the walk or just talk the talk? When was the last time you worried? When crisis strikes, today's lesson will help you be ready.

SCRIPTURAL CONTEXT On March 20, Oswald Chambers quoted from Psalm 37. Today that chapter gives us our theme verse. Did you know that this psalm is an acrostic poem? For example, today's verse begins: "Cease anger." The word *cease* starts with the fifth letter of the Hebrew alphabet.

There are twenty-one poetic passages in Psalm 37. The first words of the passages (don't, trust, commit, etc.) start with Hebrew letters that spell out the alphabet, minus one letter. Poetically, this letter's absence mirrors the dis-

appearance of the wicked (which is the theme of this psalm). What else in the psalm teaches us not to worry about the wicked?

WHAT'S THE DEVOTIONAL SAYING? If God's command not to worry can't be obeyed in "tumult and anguish" (Classic Edition), then it's not very helpful. After all, who needs this command when life is going well? Chambers reassures us that God's command *can* be obeyed in all circumstances, because it only depends on our relationship with God, and He never changes.

If circumstances don't affect the command, why don't we obey it? Our relationship with God has two parts: <u>God</u> and <u>us</u>. Since God isn't the problem, it must be us! If we find ourselves worrying, it's because *we're* not participating in the relationship. Chambers says we don't participate because we want our own way. Decide to be like Jesus today. He never wanted His own way—only God's.

APPLICATION

When have you fretted? When didn't you, despite fretful events? What was the difference?

In what way do you think that fretting reflects foolishness or that God can't handle your life?

Finish this prayer: "God, I know for certain that I've been fretting, and I want to stop right now. Please . . ."

DON'T PLAN WITHOUT GOD

What are your plans? Is God part of the equation?

◄

BACKGROUND Today continues yesterday's lesson on worrying. Yesterday taught us more about God's command not to worry. Today's lesson challenges us to make our plans using God as the main variable in all our equations.

What projects are you working on? Has God upset any of them? This may be the way He helps you put Him first. Your projects might be just what He wants you to do. But if you do them and don't include Him as the biggest factor, He may decide to upset them. Thank God for all your plans that He's upset. Thank Him also for preparing you, using today's lesson, for any future plans that He may upset.

SCRIPTURAL CONTEXT Oswald Chambers used three verses to make his three points in the original sermon "One of God's Great Don'ts" (see July 4, *Companion*). Biddy gives us two of these three and also adds a theme verse from yesterday's psalm. Look at John 14:1, 1 Corinthians 13:4–5, and Matthew 6:34. In the original sermon these three passages went along with the three points: Do calculate with God, don't calculate with evil, and don't calculate with tomorrow. How do the verses relate to the three points?

Yesterday we saw that Psalm 37 is an acrostic. Each word that begins a new poetic section was specially chosen to start with the right letter.

We saw that "commit" is the third such word. How does the emphasis the acrostic structure places on "commit" help us better understand this verse?

WHAT'S THE DEVOTIONAL SAYING? The three points of today's lesson, which follow the points of Chambers' original sermon, help us follow the meaning of the devotional. First, we can't calculate without God, or He will upset our plans. Second, we can't calculate while thinking about evil. We can't be ignorant of it and we can't use it in our calculations. Third, we can't focus on tomorrow when we make our plans.

The third point doesn't seem to make sense. How can we make any plans without thinking about the future? Chambers, in his original sermon, said, "Christ is not telling us to be careless, but to be carefully careless about everything saving one thing, seeking first the kingdom of God." Biddy further clarifies this third point by changing tomorrow to "rainy day." We all know people who do everything as if they were saving up for a rainy day. The wrong in that approach is that it keeps us from the reckless abandon that is the only way to live out the true Christian life. Put Christ first in all your practical everyday issues today, and live in reckless abandon!

APPLICATION

Do you notice times you put on a "spiritual face"? How can you always put God first? What's the difference between not factoring in evil and not realizing the reality of sin? Finish this prayer: "Lord, I don't want to plan without you. Please help me . . ."

VISIONS BECOMING REALITY

In a rush to live out God's plan? Relax, He has plenty of time to make you able.

BACKGROUND Back on March 10, we saw the first of three times Oswald Chambers quotes from Tennyson's *In Memoriam*. The lesson on that day reminded us how God batters and shapes us so we don't merely parrot His words but live them. Today Chambers teaches us about how we learn to live out God's words.

Chambers says that God first gives us vision for what it looks like to live out His words. Then we realize that we are far from this vision. Our realization makes us depressed. Satan sees our vulnerability and tempts us to give up. But this is all part of God's process. He needs us to "get to the place where He can trust us with the veritable reality." Once we do, He makes the vision real in us. We don't learn to live God's words. His supernatural gift makes us live them. We only learn to be trustworthy vessels for God's gift.

SCRIPTURAL CONTEXT Isaiah 35 completes 35 chapters of prophecy. The next section of Isaiah records a historical account that can also be found in 2 Kings and 2 Chronicles. The 35 chapters of prophecy include stinging indictments against both God's people and their enemies. But chapter 35 ends on an extremely positive note and lists several bad things that God is making good. Do you relate to this list of things that are becoming good? Is your heart like parched ground? Do you have feeble hands? Blind eyes? Deaf ears? In what ways do you realize how far you are from God's vision?

WHAT'S THE DEVOTIONAL SAYING?

How can we learn to be trustworthy vessels for God's gift of the vision-made-real? Chambers says we learn by being patient. Don't give up and don't settle for anything less than the vision God gives you of how you *will* live out His words.

God is working in your life. Don't despair. Trust in Him and His flawless character. Does He know that Satan is tempting you? Absolutely! Don't be in a hurry. Know that God's vision will be accomplished.

APPLICATION

What does God want you to be? Have you fully pursued that vision, or have you given up? Why?

What's the point of God's battering? In what ways are you (or aren't you) trustworthy?

Finish this prayer: "God, I know this vision is real, but it's not real in me yet. You will make it real as I . . ."

JULY 7
ALL EFFORTS OF WORTH AND EXCELLENCE
ARE DIFFICULT

The sermon on the Mt is the life we will live when the HS is having its way with us

Are you sad you face a hurdle? Be glad! God is shaping you.

BACKGROUND Three months after her husband's death, Biddy Chambers wrote to her mother, "Bishop Moule says ["heaven"] means better than the earthly at its very best . . . that life is for us too when God's time comes. It makes each day of the 'in between' time so full of significance. Oswald always used to say, 'Lay out each day as you do a sovereign [a British monetary unit] and spend the hours for Him.' " Today's lesson comes once again from Chambers' *Studies in the Sermon on the Mount* (see May 18, *Companion*). In this original source material, Chambers says, "Lay out your life deliberately for [Jesus], take time over it."

If you were given $160 per day, which is what a sovereign was worth to Chambers, what would you spend it on? How much would be for food? What kind of food? Where would the rest go? Today's study will help you spend the hours of each day in the same careful way you might spend a $160 per diem.

SCRIPTURAL CONTEXT Matthew 7:13–14 doesn't usually encourage people, even if they are Christians. But Chambers spent over 2,000 words lecturing about these verses in his *Studies in the Sermon on the Mount*. One of the three sections of this lecture was titled "My Utmost for His Highest." Chambers uses this phrase only five times in all his works: once here, once in his commentary on the Psalms of Ascent, and three times in *Utmost* (January 1, September 15, and December 27). In Chambers' view, Matthew 7:13–14 was a perfect passage for inspiring and encouraging his listeners to live their utmost for God's highest.

How do these verses strike you? What do you learn from Luke 13:22–30? How does this relate to Philippians 2:13 and Hebrews 2:10? How will you apply these truths today?

WHAT'S THE DEVOTIONAL SAYING?
So how should we spend the hours of each day? Chambers says we should spend them practicing God's commands. We know we haven't been spending our days practicing if we fail to obey God's commands when a crisis comes.

Practicing God's commands is hard work. At the beginning of each day, decide how you will practice each one ("Love God," "Love your neighbor," "Don't worry," and so forth). Your hard work will pay off!

The bedrock in JC Kingdom is poverty of spirit. I cannot do it - once we realize our poverty we are brought to where JC works

APPLICATION
What is difficult for you? Do you consciously base your efforts on Christ's redemption? How would "worth and excellence" look in you? What can you do to be less spoiled?
Finish this prayer: "Holy Spirit, I want to obey you and practice what you've put into my life. Today I'll . . ."

The HS is the only expounder of JC teaching. It is the HS in our hearts who applies this principles to the circumstances in which you are placed. Paul said be renewed by the spirit of your mind so you will know the good, acceptable, perfect will of God.

WILL TO BE FAITHFUL

"To will" is the ultimate verb. It takes all our being.

➤

BACKGROUND The concept of free will has come under attack in our day. We read scientific reports that tell us we are merely animals, controlled like robots by external stimuli and preprogrammed brain networks. But Oswald Chambers had a high view of our will. On June 6 we compared will to a new manager able to do all she is supposed to do.

What vision has God given you about how you can live out His Word (see July 6, *Utmost*)? Today Chambers gives us advice about how to make that vision real.

SCRIPTURAL CONTEXT Only in today and tomorrow's readings in *Utmost* do we see verses from Joshua. The only other place we see Joshua 24 in Chambers' *Complete Works* is in connection with Chambers' 1912 book *Biblical Psychology*. There he discusses the heart, which, he says, "is best understood by simply saying 'me.'" In this same section he quotes Deuteronomy 11:18 and Proverbs 3:3. What links to Joshua 24 do you see in those verses?

Today we also see Galatians 1:16, which we saw on January 30, February 3, and March 18, and will see again on November 11. Why does Chambers like this verse so much? *Our commitment is between us + God—nothing to do w/ others*

WHAT'S THE DEVOTIONAL SAYING?

What does the first sentence, which says, "Will is the whole man active" mean? Elsewhere, Chambers writes, "will is the whole man active—body, soul and spirit" and "Heart is the centre of all the vital activities of body, soul and spirit." So my will is my heart, which is best understood as "me." If we do not exercise our will to believe, receive, and obey, we end up yielding our will to Satan and the world, thus becoming slaves. Only when we yield our will to God are we free.

Chambers tells us that the reason it's hard to will to be loyal is that other people's opinions matter to us. Plus, we want to know where God is leading, but He won't tell us. He just tells us about himself. The thing to do is *"will* to be loyal," as Chambers says.

APPLICATION

Have you ever tried to passively give up your will to God's proposals? What happened?

What is God proposing you do? What do others say? How can you will to be faithful?

Finish this prayer: "Lord, I declare openly that I will be faithful. I'll choose you over others' advice and . . ."

WILL YOU EXAMINE YOURSELF?

True, you can't live holy on your own. But by God's help, you can.

◄

BACKGROUND Today continues yesterday's theme about will. The pressing issue for Oswald Chambers' audience was the realization of "big propositions" ("proposals," Updated Edition). We don't know what these propositions were or even when he gave this devotional. Perhaps it related to World War I and the choices his students faced. Today's lesson tells us that God gives us propositions to probe our hearts.

What choices has God given you? Do you think He has the wrong person? If you don't feel up for the challenge, all the better! When we stop trusting in our own power, God can start working through us.

SCRIPTURAL CONTEXT What did you learn yesterday from reading Joshua 24? Did you make a decision of your will that "as for me and my house, we will serve the Lord"? Is it strange that Joshua says he will serve the Lord but then tells the people that they aren't able to serve Him? *They cannot serve other Gods which they did.*

Chambers quotes Matthew 13:58. What was the setting for this verse? Why is unbelief so deadly? *Jesus home town – can't get honor in your own town. Didn't do many miracles there. lack faith*

WHAT'S THE DEVOTIONAL SAYING? Chambers directs today's lesson both to those who face "big propositions" and to the rest of us who are in between big decisions and are trying to live holy lives in our day-to-day routine. To both groups he has the same advice: Decide to let Christ work in and through you.

As you start a new project or live your day-to-day life, what power are you trusting? If it has anything to do with yourself, stop! Only God's power can help us do what He wants us to do.

APPLICATION

Do you rely on something or someone other than God? Why is your weakness a plus?

What has God called you to? Do you believe you can do it? Why is unbelief a sin?

Finish this prayer: "Jesus, I want you to exhibit your wonderful life in me. I'll start by willing to believe that . . ."

Moses's generation failed miserable when they committed to do as God expected from them. They made a golden calf + refused to enter the Promised land – not trusting God would protect them + honor His part of the covenant. They died in wilderness.

Before his death Joshua told his people they must choose. He expressed his commitment to the Lord

Christ realization

THE SPIRITUALLY LAZY SAINT

When life is not fair, do you throw in the towel or fight all the harder?

➤

BACKGROUND Today begins three days of lessons about Christ-realization. First, we see how it is the opposite of self-realization, which leads to laziness that is often masked by self-focused busyness. Then we see how all our circumstances are there to help us realize Christ. Finally, we see the importance of realizing Christ as members of a community, not just as individuals.

Are you hiding your laziness behind a façade of frenzied activities? Is your Bible study or prayer time just an excuse for getting away from the "rough and tumble of life"? Today's lesson is a poke in the ribs, stirring us to love and good works.

SCRIPTURAL CONTEXT Oswald Chambers says that Hebrews 10 teaches two things. What are they? Can you find other places in Hebrews 10 that talk about them?

Chambers also quotes 2 Peter 1:13 and Matthew 28:10 (see also John 20:17). Whom did the women tell? How did these "brethren" tell others? How will you stir people up by reminding them "these things"?

WHAT'S THE DEVOTIONAL SAYING?
Chambers quotes from Hebrews 10:24–25 only one other place in his *Complete Works*. There, he discusses the problem with a secluded Christian life, such as in the monasteries of the Middle Ages. He points out that Jesus was known as a "friend of publicans and sinners." He wouldn't have earned this nickname if He had retired from the rough-and-tumble of life.

What about you? Are you willing to go to the rough places of life? Stir up yourself and your friends to go where God's light is not yet shining!

APPLICATION

What rough roads are you avoiding? Has anyone's spiritual activity hit you in the ribs?
How would someone describe your active work? Is it really as spiritual as people think?
Finish this prayer: "Jesus, you don't want me holed up as a spiritual recluse; you want me active. Please . . ."

Hebrews teaches us to have confidence in the new way to God thru JC. JC was a man - was lower than the angels. Death sacrifice + humanity raises Him to role of Lord + Savior. The way of JC is so much better. Supremacy of Christ + Perseverence in Christ, Integrates the gospel w/ the O.T. Run the race before us in faith + perseverence.

Christ realization

⌘ JULY 11 ⌘
THE SPIRITUALLY VIGOROUS SAINT

First know yourself or your God—it's your choice.

◁ ▷

BACKGROUND Yesterday we saw that to spur one another on and to avoid laziness we need the initiative of God-realization, not of self-realization. Today we look in depth at God-realization.

Are your circumstances random or orchestrated by God? Oswald Chambers says they are God-engineered to help us know Him. Is your life divided between sacred and secular? Chambers says there is no such divide. All of life is controlled by God, and we must recognize God in all domains.

SCRIPTURAL CONTEXT We saw today's theme verse, Philippians 3:10, on April 8. Did you ever find an answer to the question "What must we do in order to know the power of Jesus' resurrection?" Today we learn that a first step is

to see all circumstances as ordained by God to help us know Him.

John 13:3–5 reminds us that Jesus saw all circumstances as from God. Why else would verse 3 be included? What else do you notice in John 13?

WHAT'S THE DEVOTIONAL SAYING? Do you enthrone your work, or do you enthrone Jesus in your work? How would it look if you enthroned Him?

The main point today is that a spiritual saint (as opposed to a spiritual sluggard) looks for ways to get to know Jesus in every situation. This saint doesn't think of work as something that needs to be done, but as something that helps us get closer to God. Will you think of your work in that way today?

APPLICATION
How is your life divided into secular and sacred? Are you tempted by self-realization?
What motivates you to Christian work? Can you see God in menial jobs? Which ones?
Finish this prayer: "Holy Spirit, if I don't realize Jesus' presence, you'll make me do things
again, such as . . ."

a first step in knowing the power of JC resurrection is to see and recognized God in all circumstances. Think of work as a way to get closer to JC. Enthrone JC in your work.

God realization
Foundation of a good church
Is God your goal or is your goal the blessing
he gives you

THE SPIRITUALLY SELF-SEEKING CHURCH

Is your church after its own glory—or God's?
Help her by focusing on Him.

◄

BACKGROUND Our final lesson in this three-day series teaches us how God-realization works to bring us together as a community. As we saw on July 10, Oswald Chambers did not like the way some Christians in the Middle Ages lived apart from the rough-and-tumble of life—and some of his contemporaries focused so much on personal holiness that they may as well have lived in monasteries! What's the foundation of a good church? Today's study gives us some tips.

SCRIPTURAL CONTEXT Ephesians can be divided into two sections: the first, theoretical, and the second, practical. Today's verse comes from the practical section. As Chambers says, the reason God gave us apostles and teachers is so that the church, Christ's body, can be realized in practice, not in theory.

How is Ephesians 4 similar to Philippians 3? How do they both relate to the lines of Frederick Brook's poem that Chambers quotes? Are you making God your goal, or is your goal the blessings He gives you and your church?

WHAT'S THE DEVOTIONAL SAYING? Our souls are designed to be in relationship with God. God wants to connect with each soul individually and with all souls together. Are our souls together more than the sum of the parts? God thinks so! There is something unique about a God-centered community that God can't replicate by one-on-one interactions with us.

As we think about this uniqueness, our reverence for all God-focused communities should grow. Do you give your church community proper reverence? Or do you go overboard and idolize it—always on the lookout to boost its organizational power? Chambers wants us to have the right balance, which is achieved only when we focus together on God alone.

APPLICATION
In what ways is the church self-seeking? What are you trying to get from God? Why?
How do you help the church to be known? How is your personal relationship with Jesus?
Finish this prayer: "Lord Jesus, my relationship with you is the most important aspect of my life, so I . . ."

⸎ JULY 13 ⸎
THE PRICE OF THE VISION
(BIDDY'S BIRTHDAY)

God removes our heroes to build our character.

BACKGROUND Today's lesson comes from the transcript of a lecture on Isaiah that Oswald Chambers gave in 1912. No doubt he thought of his own "Uzziah," Reader Harris, who died in 1909 (see April 22, *Companion*). But when Biddy compiled these transcripts in 1941 (or used snippets of them in 1927 to write *Utmost*), the words about losing a hero must have made her think of her own loss. Isn't it amazing that she used this lesson on her birthday?

Not a sparrow dies without God's consent. Any loved one who dies is worth far more than a sparrow. God's plans are far above ours, and demanding to understand them is foolishness. Today's lesson is a reminder that God can use even death to help us.

SCRIPTURAL CONTEXT Who was Uzziah, and why was he so important to Isaiah? We first hear about him in 2 Kings 14:21, where he is called Azariah. Read 2 Chronicles 26

to get a flavor for this king. What do you learn about him in verse 10?

Now read Isaiah 6. Review the progression from guilt to gospel to gratitude that we learned about on January 14. How might Uzziah's death have aided this progression?

WHAT'S THE DEVOTIONAL SAYING? There's more to the story today than "God lets our loved ones die so that we can put Him first." For example, we also learn that our character controls how we respond to tragedy. If there is something divine in our character, we won't give up, get ill, or get discouraged when our hero dies. Instead, like Isaiah, we will see the Lord.

Do you see the Lord in the midst of tragedy? Ask God to use external events and internal purification to make your character divine. Don't skimp on the price of the vision! Let God do whatever it takes.

APPLICATION

Which of your heroes has God replaced with himself? How did it affect your character?

What are your priorities? Are you paying the price? Is God able to reveal truth to you?

Finish this prayer: "God, you are my everything. Please let me see my circumstances as the ways you are . . ."

Uzziah - King of Judah (10th King). Reigned 52 yrs. Co-regent w/ father first 24 yrs. Reign marked height of Judah's power. He exacted tribute for on Ammonite. Also called Azariah

Do you see the Lord in the midst of tragedy?

JULY 14
SUFFERING AFFLICTIONS
AND GOING THE SECOND MILE

Ready for insult?
As Christ's disciple, expect no less!

BACKGROUND Oswald Chambers was a true Renaissance man, well versed in all subjects. When he gave the source material for today's devotional, he referenced an obscure statement attributed to Epictetus, a philosopher and former slave. This statement, "A slave would rather be thrashed to death than flicked on the cheek," serves to teach us how hard it would have been to "turn the other cheek" in Jesus' day.

Are you willing to endure the ultimate insult for Christ's sake? Today's study will motivate us to endure any insult, no matter how degrading, for the sake of our Lord and Savior.

SCRIPTURAL CONTEXT Not only was a cheek-slap more degrading than a thrashing, but Jesus also talked about a slap on your *right* cheek. This meant that someone either gave you a backhand slap, which was more humiliating that a normal slap, or slapped you with the left hand, which was the hand used for toilet purposes. What an insult!

Chambers links bearing our insults to Colossians 1:24. Do you think they connect? How has your body paid what is unpaid from Christ's original afflictions?

WHAT'S THE DEVOTIONAL SAYING? On June 27 we read, "Never look for justice in this world, but never cease to give it." Today we read the same words in a slightly different context. The emphasis today is not so much on letting go of our need for justice but on holding on tightly to the call to give others justice. This call is not our duty. It's way *beyond* our duty.

Are you only giving others the justice that you reasonably could be expected to give them? Even the pagans do that! God wants you to do what is not your duty. He wants you to endure the worst insults and still go the extra mile for your attackers. Only with His power will you be able to do that!

APPLICATION

When were you last humiliated? How did you respond? Why must we "turn the other cheek"?

Where are you looking for justice? How does demanding your own rights hurt God?

Finish this prayer: "Jesus, I want to fill up the affliction you left for me to experience. It will be hard but . . ."

∾ JULY 15 ∾
MY LIFE'S SPIRITUAL HONOR AND DUTY

Feeling smug?
We are deeply in debt to God!

BACKGROUND In January's issue of the League of Prayer's 1915 monthly magazine (see January 10, *Companion*), Oswald Chambers wrote: "Eight of our students are now in the foreign field on active service. . . . Six more will be appointed to active foreign service this year. . . . Our duty is to see that this house maintains the honor of God." It was vital to Chambers that his Bible Training College "house" maintained God's honor by sending students to foreign mission fields and World War I battlegrounds.

Is maintaining God's honor a matter of "spiritual honor" to you? Today we learn how we as saints can maintain spiritual honor.

SCRIPTURAL CONTEXT So far in *Utmost* we have looked at only the first verse of Romans 1. Today's theme verse takes us to verse 14. What's the connection between being set apart and being a debtor? In what ways are we both?

First Corinthians 6:19–20 tells us we are debtors, but for a different purpose. Why does Paul mention our indebtedness to God? Does this motivate you to avoid sexual immorality?

WHAT'S THE DEVOTIONAL SAYING? Chambers says that we can't do anything to bring God's redemption to others unless God first makes us feel our indebtedness to Him. Do you think that's true? How indebted do you feel on a daily basis?

Today we are given a delightful paradox. When we earnestly protect our spiritual honor, we become slaves to everyone. People who defend their honor are typically the least likely to serve as slaves. But protecting our spiritual honor means we fulfill our debt to God, which we do by sharing His redemption with others. What about you? Will you share His redemption today by being broken bread and poured-out wine to those around you?

APPLICATION

Do you feel indebted to Christ? How do we know this was Paul's greatest inspiration?
What parts of your life have value? Do you pray more for yourself or others? Why?
Finish this prayer: "Lord, I'm only free when I'm a slave to you. Today I'll try to not feel
    superior when I . . ."

THE CONCEPT OF DIVINE CONTROL

God is not ignoring you. He's behind the scenes teaching you total trust.

BACKGROUND It must have been helpful to Biddy Chambers, as she compiled *Utmost*, to have her husband's book *Studies in the Sermon on the Mount* (see April 18, *Companion*) on hand. Today's devotional comes once again from this commentary on Matthew 5–7 and teaches us to "notion" our minds with the concept of divine control.

Oswald Chambers uses *notion* as a verb. What does that mean? The Updated Edition explains that it means to "truly fill." Is your mind truly filled with the idea that God is there for you? Or are you living like an orphan? Sometimes God seems like an unnatural father, but He is not. Don't live like you are fatherless!

SCRIPTURAL CONTEXT In *Studies in the Sermon on the Mount*, today's lesson appears as the commentary on Matthew 7:7–10. Today's theme verse (Matthew 7:11), therefore, appears in a later section. But as you read these verses, which ones seem to best match today's lesson? It's almost as if Chambers were speaking on verses 7–10 while anticipating verse 11.

What other Bible verses help you "notion" your mind with the idea that God is totally in control? As you face the difficulties of the day, read those verses and truly fill your mind with them.

WHAT'S THE DEVOTIONAL SAYING?
How does knowing that God is in control help us ask and seek? It would seem that people who are *not* sure that God is with them would be the most fervent in their prayers. Chambers explains that the kind of asking and seeking we need to cultivate is the kind that is completely natural, as easy as breathing. That kind of asking happens only when we trust that God is there for us.

Has it always felt as if God is there for you? Chambers says it won't always feel that He is. This is when it is most vital we "notion" our mind properly and remember God really is in control.

APPLICATION
What trials or uncertainties arise in your life? Do you take them to others or to God?
What attitude would make it natural to ask from God? How can you develop this more?
Finish this prayer: "Father, you know all that I need before I ask, which makes it even easier to ask, since . . ."

THE MIRACLE OF BELIEF

The Spirit reaches others through your words, not because of your words.

➤

BACKGROUND Reading Oswald Chambers' sermons takes full concentration. His difficult language and references require several Internet searches to track down their meaning. Yet to their original audiences they seemed full of jokes and lightheartedness. Indeed, one listener commented in broken English, "Ah, I see, your jokes and lightheartedness plough the land, then you put in the seed. I feel in my insides that that is right."

Today's lesson teaches that God doesn't use our eloquent language or humor to preach redemption. We can still use those things as God allows, but they shouldn't be the reason people want to live better. Do you ever tell people about God? You should! Today's lesson tells you what to focus on when you do.

SCRIPTURAL CONTEXT In Paul's day the people of Corinth liked good oration. But when Paul rebukes them, he reminds them that his own preaching was not eloquent. Read the first two chapters of 1 Corinthians. Where else can you find Paul reminding them of this fact?

In 2 Corinthians, Paul reconciled with the church at Corinth and taught them how God uses us as His ambassadors of reconciliation. Chambers quotes 2 Corinthians 5:20 to remind us that we represent God alone and must not represent our own human ideals or gifts.

WHAT'S THE DEVOTIONAL SAYING?

The final words of today's lesson come from John 12:32. They aptly sum up what Chambers is trying to say: All we need to do is lift up Christ, and people will come to Him and be changed.

Have you had any successes or failures as you share the gospel? What has been the difference? Chambers tells us that the only thing that ruins our efforts to share the gospel is *our* effort. God's power, not ours, is what we need. Today, preach Him alone!

APPLICATION

How do you tell others about God? Are you "eloquent"? How do you represent God?

Do you fast from anything? How do our lives hinder God's work? What can you do?

Finish this prayer: "Jesus, I want to lift *you* up, not me. Please help me to represent you as I share with . . ."

THE MYSTERY OF BELIEVING

What rules you?
If it's not Jesus, then throw it off!

BACKGROUND Today continues a three-part series on how people become believers. Yesterday we saw that they don't become Christians through our eloquent speaking. Today and tomorrow we learn that they don't turn to God because of religion or because God insists they follow Him. Religion, in fact, can be a snare. Anyone who tells people, "Do this, don't do that!" breaks their spirit and keeps them from being ready for God.

Does your church break people's spirits? Ask God to use today's lesson to free you from religious snares and to keep you from being a snare to others.

SCRIPTURAL CONTEXT Our theme verse captures the first time Paul (then still Saul) speaks to Jesus. Do you remember your first words to Jesus? How long was it before you turned into His devoted servant? How long did it take for Paul?

Oswald Chambers also references John 3:19–21. What happens to people who refuse the light? Have you ever refused God's light? What happened?

WHAT'S THE DEVOTIONAL SAYING? Today's lesson teaches us several things. First, a person can be turned into God's humble slave surprisingly quickly. Second, disagreeing with a leader can be the first step in turning to Jesus, especially when the leader is overbearing and religious rather than humble and Christ-centered. Finally, God never insists we obey, but when we don't, we cut ourselves off from His re-creating power.

Take time to compare your church's approach to changing people with God's method. If you are part of a "You must!" or "You shall!" mentality, repent and mend your ways. If no one's life has changed through your church's ministry, pray for more of God's miraculous power and less of the things that you and your fellow church members can explain and control.

APPLICATION

What do you try to explain/control? What controls you? Should you stop obeying?

Have you ever come face-to-face with Jesus and not obeyed what He was telling you?

Finish this prayer: "Jesus, the last thing I want is to sign your death certificate in my soul, so today I vow . . ."

THE SUBMISSION OF THE BELIEVER

Do you like the word obey?
It's not a word for slaves; it's for friends!

[handwritten: I and the Father are one]

◄

BACKGROUND Have you met someone more holy than you are? Not holier-than-thou but with truly divine character? If you have, then you responded in one of two ways. Either you ignored what that person said, thus revealing the unworthiness in you, or you were educated by him or her and in some sense "obeyed" that person.

Today's lesson focuses on obedience. It tells us we need to rescue this word from the negative way it's been used. "Obey me!" shouts the frazzled mom at her three-year-old. We imagine a plantation owner yelling the same words to his beaten-down slave. But Oswald Chambers says we should use the word "obedience" for relationships between equals. Today, we will learn why we should obey our Master.

SCRIPTURAL CONTEXT Today's theme verse tells us that Jesus is our Master. But the rest of John 13 shows our Master in a different light. Do you know any masters who serve others as Jesus did? In Revelation 4:11, the twenty-four elders speak to God in poetic praise. Have you ever praised God in this way?

Jesus is our best example of obedience, and Chambers quotes John 10:30 and Hebrews 5:8 to show how He obeyed God. Do you think these verses prove Chambers' point that obedience is between equals?

WHAT'S THE DEVOTIONAL SAYING? "He is easily Lord." What a phrase! But it's only true once we see Him. Do you want Christ to be Lord? If you think of obedience as something you *have* to do, you are not growing in grace. But if you remember the way Jesus obeyed His Father out of reverence for His worthiness, and then follow in His steps, Yahweh truly will be your Lord.

How can we follow in Jesus' steps? At first, God educates us by those who are more holy. Ask Him to send someone like that into your life. Ask Him also to remove your unworthiness, which will tempt you to ignore those who are more holy.

APPLICATION

Do you know people who are more holy than you? Who are they? Do you listen to them?
In Scripture, have you ever truly seen Jesus? How? Has He insisted on your obedience?
Finish this prayer: "Lord, you are so worthy and I'm not. I don't want my unworthiness to keep me from . . ."

[handwritten: Hebrews 5:8 Son though he was, he learned obedience from what he suffered]

DEPENDENT ON GOD'S PRESENCE

Faced with decisions?
Depend on God's presence to keep you on track!

BACKGROUND In his book *Decision Making and the Will of God,* published in 1980, Garry Friesen makes a case against the idea of God directing us using circumstances (or "fleeces") and our inner impressions. He says God doesn't have a secret, individual plan for each of us that we must find or be forever outside of God's will. Instead, we must use God's gift of wisdom to choose our own path. Once we choose, God secretly works all the tiniest unknowns for our good.

Too bad we couldn't get Oswald Chambers and Friesen to host a joint seminar on decision making! They both have so much to say. Today, at the end of his teaching about God's presence, Chambers tells us how to make decisions—big ones and small ones.

SCRIPTURAL CONTEXT How often have you read Isaiah 40:31? Have you ever heard an interpretation like Chambers'? What about the parts of this verse he omitted? Is there anything else in Isaiah 40 that supports his view? How does Chambers use "wings like eagles" in today's second paragraph?

Chambers also quotes John 1:35–36, Genesis 17:1, and Psalm 46:2. What do these verses say about our dependence on God's presence?

WHAT'S THE DEVOTIONAL SAYING? The four paragraphs in today's lesson (see the Classic Edition) teach us four truths about depending on God's presence. First, we depend on God's presence to give us the stable, enduring qualities we need to "walk" in our daily lives. Second, without God's presence we become thrill-seekers. Third, we depend on God's presence without being conscious of it. Chambers says elsewhere, "A saint is never consciously a saint; a saint is consciously dependent on God." Similarly, we are consciously dependent on *God* without being conscious of His *presence*.

Finally, we depend on God's presence in big decisions and small. In big decisions, we directly ask God for wisdom. In small ones, we proceed using the wisdom He already worked into us. But even then, we depend on His presence to "check" us (see March 18, *Utmost*) in case our decisions are not His "order" or "according to His will" as the Updated Edition says. What decisions do you face today? Ask God for wisdom, or for most things just use the wisdom He's already given you. He will keep you on track!

APPLICATION
Are you seeking thrills? Physically or spiritually? Why is "walking" a better test?
Are you conscious of God's presence or only of your dependence on Him?
Finish this prayer: "Father, I have many decisions to make as I walk through today. Please help me . . ."

THE DOORWAY TO THE KINGDOM

God breaks our haughty spirit, so we can receive His light and His re-creation.

BACKGROUND Today's lesson has its origin in the very first section of *Studies in the Sermon on the Mount* (see May 18, *Companion*). It is the key to understanding the rest of Matthew 5–7. But it's a good thing we didn't read this devotional earlier in the year, because its truths can be understood only when the Holy Spirit opens our hearts. The more we read *Utmost,* the more likely that is to happen!

Has God broken your haughty spirit? It may have hurt, but it's the only way He can start working in our lives. Let today's lesson prepare your spirit to be poor!

SCRIPTURAL CONTEXT As you read the Beatitudes, which ones are positive in the world's eyes? Not many! That's why it's so hard for us to be blessed. We want what the world wants, and it isn't poverty, mourning, meekness, or many of the other things on Jesus' list.

What from the list do you need most today? Ask God to cultivate that in your heart so He can begin to *make* you what He *teaches* you to be.

WHAT'S THE DEVOTIONAL SAYING? As Oswald Chambers began his five-part series on Matthew 5–7, he wanted his listeners to know that Jesus' sermon was not a list of things we need to learn and follow, but an ideal that brings despair to our natural selves. As the natural in us despairs, we will realize that our natural selves are not enough, and we will desire the spiritual. At that point, our spiritual poverty will become clear as day, and we can finally "receive from Him."

It takes a long time for us to believe we are poor in spirit. We can say it to ourselves and to our friends, but there is always part of us that clings to our old self-righteous conceit. Are you willing for God to break you over some obstacle? Be willing today!

APPLICATION
Read Matthew 5–7. What is your gut response? Is this how Jesus meant you to respond? What does "Christ our Savior" mean? Is that how you see Him? Or is He just a teacher? Finish this prayer: "Jesus, I despair when I think how often I fall short of your ideal. Please help me see . . ."

JULY 22
SANCTIFICATION

Have you given yourself to God?
Die to self and be free!

➤

BACKGROUND Today begins a two-part series on sanctification. (For a quick review of sanctification, you may want to look back at the notes in *Companion* on February 8.) Today we see that God cuts us off from the way we pretend to be to ourselves and to others. Tomorrow we will learn about how God fills us with all of Jesus' holiness.

Are you still clinging to the way your friends perceive you or the way you perceive yourself? God will give you a miserable time! As Oswald Chambers wrote elsewhere, "When God deals with us on the death side He puts the sentence of death on everything we should not trust in, and we have a miserable time until we learn never any more to trust in it. . . . Then He deals with us on the life side and reveals to us all that is ours in Christ Jesus, and there comes in the overflowing strength of God."

SCRIPTURAL CONTEXT In addition to the theme verse and the two verses Chambers quotes (Luke 14:26 and Matthew 10:34), the Updated Edition points us to two more passages: 1 Thessalonians 5:23–24 and 1 Corinthians 1:30. What does each of these verses say? What do they teach us about sanctification?

WHAT'S THE DEVOTIONAL SAYING?
Sanctification is a confusing word. Nowadays, people talk about "living the Spirit-filled life" or "being controlled and empowered by the Holy Spirit." Chambers lived in a time before some of the new denominations and parachurch movements gave sanctification a variety of meanings. So he could use the biblical words *sanctify* and *sanctification* without all of the baggage they have more recently accumulated. The main thing that Chambers teaches us about sanctification today is that it means the "death" of a lot of the things that distract us from God.

What distracts *you* from God? Is it the things you think are good about yourself or that others have told you are good? Let God break you over some obstacle (see July 21, *Companion*) to strip you of all those things!

APPLICATION
How long did you spend struggling when God first tried stripping you to your bare self? What self-interests separate you from your death? Are you willing to let them go? How? Finish this prayer: "Lord, please show me what sanctification means. I want to be made new, even if . . ."

JULY 23
SANCTIFICATION

Are you trying to copy Jesus?
If you invited Him in, let Him shine out!

◄

BACKGROUND As we move from the death side to the life side, our understanding of sanctification grows. Today Oswald Chambers teaches us that Jesus really lives in us and through us from the moment we become sanctified, which happens when we ask God for the Spirit according to His promise (Luke 11:13). We also learn that the *process* of sanctification is not the same as this one-time *event* of sanctification. In today's final sentence, Chambers makes it clear that the process of sanctification is slow but sure.

Have you experienced the one-time event of sanctification? If so, are you allowing the process of sanctification to take place? Or are you blocking it by refusing to obey what you know God wants you to do. Let today's lesson challenge you to continually be sanctified!

SCRIPTURAL CONTEXT Yesterday, in the Updated Edition, we saw 1 Corinthians 1:30, which is today's theme verse. In some translations of this verse, Christ becomes wisdom for us but doesn't necessarily become our righteous-

ness, sanctification, and redemption. Can you find other places where the Bible clearly says Jesus became these three things for us?

Chambers links Colossians 1:27 and 1 Peter 1:5 to sanctification. What additional clues does this give us about what he means when he uses the word *sanctify*?

WHAT'S THE DEVOTIONAL SAYING?
What's the difference between "Christ in you" and "follow in His steps" (see 1 Peter 2:21)? Both are important, but today we learn that "Christ in you" is more profound. When we realize that all of Christ's perfections—His perfect obedience, His perfect wisdom—are in us through our sanctification, only then can we "follow in His steps." We can't follow before we realize this.

Do you want to live a holy life? Chambers says that the one secret to doing so is to let Jesus—and all His perfections—shine out from inside your life. Jesus is in you. You just need to let Him out!

APPLICATION

What good interests distract you from holiness? What will it cost to be right with God? How do you know that your life now is more orderly, sound, and holy than it was before? Finish this prayer: "God, you keep me by imparting to me all of Christ's perfection. Please help me to . . ."

JULY 24
HIS NATURE AND OUR MOTIVES
(OSWALD'S BIRTHDAY)

Our nature follows our heritage. God's solution was to swap our heredity!

BACKGROUND Today's lesson takes us back to the *Studies in the Sermon on the Mount* (see May 18, *Companion*). The theme today is our disposition, or "nature." We learn that God completely swaps out our old nature for Christ's nature, which is the only way He can make us 100 percent pure in all our thoughts and motives.

If you read this lesson in its original, Oswald Chambers tells you exactly how you can know if your nature has been swapped. He says that when you get into a difficult situation, one that would have made your old nature "sour and irritable and sarcastic and spiteful," you will instead find "a well of sweetness" that you know couldn't have come from yourself. Has this ever happened to you? Does it happen regularly? If not, ask God to swap your nature for Christ's nature once and for all!

SCRIPTURAL CONTEXT Who were the Pharisees? Chambers tells us, in *Studies in the Sermon on the Mount*, to think of the most upright, moral, sterling, religious person you know who hasn't received the Holy Spirit. He says *that* is what the Pharisees were like. Can you imagine that person conspiring to put someone to death in the most painful way imaginable? Probably not! Yet even the most upright person you know, in the appropriate circumstances, would easily do that.

Today's theme verse tells us that we must exceed the uprightness of the most upright person we know. We must *do* better things than that person does in any circumstance, and we must *be* better than he or she is, even in our deepest motives. Can you do and be like that? Not without a swap of your nature!

WHAT'S THE DEVOTIONAL SAYING? Today's first sentence might lead you to believe that *being* is the only thing that matters. But *Studies in the Sermon on the Mount* tells us that *being* without *doing* is also wrong. If Jesus had wanted only for us to be good, he would have said, "Except your righteousness be *different* than that of the Pharisees . . ." The Pharisees were masters of doing, and we must *do* if we want to exceed them.

What circumstance makes you "sour and irritable and sarcastic and spiteful"? God may put you in that circumstance again today to prove to you that He has made you a new creation.

APPLICATION
When did you do a good deed with bad motives and vice versa? Which one was worse?
Do you have a new heredity? How do you know? In what ways are you more righteous?
Finish this prayer: "Jesus, help me search the caverns of my mind for wrong motives right now, such as . . ."

AM I BLESSED LIKE THIS?

Been jarred by Jesus?
In time you'll adjust to it!

BACKGROUND On July 21, we looked at the first Beatitude (poor in spirit). Today, Oswald Chambers tells us what they all have in common: spiritual "dynamite"!

What are the Beatitudes? In order, they bless the poor in spirit, those who mourn, the meek, those who hunger/thirst for righteousness, the merciful, the pure, the peacemakers, and the persecuted. Are any of these "dynamite" to you yet? Chambers says they won't be until you hit the right kind of circumstances. And once they explode, it will take time to conform your walk and conversation to the precepts that Jesus gives you in the Beatitudes, in the Sermon on the Mount, and in all His teaching.

SCRIPTURAL CONTEXT How many times can we read Matthew 5:3–10 without experiencing the Beatitudes' true power? We hear them. They sound familiar. They have a nice ring to them. But do they ever impact us in the way Chambers describes?

Why not let today be the day you commit them to memory? One trick is to learn the two groups of four by memorizing the first letters: p-m-m-m (where the final "m" stands for a "mix" of hunger and thirst) and m-p-p-p. After that, you need to think about why the first and last rewards are the same, why the meek inherit the earth, why the pure see God, and why the peacemakers are sons of God. If you haven't memorized Scripture for a while, this is a good place to get started again.

WHAT'S THE DEVOTIONAL SAYING? Have you caught the meaning of today's lesson yet? The Sermon on the Mount and the Beatitudes are not rules to follow but descriptions of how Spirit-led believers live. Don't read Matthew 5–7 just so you know what to do. Study these truths so you can rejoice as you see the Holy Spirit change your life to conform to what you read in these chapters.

Only God can help us live the truths in Matthew 5–7, and His help comes only after we allow Him to swap our disposition (see July 24, *Companion*). But just because we can't do it without God doesn't mean there's nothing for us to do. It's the stern, difficult work of a saint to interpret the truths. This stern work takes concentration. As Chambers put it, "Concentration means pinning down the four corners of the mind until it is settled on what God wants." Will you patiently pin down your mind? The sanctification process awaits your steadfast concentration.

APPLICATION

The last time you thought about the Beatitudes, what was your opinion of them? Why? How do you think about the Beatitudes now? Will you apply them today? Which ones? Finish this prayer: "Lord, I know it costs a lot to follow you, but please give me an opportunity to . . ."

JULY 26
THE WAY TO PURITY

Hiding behind ignorance?
Jesus will expose the truth of your sin and heal you!

BACKGROUND Even though today's theme verse is from Matthew 15, the original source material is again *Studies in the Sermon on the Mount.* That five-part lecture series was chock-full of insight!

Have you used the excuse that you didn't *mean* to hurt someone? You didn't *intentionally* do (or say) that cruel thing? Oswald Chambers says that these excuses are a "fool's paradise." Someday God will show you that your "innocent ignorance" was just a cover for a horrifyingly evil heart. Read today's study to prepare yourself for that day of reckoning.

SCRIPTURAL CONTEXT Biddy deleted the sordid list in today's theme verse. Her original readers may have known this list so well that they only needed the first five words of the verse to remind them of the "evil thoughts, murder, adultery, sexual immorality, theft, false witness, and slander" that proceed out of the heart.

The Amplified Bible adds "such as" after "evil thoughts." How does this change the meaning? Has God shown you how bad your thoughts can be? Do you realize that your heart must be equally evil?

WHAT'S THE DEVOTIONAL SAYING? Biddy Chambers was a master seamstress. Not literally, but with words. Every lesson in *Utmost* is carefully trimmed from longer sermons. Many of them are woven together from several of Oswald's talks. Today, she has sewn together individual sentences to capture an important truth: Innocence can be dangerous.

How can we protect ourselves from this danger? By being pure. But only God can give us purity. Don't wait for Him to show you the evil your heart is capable of doing. The price is too high! Instead, cry out for the Holy Spirit—the Spirit of perfect purity—to come into the center of your life.

APPLICATION

Has Christ revealed your sin? Did you believe Him? Resent it? Trust His redemption?

What bad things proceed out of your mouth? How do you explain them? Correct them?

Finish this prayer: "Jesus, you're right—my words and my heart defile me. There's no use pretending that . . ."

THE WAY TO KNOWLEDGE

Need to fix something?
Do it now. Don't delay!

BACKGROUND Today we return to an important theme: We learn more spiritually only after we obey what we've already learned (see January 12 and March 27, *Companion*) Oswald Chambers compares spiritual learning with scientific learning. He asserts that while curiosity helps us learn science, obedience is the *only* way to learn spiritually. Curiosity can't help us on that front.

Are there things you've learned and need to fix? Today's lesson urges you to fix them now! The longer you delay, the more you shrug your shoulders and lose your nerve to tackle that issue, the more of a "religious humbug," or fake, you will become.

SCRIPTURAL CONTEXT In the *Complete Works*, Chambers references today's theme verse (John 7:17) sixteen times. This is not a huge number (he quotes Luke 11:13, his life verse, forty-two times), but it shows that he finds this verse important. If you read John 7, verse 17 might slip by unnoticed. How does this verse perfectly prove Chambers' point about learning by obedience?

Since the original source material is again from *Studies in the Sermon on the Mount*, Chambers quotes Matthew 5:23–24 as an example of something God might ask you to obey. What has He asked you to obey? Will you do it?

WHAT'S THE DEVOTIONAL SAYING?
What does Chambers add to the lessons he's already taught us about obedience? For one, he tells us that we will instantly be tested on what God reveals to us. Second, he mentions self-vindication as a sin that God specifically targets. Third, he uses the word "humbug" ("imposter" in the Updated Edition), twice, since that's what we become when we don't obey. Finally, he says people will think us fanatical when we obey.

What has *Utmost* revealed to you? Did God test you on it immediately? Do you vindicate yourself? How does that usually end? Has anyone considered you a fanatic, or just a fake? Decide today to act on whatever God shows you that you need to do!

APPLICATION
What spiritual truths make you curious? Which ones are dark and hidden? Why is that?
What does God want you to do right now? Could you be seen as fanatical if you did it?
Finish this prayer: "God, dark, hidden things are my cue to start obeying. Right now I can't
   understand . . ."

wed

GOD'S PURPOSE OR MINE?

Do you think getting there is half the fun?
For God, it's the main thing.

BACKGROUND Yesterday's lesson said that obedience is the key to spiritual learning. Today, we learn that we shouldn't obey in order to get anything—not success, not peace, not even spiritual learning! Instead, we obey God moment-by-moment simply because we owe it to Him as His creatures. And the only thing we are guaranteed to get as a result of obeying is the good habit of trusting God in every situation.

What chaos do you face? Jesus can walk on our chaos the way He walked on the waves in the middle of the storm. He wants you to see how well He can handle everything. He wants you to walk too—with assurance that God is with you.

SCRIPTURAL CONTEXT On March 28 and June 18 we looked at the same story Oswald Chambers references today, but in a different gospel. What are the differences? Which version talks about Peter? Does John 6 have this detail?

When have you felt as if God made you "get into the boat"? What were you more interested in—what was on the other side or the journey to get there?

WHAT'S THE DEVOTIONAL SAYING? The final line in today's lesson is priceless: "If we realize that obedience is the end, then each moment as it comes is precious." Is each moment, even times of drudgery (see February 19, *Utmost*), precious to you? If not, perhaps you are focused on future goals rather than on the steps along the way

What are your goals, anyway? If you've been using *A Daily Companion* this year, review your answers on January 24 and March 17. Ask God to replace your goals with His goals for your life.

APPLICATION

When did you obey God? Did you then expect success? How does God define success?

What are your goals? How are you preparing? How does God see your preparation?

Finish this prayer: "God, the time I'm spending with you right now is as much a goal as what I do. Please . . ."

DO YOU SEE JESUS IN YOUR CLOUDS?

Pain isn't evil. It's how God builds faith in us.

Which sermon reflected Oswald's dark time?

BACKGROUND Gertrude "Biddy" Hobbs didn't meet Oswald Chambers until after his time of "clouds and darkness" (see January 3, *Companion*). But surely he shared with her what he "unlearned" during those four years. As he gave the original 770-word sermon on this subject, he must have been thinking about that dark time. And as Biddy edited it into today's 300-word devotional, she must have been thinking about her own time of clouds and darkness—the months after Oswald died. What about you? When have clouds rolled into your life?

Today's devotional helps us better understand times of pain and sorrow. It's not God teaching us, it's Him "unlearning" us from our complicated ways and building simple faith in us. Are you ready for clouds?

SCRIPTURAL CONTEXT When was the last time you read either Revelation 1:7 or Nahum 1:3? Chambers quotes both of these today as he explains God's clouds. He also references the transfiguration (Luke 9:34 and Mark 9:8). In all cases, clouds are associated with God, not Satan.

When Oswald died, Biddy's world fell completely apart. Losing him meant losing her best friend, her financial provider, her young daughter's father, and more. And all this happened in a scorching hot foreign country thousands of miles from any of her relatives. This was no small cloud! How can we be sure that "clouds are always connected with God," as the first sentence says?

WHAT'S THE DEVOTIONAL SAYING? The four paragraphs in today's study each build on Chambers' clouds-are-connected-to-God theme. First, God teaches us faith using clouds. Second, the kind of faith He teaches is simple faith—He strips us of others until He is the only one we see. Third, a test of whether we know God is if we can still trust God's goodness even in the clouds. Finally, Chambers challenges us to get to a place where God is first and all else fades.

Are you ready for God to be first? Will He need to send more clouds before you're ready? Probably! When He does, trust that He's still as good as ever.

APPLICATION

What clouds are in your personal life? Do you think they are from God? How do they affect your faith?

What have you unlearned? Is your relationship with God simpler today than a year ago?

Finish this prayer: "God, I want to come face-to-face with the pain in my life and in the world and still say . . ."

JULY 30
THE TEACHING OF DISILLUSIONMENT

Let down by someone?
God's disillusionment gets rid of all our pretenses.

BACKGROUND February 7 began a six-part "Discipline of . . ." series (in the Classic Edition). Today is part five, and it tackles the sad subject of disillusionment. Oswald Chambers' deepest time of disillusionment may have been his failed career as an artist (see February 2, *Companion*). His letters reveal that he couldn't even pay his rent. Add to that his father's pressures (see January 11, *Companion*) and you have the making of major disillusionment.

How well are you coping with the endless string of disillusionments we call life? Today's lesson encourages us to avoid cynical disillusionment and to embrace the disillusionment that comes from God.

SCRIPTURAL CONTEXT The last time we saw today's theme verse was on May 31. The main point that day was to put God first. Today's lesson is about how God helps us put Him first—through disillusionment.

An example of how Jesus "trusted no man" is John 7:1–10. Whom didn't He trust? What happened to them (see Acts 1:14, 1 Corinthians 9:5, Galatians 1:19, and Jude 1)? Was Jesus right to trust in God and "what His grace could do"?

WHAT'S THE DEVOTIONAL SAYING?
Who has let you down? Did it make you cynical? Chambers tells us how disillusionment leads to cynicism. First, we love someone instead of God (see July 29, *Companion*). Then, this person lets us down, and since we didn't let God "satisfy the last aching abyss of the human heart," we get bitter over this person's disappointing us.

Do you want to break this cycle? Put God first! Trust what God's grace can do. See people as "facts," not as the "ideas" you have about who they are and what they should be able to do for you. The fact is, everyone is a sinner and lets others down.

APPLICATION
What or who has deceived you? When were you disillusioned by this deception? How?
Whom do you love? Do you demand more perfection than they are able to give? Why?
Finish this prayer: "God, I want to be true to the facts about others, not my ideas of them. But I need you . . .

⚛ JULY 31 ⚛
BECOMING ENTIRELY HIS

Don't complain when God pokes and prods. Instead, marvel at His patience!

BACKGROUND On June 23, 1915, three weeks before the Bible Training College closed its doors for the last time, Oswald Chambers gave today's lesson. Months earlier, he had signed up to give "spiritual first-aid" to the troops fighting in World War I. Just a few weeks before he gave this lesson, the YMCA accepted him as one of that organization's workers in Egypt. Imagine listening to this talk—one of the last devotional hours Chambers gave at the college. Chambers' students must have hung on his every word, knowing that they might never see his face again.

What can we learn from this momentous talk? Chambers' main point is that even after our white funeral (see January 15, *Utmost*), there are minor battles that still must be fought. God will relentlessly fight these battles until we are "entirely His." How fitting that at the end of the college's four-and-a-half-year journey Chambers reassured his students that they were "right in the main." Then he challenged them to remove, at every instance, the remnants of their carnal life.

SCRIPTURAL CONTEXT Chambers quotes today from the Moffatt translation (see January 1, *Companion*). How do "Let your endurance be a finished product, so that you may be finished and complete, with never a defect" (Moffatt) and "But let patience have her perfect work, that ye may be perfect and entire, wanting nothing" (King James Version) differ? What part of this theme verse does Chambers quote a second time? Whose patience is James talking about—ours or God's?

WHAT'S THE DEVOTIONAL SAYING? Chambers knows that James 1:4 is about *our* patience. But today's lesson focuses on *God's* patience. God's patience strengthens ours as we avoid laziness and work out the external expression of our internal salvation, which God bought for us with the blood of Jesus.

Is God bringing you back, again and again, to a certain problem? What is it? Will you commit today to avoid laziness? God is patient! Are you?

APPLICATION

What are your faults? How do they affect the outward expression of your love for God?
How has God dealt with your faults? Are you working with Him to become entirely His?
Finish this prayer: "Lord, you've been so patient in sanding down my rough edges. Lately you have been . . ."

◌◌◌ AUGUST 1 ◌◌◌
LEARNING ABOUT HIS WAYS

Are you a Christian busybody?
Your activity blocks God's productivity.

BACKGROUND Nine years after *Utmost* first appeared, Biddy Chambers took forty-four of the readings and put them into a smaller book. The focus of this book was the missionary call. Today's lesson was among those chosen for this book, *Called of God*.

Have you ever felt called into a missionary life? Oswald Chambers stressed the importance of being sure of one's call. He felt the mission field was littered with the casualties of spiritual warfare. In 1907, he wrote, "Our training for both home and foreign work is all too slight." From the very first day of the Bible Training College in 1911, his goal was to uproot "missionary ignorance," which he said had "at its heart laziness or a mistaken notion that the Holy Ghost puts a premium on ignorance." Today's lesson is part of his efforts to train us for when God calls.

SCRIPTURAL CONTEXT Chambers' message is divided into three parts, each with its own theme verse. First, Matthew 11:1 says that Jesus asks us to physically leave so He can teach those who are left behind. Second, Luke 9:33 tells us not to keep talking when God is trying to say something. Third, Luke 24:49 shows how God wants us to wait on Him, not run ahead of His timing.

Which of these verses applies most to your situation? If you have the Updated Edition, did you read the verses in Psalm 37 that its editor, Jim Reimann, suggested? How do they connect to the third section?

WHAT'S THE DEVOTIONAL SAYING? Have you ever wondered what Paul meant by "busybodies" in 2 Thessalonians 3:11 and 1 Timothy 5:13? In English, this word comes from "busy" (as in the old sense of "meddling"). For Paul, it was from two words: "all around" and "work." Today's lesson implies that we meddle into God's affairs when we "work all around" and go where He says is off-limits.

Let's review what God says is off-limits: Anywhere He tells us not to be, anything He tells us not to teach, and anytime He tells us to wait. Has He asked you to leave, to stop teaching, or to wait? Listen to Him, or you will be blocking what He wants to do.

APPLICATION

Has God ever asked you to leave/wait? Did you? What was your attitude/outcome?

What things do you tell other people to do? What things does God want you to do? Will you do them?

Finish this prayer: "God, I don't listen to you enough. Please help as I write down what I hear you saying . . ."

⟿ AUGUST 2 ⟿
THE TEACHING OF ADVERSITY

Evading strain?
Embrace it, and you will overcome!

BACKGROUND "God does not give us overcoming life: He gives us life as we overcome." So says today's devotional. This was certainly true for Biddy Chambers. After Oswald died, Biddy found a letter that Oswald had written to his former students. Biddy decided to send it out as a New Year's letter to his students who were now scattered all over the globe. This 250-word letter was her first effort after his death to bring Oswald's messages to the world. From that moment, publishing Oswald's words became her life's work.

Do you face a situation that must be overcome? Take the first step, and God will give you overcoming life!

SCRIPTURAL CONTEXT Back on April 4, we saw today's theme verse in the context of "spiritual grit." Today Chambers complements John 16:33 with quotes from Psalm 91:1–10 and Revelation 2:7. Read these three chapters looking for descriptions of overcoming and examples of God's protection.

Are you trampling any "lions and cobras"? Do you feel God feeding you from the "tree of life"? Buck up your resolve today and be an overcomer!

WHAT'S THE DEVOTIONAL SAYING? Today is the final lesson in the six-part "Discipline of . . ." series. The main point is that Christians should expect to face trouble. If we don't realize this, we will whine and complain *more* than we did before we were Christians because we think God promises to take us out of our troubles.

If you read the Classic Edition exclusively, you will miss out on a wonderful paraphrase of Chambers' final sentence: "a saint can 'be of good cheer' even when seemingly defeated by adversities, because victory is absurdly impossible to everyone, except God." Do you believe this? Ask God to increase your faith!

APPLICATION

Did you have a typical view of Christianity? Until when? Were you delivered *in* trials?

How can you be certain of adversity but still be unafraid? Are you able to do this? How so?

Finish this prayer: "Father, there is so much strain on my life right now. I want to embrace the strain by . . ."

◠◡◠ AUGUST 3 ◠◡◠
THE BIG COMPELLING OF GOD

Our efforts merely frame God's ultimate purposes.

➤

BACKGROUND On March 18, 1917, Oswald Chambers held the Sunday evening service in the El-Zaytoun YMCA hut and spoke on "The Big Compelling of God." For the next three days we get to read the same sermon, edited by Biddy's careful hands.

What are your goals (see July 28, *Utmost*)? Today, we see how our goals, and even the vision God gives us for our life, are nothing compared to God's goals. Will you follow God even though you don't understand His plans?

SCRIPTURAL CONTEXT The Synoptic Gospels (Matthew, Mark, and Luke) all record three times when Jesus predicts His death. The first two straddle the transfiguration. The third is today's theme verse and occurs just before Jesus goes to Jerusalem to die. As Chambers says, Jerusalem represents the place where Jesus fully accomplished God's will. When have you accomplished His will and not your own plans?

Chambers also quotes from John 5:30, Luke 9:51, and John 15:16. Who was Jesus addressing

in the two verses from John? Why did it take so long (ten chapters later) for Jesus to get to Jerusalem if he "steadfastly set His face" to go there? Have you ever shown long-term commitment to do God's will?

WHAT'S THE DEVOTIONAL SAYING? Chambers begins by showing us Jesus' example of putting God's will first. In the second paragraph, he contrasts our typical way of pursuing our own goals with the way God wants us to pursue His goals. This section demonstrates that Chambers understood clearly that it is all by God's grace—we don't *decide* to be Christians.

Does it seem like God is aiming at the wrong thing? Is His plan getting more and more vague? It's normal to feel that way! Trust that He has everything under control, and enter into *His* great purpose.

APPLICATION

What are your goals? Has God called you to a special task? What lies beyond that task?
How good are you at seeking God's will? How can you "set your face" to do it today?
Finish this prayer: "Jesus, I want to be like you. With your help I can steadfastly do God's will today by . . ."

AUGUST 4
THE BRAVE COMPANIONSHIP OF GOD

God is brave enough to be our friend—once we realize we are of no use to him.

◄ ►

BACKGROUND Today we continue the edited version of Oswald Chambers' 1917 sermon. The original title was "With God at the Front." Many of the soldiers at the Imperial School of Instruction (see April 30, *Companion*) had been to the war front and could imagine what it would be like to have God with them there.

Does your life feel like a war zone? Would you like God to be with you in the trenches? The only way to have God with you is to be with *Him* and to continually maintain your relationship. Today's lesson puts all that in perspective.

SCRIPTURAL CONTEXT Yesterday we examined Luke 18:31. Look at it again today. What else do you notice? Can you relate to verse 34?

Chambers also references 1 Corinthians 1:26–31. Do you see yourself as weak, lowly, foolish, and despised? Why or why not?

WHAT'S THE DEVOTIONAL SAYING? When Jesus walked the earth, He chose twelve men to be His apostles. We know that some, like Peter, were already aware to some extent of their sinfulness (see Luke 5:8). Now that Jesus is at His Father's right hand, He still chooses people to follow Him. The only requirement is that we let Him bring us to the end of our self-sufficiency.

Has God brought you to the end of thinking you can accomplish anything? Have you realized that the only cause we work for isn't our cause at all? We can't even know it, since it is God's and far, far above our understanding.

So, where *should* our focus be? Today's lesson says it well: "The main thing about Christianity is . . . the relationship we maintain. . . . That is all God asks us to look after." Defend that relationship at all costs!

APPLICATION

What are your strengths? Can you acknowledge them and still see your total poverty?

How is your relationship with God? Why is it always under attack? What can you do?

Finish this prayer: "Lord, I've been serving my own purposes, but I want to serve your purposes, which . . ."

⟁ AUGUST 5 ⟁
THE BEWILDERING CALL OF GOD

What are your goals?
Worrying about them keeps you from God.

◄

BACKGROUND Today ends our three-day series about God's goals versus our goals. The main point has been that our work is only "scaffolding" (see August 3, *Utmost*) around God's larger purposes. Today's lesson develops this theme, reminding us that we can't understand God's purposes and that they may seem a "disaster" to us.

Is your work like scaffolding for God's purposes? Has God's call seemed like an utter disaster to you? Today's lesson urges us to heed God's call despite all appearances.

SCRIPTURAL CONTEXT Besides the theme verse, which today includes verse 34, the only other quotation that Oswald Chambers uses is from Shakespeare's *Hamlet:* "There's a divinity that shapes our ends" (Act 5, Scene 2). Does Hamlet agree with the Bible in this? What Bible verse says the same thing?

Do you feel as the disciples did in Luke 18:34? Why are God's ways so hard for us to understand? Is it so that we have no choice but to trust His understanding and not our own?

WHAT'S THE DEVOTIONAL SAYING? Today's three paragraphs walk us through a good summary of what we've learned these past three days. First, God's plans seem like disaster, even though they are a triumph. Second, we can't understand God's plans; our job is to trust that God knows what He's doing. Third, once we trust that God has it under control, our life gets simple and has the "leisureliness" of a child.

Is your life too hectic? Instead of focusing your efforts on streamlining and being more efficient, spend your energy on trusting God. It's hard work, but the reward is a more relaxed pace of life!

APPLICATION

Why was Jesus' "failure" a triumph from God's view? Have you had such "failures"?

What has God called you to? How do you know? Have you tried to explain it to others?

Finish this prayer: "Lord, I always ask you why you allow things, but I want to be your relaxed child by . . ."

THE CROSS IN PRAYER

Did you pray? Didn't get an answer?
God always answers—to draw us close.

➤

BACKGROUND Today begins a new series, this time on prayer. For the next four days we will look at how prayer relates to the cross, God's house, His honor, and His hearing. If your prayer life is floundering, this series will give you a boost.

Do you feel too busy to pray? Here's how Oswald Chambers' biographer David McCasland (see January 19, *Companion*) described Chambers' reaction to increased busyness: "In the face of increasing demands on his time and energy [in Egypt], Chambers stringently maintained his early mornings alone with God. A double-fly bell tent pitched outside the bungalow gave him an open-air study for daily Bible reading and prayer. By 6 a.m., he was in the tent awaiting the sunrise." What a great example! Will *you* do that too?

SCRIPTURAL CONTEXT On May 29, we had the same theme verse and a similar main point: The purpose of prayer is to increase our intimacy with God. As you read John 16 again, what message do you hear Jesus telling you? Is it surprising that He doesn't pray to God for us? Doesn't He intercede for us (Romans 8:34 and Hebrews 7:25)? How can we understand these verses?

Chambers also quotes Matthew 6:8. Do you like his explanation of why we still need to ask? Is there another explanation?

WHAT'S THE DEVOTIONAL SAYING? On January 4, we saw that hundreds of *Utmost* readers on Kindle had highlighted three sentences at the end of the first paragraph that they found helpful. Are you curious which day has the *most* highlights? As of this writing, the winner is today! (Though the top spot seems to change weekly.) Interestingly, the most highlighted section in the Updated and Classic Editions are different. The Updated Edition has over five hundred highlights at "The point of prayer is not to get answers from God, but to have perfect and complete oneness with Him." The Classic Edition has more than seventy at "We are not here to prove God answers prayer; we are here to be living monuments of God's grace." Both of these sentences nicely summarize today's main point: Getting God to say "yes" is less important than getting *to* Him.

Do your prayers bring you closer to God? If not, keep praying! Jesus' prayer life must become yours.

APPLICATION
What is your goal in prayer? Do you get unexpected answers? Is it irritating? Why?
Have you tried to prove that God answers prayer? How could you be God's trophy of grace?
Finish this prayer: "Jesus, I want to get into your cross and identify with you as I pray. I'm asking you . . ."

PRAYER IN THE FATHER'S HOUSE

Jesus always talked to God; and He still does, if we let Him.

◄　►

BACKGROUND Jesus' childhood intrigues us. How could Jesus, who is God made flesh, have "learned obedience" (Hebrews 5:8)? Did He always know He was God? F. LaGard Smith, in his must-read work *The Daily Devotional Bible*, speculates that Jesus realized His divinity in today's theme verse. If that's true, then His question to His parents takes on new meaning: "Did not *you* [of all people] know [what I have just now finally realized] that I must be in My Father's house?"

Whatever the truth about today's theme verse, Oswald Chambers' point about Jesus' childhood being an eternal fact is profound. It also helps us prepare our hearts as we come to God in prayer as His children.

SCRIPTURAL CONTEXT Have you ever sung the song suggesting that one day in God's house is better than thousands spent somewhere else? Read the basis for that song in Psalm 84:10. How did the psalmist feel about God's house? Do you feel this same childlike wonder when you pray?

In today's lesson and elsewhere in his *Complete Works*, Chambers quotes Luke 2:49 to show that Jesus had childlike, innocent wonder about His Father. If He, though He was God, had wonder, we should all the more!

WHAT'S THE DEVOTIONAL SAYING? Yesterday's lesson focused on how we gain intimacy with God through prayer. Today points out that the ordinary moments in daily life also draw us closer to God. In both cases, we can break the closeness. In prayer, we break the closeness by fretting over "unanswered" prayer. In daily life, we break it by complaining about our circumstances. Chambers reminds us that we go through circumstances *because* of our relationship to God.

Look back at what we learned on May 3 and 4 about intercession. We intercede with vital, living power because of Jesus' vicarious intercession for us. Yesterday and today, we learned the same thing: We can pray and walk through daily life *because* Jesus' life is living in us. Thank Jesus that He gave you His life by paying the ultimate price!

APPLICATION

How is Christ eternally like a child? Is He this way in your life? How does God order you?

What gets you praying? Do you continually talk to God? How can you do this more?

Finish this prayer: "Jesus, you are God's perfect Child; and since you're in me, I can be His child too as I . . ."

It's time to let Jesus do the Father's business in you.

BACKGROUND From the age of fifteen until he was twenty-one years old, Oswald Chambers lived in London. He summed up his view of this bustling city in a poem he wrote the year before he left for Edinburgh (see February 2, *Companion*). The first verse reads:

> *Busy, driving, rushing Londoners,*
> *Driven, palefaced, wiry blunderers,*
> *Striving ever,*
> *Praying never,*
> *Busy, driving, rushing Londoners.*

Today's lesson discusses "quiet holy communion" with God. This is yet another facet of prayer—being quiet before God. Oh, how we need that today!

SCRIPTURAL CONTEXT Here at the beginning of August, we are a long way from Christmas. Today's theme verse, however, brings back memories of Advent Scripture readings, church pageants, and the mother of Jesus, who, though young, pregnant, and unwed, filled her role in history so bravely and so well.

What other verses does Chambers quote? How do these help us apply the main point (to let Christ's life shine out of ours so we can have quiet fellowship with God)?

WHAT'S THE DEVOTIONAL SAYING? In the first paragraph, Chambers compares our life to that of Mary and of Jesus (when he was twelve years old). The miracle that forms Christ's life in our lives is no less of a miracle than when He became flesh inside Mary. And we should rebuke our common sense the way young Jesus rebuked His parents for not knowing that He needed to do God's business.

The second paragraph warns us of the kind of clamor Chambers saw in London more than one hundred years ago. We need to be simple so Christ can be formed in our lives.

Finally, Chambers holds up the example of mature Christians ("God's ripest saints" in the Classic Edition). Are you like them in any way? Are you willing to be filled with suffering? Whatever suffering is in your path, embrace it without dictating your demands to God!

APPLICATION

Are you exhibiting Christ's innocence, simplicity, and oneness—or dictating demands?
What is left to "fill up" in you? How can you allow Christ to minister through you more?
Finish this prayer: "Son of God, I get so busy and push you away, which is like putting you to death. Right now I . . ."

AUGUST 9
PRAYER IN THE FATHER'S HEARING

Want your prayers heard?
If Jesus prays, they will be!

◄

BACKGROUND Today ends our four-day series on prayer. What have we learned so far? First, we learned that prayer mainly helps us be closer to God. Second, we saw that the daily moments of life are part of prayer. Next, we looked at how prayer is being quiet before God. Today, we will see that prayer is about letting Christ, who lives in us, talk to His Father the way He did when He was on earth.

How did Jesus talk to God? We know that He woke up to pray "before it was light" (Mark 1:35). He spent the night praying (Luke 6:12). And He prayed in His disciples' presence (Luke 9:18). But none of the mechanics of Jesus' prayers are as important as the oneness He had with His Father—a oneness He offers to us.

SCRIPTURAL CONTEXT Oswald Chambers refers to at least five verses today: John 11:41, Galatians 4:19, 1 Corinthians 6:19, John 16:26, and 2 Corinthians 4:11. Find something about each verse that you haven't seen before.

Why did Jesus say what He did in John 11:41? If the Galatians weren't letting Christ be formed in them, what *were* they doing (see verse 21)? Where did the Corinthians go when they practiced immorality? In John 16:26, was Jesus talking about Pentecost? How will you be "given over to death" today?

WHAT'S THE DEVOTIONAL SAYING? Chambers asks five pointed questions. First, are you letting Christ have a chance to shine from your life? Second, can anyone see that you have Christ's simplicity? Third, is your reaction to daily circumstances like one of Jesus' prayers to His Father? Fourth, is your life a "strut," where you parade around as if you were superior? Finally, do you completely depend on Jesus?

These questions can help you work out the salvation God worked in you. Remember: It is *God* who allows you to will and accomplish all of His good purposes.

APPLICATION
What actions exhibit Christ working in you? What would let Him influence you more?
Have you exhibited spiritual pride or "forceful" common sense? What prevents these?
Finish this prayer: "God, I want to worship you in spirit and truth. Please transform my abilities so they . . ."

THE HOLY SUFFERING OF THE SAINT

Jesus didn't want human sympathy, nor should we!

BACKGROUND When Gertrude Hobbs (Biddy) was young, her goal was to become the secretary to the prime minister. She left school so her widowed mother could focus on paying tuition for her older brother and sister. She taught herself typing and shorthand. She worked at two different jobs in London before setting sail for New York, where her friend said secretarial work was plentiful. It was on that voyage that she and Oswald Chambers spent time together and fell in love.

Did Biddy regret having to quit school? Might she have questioned why God put her in that situation? Today's lesson teaches that God puts His people wherever it glorifies Him most. Biddy's lack of formal schooling resulted in her learning shorthand and later transcribing what we read today—all to God's glory!

SCRIPTURAL CONTEXT As we discussed on June 21, 1 Peter is a book for suffering Christians. Today's theme verse ends a two-chapter treatise on godly living and suffering. How does this verse sum up all that Peter was trying to say? How does it sum up today's lesson?

Chambers mentions Matthew 16:21–23 and Luke 15:10. The connection to Matthew 16 is clear: Jesus rebuked Peter's sympathy, and we should rebuke human sympathy in the same way. But the Luke reference is a bit less clear. Chambers says that this description of the angels rejoicing over the repentant sinner shows that Jesus accepted sympathy from angels. Do you agree?

WHAT'S THE DEVOTIONAL SAYING? Chambers asks us to notice "God's <u>unutterable</u> waste of His saints." This is such a vivid description of how we often feel! Do you feel as if God is wasting your life? Today's lesson ends by reminding us that God's glory is the ultimate measure of what is wasted and what is not.

The first two paragraphs teach us other lessons about suffering. First, we learn that we shouldn't choose suffering just for suffering's sake. We should suffer only if it comes from following God's will. Second, we see how Jesus refused human sympathy. Chambers urges us to do the same. Have you been accepting or giving out sympathy? Be careful! Compassion is good, but don't block God's plans.

[handwritten margin note: so great to describe]

APPLICATION

Have you followed God's will into suffering? Have you interfered with God's lessons?
Who has strengthened you the most? How? Have you been hindered by sympathy?
Finish this prayer: "Lord, I need to stop my self-pitying and start blooming where you plant me. I need to . . ."

AUGUST 11
THIS EXPERIENCE MUST COME

Have your mentors left you?
Make them proud by doing what they taught you!

BACKGROUND When might Oswald Chambers have preached the original sermon that became today's lesson? Was it right after Harris Reader died (see April 22, *Companion*) or right before he left his students to go to Egypt? The message applies in either case: When God inevitably takes away our teachers, we must do the things we learned from them.

Has God taken away any of your mentors? How are you faithful to the things you are learning from others? Today's lesson will help you stay true to what you've learned.

SCRIPTURAL CONTEXT Chambers (or Biddy) often used theme verses without tying in the larger context. But today, the whole lesson is about 2 Kings 2:11–25. What do you notice about this story? Would you have wanted to look for Elijah? What if the jeering youths were your friends? How would you feel?

In the original sermon, Chambers linked the three verses (14, 15, and 23) to your seal, sin, and sacrament. Can you see those connections?

WHAT'S THE DEVOTIONAL SAYING? In 2 Kings 2, God sends Elijah to Bethel, to Jericho, and then to the Jordan River. When Elijah leaves, Elisha retraces this route. What happens at each location? Chambers uses this route to teach us three lessons about the experience of losing a mentor. First, we must do alone the things we used to do with our mentor. Second, we must ignore the "clamour of the educated prophets," as Chambers put it in the original sermon, and trust in God. Third, we come to our wits' end and God makes our life a sacrament. As Chambers described it: "The abiding presence of God will come through the simple elements of your life."

Will you do what you've learned from your teachers to do? Will you ignore educated prophets and cling to God? Will you let God make your everyday life a sacrament? Doing these things is the best and only way to honor any dear mentors God has removed from your life.

APPLICATION

Who have been your Elijahs? Have they left? Was that best? How did you respond?

When have you been separated from fellowship? From mentoring? At your wits' end?

Finish this prayer: "God of Elisha, you hold me in the palm of your hand. Please help me to trust you as . . ."

⁖ AUGUST 12 ⁖
THE THEOLOGY OF RESTING IN GOD

Want to make God smile?
Be confident in His power!

BACKGROUND How can we give God joy? On January 21, we were encouraged to cheer and gladden God's heart. Today's lesson, which comes from a longer sermon by the same title, gives a clear description of how we bless God. First, we are filled with the Holy Spirit (Luke 11:13). Then, as God works in us, we work out our salvation and sanctification (Philippians 2:12–13) and convert these precious gifts into an attitude of resting in God. This rest means oneness with God and results in two things: our blamelessness and God's joy.

Have you blessed God in this way? It's obviously not a one-time thing. You must constantly work out your salvation, convert it into rest, and reap the reward of being a blameless blessing to God.

SCRIPTURAL CONTEXT

On July 28 we looked at the other time when Jesus calmed a storm. How do the two times differ? Which came first? Did the disciples get less fearful after the first time?

Imagine being the disciples. They kept missing opportunities to delight their Master's heart the way the centurion did in Luke 7:9. Have you felt this stinging pang?

WHAT'S THE DEVOTIONAL SAYING?

As we walk through today's four paragraphs, we get a clear picture of the kind of rest Oswald Chambers urges us to cultivate. First, it is a responsible rest: We ought to be the bravest in any crisis. Second, it is a joy-producing rest, since it blesses God's heart. Third, it is confident rest and is best revealed in crisis. Finally, it is oneness with God—the kind of rest that gives us complete blamelessness.

Will you cultivate rest today? Chambers makes the process crystal clear. Not all parts of the process are in your control. But will you do the parts that are your responsibility? God expects nothing less. And He will send crises to show you how you are doing with the responsibility He has given you.

APPLICATION

When have you been in crisis? How did you respond? Did you feel like an unbeliever?

Is God's heart important to you? What do you need to do—*right now*—to give Him joy?

Finish this prayer: "God, I bounce from one crisis to another. Please help me get ready for the next one by . . ."

"DO NOT QUENCH THE SPIRIT"

Is the Spirit muffled by your disobedience?
Cut off what mutes His voice!

➤

BACKGROUND On June 3, we discussed what it means for God to "check" us (Updated Edition: sense of restraint, conviction, or warning). Oswald Chambers uses this expression throughout *Utmost*, starting on March 18, to explain how the Holy Spirit guides our life.

Have you learned to be more sensitive to the Spirit's leading? Today and tomorrow we will learn how to better respond to the Spirit and to avoid grieving Him.

SCRIPTURAL CONTEXT For this two-day series on the Spirit's leading, Chambers picks interesting theme verses. Today's verse forbids quenching the Spirit. What does that mean? Chambers says it's when we don't heed the "checks" He gives us. Do you get that meaning from the context of 1 Thessalonians 5? What else might it mean?

"Still small voice" is a fairly common expression that comes from 1 Kings 19:12. How does this "voice" relate to the Spirit's "checks"? Chambers also mentions walking in the light. What verses discuss this (see January 9, *Com-*panion)? Are you refusing to walk in the light while distracting yourself with past spiritual experiences?

WHAT'S THE DEVOTIONAL SAYING? Let's look at what each paragraph says about the Holy Spirit. First, we must live in oneness with God if we want to hear the Spirit, since His voice is quiet. Second, we must not rest on our laurels when we ought to be obeying. Like the servant in Luke 17:7, we don't dwell on past achievements. They're the background for our present obedience. Finally, our best chance to give our utmost to God is the *first* time we face a God-given crisis (see January 1, *Utmost*). If we fail to choose God that first time, each subsequent time it will be harder.

How sobering to realize that the Spirit speaks quietly; we often miss Him because we'd rather daydream about our past successes; and our best shot is our first one. Keep these three things in mind as you face the day. Chances are the Holy Spirit is trying to lead you right now!

APPLICATION

Have you told others the story of your testimony? Do you refer more to the past or the present? Why?

What are you attached to? Has God sent you a crisis to help free you? What happened?

Finish this prayer: "Holy Spirit, I'm glad your voice is so soft that I have to change my life to hear it. I . . ."

AUGUST 14
"THE DISCIPLINE OF THE LORD"

Are things not going well for you?
Don't pout. Let God have His way in you.

◄

BACKGROUND Today we finish the two-day series on how the Holy Spirit leads. Has He been leading you? Did you stop something or try doing something based on what you thought He said or how He "checked" you?

Oswald Chambers begins today's lesson with a discussion about our sanctification. He says that initially our sanctification is shallow: We see only a "shadow" of the life God wants us to live. Because of our shallow view of what God wants for us, we miss God's voice. Even worse, when God speaks, His words seem different from the inferior shadow of His plan that we are so used to seeing. As a result, we attribute His voice to Satan!

SCRIPTURAL CONTEXT Chambers discusses both parts of today's verse. Found in Hebrews 12:5, it was originally a poetic couplet from Proverbs 3. What does Chambers say about the first part ("do not despise . . .")? What about the second part ("nor faint . . .")?

Yesterday we didn't get to see much of the theme verse's context. Today Chambers says that God will sanctify wholly, which is Paul's benediction in 1 Thessalonians 5:23. Does this prove that grieving the Holy Spirit means not heeding His "checks," as we saw yesterday?

WHAT'S THE DEVOTIONAL SAYING? In four paragraphs, Chambers takes us through deep truths about God's discipline. First, he repeats yesterday's lesson about how we grieve the Holy Spirit by not listening when He checks. Second, he reminds us that if we are not yet ready, God doesn't tell us when something is wrong in our lives. But as soon as He does, we need to obey! Third, Chambers chastises us for having less grit spiritually than we have for other things. Finally, he says that at all costs we must want God to sanctify us.

Are you ready for God's sanctifying discipline to change you at any cost? Demonstrate your spiritual grit today!

APPLICATION
How do despising discipline and being discouraged by it differ? How do you respond?
Do you mistake God's warning for something else, or do you give up trying to be sanctified?
Finish this prayer: "Father, please grip me and make me worthy—no matter what it takes; for example . . ."

ꙮ AUGUST 15 ꙮ
THE EVIDENCE OF THE NEW BIRTH

Born into God's family?
If so, you'll stop sinning and know Him firsthand.

BACKGROUND Today Oswald Chambers uses the curious expression "rag rights." George MacDonald (see April 15 in *Companion* for more about MacDonald) coined this phrase in his daily devotional *The Diary of an Old Soul*. MacDonald had a big effect, not only on Chambers, but also on J. R. R. Tolkien, C. S. Lewis, and Madeleine L'Engle. All of Mac-Donald's works are helpful. (*The Wise Woman* is particularly good.) The poem below gives a taste of his writing and introduces the phrase "rag rights":

Lord, I have fallen again—a human clod!
Selfish I was, and heedless to offend;
Stood on my rights.
Thy own child would not send
Away his shreds of nothing for the whole God!
Wretched, to thee who savest, low I bend:
Give me the power to let my rag-rights go
In the great wind that from thy gulf doth blow.

SCRIPTURAL CONTEXT Chambers focuses on the theme verse (John 3:7) by using four other verses from the pen of the apostle John. First, Chambers answers Nicodemus' question in John 3:4. Second, Chambers uses John 1:12 to show that we must receive our knowledge

from God, not just from humans. Third, he returns to John 3 and says that we see God's kingdom if we are born again. Finally, he looks at what 1 John 3:9 means by "does not sin."

Can you find evidence of new birth in your life? Let's look specifically at four signs that we are born again.

WHAT'S THE DEVOTIONAL SAYING?
Our first signs of new birth are conscious repentance, unconscious holiness, and willingness to see our righteous deeds as "filthy rags" (Isaiah 64:6). Second, we have knowledge that is not just regurgitated from what we heard someone say. Third, we stop seeking proof that God is working because we can see His work. Fourth, we stop sinning.

This fourth sign seems far-fetched. How can we really stop sinning? When discussing Christians who do things based on their understanding, not God's, Chambers said "there is no sin in it" (February 28, *Utmost*). Perhaps he had a narrower definition of sin than we do. Still, isn't it time we stopped *trying* and started *not* sinning? Read 1 John 3 again and ask God to help you claim the power not to sin. You don't *need* to sin, so why keep sinning?

APPLICATION
Keeping in mind today's lesson, what's your proof of new birth? Are you Jesus' personal friend? Read John 3. Is Nicodemus sign-seeking or perceiving God's rule? (Notice verses 2 and 12.)
Finish this prayer: "Almighty God, I know I have the power to stop sinning, but I want to actually *stop*. Please help . . ."

DOES HE KNOW ME . . . ?

It's not what you know or even who you know; it's Who knows you!

BACKGROUND Today Oswald Chambers looks poignantly at how deeply Jesus knew His three disciples Mary Magdalene, Thomas, and Peter. Their stories are our stories. We do well to see how lovingly their Master treated them despite their failures.

Who knows you? How would they treat you if you misunderstood, doubted, or denied them? Do you believe Jesus will treat you kindly in these situations? He really will!

SCRIPTURAL CONTEXT Read John 20 and 21. Picture Jesus as He speaks to each person. Is He angry, disappointed, or smiling?

Now do some background reading. What do you learn about Mary in Luke 8, Thomas in John 11, and Peter in Matthew 26? Can you identify with any of their struggles?

WHAT'S THE DEVOTIONAL SAYING Today, Chambers teaches us how Jesus loved three of His friends. First, He loved Mary, whose life is a great example of putting Jesus, not doctrine, first. But even though Mary put Him first, she still didn't recognize Jesus until He spoke. Has He spoken to you? Ask Him to remind you of your personal history with Him.

Second, He loved Thomas. Would you have humored Thomas' requests? Wouldn't it have been better to put him in his place? But Jesus welcomed him to touch His wounds, even the place where the spear had pierced, which Thomas hadn't asked to touch. What a loving Savior!

Finally, Jesus loved Peter, the man who denied ever knowing Him. Isn't it interesting that Jesus had to privately restore Peter before the public scene we read about in John 21? Get with Jesus privately and confess your selfishness to Him. He will treat you more lovingly than you could ever imagine!

APPLICATION

When have you misunderstood or doubted Jesus? How did He make himself known?

In what little ways have you denied Jesus among your peers? How were you restored?

Finish this prayer: "Jesus, it's easy for me to let my knowledge of doctrine obscure my knowledge of you . . ."

ARE YOU DISCOURAGED IN DEVOTION?

Despair takes us right ... Once lost ... , it's gone!

BACKGROUND Today we begin a two-day series on the rich young ruler. Just as in yesterday's lesson, we can learn from examples of how Jesus loved others.

In his original talk, Oswald Chambers used the two parts of Luke 18:23 as his outline. Today's lesson comes from the section "And when he heard this . . ." Tomorrow's source material comes from the phrase "he was very sorrowful, for he was very rich." Are you sad about something you know God has said? Look at today's lesson. It will encourage you: There is hope ahead!

SCRIPTURAL CONTEXT Read Luke 18:18–30. What stands out to you? Is it how Jesus rebukes the man's use of the word *good*? Is it Peter's proclamation? Chambers focuses on verse 23 and the fact that the man "heard" what Jesus said.

When have you heard Jesus? When have you seen a trouble coming and not heard, thus preventing God's Word from bearing fruit? Commit to obeying no matter how hard His sayings are.

WHAT'S THE DEVOTIONAL SAYING? Chambers says God's "living word" always bears fruit. If, in abandoned devotion, you have deep despair, know that God's Word will not return void. Eventually, you will make up your mind to be devoted to Him in whatever it was He told you to do.

But why wait? Decide today to do what He wants you to do. It might be something small. But as we've learned in *Utmost,* you won't move forward until you obey, in abandoned devotion, whatever God wants.

APPLICATION
When has God said something difficult to you? Did you listen? Were you discouraged?

How might you be preventing God's Word from bearing fruit in you? What will you do?

Finish this prayer: "Jesus, I've ignored you. Thank you for not rubbing it in my face as I finally come to . . ."

HAVE YOU EVER BEEN SPEECHLESS WITH SORROW?

Despair is the first step in giving up our preconceived ideas and self-love.

◄

BACKGROUND How many sermons have you heard about the rich young ruler? Some pastors speculate that this man eventually became a Christian. But all we know is what Oswald Chambers points out today—that this young man left Jesus completely broken, without a word to say in his own defense.

Chambers tells us that being broken like the rich young ruler is a first step in becoming abandoned to Jesus. Have you felt this kind of sorrow? What happened as a result?

SCRIPTURAL CONTEXT Can you think of anyone else in the Bible whose sorrow over God's command led to repentance? Jonah? The Corinthians? The son in Matthew 21:29? It's a rare occurrence, but see if you can track down other examples that give you a picture of sorrow that leads to repentance.

WHAT'S THE DEVOTIONAL SAYING? "Undress yourself . . . until you are a mere conscious human being." Does this sentence confuse you? Does the Updated Edition help? On July 22, Chambers said a similar thing: "Am I willing to reduce myself simply to 'me,' determinedly to strip myself of all my friends think of me, of all I think of myself, and to hand that simple naked self over to God?"

You face the same decision the rich young ruler faced. How long will you walk away sorrowful? God wants your utmost for His highest. He wants you to give everything "good" away and trust only in Him. Will you do that today?

APPLICATION

When have you been the most speechless with sorrow? Did you yield to God? How so?

How are you more devoted to what Jesus wants than to Jesus himself? Can you change?

Finish this prayer: "Lord, sometimes I get so aware of my poverty that I lose sight of being your disciple . . ."

SELF-AWARENESS

Is introspection sapping your energy?
Come to Christ and be refreshed!

➤

BACKGROUND Today begins a two-day series on self-consciousness, which is the main disturber of our spiritual peace. Oswald Chambers uses the word *self-consciousness* differently from how we do. We think of self-conscious shyness. But he means someone who obsesses over his or her own spiritual temperature.

Are you self-conscious in the way Chambers means? This two-part series helps you come to Jesus to have Him cure your overactive self-obsession.

SCRIPTURAL CONTEXT The theme verse for today and tomorrow is one we've heard many times. But look at the context: Jesus has just sent out the Twelve and then followed them to preach where they had prepared the way. Many "wise and learned" rejected Him, but some "little children" accepted Him. For this, Jesus thanked His Father (as He did later, when the seventy-two returned; Luke 10:21). It was right after thanking God that He spoke today's theme verse.

Are you "wise and learned," or more like a child? Jesus' invitation to "come" is for those who are weary and heavy laden, and for those who are like little children. Ask God to give you a childlike heart today.

WHAT'S THE DEVOTIONAL SAYING?
Oneness with God is the biggest theme in all of *Utmost*. Unity with God is the only way we can give our utmost for His highest. Today we learn how introspection breaks our childlike oneness with our Savior. Have circumstances or nervousness made you overly self-aware?

The only cure for this kind of self-consciousness is to come to God and ask Him for Christ-awareness. Will you humble yourself and ask for this today? He is ready to give you rest!

APPLICATION
How are your friends and circumstances influencing your life of oneness with Jesus?
Have you felt your spiritual growth slowed? How so? What will you do to change this?
Finish this prayer: "Jesus, I need to prioritize my oneness with you above anything else. I'll come to you . . ."

CHRIST-AWARENESS

Feeling misunderstood?
Let it go. God has better things in store for you.

◄

BACKGROUND As we end our two-day series on being too introspective, Oswald Chambers gives us more examples of what leads us into unhealthy introspection. For instance, we get too self-aware when we are hurt by others.

Have you been wronged? How does it affect you? Have you spent mental energy thinking about it? Chambers says our self-pity is satanic. Today's study gives us the warning we need in order to avoid the pity-party trap.

SCRIPTURAL CONTEXT In today's theme verse, another translation for *weary* is "laboring." Jesus is calling both the people who push themselves to labor hard and those who have to work hard because others load them with heavy burdens. Do you fall into either category? Do you push yourself? Do you feel like an ox whose owner piles on more and more for you to pull? Or can you relate to both pictures?

Contrast that picture with an ox that is yoked to SuperOx, the two-horned wonder. SuperOx does all the pulling, and its partner is just along for the ride. That's the image Jesus is trying to give us. He's offering His yoke to us—the one He's still pulling or the one He has made especially light. Either way, it's a big change from the yoke we used to have to pull!

WHAT'S THE DEVOTIONAL SAYING? God's goal for us is that we become "fully-orbed" and have a well-rounded, complete life in Him. On June 29, we saw that God has us cut off things initially but later wants us to regain every good aspect of life so we can be whole in Him. Today and yesterday we see that our worries and self-awareness keep us from the whole life God wants for us. The only way to get it back is to turn to Him at once. Wrestle against self-awareness, but don't use common-sense methods. Wrestle by turning to God over and over for as long as it takes.

Do you want childlike oneness? All your worrying and introspection proves you're not there yet. Turn to God now and ask Him for rest. It's a constant battle to turn to Him, but He wants you to keep fighting!

APPLICATION
Has anything caused your life with Christ to disintegrate? If so, how did you respond?

What are our tasks and God's in developing Christ-awareness? Are you doing enough?

Finish this prayer: "Lord Jesus, in the end it's your job to make me more aware of you, but first I must . . ."

ᕮᕮ AUGUST 21 ᕮᕮ
THE MINISTRY OF THE UNNOTICED

Did you yield to Christ or make a decision for Him?
The two are not the same!

BACKGROUND Today's lesson has its roots in a talk Oswald Chambers gave at his weekly devotional hour. Biddy shortened this talk to ten percent of its original length. It only takes about two minutes to read today's devotional out loud, so the original talk was about twenty minutes. What happened during the other forty minutes of the devotional *hour*? Undoubtedly, Chambers prayed. He might have played hymns on the school's small organ. One thing is certain: For the Bible Training College students, this hour "marked an epoch in their life with God" (see January 1, *Companion*).

Do you have an hour a week during which your heart is brought closer to God? If not, cry out in your poverty to God. As today's lesson says, it is through your poverty that you enter God's kingdom.

SCRIPTURAL CONTEXT When we last read Matthew 5:3–11 on July 25, we learned that the Beatitudes are like dynamite—they detonate when God puts us in the right circumstances. Since that day, have any of them

exploded in your heart? Have circumstances shown just how spiritually poor you are?

Chambers also quotes John 7:38. Where and when did Jesus say this? Who was His audience? Is the Spirit flowing out of you to other people? Or are you examining the flow so much that His touch on your life has gone away?

WHAT'S THE DEVOTIONAL SAYING? Biddy did a heroic job of capturing Chambers' original message while using only a tenth of his words. In three paragraphs, she covers the main points. First, we don't decide for Christ; we yield to Him as the poor, ordinary, unpretentious people we are. Second, we mustn't wonder if we are useful to God. We'll be most useful if we don't think about whether we are or not. Third, we know Jesus is in anything that seems ordinary but somehow inspires.

Are you ordinary-yet-inspiring? That's what God wants you to be. Model your life on those who have influenced you most. They're sure to be ordinary!

APPLICATION

Who influences you most? Are they conscious of influencing you? Are you conscious of influencing others?

What's the difference between deciding and yielding? Which have you done for Christ?

Finish this prayer: "Holy Spirit, please let your living water flow out of me without me being prideful, so . . ."

ᘒᘙᘚ AUGUST 22 ᘒᘙᘚ
"I INDEED . . . BUT HE"

Stop making excuses! They're a sign you won't repent and come to Jesus.

BACKGROUND Today's lesson, which was taken from a much longer sermon, gives us both hope and a warning. Hope springs from the fact that God does the things we can never do ourselves. The warning is that He won't come into our lives if we do not first repent.

Are there things, either good or bad, that are blocking Jesus' way into your life? Let today's lesson motivate you to repent of them and open your heart to God.

SCRIPTURAL CONTEXT When the great Bible teacher R. C. Sproul wanted to stump his students, he would ask, "Who was the greatest Old Testament prophet?" Answer: John the Baptist! Sproul explained that since John lived before the new covenant (testament), he was an Old Testament prophet. He was also the greatest, according to Matthew 11:11.

Today's theme verse is another example of how John was the greatest. Long before anyone else, he realized that Jesus could do what no one else could. John also knew that repentance was the only way to allow Jesus to work. Will you follow in John's steps today?

WHAT'S THE DEVOTIONAL SAYING? Looking at today's three paragraphs (in the Classic Edition) helps us understand this meaty lesson. First, repentance of both "good" and bad things is absolutely essential. It gives you awareness of your helplessness, which opens the door for Jesus to be your help. Second, the only thing you notice when you ask God to fill you with the Spirit (Luke 11:13) is your unworthiness. Third, you must "get to the margin," or as the Updated Edition says, "get to the end of yourself" so God can do *everything*.

Are you letting God do everything? Or is there something in your life you think you can control? The only thing He wants us to do is to work *out* the things He works *in* (Philippians 2:12). He has worked in everything and will continue to work in it as long as we open the door through our repentance. Repent today and let Him continue to work!

APPLICATION

What brings you to the end of yourself, willing to shine light on all your wrongs?

What blocks Jesus' way in you? Do you defend your actions? Or are you repentant?

Finish this prayer: "Lord Jesus Christ, I'm so unworthy, but you are so powerful. Please start your work . . ."

PRAYER—BATTLE IN "THE SECRET PLACE"

Do battle by prayer first; then gather the spoils all day!

BACKGROUND In his *Complete Works,* Oswald Chambers mentions "wool-gathering" twenty times. Where does this strange expression come from? According to the *Dictionary of Animal Words and Phrases*, it comes from the practice of collecting tufts of wool that get caught on twigs as sheep walk by. Not much wool can be collected like that, and you have to move all over the place to get it!

In the same way, our thoughts sometimes move all over the place when we are trying to pray. The way to stop this, according to today's lesson, is to shut the door on our emotions as an act of will and to bring God to mind, recalling who He is. Will you try that today?

SCRIPTURAL CONTEXT Jesus' teaching on prayer is so refreshing! Other rabbis taught their disciples to pray publically with fine-sounding words. Jesus taught by His example of long nights and early mornings in prayer. He gave His disciples the Lord's Prayer as a model, and today's theme verse shows how He taught them about prayer.

What does the theme verse tell us? Have you ever done this literally? Do you think Jesus meant for us to only do it literally? How can we expand the literal meaning in the same way we expand on the Lord's Prayer?

WHAT'S THE DEVOTIONAL SAYING? The opening sentence sums up the lesson: We must pray, not dream! Dreaming is easy. Our thoughts wander from topic to topic. Prayer is hard. We have to continually corral our thoughts by the act of our will.

Contrast the idea of gathering wool with gathering the winnings of a victory. With wool, you wait passively until the sheep walk by. With winnings, you have to do the hard work of defeating the enemy. With wool, you might get enough to make a sweater after months of gathering. With winnings, you can take as many sweaters as your enemies were wearing!

Chambers says that if we go to God in secret, our public life will have His stamp. The "common round" of trivial tasks will have "God" written all over them. Do you want Him written all over your life? Then do the hard work of battling the enemies of distracting ideas and thoughts.

APPLICATION

What makes praying difficult? Does selecting a special place help? What else helps?

When have you doubted God? Why does "the secret place" help us to be sure of Him?

Finish this prayer: "Lord, I open my life completely to you, knowing that you order my steps and mark . . ."

AUGUST 24
THE SPIRITUAL SEARCH

Were your prayers not heard?
Find out why!

BACKGROUND If you were to read the Classic Edition for today, you would notice that Oswald Chambers uses the word *index* in a way we might not understand. "Index" has always meant the pointer finger, and it's come to mean many things that point to something. Today we read, "turn up the index," "look at the index," and the title "The Spiritual Index."

Chambers is telling us that our unanswered prayers *point* to problems in our lives. Have your prayers gone unanswered? What's the reason? Today's lesson may give you some ideas.

SCRIPTURAL CONTEXT Yesterday we saw Jesus' first instructions about prayer in His Sermon on the Mount. Today we look at His return to the topic in Matthew 7. What does He add that we didn't get the first time?

Chambers refers to Matthew 5:45 to show how we think God showers down answers to prayers in the same way He makes rain fall on the righteous and unrighteous. Do you think that? How does our behavior affect prayer (1 Peter 3:7)? Does it affect how God loves us?

WHAT'S THE DEVOTIONAL SAYING?
The second paragraph in the Classic Edition begins with a priceless quote: "We mistake defiance for devotion; arguing with God for abandonment." Does this describe you? When you think you've finally abandoned all to God, could it be that you're just arguing?

Today's lesson is that we must trace unanswered prayers back to the source. Are you willing to search for the reason and correct the problem? Do it now!

APPLICATION
Which answers to prayers haven't you received? Why? Have you argued with God about them?
How are your relationships? Will God answer prayer regardless of your relationships?
Finish this prayer: "Father, you promise I'll receive what I ask for when I'm your child. Please help me . . ."

⌒⌒ AUGUST 25 ⌒⌒
SACRIFICE AND FRIENDSHIP

"Yes . . . but" is no way to follow Jesus. Just dive in!

BACKGROUND On June 16, we looked at part of a talk Oswald Chambers gave in 1916. Today we have the title and theme verse from another section of this talk, but the words are a patchwork from other talks Chambers gave. Once again, Biddy shows herself to be a master seamstress!

Do you wonder what it's like to give your utmost to God in absolute abandon? Biddy has provided a beautiful description in today's study. Read and enjoy!

SCRIPTURAL CONTEXT What kind of friendship does Jesus discuss in John 15? Is it friendship with Him, with one another, or both? Today's lesson follows the same line. Can you find examples in John 15 that match the different parts of today's study? What does Psalm 40:8 tell us about how Jesus was God's friend? What would this look like in your life today?

WHAT'S THE DEVOTIONAL SAYING? Today's lesson in the Classic Edition has a record five paragraphs. Each one teaches us about friendship. First, the fruit of our friendship with Jesus is the feeling of pure joy that we get once we've abandoned to God each detail of our life. Second, once we've abandoned it all, the Holy Spirit in us has a "love passion" for sacrifice. His passion becomes ours, so we joyfully lay down our lives for Jesus. Third, sacrifice alone does nothing. Sacrifice based on friendship with Jesus transforms us. Fourth, our friendships with one another, like our friendship with Jesus, must not be based on our natural taste in personalities and common interests. Finally, our friendship with Jesus is possible only because God puts His life in us. Jesus is God and can only be friends with God. Thankfully, God the Holy Spirit can live in us so we can be friends with Jesus too!

APPLICATION

Have you sacrificed yourself to God? Was it begrudgingly, conditionally, or wholeheartedly?

How do natural love and desires differ? What natural desires hinder your love for God?

Finish this prayer: "Jesus, you sacrificed yourself joyfully to God. If my sacrifice is not that way, it's not . . ."

∞ AUGUST 26 ∞
ARE YOU EVER TROUBLED?

What worries you today?
If you can't seek God now, you've got big problems!

BACKGROUND On Wednesday, May 27, 1914, Oswald Chambers gave the Bible Training College weekly devotional hour. Today we read a shortened version of his talk. No one could have guessed that just over one month from that day, Archduke Ferdinand of Austria would be assassinated and nations would be plunged into war. Who knew that the "waves and billows" Chambers said were painfully disturbing his students would only get far worse?

Are you at peace? If so, is it based on ignorance or on Jesus' peace? If not, would you like peace that surpasses understanding? Today's lesson will help!

SCRIPTURAL CONTEXT John 14 begins, "Let not your hearts be troubled." In today's theme verse, Jesus repeats this admonition. He also promises His peace to us. What else does He promise in this chapter? How would those promises help the disciples in years to come? How do they help you?

Chambers also quotes John 6:63, linking Jesus' peace to the spirit and life that His words are to us. How are "spirit and life" similar to peace? Did Peter have Jesus' peace (verse 68)?

WHAT'S THE DEVOTIONAL SAYING? Is it harsh for Chambers to say that we "deserve what we get"? Yes, harsh but true! We deserve a "barren" life, devoid of peace if we aren't "looking unto Jesus" (Hebrews 12:2).

Looking to Jesus is difficult, especially as "waves and billows" hit us from every side. The first step is to realize that anything besides Christ's peace is false security and ignorance, even if you've turned over all the "boulders of your belief." Then realize that your worrying is obliterating God's power in you. Finally, recognize that Jesus' words are peace. Then open the Bible and look for His peace; don't turn to any other source!

APPLICATION

What is stressing you? How does it affect you? Have your "stones" not given comfort?

How do you seek God's face? What can you do differently? Do you think it will work?

Finish this prayer: "Jesus, you promise the perfect peace you had in the midst of incredible stress. Please . . ."

LIVING YOUR THEOLOGY

Feeling spiritually puny?
Check to see that you're obeying what you know is true.

BACKGROUND Today's lesson once again seems to be a patchwork of Oswald Chambers' talks (or there may have been a talk, now lost, that shared the phrases of other preserved lectures). For example, the last sentence in today's lesson matches one from the talk on "abysses" that we saw on May 5 and 6. Looking at the original talk will show what Chambers meant by "measured by the standard of the atonement" (Updated Edition), since he explains that by *atonement* he means "holiness."

If you measured your physical, moral, and spiritual life by the standard of holiness, how would you fare? Let today's lesson challenge you to give up pretense and really live a holy, sanctified, obedient life.

SCRIPTURAL CONTEXT Have you ever wondered how the "light" in you could be "darkness," as it says in Matthew 6:23? Today's theme verse gives us a clue, as does today's study. Who is the light? How do we walk in Him? What happens when we don't?

Chambers also quotes Matthew 5:20, which we studied on July 24. How can we strive for this level of righteousness without falling into legalism?

WHAT'S THE DEVOTIONAL SAYING? Jesus is the Light of the World. He reveals himself to us in mountaintop experiences. If we don't obey what we learn in those experiences, we won't have the light. So Matthew 6:23 means that God puts light in us, but when we don't obey it, what we learned and what inspired us rots away. When this happens, our "darkness" is even greater than before we received God's light.

Today's study warns us against smugly resting on our laurels when we should be working out in our everyday life what God teaches us. Don't be the "most difficult person to deal with," as described by Chambers in this lesson. Instead, continually strive for a righteousness that exceeds the Pharisees: one with good doing *and* good being (see July 24, *Companion*).

APPLICATION

What visions have you seen on the mountaintops? What are you doing to obey them?
Are you hypocritical in claiming to be sanctified? How are you working out God's truth?
Finish this prayer: "Lord, you've set high standards for me, but I'm capable of reaching them if I'll only . . ."

THE PURPOSE OF PRAYER

Prayer changes you so that you can change things.

BACKGROUND On Thursday, November 4, 1915, and the following year on Monday, November 13, 1916, Oswald Chambers gave lectures on "What's the Good of Prayer?" He could give the same talk each time because the audience of soldiers had completely changed.

The first time Chambers gave this talk he had been in Egypt only eleven days. (On that occasion, four hundred soldiers showed up—a huge change from his YMCA predecessor, who didn't attract more than a handful of people to his daily prayer meeting.)

What a different man he must have appeared when he gave the talk the following year. In the intervening time, he had spent a summer in Suez (see April 30, *Companion*) and had become as accustomed to the blazing heat, maddening flies, and raging sandstorms as the soldiers he served. Though the talk was the same, the prayer life of the man who delivered it may have been dramatically different!

Biddy beautifully summarized Chambers' lessons on prayer. Do your prayers need a boost? Today's devotional will give you just that!

SCRIPTURAL CONTEXT Why did the disciples ask Jesus to teach them to pray? Had any of them been John the Baptist's followers? How does the prayer differ from the one Jesus gave at the Sermon on the Mount? Hadn't they already heard that one before?

John 16:24 and Matthew 18:3 remind us to ask boldly as children do. Have you asked God like this?

WHAT'S THE DEVOTIONAL SAYING?
Chambers' teaching on prayer looks like a paradox: He warns us against seeing prayer as a "means for getting things for ourselves," yet he urges us to ask God for more than we normally do. Which is it? Should we ask for more things, or fewer? We should pray for more things, knowing that the goal isn't to get the things but to have more knowledge of God, which changes our whole disposition (see July 1, *Utmost*).

We don't live on bread alone. What nourishes us? God's Word. Today's lesson teaches us that it actually nourishes our new life, which is Christ's life in us. Are you feeding Christ in you today by prayer?

APPLICATION
When have you really prayed—coming in contact with God? What did you learn?
What keeps you from asking God for things? What can you ask Him for today?
Finish this prayer: "Father, I want to get to know you, starting with asking you for things as your child . . ."

AUGUST 29
THE UNSURPASSED INTIMACY OF TESTED FAITH

Want your faith purified?
It takes conflict to do so!

BACKGROUND "The last great test is death," says Oswald Chambers in today's lesson. He didn't know he would die at 43, but he knew he would die. We all will. How do you think you will do on this final exam? Will your last words be Scripture? Chambers' were from John 14:12: "Greater works than these shall he do, because I go unto my Father." Chambers passed his final test with flying colors and gave Biddy a verse that would comfort her in the dark days after his death.

Today's lesson is about faith. Daily circumstances fly in the face of what we hold by faith to be true. So how do we know what's true? Chambers says our physical eyes deceive us. Faith is true; circumstances are not. But the only way to purify our faith is by going through the circumstances that defy our faith. Are you going through them right now? Take heart and have faith!

SCRIPTURAL CONTEXT The story of Lazarus, which we looked at on February 13, pulls at the heartstrings. Imagine Mary's grief, knowing that Jesus could have saved her brother. And poor Martha keeps trying to be practical and have the "right" answers. What else could she do in the midst of seeing her world turned upside down? Today's theme verse is Jesus' loving response to her warning about the stinking body. Can you relate?

Chambers also quotes Matthew 11:6. Are you offended in Jesus? When life's realities say Jesus is a fraud, are you ashamed of Him? You will be blessed if you stick with what He says!

WHAT'S THE DEVOTIONAL SAYING?

If Chambers hadn't gone through life—and even death—practicing what he preached, this lesson on faith would ring hollow. How many times have people tried to comfort those who struggle with unhelpful talk about "developing faith"? Such words don't help unless they come from someone who went through a similar struggle.

Jesus went through the darkest valley and still passed the test of faith. He tells us we'll be blessed if we are not offended in Him and that, if we believe, we will see God's glory. Trust in what He says, not in what you see around you. He is the truth!

APPLICATION

Do you believe God will meet *all* your needs? What are your needs? What are your trials? What's wrong with common sense? Is it of any use? Why is it at odds with faith?
Finish this prayer: "Father, I've been born again into Christ's wisdom, which the world thinks is foolish, so . . ."

AUGUST 30
USEFULNESS OR RELATIONSHIP?

God cares more about us than about what we do.

BACKGROUND When it comes to fame, Oswald Chambers was no Billy Graham. The only newspaper that mentioned his death was the English-language daily *The Egyptian Gazette.* Two services—one in London, the other in Manchester—commemorated his life. He never spoke in football stadiums, was never featured on magazine covers, was never friends with presidents. His life should have been quickly forgotten by all but his closest friends and family. Yet here we are, reading his words over a hundred years after he spoke them. Was he useful to God? Not by some measures. But as today's lesson says, God is not interested in your usefulness. He wants *you.* And when you give Him *you,* with no holds barred, your life blesses *His* heart and others.

SCRIPTURAL CONTEXT On August 19, we saw that Jesus thanked His Father after the seventy-two returned. Right before He thanked God, He spoke today's theme verse. In what does *Jesus* rejoice? Is that consistent with what He told the seventy-two?

Today's lesson is sprinkled with Scripture. Where in the Bible can you find "living water," "in the light as God is in the light," and Jesus "bringing many sons to glory"? Chambers' familiarity with all parts of the Bible should inspire us to likewise grow in the knowledge of the Word!

WHAT'S THE DEVOTIONAL SAYING?
Why would it be God's mercy not to let us know we are pouring living water into those we meet? Why shouldn't God have revealed to Chambers, for example, that his life would have such a profound effect on so many?

We humans are weak and easily tempted. The slightest fragrance of self-love sets our heads reeling. God knows our weakness and spares us the wretched pride that would come from seeing how He uses us. How much better that He reveals himself, rather than our usefulness. Focus on Him alone!

APPLICATION
When has God used you? Did you rejoice? Was your relationship with God still first?

What are your circumstances now? Do you see them as from God? How do you react?

Finish this prayer: "Jesus, people might say your life was useless, but now we see its impact. Thank you . . ."

〜 AUGUST 31 〜
"MY JOY . . . YOUR JOY"

Do you have joy?
It isn't hard if Jesus lives in you.

BACKGROUND On August 25, we saw that Jesus is our best example of self-sacrifice and the joy it produces. Today we explore more of this joy. Joy comes from being poured out. Have you had this joy? Do you feel it when you pour yourself out for a project at work or for your family? Oswald Chambers knew it well. Listen as he tells us how we can have it too.

SCRIPTURAL CONTEXT Can you see the connections between the parts of Jesus' Upper Room Discourse (John 13–17)? Can you find where Jesus modeled these things? Was His heart troubled? How did He experience joy? How did He show us how to love one another? Every piece of this amazing five-chapter speech is filled with truths He also demonstrated.

Chambers continues to sprinkle his words with Scripture. If you read the Updated Edition, you'll see five Bible references scattered across the three paragraphs. If you only have the Classic Edition, see how many of these five you can find!

WHAT'S THE DEVOTIONAL SAYING? At first glance the three paragraphs might seem unrelated, but they all describe Christ's joy. First, Christ's joy comes from His self-sacrifice, and it is a far cry from mere "happiness." Second, worldly cares choke Jesus' joy out of our lives. Third, Christ's joy and His rivers of living water become ours when we have a right relationship with God.

Is your focus where it should be, on a right relationship with God? Spend time with Him today. If you don't, your efforts to keep your health, to keep your activities going, and to successfully do God's work are wasted.

APPLICATION

How do joy and happiness differ? Which one do you exhibit concerning God? Why?

What thought-provoking circumstances are you experiencing? Do they hinder your joy?

Finish this prayer: "God, I want to have a natural, right relationship with you. Today, please help me avoid . . ."

SEPTEMBER 1
DESTINED TO BE HOLY

What's on your mind?
Let God scrutinize it.

BACKGROUND As part of the League of Prayer (see January 10, *Companion*), Oswald Chambers worked to spread holiness to each Christian. Today's lesson tells us that holiness is our life's purpose. Chambers is clear that God alone gives us holiness. But it's our responsibility to exhibit and make manifest the holiness He gives us.

Are you up to the task of manifesting the gift of holiness? It's hard work, and it requires "minds alert and fully sober"!

SCRIPTURAL CONTEXT We read about a sober mind in 1 Peter 1:13, and our theme verse follows soon after this. What does a sober mind look like? For those who know J. R. R. Tolkien's famous story *The Hobbit*, a good example of a sober mind is Bard, the archer who killed Smaug the Dragon. While the rest of his kinsmen were reveling in the return of Thorin Oakenshield to Lonely Mountain, Bard's mind was alert and sober. Tolkien calls him "grim faced."

In the end, his grim sober-mindedness carried the day and saved his people from destruction.

Peter counsels us to soberly set our minds on hope. What hope does he mean? In order to be holy, to what must we *not* conform?

WHAT'S THE DEVOTIONAL SAYING? Chambers says that God scrutinizes every part of our life: our walk, our speech, and our thoughts. We know what our thoughts and speech are, but what is our walk?

If you have a dog, you may have noticed that it can recognize you from far away—that is, unless you're injured and have a limp. Each of us walks in our own particular way. God scrutinizes the things we do that make us who we are. The lesson is that we must make everything we do conform to His holy standards. Another lesson is that we can't scrutinize other people's walks. They might have a funny walk, but that's for God to deal with, not us!

APPLICATION

What good interests distract you from holiness? What will it cost to be right with God?

When have you preached holiness? How did people respond? Did God save us for pity?

Finish this prayer: "God, I want my thoughts, words, and actions to be clean and holy. I vow to no longer . . ."

SEPTEMBER 2
A LIFE OF PURE AND HOLY SACRIFICE

Want to bless others?
Forget self-fulfillment. Just pour out your best!

➤

BACKGROUND We don't know when Oswald Chambers gave the original sermon for today's devotional. To edit it into today's lesson, Biddy took the opening and two closing paragraphs. Tomorrow, we see part of the middle.

A pre-1928 song, which is attributed to George Liddell, begins:

> *Give me a man of God—one man,*
> *Whose faith is master of his mind,*
> *And I will right all wrongs,*
> *And bless the name of all mankind.*

Today's reading ends with the question: "It is time to break the life, to cease craving for satisfaction, and to spill the thing out. Our Lord is asking who of us will do it for Him?" Will *you* break the jar of perfume and pour yourself out? This lesson will inspire you to that!

SCRIPTURAL CONTEXT The theme verse is John 7:38, which we last discussed on August 21. Do you remember the audience? What was their excuse for not believing?

Today's lesson is equally about Mark 14:3–9. When did this take place? Why did Mary anoint Jesus? Who disapproved? (See February 21, *Companion*.) Are you willing to be a fool for Christ?

WHAT'S THE DEVOTIONAL SAYING?
The first half of today's lesson teaches us that our lives should be marked by expenditure—by God squeezing us like grapes. The second half holds up Mary of Bethany and God the Father (who spent His Son) as examples of expenditure.

Will you let God pour himself out through you? Letting Him do so means you will be crushed like a grape. Are you willing to be sacrificed? We will be willing only if we feel the debt of gratitude as Mary did. Has Jesus forgiven you much, or only a little?

APPLICATION
How did God "squeeze sweetness" out of Jesus? Is He doing the same to you? How so?
Are there ways you can be more extravagant for Jesus? What rules prevent you? Why?
Finish this prayer: "Jesus, you are worthy of the very best I can offer; so I won't hold back today on how . . ."

❦ SEPTEMBER 3 ❦
POURING OUT THE WATER OF SATISFACTION

Did you get something good?
Give it back to God, and He'll multiply it!

◄

BACKGROUND As we continue with our two-day series on "self-expenditure," Oswald Chambers makes it even clearer what we will need to pour out; namely, all the blessings God gives us.

Has God recently given you what you've been longing to have? Is it peace in a broken relationship or evidence that the Spirit is indeed filling you? Those are good things, but today we learn that unless we pour them out they become a trap for us and others.

SCRIPTURAL CONTEXT Read 2 Samuel 23:8–23. Have you heard these stories? They are no bloodier than the story of David and Goliath, but we rarely learn them in Sunday school. What strikes you most in the story of Jashobeam, Eleazar, and Shammah getting water for David? Why didn't David just drink it? Sacrifice

WHAT'S THE DEVOTIONAL SAYING? The big question after reading today's study is this: But *how* do I pour out my "Bethlehem water"? We know what this water is—all our blessings—but how do we give them to God?

You may have already figured it out. After all, Chambers' answer is this: *in the determination of my mind.* But for those of us who are still scratching our heads, the original sermon comes to our aid. It adds: *and that takes about two seconds.*

Our "pouring out," therefore, is a mental determination that takes two seconds. It's a simple deciding, like when a child decides to give a cookie to his father or mother instead of eating it himself. His decision takes all of two seconds as he thinks about whether he wants to eat it or bring it as a trophy gift to his parent. After the decision not to keep the cookie, the rest of the story unfolds rather easily. He presents the cookie and then watches with pride as his parent eats it in gratitude.

Will you make this same decision about the blessings God has given you? If you have gotten to the point where you finally know you have the Holy Spirit at work in you, thank God for that confidence. But quickly *decide* to give this great blessing back to Him. If you do, He'll multiply the blessing to others!

APPLICATION

What is blessing you most? How can you pour it out? What could happen if you don't?

Are you sweet or bitter to those around you? Why? What can you do differently today?

Finish this prayer: "Father, you've heaped blessings on me, but I need to be careful not to hoard them, so . . ."

HIS!

Who owns you?
Jesus Christ or others you love?

➤

BACKGROUND For twenty-two weeks, until two weeks before the Bible Training College disbanded (see July 31, *Companion*), Oswald Chambers taught a series of missionary studies. Today's lesson comes from his very last recorded lecture in this series. Imagine the feeling in the room as he delivered this talk. Students who had lived, eaten, sung, laughed, and studied with Mr. and Mrs. Chambers would now be saying goodbye. Some would never see their teacher's face again.

The most important part of being a missionary is also the most important part of being a Christian: to be "not your own" but to be completely His. Have you come to this realization?

SCRIPTURAL CONTEXT In today's theme verse, Jesus is talking with His Father in the presence of His closest friends. What else does He tell God? How does it show that we are His? When did He tell them, "Go"?

Each paragraph has a key verse: 1 Corinthians 6:19, Luke 14:26, and Acts 1:8. How do these three verses form the outline of our lesson? Why aren't you your own? What competes with being all Christ's? How is being a witness different from being a worker?

WHAT'S THE DEVOTIONAL SAYING?
Chambers saved the best for last in his twenty-two-week series. Today's lesson really is the crux of the matter: We can't be Jesus' disciples until we give up all competing relationships and know beyond a doubt that He owns us. Once we have done this, we will delight God's heart and be His witnesses.

Today's lesson completes what we learned on June 16: We are Jesus' friends *and* He owns us. We are not just His friends; we are His possessions. And we are not merely possessions; we are His intimate friends. Will you deliberately give yourself up today?

APPLICATION
  Are you a missionary? Do you put Jesus first? Can you be saved but not entirely His?
  What has Christ done for you? What is His true nature? Why does He send us out?
  Finish this prayer: "Holy Spirit, you reveal Christ's true nature as my Lord so I can tell others
    about you. Today I . . ."

SEPTEMBER 5
WATCHING WITH JESUS

Do you see what God is doing?
The Spirit can open your eyes so you will.

BACKGROUND Today's reading comes from the same original lecture as yesterday's lesson. It's no surprise that the message is similar: We watch with Jesus, not with ourselves, because we deliberately gave up self to Him.

What does "watching with Jesus" mean? Oswald Chambers contrasts it with watching for Jesus, which is about what He brings for me, like a child watching for Santa. Do you watch *with* or *for* Jesus? Let today's study help you watch *with*!

SCRIPTURAL CONTEXT Jesus spoke today's verse just a few hours after He spoke yesterday's verse. Here He asked those He called "His" to stay and watch with Him. Did they? Why not? Whose sorrow was more severe? What do we learn from Matthew 26:56 and its context?

Fifty days after forsaking Jesus, the disciples are completely changed by the Holy Spirit (Acts 2:4). What change do you notice as you go from Acts 1 to Acts 2?

WHAT'S THE DEVOTIONAL SAYING?
The first paragraph teaches us three things. First, "watching with" and "identifying with" are synonyms. We identify *with* Jesus when we put away our personal opinions about the world and deliberately give ourselves up entirely to Him. Second, the difficulty is that we don't understand Jesus' goals, just as the disciples didn't understand why Jesus was suffering. Our lack of understanding makes us unable to watch with Jesus. Third, we like it when Jesus watches with us, but we have little practice in watching with Him.

The second paragraph talks about how the disciples slept for their *own* sorrow; they had no clue about *Jesus'* sorrow. But the good news comes in the final paragraph: The Holy Spirit completely changed these clueless disciples, just as He can change us this very moment. Do you want to "watch with Jesus" the rest of your life? You can if the Spirit invades you!

APPLICATION
What does "no private point of view" mean? Are you watching with Jesus like this?
What Gethsemane have you gone through? How did it help you to identify with Jesus?
Finish this prayer: "Holy Spirit, please come upon me, fill me, and invade me so I can watch with Jesus by . . ."

SEPTEMBER 6
THE FAR-REACHING RIVERS OF LIFE

Can't see your way out?
Stand in God's spring—He'll push you through.

➢

BACKGROUND For the next six days we will encounter three two-day series. Today and tomorrow the theme is water—river first, then fountain. What ideas does fresh water bring to your mind? Running through a sprinkler? The sun's reflection on an endless, snaking river?

Today Oswald Chambers compares life to a mighty river, unstopped by any obstacle. Is that how you feel, or do obstacles seem to completely block your way? Let today's lesson give you hope that God will help you overcome.

SCRIPTURAL CONTEXT Over the past three weeks, John 7:38 has been a recurring verse for us. What new thoughts do you have about this verse? Do you think the idea of someone pouring out huge rivers of water is a bit humorous?

Chambers uses John 6:29 to teach us that the key is our belief in Jesus, not the output of our rivers. What was the original context? Do you think the crowd's question was genuine?

WHAT'S THE DEVOTIONAL SAYING? There are three main points today. First, the key to our river-like life is attention to the source. If we lose focus on Jesus and worry about our influence, our lives will dry up. Second, our influence is not readily apparent, but it's sure to happen. Third, our river-like life will overcome all obstacles.

When we see our lives as God's river, we get things in proper perspective. We stop worrying about how much we are doing. We focus on our relationship with God, our source. And we maintain an attitude of persistence. Be God's river today!

APPLICATION

What obstacles do you face? Are you focused on them? How can you overcome them?

How has your life been a blessing for others? Did you find out about it much later? How?

Finish this prayer: "God, my Living Source, I know you will carry me through all obstacles and make me . . ."

SEPTEMBER 7
FOUNTAINS OF BLESSINGS

Your relationship with God is not just for you. It's also to bless others.

≺

BACKGROUND What's the difference between a simple channel and a fountain? The channel connects two bodies of water and is sometimes dry. The fountain continually sends hidden water up to the surface.

Yesterday's lesson taught us to think of our lives as overcoming rivers. Today we learn to also think of our lives as fountains, continually pouring forth God's blessings to others. Are you always taking from God and rarely giving out? When you are rightly related to God, the outflow happens naturally.

SCRIPTURAL CONTEXT John 4 gave us our theme verse on February 26 and 27. What did you learn on those days about this chapter? What else can you learn? Why did Jesus bother to teach the woman at the well that life was supposed to be like a fountain? Wasn't that a rather advanced lesson for one who didn't know anything about the Holy Spirit? How do you suppose John learned of her conversation with Jesus?

Oswald Chambers often translates Ephesians 5:18 as "be being filled." How is this different from your translation? How does this verse connect to our two-day "water" series?

WHAT'S THE DEVOTIONAL SAYING? Can you find the same three points that we saw yesterday? The third point is missing, but in its place, Chambers tells us that if our rivers are not overflowing and going around all obstacles, we are to blame. We have obstructed the flow. The second paragraph asks probing questions about what might be blocking the flow. Is God flowing through you? If not, why is that?

In today's final sentence, Chambers says God's work always starts with somebody who, though obscure (like Chambers, see August 30, *Companion*), is true to Jesus. Will you be that obscure, faithful somebody today?

APPLICATION

What's your motivation to improve your relationship with Jesus? What do you lack?

Do you doubt God's plan to use you in order to bless many people? Why?

Finish this prayer: "Jesus, I want to be steadfastly true to you so you can use me to bless others. Please . . ."

DO IT YOURSELF

What's blocking God's will?
Use His power to demolish whatever it is!

➤

BACKGROUND Do-it-yourself home repair frequently proves more difficult than anticipated. Today and tomorrow Oswald Chambers teaches us that the same thing often happens in the spiritual realm, where the stakes are far higher.

Have you found that it isn't easy to live the Christian life? Every day we are faced with tough choices, yet the holiness God gave us will be complete only if we make consistently right decisions. Today's lesson reveals the battle lines in our fight for holiness.

SCRIPTURAL CONTEXT On first read, 2 Corinthians 10:5 and today's first paragraph seem to be pointing to philosophical or scientific theories that go against God's Word. Read today's second paragraph and the context for our theme verse. What "arguments" is Paul talking about? What are Chambers' "ramparts" ("barriers" in the Updated Edition)?

When trapped between the Egyptians and the Red Sea, the Israelites panicked, but Moses displayed incredible faith: "Stand still and see the salvation of the Lord!" He didn't even know how God was going to do it, but he was confident that God would keep His promise. Do you have that faith? When does Chambers say we must stand still?

WHAT'S THE DEVOTIONAL SAYING? If we are going to fight for holiness, the first thing we need to know is where to fight. Chambers helps by giving us the boundary lines of our battle. We do not have to fight against sin (that's God's fight, which He already fought and won) nor against our faulty presuppositions and prejudices (we defeat those by not using them in our decisions). Instead we have to fight against "the entrenchments of our natural life."

What are your entrenchments? With Jesus as your commander, will you fight against them with all your might? If you succeed, the glory will go to Jesus—not you, which is just as it should be. He is the One who gives us the divinely powerful weapons and clears us of our sin so we can fight on His side!

APPLICATION

What are some examples of your human nature? How will you destroy them?

How can you be made innocent but not holy in character? What choices must you make?

Finish this prayer: "Father, I've stood still and watched you transform me. Now I need to start fighting . . ."

ᖇᖇᕈ SEPTEMBER 9 ᖇᖇᕈ
DO IT YOURSELF

Did God commission your work?
If not, don't do it!

◄

BACKGROUND Has anyone accused you of not being "on fire" for God? Or not being pumped up enough about saving souls? Have you thought this about others? Today's lesson reminds us that being "on fire" is often our undisciplined response to a "vivid religious experience" (in the Classic Edition). If we love God, we will bring every project into captivity to Christ, as today's theme verse tells us. Are you being this disciplined in your work for the Lord?

SCRIPTURAL CONTEXT Today we finish off yesterday's theme verse. First, we demolish the strongholds of our natural life. Then we make all our new projects prisoners of Christ. If we do the first step and not the second, we risk launching out on a venture that looks new and different from our old, natural life, but which is just as self-driven, even if it is supposedly for God.

What is Jesus' example in all of this? Chambers quotes John 5:19. What does this teach us about Jesus' projects? How can you follow His lead?

WHAT'S THE DEVOTIONAL SAYING? We have already looked at the meaning of the first two paragraphs. What does the third one tell us? Chambers elaborates on this paragraph elsewhere in his *Complete Works*. From this, we know that he is teaching against a "believer" being someone who merely believes in God to get saved. Being a "believer in Jesus" is the best way to describe a Christian, as long as we know what we mean by belief—"a mental and moral commitment to our Lord Jesus Christ's view of God and man, of sin and the devil, and of the Scriptures."

Are you a believer in Jesus according to this definition? Have you committed, in your mind and in your heart, to see everything the way Jesus sees it? Make the decision today to believe like this. Fight against both the entrenchments of your natural life *and* the temptation to launch projects before they've been brought into Christ's captivity.

APPLICATION

What are your projects now? Are they disciplined to God's will? How would that look?

Have you criticized others (or been criticized) for not working on Christian projects?

Finish this prayer: "God, my projects have been my own thing, not yours. I commit to renew my mind so . . ."

SEPTEMBER 10
MISSIONARY WEAPONS

What do you do in secret?
Let God scrutinize it!

➤

BACKGROUND As World War I hit the six-month mark without signs of ending, Oswald Chambers launched a twenty-two-week series on missionary issues (see September 4, *Companion*). His goal for the Bible Training College had always been to equip missionaries. But with men leaving England daily by the thousands, Chambers' students would be missionaries sooner than expected. Chambers embraced this new timeline. For example, right before he started his missionary series, he published a letter thanking God for the fourteen students who were, or were soon to be, on active duty.

The readings today and tomorrow come from a talk that was given toward the middle of the twenty-two-week series. Chambers had read a quote from Britain's minister of munitions (weapons) stressing the importance of munitions factories. He titled his talk "Missionary Munitions," and he said that the Christian's hidden worship is the weapons factory for future missionary work.

SCRIPTURAL CONTEXT Chambers picks an interesting verse to go along with the subtitle "Worshipping as Occasion Serves" (John 1:48).

Who was under the fig tree? Do we ever see him appear again? Could he also be known as Bartholomew?

The point of this verse is that sometimes our lives have a slower pace ("under the fig tree"). During those times we must worship God so we are ready for being "out into the open." Is your life slow? Are you worshiping in secret?

WHAT'S THE DEVOTIONAL SAYING?
The four paragraphs today each teach us about worshiping in secret. First, secret worship means we do the things God gives us to do long before there's a crisis. Second, once the crisis comes, it will show whether we have been secretly worshiping Him in the everyday decisions. Third, we deceive ourselves if we think we will be holy in crisis if we haven't worshiped God during the slower times. Finally, our secret worship is as important as a weapons factory during wartime.

How do you secretly worship God? Do you pray, read the Bible, and do what He puts before you? Ask Him to help you worship in secret today, so you will be ready for whatever is in store for you.

APPLICATION
What crisis have you experienced? What did it reveal? Are you ready for the next one?
What are your "closest tasks"? Are you doing them well? Do you worship God in them?
Finish this prayer: "God, I worship you as the great One, the perfect engineer of circumstances, such as . . ."

MISSIONARY WEAPONS

We need more of God's power to wash dishes well than to preach a sermon.

◄

BACKGROUND Just as it would be crazy to have troops make their own munitions while in the trenches, so it is crazy to prepare for spiritual battle when you are already in the battle. Rather, God provides slower times—"under the fig tree," as we saw yesterday—to prepare us for future battles.

Today Oswald Chambers makes the point that the slow times also show what we are made of. What are you made of? Can you see the true you coming out as you do dishes and other menial tasks?

SCRIPTURAL CONTEXT Chambers loves to quote from the story of Jesus washing the disciples' feet. What new insights do you gain by reading John 13 again?

Where else does Jesus teach us to do menial tasks? Chambers mentions the "second mile," which is from Mathew 5:41. Can you find other places like this? (See Luke 17:7-10 and note on August 13, *Companion*.)

WHAT'S THE DEVOTIONAL SAYING?
Today we have another record number of paragraphs. Let's look at each one: First, we mustn't try to choose our circumstances but only to choose God in our circumstances. Second, we shouldn't underestimate how much of God's power we need to do menial tasks. Chambers says that God gives us those tasks, almost like a final exam, to test our character. Third, it's humbling to think about how we've treated the people God put in our lives. Some of them are undoubtedly difficult for us to love, but we must follow Jesus' foot-washing example with all of them! Fourth, we shouldn't kid ourselves that we'll be able to love difficult people on the mission field. If we don't do it on the home front, we'll never do it. Finally, we must not give up doing hard things just because we can't see what God is doing.

Yesterday we saw the importance of worship. Today we see that ministering to others is harder than it appears and involves a lot of menial tasks. Spend today worshiping and ministering as opportunities arise, always relying on God's power.

APPLICATION
Make a list of the "random" events in your life. Are they from God's engineering?

Your character is revealed by menial tasks. What are your tasks, and is Christ in them?

Finish this prayer: "Almighty Jesus, if you aren't incarnate in me, I'll never be able to do (as I ought to) things like . . ."

⌘ SEPTEMBER 12 ⌘
GOING THROUGH SPIRITUAL CONFUSION

Confused?
Don't worry—God has it under control.

BACKGROUND "Spiritual Confusion" was the title of one of Oswald Chambers' many sermons. Biddy shortened it for today's lesson, keeping the same three subtitles.

Do you ever doubt that God is a good friend? A loving father? Faithful? The lesson today tackles all of those doubts.

SCRIPTURAL CONTEXT Read Matthew 20:17–28. Did Zebedee's wife feel confused? Was she? Might she have felt confused after talking with Jesus? "Ye know not what ye ask" might be spoken to you long before you start feeling confused. But once you are confused, God will bring it to mind to remind you it's normal to feel confused.

Now read Luke 11:5–13 and 18:1–8. Why did Jesus tell the two parables and compare earthly fathers to our Father in heaven? Is Jesus saying that God will appear as an uncaring friend or a callous father?

Jesus implicitly acknowledges that God at times seems far off. He tells the parable of the friend at midnight to show us that even when it seems God doesn't want to answer, we must keep asking Him. Do you ever feel as if God doesn't want to be bothered with your requests?

WHAT'S THE DEVOTIONAL SAYING?
The key to applying today's lesson is to look at the questions in each section. Will you hang on in confidence that God is still your friend? Will you trust that God will eventually show himself to be a good father? Will you bank on Him despite the confusion?

What's your situation right now? Does God seem more uncaring or more confusing? If you are tempted not to trust Him, face your temptation squarely and decide to count on Him no matter what. Take comfort in the fact that Jesus knew ahead of time that we would often be confused.

APPLICATION

What is most confusing to you? Is God using this to encourage you to practice trusting in Him?

How is your relationship with your father? From this, what are you projecting on God?

Finish this prayer: "Father, I want to count on you despite confusion; so, although I'm asking you for . . ."

SEPTEMBER 13
AFTER SURRENDER—THEN WHAT?

When God offers you a trade-in, you'd be a fool not to take Him up on it!

BACKGROUND Today Oswald Chambers again teaches us the most important aspect of our relationship to God: surrender. This is the great trade—our right to our self in exchange for oneness with Him. To be one with His glorious life—what a deal! But what is surrender? Today's lesson helps us better understand three aspects of this process.

SCRIPTURAL CONTEXT Each aspect of surrender has a verse. First, Matthew 11:28 relates to surrendering for rest. The one calling us to "come" is Jesus, but He calls us using the things that vex us. The second aspect is also about rest—long-term rest in devotion to God rather than the immediate rest of deliverance from our troubles. Matthew 16:24 best describes this rest in devotion. Finally, John 21:18 points us beyond long-term surrender to the "surrender for death."

How does the theme verse relate to surrender? The answer lies in remembering how Jesus did His work on earth. He did it in unbroken communion with God. So after we surrender our will, we must do the same thing He did. If we do, we will "finish the work" God gave us to do and bring Him glory as a result.

WHAT'S THE DEVOTIONAL SAYING? In the "surrender for death" section, Chambers warns us of taking back our surrender. So when Chambers says "surrender of will; when that is done, all is done," he means that no other surrender is necessary once we surrender our will. However, we must always be alert to the possibility of taking back our surrender. Have you taken back your surrender? If so, it's time to surrender again. This time let your perplexing circumstances call you to surrender, not an "ecstasy."

Today is yet another opportunity for you to trade yourself to God and receive a true relationship with Him. Will you make the trade?

APPLICATION

What externals have you given up to God? Have you also surrendered your will? How?

When were you saved? When did you experience what it means? How restful are you?

Finish this prayer: "God, I trade my will, self, and desires for your rest, sufficiency, and fellowship. Please . . ."

SEPTEMBER 14
ARGUMENTS OR OBEDIENCE?

Confused?
Your pride, not your circumstance, is to blame.

BACKGROUND On July 27, we saw that trying to think through spiritual darkness is the wrong approach. Only *obeying* will shed light on spiritual issues. Today we return to this same point, and we see how Oswald Chambers ties it to the concept of imagination (see February 10, *Utmost*).

What parts of your spiritual life are muddled? Is it strange that any part of our life is murky? Why won't God just clear things up? Chambers says it's due to something we haven't let the Holy Spirit control. What is that something for you?

SCRIPTURAL CONTEXT Today Chambers specifies only two verses: 2 Corinthians 11:3 and Matthew 11:25. We looked at the context for Matthew 11 on August 19. What is the context for today's theme verse? Some scholars think Paul sent 2 Corinthians 10–13 before he sent the first nine, friendlier chapters. Paul pulls no punches in these final four chapters!

Do you have the simplicity that today's theme verse describes? What keeps you from it? What was keeping the Corinthians from it? Can you relate?

WHAT'S THE DEVOTIONAL SAYING? Does Chambers shock you when he says that a Christian won't *think* clearly for a long time? Do you feel that you're still in the unclear-thinking phase? He says, though, that we should *see* clearly from the very first day. Was that true of you? Are you still seeing clearly?

Seeing comes from obeying. Even a child can see in that way. Are you being an obedient child? Chambers tells us to bring our imagination, which is the part of our mind that reasons and perceives, into captivity to Christ. Will you do that today?

APPLICATION
Do we really have to obey before things become clear? Why? Do you "try to be wise"?
Are all your "smallest things" under the Holy Spirit's control? What will you do to ensure they are?
Finish this prayer: "Holy Spirit, I submit all of my thoughts to you. Please change my thinking as I obey . . ."

WHAT TO RENOUNCE

Evangelizing with tricks?
God wants us to speak truthfully.

BACKGROUND In Egypt, Oswald and Biddy Chambers instituted "free teas" for the troops. The soldiers were surprised they weren't forced to hear a sermon in exchange for the eggs, sandwiches, cakes, and tea. Chambers said, "They came to eat, not to hear a sermon. There's a meeting later tonight if they want to stay and hear someone preach."

Today's lesson teaches us to make our points honestly, without trickery. It also urges us to rid our lives of anything dishonest. Do you ever stretch the truth? Let this lesson help you live more honestly.

SCRIPTURAL CONTEXT Second Corinthians 4:2 gives a taste of how Paul saw his ministry. He felt that although some accused him of forcefulness (2 Corinthians 10:10), at least no one could accuse him of trickery. What else does he say in chapter 4?

WHAT'S THE DEVOTIONAL SAYING? Today's lesson is neatly divided into two parts. First, we're urged to rid our lives of anything that would cause us shame—although it's tempting to hide those things, since they are easily hidden. Chambers says they don't necessarily come from our sin. They may just be old habits of the "flesh." Here we see again how Chambers defines sin differently from how many of us do. Would you ever consider envy, jealousy, and strife *not* sins?

In the second part, we are told that if dishonesty is involved we are not to let our ends ever justify the means. Are you tempted to use dishonest means and to hide your shameful things? Decide to be continually watchful about your hidden things and to give your utmost for God's highest!

APPLICATION

Would any of your recent thoughts embarrass you if brought to light? Renounce them!

What dishonesty or craftiness do you need to renounce? How will you stop these behaviors?

Finish this prayer: "Lord, there's so much envy, jealousy, and strife in me. Please help me stop thinking . . ."

SEPTEMBER 16
PRAYING TO GOD IN SECRET

He who prays but doesn't ask is like one who chews food but won't swallow!

BACKGROUND Today we return to the rich material of *Studies in the Sermon on the Mount* (see May 18, *Companion*). In three paragraphs we learn about three aspects of prayer: its secrecy, simplicity, and surety.

Are you convicted by the last sentence of Oswald Chambers' first paragraph? Make prayer an essential priority! And don't worry about needing an actual prayer closet. Chambers explained, in his original 1911 talk, that our definite times of secret prayer are "in your business, as you walk along the streets, in the ordinary ways of life, when no one dreams you are praying."

SCRIPTURAL CONTEXT Matthew 6:6 and 6:7 inspire the first two paragraphs, while Matthew 7:8 and John 15:7 provide the teaching for the last paragraph. Read these verses and compare them with what today's study says. How does your Bible translate John 15:7? Is Chambers' point about "will" still valid?

The Bible teaches us how to pray, why to pray, and what happens when we pray. But mostly it tells us *to* pray. Will you pray more today than yesterday?

WHAT'S THE DEVOTIONAL SAYING? Secrecy, simplicity, and surety—these words guide us as we apply today's lesson. Are you praying in secret, or do you make it a point to tell people, "I'll pray for you"? Do you think God hears you because you pray for the right things—things you think He would want? Or do you know that the reason He listens is simply because of *redemption* (a word Chambers used more than seven hundred times in his *Complete Works*!). Finally, do you have childlike surety that you can ask God for anything? Do you *want* anything? Or are you so unsure that God gives you things that you don't have any strong desires?

Prayer is God's way of getting us closer to Him. Will you *ask*, or will you just go through the motions?

APPLICATION

What is your motivation for praying? When and where do you pray? Is it an act of will?

For what or who are you praying? How's your attitude? Does it need changing? Why?

Finish this prayer: "Jesus, you commanded me to ask in keeping with your character, so I'm asking . . .

SEPTEMBER 17
IS THERE GOOD IN TEMPTATION?

Yielding to temptation makes yielding a habit.

➤

BACKGROUND Today we begin a three-day series on temptation. The source material for this topic comes from the book *The Philosophy of Sin*. Although the lectures in this book were mainly from the Bible Training College, Oswald Chambers had spoken on this topic three years before he started the college. Learning about sin had long been his focus.

Do you understand temptation? Is it "a suggested short cut to the realisation of the highest at which I aim," (Classic Edition) or something else? Listen to Chambers about temptation so you can resist it!

SCRIPTURAL CONTEXT First Corinthians 10:13 is a favorite temptation verse. We like that our temptations won't get any worse than what other people face, that God won't let us be tempted more than we can bear, and that He will give us a way out. But what do these three things really mean? Think how they apply to the temptations you face now.

Chambers points us to Hebrews 2:18 (4:15 is also good). What is encouraging about this verse? If Jesus hadn't been tempted, couldn't He still have helped us?

WHAT'S THE DEVOTIONAL SAYING? Each paragraph today teaches us new things about temptation. First, being tempted is far better than not being tempted, and the kind of temptation we face tells us how mature we are in our faith. Second, we are tempted by what matches our disposition (see July 1, *Utmost*). Third, temptation is a shortcut to something good. Finally, God doesn't keep us from temptations. He saves us when we go through them.

What temptation did you yield to most recently? What did you learn from it? Did it teach you that all the times you resisted temptations in the past were only because you were afraid of doing something difficult? Did you see how, as soon as a temptation gave you an easy way to yield to it, you yielded? The most important lesson to learn today is that we are weak and need God so badly!

APPLICATION

What things tempt you? Are they low- or high-level things? How are we lifted to a higher level of temptation?

What are your big goals and big confusions? What shortcuts are you in danger of taking?

Finish this prayer: "Father, you have sustained me through so many temptations. Right now I'm prone to . . ."

HIS TEMPTATION AND OURS

What's inside?
Temptation makes your insides public!

BACKGROUND What else is there to learn about being tempted? Today we learn that Christians are mainly tempted to *be* wrong, not to *do* wrong. Nonbelievers don't have God in their hearts, so Satan can't tempt them to push God out. But for us, Satan's tricks *do* come along these lines. Getting us to do wrong might be part of the way he tempts us, but the main result is wrong *being*.

Think back on your last temptation. How were you tempted to be something other than what God re-created you to be? Today's lesson will help you be on your guard for the next time you are tempted.

SCRIPTURAL CONTEXT After you look at today's theme verse, read about Jesus' temptation in Matthew 4. Are we ever tempted the way Jesus was? That's what the theme verse says! Do you think Oswald Chambers has it right? Are we tempted as Jesus was only after we become Christians?

What was Jesus' mission (see John 1:29)? What is yours? Will you take a shortcut to accomplish your goals?

WHAT'S THE DEVOTIONAL SAYING? Look at James 1:14. Does this apply only to unbelievers? Chambers says it's the only kind of temptation that unbelievers face—not that it only applies to them. We can face both this kind and the kind Jesus experienced. What is the difference? Did Jesus have "evil desire" or "lust"?

A confusing word today is "possessions." What are the possessions of Jesus' "personality" ("nature" in the Updated Edition)? In the original sermon, we read, "A man's disposition on the inside, i.e. what he possesses in his personality, determines by what he is tempted on the outside." So "possessions of His personality" is the same as "His disposition."

That same sermon says, "Temptation is also a severe test to fulfill the possessions of personality by a short cut." Comparing this with what yesterday's lesson said ("Temptation is a suggested short cut to the realisation of the highest at which I aim," Classic Edition), we see that our disposition, besides being our nature, can also be thought of as our highest aim.

Linking disposition to our aim adds new meaning to the phrase, "my utmost for His highest." Have you asked God to swap your disposition (see July 24, *Utmost*) for Christ's disposition? If you have, and haven't taken your surrender back (see September 13, *Utmost*), then your highest aim will be the same as Christ's: giving His utmost to God's highest purposes for His life!

APPLICATION
What ungodly desires have enticed you? Are you tempted to an ungodly point of view?
How do you understand Jesus' temptation? Does this help you in your temptation?
Finish this prayer: "Jesus, you were tempted and learned obedience. Please help me . . ."

ARE YOU CONTINUING TO GO WITH JESUS?

We stay close to Jesus by sharing in His trials.

◄

BACKGROUND Today we end our three-day series on temptation with source material that comes from a different book (*Now Is It Possible*). The three talks found in this book were given to Oswald Chambers' students at the Bible Training College. Chambers knew that some of his students would turn back and no longer follow Jesus. So today's message is a plea to remain loyal to Jesus no matter what temptations arise.

SCRIPTURAL CONTEXT If you read Luke 22, verse 28 can slip right by. Why might the disciples have paid special attention to this verse and to verses 29 and 30? Chambers contrasts Luke 22:28 with John 6:66. Which of these two verses fits you right now?

The final paragraph paints a vivid picture of what it means to continue with Jesus in His trials. Read Hebrews 13:13. The first-century Hebrew readers would have been shocked! "Outside the camp" was only for the sin offerings on the Day of Atonement. But since Jesus became sin for us, let us become little sin offerings for those around us, bearing up under shame and abuse and pouring ourselves out for their salvation.

WHAT'S THE DEVOTIONAL SAYING? What does "the moment we have an experience of what He can do" mean? Thankfully, Chambers uses this expression elsewhere in his *Complete Works,* where he says, "Do not profane the holiness of God by refusing to abandon yourself away from your experience of what He has done for you to God Himself." In other words, *don't put what God can do for us in place of God himself.*

Have you stopped going with Jesus because you have experienced enough of His blessings that you didn't think to keep seeking Jesus himself? As Chambers said in Egypt on February 25, 1917, "We may have had an experience of what Jesus Christ can do and yet not have known Him. . . . It takes all time and eternity to know God." Take time to get to know Jesus and His trials today!

APPLICATION

Does Satan tempt *your* life or the life of *Jesus* in you? Is this always true? How do you know?

When you yield to temptation, with whom are you siding? How does Jesus feel? Why?

Finish this prayer: "Jesus, I've been trying to face temptations alone, but your life in me is what is really being tempted . . ."

SEPTEMBER 20
THE DIVINE COMMANDMENT OF LIFE

Trying to be good?
God wants total perfection!

➤

BACKGROUND Today's devotional launches us into an eleven-day missionary series. Starting tomorrow, each lesson will be taken from a series of missionary studies by Oswald Chambers (see September 4, *Companion*). But today's lesson is from his *Studies in the Sermon on the Mount*, which Biddy used many times to create *Utmost* devotionals.

Loving others no matter what is what connects today's lesson with the next ten. Are you able to love even the people you don't like? That's one example of how you are called to "be perfect, as your Father in heaven is perfect" (Matthew 5:48).

SCRIPTURAL CONTEXT The Sermon on the Mount had no chapter breaks when Jesus preached it. But today's theme verse is a clear segue between two parts of his sermon. What phrase introduces each topic in the section

from 5:21–47? Does verse 48 summarize verses 43–47 or the whole section?

Chambers bases this lesson on the assumption that verse 48 is closely tied to verses 43–47. What other verses help make his points (for example, John 13:34)?

WHAT'S THE DEVOTIONAL SAYING?
If you read 1 John 1:7, you see that we will have "fellowship" with one another. In *Studies in the Sermon on the Mount*, Chambers quotes this verse and then says, "God gives us fellowship with people for whom we have no natural affinity."

For which people in your life do you have less natural affinity? What will you do to love them? Over the next ten days, pray that God will send you to the right people as His witness. It might turn out that the people you dislike the most are the ones you can love the best!

APPLICATION
Who don't you like? Are you generous to them? How? Did you prove you're perfect?
How natural is the supernatural to you? How are you responding to your "flurries"?
Finish this prayer: "God, I want to treat others as you have treated me. I'll identify with your
   interests in . . ."

THE MISSIONARY'S PREDESTINED PURPOSE

Do you glorify God?
If not, you're distracted!

◄　►

BACKGROUND Oswald Chambers' original sermon "Missionary Predestinations" had three sections: fitness, finish, and fittedness. Each of these had subsections (the purpose of our creation, the preparation of our characteristic, and the plan of our concentration). Chambers had a lot of fun with alliteration!

For today's *Utmost* lesson, we don't get all of these catchy section and subsection titles, but we do get the meat of Chambers' message, which is this: We are predestined to glorify God.

SCRIPTURAL CONTEXT In three places (chapters 42, 49, and 50–53), Isaiah talks about "The servant of the Lord." What does he say in chapter 49? How is this servant like Israel, like Christ, and like us?

WHAT'S THE DEVOTIONAL SAYING?
The poem *Saint Paul,* which we first encountered on April 9, appears again today when Chambers tells us what to expect after we are filled with the Spirit. Have you felt God force the world's anguish through your heart? We read John 3:16, but do we have the same heart anguish that God feels for the world?

The main point today is that to be a missionary to anyone (even our own family), we have to see that our purpose is to glorify God. If we don't, God will have to deal ruthlessly and relentlessly with all that we put in place of Him. Realizing that we are created for God's glory gives us joy. (The answer to the Westminster Shorter Catechism's first question says the same thing: We can enjoy God if we know we're here to glorify Him.)

Do you muddle God's creative purposes with your own intentions? Refocus your mind and heart on the only thing you need to do: glorify God!

APPLICATION

What is God's purpose for you? For the human race? How are you conforming to His will?

What prejudice, parochial thinking, and patriotism stop you from doing God's purposes?

Finish this prayer: "Father, it's hard to believe that you love the world and that you want me to do the same, so please . . ."

SEPTEMBER 22
THE MISSIONARY'S MASTER AND TEACHER

Jesus never forces us. That's why we need to know Him so intimately.

◄ ►

BACKGROUND Oswald Chambers aptly distinguishes between "being mastered" and "having a master." Have you been mastered by a master that doesn't even know you? If your master was a *thing*, you can be sure you didn't "have a master" the way Chambers describes.

Other than in its title, today's lesson never mentions missionaries. But its main point (Jesus must *be* our master—we can't be *mastered* by Him, since that's not an option) is a prerequisite for all missionaries. Is Jesus your master? Or are you wasting time hoping He will master you?

SCRIPTURAL CONTEXT When was the first time Jesus told the disciples He was their master? Depending on which version of the Bible you use, you may never notice it! But in the version Chambers used (KJV), Jesus says it both in our theme verse and in Matthew 23:8, which Chambers quotes. What do these two verses say in your Bible?

Now turn to Hebrews 5:8. We already discussed this verse three times (see especially July 19, *Companion*). Read it once more and decide again if you think obedience occurs between equals.

WHAT'S THE DEVOTIONAL SAYING? As you read today's first paragraph, what kind of master does Chambers describe? It barely seems like a master at all! That's the point. Jesus is unlike any master we've ever had. He invites us—never forces us. That's why it's so important that we know Him personally. Otherwise, how will we know what He wants us to do?

Do you wish God would just tell you what to do? You're not alone. But Chambers wants us to have Jesus as our master, not to be mastered by Him. Ask Him to expand your understanding of "master" today!

APPLICATION

Is Christ your master and teacher? How do you know you aren't just "being mastered"?
What does it mean to be "His to obey"? What should you change to be more like that?
Finish this prayer: "Jesus, you know the deepest abyss of my heart and fill it completely. Please help me . . ."

SEPTEMBER 23
THE MISSIONARY'S GOAL

If Jesus is your goal, then nothing can deter you.

◄ ►

BACKGROUND "Christ, Christ, none but Christ!" So shouted the sixteenth-century reformer John Bradford on his way to be burned at the stake. Today's lesson, in the same vein, reminds us, "We start with Christ and we end with Him." He is our only goal, from first to last.

Will you make Christ your only aim, even if you are shown mostly "gross ingratitude" as a result? Will you focus only on doing God's will—not winning the lost or anything besides that one thing? Everything else will happen as a side effect of putting Christ first.

SCRIPTURAL CONTEXT Luke 18:31 was our theme verse on August 3. Did you think of a time when you did God's will and not your own? Has there been a new example in the meantime?

What is the "fullness of Christ" in Ephesians 4:13? Have you attained this fullness? What gives us this fullness (verse 11)?

Oswald Chambers also quotes Matthew 10:24 and Luke 23:33 and says seemingly opposite things about them. First, we will suffer the same thing as Jesus (ingratitude). Second, we won't suffer the same thing as Jesus (crucifixion). We can best understand this contradiction by remembering that we go through everything that Jesus went through except the ultimate payment He paid for our sins.

WHAT'S THE DEVOTIONAL SAYING? Have you tried to be a missionary—in the broadest sense of the word? When you do, remember today's lesson: The goal of a missionary is not to win souls or to be useful to God. The missionary's goal is to *do God's will!*

What stops you from being a missionary? Is it the ingratitude you think you'll receive? You *will* receive it, but don't let that deter you. Ask God for boldness to go with Jesus "up to Jerusalem," and decide to make Him your all-in-all today.

APPLICATION

How have your natural goals changed? What tempts you to change your spiritual goal?

What is your Jerusalem? Is it the same as other believers' Jerusalem? Does ingratitude affect you?

Finish this prayer: "Jesus, you are my model for resolutely sticking to the goal. My goal is clear: to be . . ."

SEPTEMBER 24
THE "GO" OF PREPARATION

The littlest things are often the hardest to give up.

◄ ►

BACKGROUND Today's lesson, though challenging, is surprisingly encouraging. Oswald Chambers tells us that we will never "arrive" spiritually—there's always more we must learn and give to God. Interestingly, the tiniest things are often most important to give to God, since behind those tiny things lies our "central citadel of obstinacy."

Is there something small God wants you to give up to Him? Let today's lesson challenge you and encourage you as you continually prepare your life.

SCRIPTURAL CONTEXT It's rare that Biddy devotes as much space to the theme verse as she does today. Usually she lets the reader look up the full context, but today she quotes two verses in their entirety. Why do you think she did that?

One possibility is that Chambers used the entire two verses as the outline for his original sermon. He broke the verses into six sections and discussed each section for a paragraph or more. How would you split up this text? What could you say about each part?

WHAT'S THE DEVOTIONAL SAYING? If you've felt battered by all the things you're learning from *Utmost*, take heart. We must constantly prepare, and being convicted of sin is the major part of preparation.

When you're convicted, do you admit your sin or do you confess it? What's the difference? Chambers implies that confessing brings humiliation, which results in godly, winsome humility. Are you willing to confess and make things right even though it will result in more humiliation than if you merely admit your sin?

APPLICATION

On a scale of 1–10, how prepared are you? What will you do to be more prepared? When?

When was your enthusiasm for God put to the test? How did you respond? Why?

Finish this prayer: "Holy Spirit, only you can reveal the attitude in me that can never serve God. Please . . ."

THE "GO" OF RELATIONSHIP

Following God is easy, but not without His grace!

BACKGROUND As we reach the midpoint of our eleven-day series on missionary issues, Oswald Chambers forcefully reminds us that we can't be disciples or missionaries without God's supernatural power. Today's lesson comes partly from yesterday's lesson, "The 'Go' of Preparation," and partly from a talk called "The 'Go' of Sacramental Service."

Are you going the second mile—beyond what your natural capacity would allow? If not, ask God for His supernatural power, since without it, you can't do anything He wants you to do.

SCRIPTURAL CONTEXT As many Bible teachers tell us, Roman soldiers could force Jews to carry their loads for one mile. In Matthew 5:39–41, when Jesus talks about going an extra mile, turning the other cheek, and giving up our cloaks, what does He mean? Is this an exhaustive list? Can we do these things in our own power?

Chambers says that we know we are *not* Jesus' disciples if we are "dead-set" (Classic Edition) on being His disciples. This seems strange.

But Chambers backs up this statement by quoting John 15:16. Do you think Chambers' point is correct?

WHAT'S THE DEVOTIONAL SAYING? How often we try to do things in our own power! But how can we work out our salvation, like Chambers urges us to do, without using our own power? Chambers explains: "We cannot do what God does, and . . . God will not do what we can do" (see May 10, *Utmost*). *The extra mile* is Jesus' illustration of something we cannot do without His power. Chambers elaborates on this, saying there can't be the "slightest trace of resentment even suppressed in the head of a disciple when he meets with tyranny and injustice." That's a tall order!

Where are you trusting your natural capacities as you serve God? Another way to think about it is this: "What does God want you to do that is completely outside of your gifts?" The fact is, when you are filled with the Spirit, those things that seemed so hard will be easy, since God is doing them through you.

APPLICATION

Which of God's commands seem most impossible to you? Is that a bad thing? How so?

What are your natural capacities? Do you feel that God built on them in discipling you?

Finish this prayer: "Lord, my enthusiasm for doing your will can't help me. I can only follow as I deepen . . ."

SEPTEMBER 26
THE "GO" OF RECONCILIATION

Don't resist the Spirit's light; He shines it down the path of true healing.

BACKGROUND Two days ago we looked at Matthew 5:23–24 and how God wants us to confess the tiniest things. Today we return to these verses and focus on confessing when someone has something against us.

Before you looked at today's lesson, had God already reminded you of a problem in one of your relationships? Oswald Chambers warns us against dredging up obscure issues with others, which could be a sign of "morbid sensitiveness" rather than a sign that you offended someone and need reconciliation. So if you weren't already reminded, then learn from today's study so you can apply it in the future.

SCRIPTURAL CONTEXT In the original talk, "The 'Go' of Preparation," Chambers divided Matthew 5:23–24 into six sections (see September 24, *Companion*). Today's lesson comes from the second, fifth, and sixth pieces ("and there remember," "First be reconciled" and "then come . . ."). How do these pieces work together?

What sacrifice do you give to God? Is reconciliation ever as "natural as breathing" for you? Think about these words, and ask God for insight.

WHAT'S THE DEVOTIONAL SAYING? In today's final paragraph, Chambers gives us a clear, step-by-step description of how we experience Matthew 5:23–24. We, especially young Christians (see September 24, *Utmost*), first feel the heroic call to sacrifice. Second, God tells us about someone who has something against us. Third, we follow the way that God's Word shows us, which gives us the "unblameable" attitude that makes reconciliation as easy as breathing. Finally, we can give to God what we first felt heroically called to give Him.

Have you ever been through this process? Now that you have learned more about it, perhaps God will take you through it soon. Pray that you will be ready and open to God's corrective nudges.

APPLICATION
What situation is like being at the altar? Could you leave abruptly to be reconciled?
Are you prone to be too introspective? Not sensitive enough? What can you do about it?
Finish this prayer: "Spirit of God, you remind me of things I need to do, and I still procrastinate. But today I'm . . ."

SEPTEMBER 27
THE "GO" OF RENUNCIATION

What's holding you back?
God will body-slam it!

◄ ►

BACKGROUND Out on the moors and hills of Scotland, Oswald Chambers welcomed the "leagues of pure air" and was no stranger to freezing north winds. Today, he captures how we all feel about Luke 9:57–62: That Jesus is as discouraging as a north wind to His would-be followers.

Don't our feelings about this passage come from identifying with the three men in Jesus' story? Can't we imagine ourselves in their shoes? We need lots of courage as we look at what Chambers says about their (and our) flimsy excuses!

SCRIPTURAL CONTEXT Read Luke 9:57–62. How does John 2:25 explain Jesus' harshness? What evils hide in your heart? Jesus sees them. How will He hurt them to the point of death?

Imagine being one of those three men and, thirty years later, reading about yourself in Luke's gospel. How would you feel? What if you had eventually become Jesus' followers? Would you feel ashamed?

WHAT'S THE DEVOTIONAL SAYING? Today's lesson looks at how Jesus handles three reasons people fail to truly follow Him. First, some people who want to follow Jesus don't *truly* want to follow Him. Their desire is to please themselves. Jesus rejects them and leaves them with nothing but desperate hope, which is the beginning of true discipleship.

Second, some put family before Jesus. How does Jesus handle this? (The lesson doesn't say, but Luke 9:59 does.)

Others have reservations about following. Jesus gives these people an "exacting call." Has He given you this kind of call? What still holds you back?

APPLICATION
Have you felt embarrassed for Jesus? What is He doing when He seems unreasonable?
What do you need to renounce (comfort, family, reservations)? Will you let them go?
Finish this prayer: "Jesus, I will follow you with no exceptions. Only you have the words of eternal life . . ."

Is your heart hard?
A look from Jesus can tenderize it!

BACKGROUND In his *Complete Works,* Oswald Chambers uses the word *identify* and its derivatives more than four hundred times. We're more comfortable describing ourselves as "adopted" or "redeemed." What does "identified" even mean?

Today's lesson explains that being *identified with Jesus* means "having a relationship with Him in which there is no other relationship." Are you identified with Jesus like this? Today's lesson says that this is God's primary consideration when He calls us to follow Him.

SCRIPTURAL CONTEXT We recently looked at the rich young ruler's story (August 17–18). As He did with the three men we saw yesterday, Jesus told the rich young ruler hard things. Why does Jesus do this? What do we learn from Mark 10:21?

Have you reduced yourself until you are a mere human being? Renouncing possessions— not just material possessions—is one of the things about which Chambers says, "We have to

do all that ourselves" (see May 10, *Utmost*), and God won't do it for us. Ask Him to empower you with His Spirit, so you will have the strength to renounce all.

WHAT'S THE DEVOTIONAL SAYING? Chambers distinguishes that which saves us (salvation) and gives us the gift of the Holy Spirit (sanctification) from that which we do to remove all competing relationships from the one we have with God. Only reliance on Jesus gives us salvation and sanctification, since only He does those things. But we must rid our lives of competing relationships; God won't do it for us.

Today ends the lessons in our five-day series that talk about "go." What does "go" mean in this sense? Chambers says *go* simply means, *"live."* Jesus doesn't tell us simply to *go* to Jerusalem, Samaria, and other parts of the world; He says to be His witnesses in all those places. Are you living your life as a witness for Him?

APPLICATION

Has your heart ever melted before God? If so, how? Where are you hard or vindictive?

What is lacking in your oneness with Jesus? What must you renounce? Are you willing?

Finish this prayer: "Jesus, I want to follow you down the road you're traveling; so I renounce my right to . . ."

THE AWARENESS OF THE CALL

God's call is mysterious, but it can't be resisted!

BACKGROUND The last two lessons in our eleven-day series come from the second lecture in a series of missionary studies (see September 4, *Companion*). Today we learn that God's call is not what we might think. Tomorrow we will see that He calls us to be "broken bread and poured-out wine."

Those who heard Oswald Chambers' missionary studies were students who would soon be scattered to the ends of the earth. They thought God might be calling them to preach the gospel. Today's lesson helps anyone, whether called to preach or not, to hear God's call.

SCRIPTURAL CONTEXT Today's theme verse is strange in light of what Paul says in the previous verse. Why does Paul want to boast (verse 15) when he can't boast (verse 16)? He is talking about boasting about supporting himself in one case and about preaching in the other.

What other examples of the call to preach can you find in the Bible? How do these compare to our call to support ourselves (1 Thessalonians 4:11 and Ephesians 4:28)?

WHAT'S THE DEVOTIONAL SAYING? In three paragraphs, Chambers teaches us about God's call. First, it is always supernatural. It might be sudden or it might be gradual, but if you can explain it easily, it is not from God. Second, it is "obliterated" when we put things ahead of God. We can't resist the call, but we can put it on the backburner. Third, circumstances, bad or good, further God's purpose and call. God wants to call us consciously and at a deeper level, so we need Him to use any and all circumstances to get through to us.

Has God called you to preach? Even if He never does, what can you learn from today's lesson? Is it that God gives His plan for us in mysterious, irresistible, supernatural ways? Listen to His voice in your circumstances. Don't put anything above Him. At any moment, His surprising call might break through!

APPLICATION

How does God's call differ from salvation and sanctification? How has God called you? What has prevented you from fulfilling God's call? How has God orchestrated things?

Finish this prayer: "Father, your call to me runs through my veins in a way I can't describe. I want to . . ."

THE ASSIGNING OF THE CALL

Who can help you suffer and be more like Christ?
God's answer is "anyone."

◄

BACKGROUND Today we finish our eleven-day series and reach the three-quarters mark of our year in *Utmost*. How appropriate that today's lesson reminds us of Oswald Chambers' favorite biblical image—broken bread and poured-out wine.

But today's lesson is not a lofty treatise on biblical imagery. It hits us in the heart and meets us right where we live each day. It teaches us why we often face people who annoy us: Because God uses them to make us more like Christ!

SCRIPTURAL CONTEXT We looked at Colossians 1:24 on February 3 and July 14, and we'll see it again in a week. What does the phrase "fill up in my flesh what is lacking in the afflictions of Christ" mean? How does Chambers describe the way this happens?

In the first paragraph, Chambers quotes Isaiah 6:8. What is the "one thing we never dreamed of"? In the full sermon, Chambers

explains that it is "the condition of real communion with God." It's in that condition when we overhear God asking, "Whom shall I send?" Isaiah experienced that communion. Have you?

WHAT'S THE DEVOTIONAL SAYING? On February 24, we saw that Paul was a "sacramental personality" (Classic Edition). We see this phrase again today: "To be a sacramental personality means that the elements of the natural life are presenced by God as they are broken providentially in His service." Are the elements of your natural life being broken by everyday circumstances?

The problem with being made into wine is the way God crushes us. We object to the people and circumstances He uses. Can you think of who and what He has used recently? Did you enjoy the experience? Probably not, but stay in His will and you will be crushed into a blessing to others!

APPLICATION

How have you set yourself apart for God? Do you try to make this consecration a call?

Whom does God use to crush you? How do you respond? How does your "wine" taste?

Finish this prayer: "Lord, I need to be right with you so I'll experience your presence in every-day things . . ."

OCTOBER 1
THE PLACE OF EXALTATION

Do you want character?
Touch it by revelation and keep it by adversity.

➤

BACKGROUND Today we start a new series on Mark 9. Oswald Chambers' original talk on this subject was given at the weekly devotional hour (see January 1, *Companion*). It had three subsections, which have the same titles as the three-day series that begins today.

Have you been to the top of the mountain with God? Have you been plunged into the valley? Has there been an "epileptic boy" problem in your life that you couldn't solve? Over the next three days, we'll hear what Chambers says about these important themes from Mark 9.

SCRIPTURAL CONTEXT Chapter 9 is pivotal in Mark's gospel. The transition begins in chapter 8. Read 8:27–9:32. Why is this section the turning point?

Have you wondered what it will be like when you get to heaven and see Jesus? That's the essence of Bart Millard's song recorded by MercyMe: "I Can Only Imagine." Mark 9:2–7 gives us a sneak peek into what heaven will be like. The song wonders whether we will be able to stand in God's presence or perhaps simply fall to our knees. What did the disciples do in this situation? Can you imagine what it might be like?

WHAT'S THE DEVOTIONAL SAYING? Today's lesson doesn't talk only about the mountaintop, but it also previews tomorrow's study about the valley. What does it tell us? First, we must not yield to the temptation of staying on the mountain. We're not built for the "air" up there! Second, the mountain is to help us be poured-out wine for other people. Finally, to be wine for others, we don't need to be taught, we need to be *made*.

How is God making you into His bread and wine? What's in your "demon-possessed" valley? For godly character, we need *both* the mountain *and* the valley.

APPLICATION

What was a mountaintop experience for you? Did it help you lift others up? Why or why not?
How do teaching and building character differ? Why is one better? Which do you prefer?
Finish this prayer: "Father, without the day-to-day grind and the mountaintop experiences, I would never . . ."

OCTOBER 2
THE PLACE OF HUMILIATION

Seeing God's power is humbling because it shows where we doubted Him.

BACKGROUND We don't read much about Oswald Chambers' "valley" experiences. His sermons, lectures, and even private diaries sound mostly upbeat. Even when his mind was "unrelieved" (see March 28, *Companion*), it seemed as if this was the exception to the rule.

But we know that Chambers didn't "presume . . . to teach" what he hadn't "by suffering bought" (see January 28, *Companion*). So we can be sure he personally experienced "things as they are . . . neither beautiful nor poetic nor thrilling."

SCRIPTURAL CONTEXT Today we learn an important distinction between seeing and living. The heart-swelling mountaintop experience is for vision, and the drab drudgery of the valley is for living. Can you find this distinction in Mark 8 and 9?

How does Jesus respond in Mark 9:23? How did his question root out skepticism in the father's heart? Do you get skeptical when in the valley? What is Jesus asking you?

WHAT'S THE DEVOTIONAL SAYING? When Jesus taught in parables, He gave the story and later explained the meaning. Chambers says a similar thing happens with the vision and the meaning of the vision. God gives us a vision, and we feel as if we can trust Him in anything. Then He brings us back to reality, where we're tempted to be skeptical. The *meaning* of the vision is still trusting God in real life.

It's humbling enough to be in the drab drudgery of real life. But the most humbling thing is to see that we didn't have as much faith in God as we thought when we were on the mountain. It would have been less humbling if God had never shown us His power on the mountain. But our humility is His goal!

APPLICATION

What has been humbling for you? Did it expose your skepticism about God's power?

If your skepticism was exposed, did you feel like leaving Jesus (see September 19, *Utmost*)? How so?

Finish this prayer: "Jesus, I want my time with you to always be rosy. When it isn't, I turn my eyes to . . ."

THE PLACE OF MINISTRY

Does your ministry make a difference?
It will when you are close to God.

◄

BACKGROUND Today we finish the three-day series based on Oswald Chambers' talk "Can You Come Down?" Do you feel more ready to come down into the valley? Can you see why God puts us up on the mountain in the first place?

Today's lesson looks closely at times when we pray but there are no results. Has this happened to you? Today's lesson encourages us to pray and keep praying more!

SCRIPTURAL CONTEXT Today's theme verse, taken from the King James Version, varies from most versions we use today, which drop the words "and fasting." Why? Scholars' best guess is that "and fasting" was probably added later and that Jesus didn't actually say that. Chambers' analysis thankfully doesn't change. Why not? Would today's lesson still be true if Jesus had never said, "and fasting"?

On March 19 and July 20 Chambers interpreted Isaiah 40:31 as he does today: We should "mount up" in mountaintop experiences *and* walk through the drudgery of life. How does Philippians 4:13 fit into this interpretation?

WHAT'S THE DEVOTIONAL SAYING? Today's study looks at what makes you powerful (or powerless) as Jesus' disciple. Chambers' answer is this: your focus on Christ. If you continually focus and refocus on Jesus, you will eventually break through all obstacles. When you do, the obstacles you faced "and all you have been through in connection with it" will bring Jesus glory. Interestingly, you won't see how you bring Him glory until you die. Why might that be?

You can choose to cling to the mountain and not face the obstacles of real life. But if you are willing to go back down the mountain and make up your mind to focus and refocus on Jesus, even when your prayers yield no visible results, you will glorify God in a way that is beyond your wildest imagination!

APPLICATION

Do you want to stop being powerless for God? If so, does your relationship reflect this?

What's going on when you pray and nothing seems to happen? What should you do?

Finish this prayer: "Lord, I don't want to avoid difficult situations just because I prefer mountaintops; so I . . ."

OCTOBER 4
THE VISION AND THE REALITY

God knows the real you, not who you are right now but who you will be.

BACKGROUND Today's lesson doesn't come from the same source material as the three-day series we just finished, but it fits in perfectly. What we learn today ties together what we saw for the past five days.

Have you explored the "valley"? Have you examined the fingers God uses to crush you into wine? The hands that knead you into bread? Today's lesson looks at all of those things and concludes that we can't escape God's crushing, kneading plans for us.

SCRIPTURAL CONTEXT Paul's greetings give us insight into what he wants to tell his readers. In today's verse, what does Paul say about the Corinthians? What does he say about himself in verse 1? Why was it important to this letter that he said these things?

In the final paragraph of today's lesson, Oswald Chambers quotes Exodus 3:14 and reminds us of an essential truth: we need to let our little "I am's" fade away in light of God's great I AM. Will you do that today?

WHAT'S THE DEVOTIONAL SAYING?
God's primary call on our lives is not to any particular ministry. He calls us to be saints. To train us to be saints, He batters us through people and situations, crushing us into the wine that will bless other people. The hardest part about God's training is not the battering or even the difficult people He uses to crush us, but the times we can't see *what* His purpose is.

In hard times like those, what keeps us going? Chambers says it is the vision God gives us on the mountaintop. Thank God right now for letting you see what He wants you to become!

APPLICATION
What bumps and bruises have you experienced? Were you prepared? How did they shape you?
Has God said *do*? How? Has He hunted you down? Is it comforting that He knows you?
Finish this prayer: "God, no matter where I sulk and hide, you will find me; so I'm giving myself to you . . ."

OCTOBER 5
THE NATURE OF DEGENERATION

We're born with sin, but God won't condemn us unless we reject His Son.

➤

BACKGROUND Today we begin a three-day series on theology. If you find yourself disagreeing with Oswald Chambers, you are not alone. Students at his Bible Training College often lambasted him over dinner about some piece of theology he had just taught them. His gentle response was, "Just leave it for now. Brood on it, and it will come to you later."

As you read the next three days of lessons, brood on what you learn and let the Holy Spirit help you understand each piece.

SCRIPTURAL CONTEXT Today's theme verse sums up Paul's teaching on original sin. This subject is always under attack. Most recently, the battle is whether one father for the whole human race is even a scientific possibility, given population genetics and data from the human genome project. But these battles come and go, while the biblical and experiential evidence for humans' sin nature remains.

What does Paul say about original sin? How is it similar to what Hebrews 9:26 says?

Chambers tells us that John 3:19 is proof that we aren't condemned for original sin, but for rejecting Jesus. Do you think that's the correct way to interpret John 3:19?

WHAT'S THE DEVOTIONAL SAYING? This three-day series comes from the book *The Shadow of an Agony*, which Biddy prepared from her notes less than a year after Oswald died. In this book, Chambers lays out his theology. Today we see that he thinks that Jesus did away with original sin, once for all humans, and that, therefore, God doesn't condemn us for original sin, but for rejecting His Son.

Do you think Chambers is right? Perhaps before you decide one way or another, you should follow his advice and "brood on it" for a while. Ask God to show you where your sin nature (disposition) continues to rear its ugly head, though Jesus stripped it of its power.

APPLICATION

How have you seen sin's heredity at work in you? What rights do you claim? Why?

Do you look more at others' morality or at their nature? Does knowing *your* nature help?

Finish this prayer: "Jesus, thank you for taking away my sinful heredity. Without your costly sacrifice, I . . ."

OCTOBER 6
THE NATURE OF REGENERATION

Do you want holiness?
Admit your neediness!

◄ ►

BACKGROUND Isn't it odd that Oswald Chambers taught these theological lessons to soldiers, many of whom were heading to the frontlines to die? If he thought *they* needed to hear these things, then *everybody* does!

Today, Chambers looks at the problem of God's demand for our holiness. If God wants us to be holy but we start life with a sinful nature, then what can be done? He can exchange our nature with the nature of His Son! Praise God, this is what He did!

SCRIPTURAL CONTEXT Yesterday it might have been hard to fully agree with Chambers' view. But today our understanding of his message deepens. We learn that he doesn't think Jesus *erased* our nature (disposition) of sin that we inherited from Adam. Rather, we keep our old disposition until we realize our need and ask Jesus for His perfect disposition. It is then— when we come to Jesus as beggars—that we become blessed (Matthew 5:3).

Today's theme verse makes it clear that we become aware of our need and ask for Christ's disposition only when it pleases God. Our salvation is entirely God's work, not ours, which is what Chambers has said all along.

WHAT'S THE DEVOTIONAL SAYING? What is our role in God's demand for holiness? Chambers says it is to agree with the verdict God gave against sin at the cross (Romans 8:3). We must agree with God's condemnation of our self-love and keep agreeing with it "until Christ is formed" in us. Will you keep doing that, as you did when you first realized your need?

APPLICATION

Which teachings of Jesus cause you to despair? How are you hit by your sense of need?

How would this week be different if you were more spotless? Do you really want that?

Finish this prayer: "God, I owe you everything: my first birth and my second. I *do* want to be holy, so I'll . . ."

OCTOBER 7
THE NATURE OF RECONCILIATION

We're reconciled when we repent, by God's power.

◄

BACKGROUND When several theologians were arguing about what distinguished Christianity from other religions, C. S. Lewis overheard their debate and famously quipped, "It's grace." Oswald Chambers might have said the same thing. But today he says that another difference is that other religions deal with *sins* while only the Bible deals with *sin*.

Our theological three-day series ends today by teaching us what part of the salvation experience is God's job and what part is ours. It tells us that God's job is to take away the sin nature of humanity, and our job is to be willing to identify with Jesus (see September 28, *Utmost*). As Chambers says in the original lecture, "Every one of us who is willing to be identified with Him is freed from the disposition of sin."

SCRIPTURAL CONTEXT Today's theme verse profoundly explains the gospel. Paul says, "Be reconciled to God," and then he gives this verse as the explanation for how we are reconciled. Is there anything this verse leaves out of the explanation? How does it compare to other biblical summaries of the gospel message? Why is it important to know this?

WHAT'S THE DEVOTIONAL SAYING? On September 17, we began a three-day series from *The Philosophy of Sin*, which is a whole book on the nature of sin. What two things do we learn about sin today? First, we learn that sin is a "fundamental relationship." What does this mean? Sin is the foundation underneath a relationship between man and the devil that allows man to be his own god. Sin is not about *doing*, since people who live moral lives can be as much "in sin" as those who are immoral. Sin is about *being*. Man *is* a rebel. He *is* independent from God. Sin is man's state of being.

Second, we learn that God took responsibility for creating the devil by sending His Son to the cross to take away our fundamental relationship to the devil. God doesn't condemn us for this relationship that Adam began. He simply removes the relationship and offers to apply the reality of this removal to each of us. We are "responsible moral" beings (see October 6, *Utmost*), so we don't experience the reality of God's removal of our sin-relationship unless we are conscious of our need—our spiritual poverty. Thank God today for His amazing gift of reconciliation!

APPLICATION

Do you focus more on sin or sins? Why? Did Christ become our sin or our sins?

What actions connected you to God's redemption? Who helped you do those things?

Finish this prayer: "Holy Spirit, without you, I would still be rejecting salvation; and even now I would . . ."

OCTOBER 8
COMING TO JESUS

What won't let you come to Jesus?
The Spirit will ask you to kill whatever it is.

BACKGROUND Today's title in the Classic Edition is "The Exclusiveness of Christ." The Updated Edition's title is "Coming to Jesus." But we've already had four lessons about coming to Jesus (June 11, August 19–20, and September 13). So what makes today's lesson different?

"Exclusiveness" is the key. We come to Jesus by *excluding* what the Holy Spirit says is blocking our path to Jesus. What blocks your path? Will you exclude it and come to Jesus today?

SCRIPTURAL CONTEXT Each time we look at Matthew 10:25–30, we learn new things. For example, did you notice verse 27? What does this mean? Why did Jesus say this right before He invited the weary to come to Him?

Today's final paragraph comes from a talk on our revealed certainties. In this talk, Oswald Chambers quotes Galatians 2:20 and says that it "is foundation truth and experimental truth in one." Which part of this verse talks about the daily life we experience? The rest of the verse is about foundational truth. What is that truth? How does this relate to Matthew 11:28?

WHAT'S THE DEVOTIONAL SAYING? Although it seems just as difficult as the three-day series we just finished, today's lesson is simple. It says that Jesus invites us to come to Him. Then the Spirit reveals what prevents us from coming. Next, any "spiritual impertinence" in us refuses to come to Jesus because what the Spirit reveals seems so foolish.

These three things (invitation, revelation, refusal) happen all the time. What happens next is up to us. We can surrender our impertinence, or we can keep refusing. If we refuse, we don't go further until we surrender. Thankfully, Jesus keeps inviting us. His patience is "invincible, unconquerable, unwearying." As soon as we surrender, Jesus not only takes us, but we also take Him. As a result, we receive far more than we could have ever hoped!

APPLICATION

What about Jesus embarrasses you? When have you felt most foolish coming to Him?

What are your requests? Do you feel you've received them? Will they help you *come*?

Finish this prayer: "Jesus, I'm sorry for all the times I haven't come to you. You're the only one I need . . ."

OCTOBER 9
BUILDING ON THE ATONEMENT

Is it about your conversion or about Who converted you?

BACKGROUND Biddy Chambers took two of her husband Oswald's talks and blended them to give us a devotional reading about the atonement. What's the atonement? The Merriam-Webster dictionary defines it as "the reconciliation of God and humankind through the sacrificial death of Jesus Christ."

How does the atonement help us in our daily life? It's the compass that points us in the right direction for everything we do and who we are. For example, if we are pious, but our piety is not based on the atonement, then our piety counts for nothing. Today's lesson will help you build your life on the atonement.

SCRIPTURAL CONTEXT Romans 6 teaches you how to "pull yourself together" practically through the atonement. Chambers focused on verses 13–18 in his original talk "You Need Not Sin." What can you learn about not sinning from these verses?

In Chambers' original "Pull Yourself Together" talk, he quoted John 15:7. How is this verse related to Romans 6 and the atonement?

WHAT'S THE DEVOTIONAL SAYING?
In the July 10 and 12 lessons, Chambers warned against the secluded Christian life typified by ancient monasteries. Today he says that if we are pious without the atonement, we won't be good for anything but a secluded life. People who spend hours reading the Bible, praying, and so forth all to bolster their feelings of spiritually superiority are destined to seclude themselves with others who subscribe to their definitions of super spirituality.

In the materialistic, hedonistic Western culture that surrounds and influences us, over-piousness is not usually our problem. However, when we don't base our lives on the atonement, we create problems every bit as dangerous as over-piousness and seclusion. Without the atonement at the center of our lives, everything we do will be tainted by our self-love. This leads directly to the problem of spiritual arrogance. We need to realize that the only reason we can ever do anything good is because of the power of the atonement.

Have you ever wondered how we are supposed to purify our hidden motives? We can't! Only God purifies what's impure. That's why we have to build on the atonement to be holy in anything we do.

APPLICATION
How can your holiness be based more on the atonement? On practical, everyday life?
What are you *doing* to be holy? What are you *believing*? Why is one more important?
Finish this prayer: "Lord, I want your atonement to show up in the little things I do and to be the basis of . . ."

293

OCTOBER 10
HOW WILL I KNOW?

Reasoning is sinking sand. Obedience is a solid rock.

BACKGROUND Oswald Chambers liked to tell his Bible Training College students that their job at the college wasn't to *do* anything but to soak before God. Today we see the first mention of "soaking" in *Utmost*. We read how "soaking in" God's Word is better than worrying about it.

How can you "soak in" God's word? You can start by reading the context of Matthew 11:25 yet again.

SCRIPTURAL CONTEXT We've read Matthew 11:25–30 many times. But if we want to "soak," we've got to keep reading verses again and again. This time, focus on verse 26. What pleased God? Does God always do what He pleases? Why is it right and beautiful when *God* does what He pleases? Why is it so wrong and ugly when *we* do what we please?

Chambers also mentions, "walking in the light." Do you remember where to find this phrase? Why does Chambers emphasize the word *are* in this phrase?

WHAT'S THE DEVOTIONAL SAYING? In previous lessons, Chambers taught that we grow step-by-step in knowledge of God and His will, in concentration during prayer, and in clear thinking (see September 14, *Utmost*). But today he says that we do *not* grow step-by-step in our spiritual relationships. We either have a relationship with God (and are cleansed from sin) or we don't.

Our obedience to God, as we've learned before, is the key to new spiritual knowledge and growth. Today we see that our obedience to God is an all-or-nothing act, like the marriage act. But how does this instantaneous act relate to the slow "soaking" in God's truth that Chambers mentions ("immersing" in the Updated Edition)? The answer is simple: When we soak in God's truth, we stop worrying about or "trying to find out" about God's truth and can focus our energy on obeying. The act of obedience takes no time at all, but getting to the point where we are ready to obey requires lots of "soaking" before God's presence. Are you willing to start soaking today?

APPLICATION

Which parts of us grow step-by-step and which parts don't? Does this change our focus?

What truths are hidden from you? How do you (or should you) try to understand them?

Finish this prayer: "God, obeying you is the antidote for all my wishy-washy uncertainty. Today I'll obey . . ."

GOD'S SILENCE—THEN WHAT?

Want to still your heart?
Listen to God's silence.

BACKGROUND The sisters experienced four long days of sorrow. And that's not even counting the anxious days of waiting for Jesus before their brother died. Mary and Martha certainly experienced grief to the full.

Then there is Biddy Chambers, editing her dead husband's sermon on God's silence. As she typed and retyped today's study, what thoughts crossed her mind? Did she envy Mary and Martha, who only had to taste a few days of sadness before their tears turned into joyful laughter? Was she comforted to know that God trusted her enough to give her silence—from the hour she first started praying that her husband would recover, until months or years later when her heart had fully realized that "this sickness is not unto death" (see May 1, *Companion*)?

Will today's lesson be a comfort to you too? It will—but only if you are willing to let go of the idea that God will always bless you in answer to your prayer.

SCRIPTURAL CONTEXT We haven't read the story of Lazarus since February 13. Read it today, and put yourself in the sisters' shoes. Although they had totally different personalities, they shared the same feelings of abandonment. If only Jesus had come earlier! Oswald Chambers also quotes Matthew 7:9 and the phrase "bread of life" from John 6:35. Have you felt as if God mocked your prayers and gave you exactly what you *didn't* want? How could what He gave you have been the "bread of life"?

WHAT'S THE DEVOTIONAL SAYING? Today's lesson is simple to understand but difficult to apply! It tells us that when we pray and don't get what we asked for, it is God's silence, which is better than getting what we wanted. Why better? It's the first sign that we are getting closer to God. We learn that prayer is all about getting closer to Him, not about getting things.

Some people think God always blesses in answer to prayer and are quick to tell you about all the ways God has blessed them. Other people see prayer as the way to get to know God and often receive silence in answer to their prayers. In which group would you like to be? Don't you want God to always bless you?

Then again, isn't getting to know God the best thing you could ask for? Even if your husband, like Oswald, or brother, like Lazarus, or any other loved one is on the brink of death, isn't drawing closer to God even more important? Until you accept that as the absolute truth, your prayer life will be hollow.

APPLICATION
Before Jesus raised Lazarus, how did Mary or Martha feel? Have you ever felt this way?
How does the silence of despair and of pleasure differ? Have you "caught" God's silence?
Finish this prayer: "God, you give the best things; so, though it seems you aren't giving . . ."

OCTOBER 12
GETTING INTO GOD'S STRIDE

God moves fast. Ask for help and stay right in step!

➤

BACKGROUND Just ten days before he developed the case of appendicitis that led to his death, Oswald Chambers gave a talk on Enoch to the Word War I soldiers gathered for Sunday service at his YMCA hut in Egypt. Today and tomorrow we read parts of this talk.

Are you getting into stride with God? Chambers influenced the world, not because he died fairly young, but because he walked day by day with God.

SCRIPTURAL CONTEXT We don't know much about Enoch. Genesis 5:24, Hebrews 11:5, and Jude 14 are our only biblical clues about his life. He captures our imagination because, besides Elijah and Jesus, he is the only person who left earth while alive.

Chambers also references John 1:36 (John the Baptist recognized Jesus' worth as Jesus simply walked) and quotes Isaiah 42:4. What things could have discouraged Jesus or caused Him to fail?

WHAT'S THE DEVOTIONAL SAYING? Anyone who has tried to get in shape physically can understand the point of today's lesson: Getting in spiritual "shape" requires pushing through pain and keeping at it.

What makes the process so painful? God has different ways of doing things, and until we learn His ways we suffer for three reasons. First, we don't get to be in the spotlight. God's strides take us through the most mundane things. Second, He makes us hang on past our first wind all the way to our second wind and beyond. Third, we can't use our intellect to learn God's ways.

Are you willing to get in shape spiritually? If you are, be prepared for pain. But the "gain" is worth it: God's stride alone will shine through your life. When you work from God's standpoint, you will not fail or be discouraged. His pain protects you from any other pains.

APPLICATION

What are you doing now to keep pace with God? Are you tired? What would help you?

How has God changed your way of looking at things? What do you still need to change?

Finish this prayer: "Holy Spirit, please clear the air around me so I can see your power and not the . . ."

∾ OCTOBER 13 ∾
INDIVIDUAL DISCOURAGEMENT
AND PERSONAL GROWTH

Feeling dry in the desert?
Let God scorch your pride!

◄

BACKGROUND Yesterday we saw that getting into God's stride is painful. Today we learn about God's first great stride and how we learn this great lesson when our individual nature gets discouraged.

You are an individual, different from everyone else. For *what* do you think God made you? There is a reason! But even after He gives you a vision for that reason, you aren't ready to serve Him. You have to first get into His stride.

SCRIPTURAL CONTEXT Exodus 3 gives a good picture of God's first great stride. Our theme verse shows us Moses' vision for what his individuality was created to do. But it's not until forty years later that he is ready and walks God's first great stride. What is this stride? Have you ever walked it?

Oswald Chambers also refers to Matthew 3:11 and says that our individual effort is nothing compared to what individuality can do in a personal relationship to God. Does this verse illustrate what Chambers says?

WHAT'S THE DEVOTIONAL SAYING?
Today's lesson is straightforward. Even though God gives us a vision for our life, we won't see that vision fulfilled until we become discouraged with our own efforts. During this time in the desert, God disciplines and trains us. Only then will we be in stride and in relationship with God, recognizing that He is the one who brings the Holy Spirit's fire.

Has this happened to you? Was it painful? God wants you to be the right person for the job. Even though He created you to be that person, you aren't actually that person until you go through this kind of discouragement about your vision and then grow as a result.

APPLICATION

What is God's vision for you? Are you doing that now? If not, is it a time for growth?

What lesson must we learn in the wilderness? Or when we're trembling in God's presence?

Finish this prayer: "Father God, I put stock in my personal effort, which is an impertinence to you. Please help me . . ."

ᗌᗑᗌ OCTOBER 14 ᗌᗑᗌ
THE KEY TO THE MISSIONARY'S LIFE

Want to reach the lost?
Jesus alone can let you!

➤

BACKGROUND At the end of September, we spent eleven days learning about missionary issues. For the next five days, we get an encore of that great series. What more do we need to learn about being a missionary? All the same things we need to learn about being a Christian.

Today's lesson is rich in vital truth. It's as if Oswald Chambers reached for all his favorite verses and threw them into one big pot to stew up a rare delicacy for us today.

SCRIPTURAL CONTEXT The lesson begins with a short exposition of Matthew 28:16–20. What is Chambers' main point about this passage? He brings in Acts 1:8 to show us we need to go (or live) in the power of the Holy Spirit. Then he quotes Matthew 11:28 to remind us that the Spirit's power is there for us when we are most weary—if we only ask for it. He also uses John 15:7 to show *how* we go— by feeding on God's Word.

What is the context of Acts 20:24? Does Paul's speech reflect what he said in Philippians 1:21? How can you make this verse your motto?

WHAT'S THE DEVOTIONAL SAYING? A key point today is that God is not the helper who aids us in our projects. He is our "absolute sovereign and supreme Lord." Have you ever caught yourself thinking of God merely as your assistant?

An even bigger point is this: If we are to really know that God is our sovereign, we have to know Him personally and know how to spend alone time with Him.

Don't worry if where you are is not where you hoped you would be. Don't worry if you're doing something that's totally not what you hoped you would be doing. Don't even worry about those who are lost. For now, focus on your "living experience" of Jesus.

APPLICATION

How do your words to the lost compare to what they see in you? Why do you live a clean life? Where are you being placed? Do you see this as God's doing? How do you keep going?

Finish this prayer: "Lord, I want my life to reflect my living experience of you. Help me not to count dear . . ."

ᏅᎠᎾ OCTOBER 15 ᏅᎠᎾ
THE KEY TO THE MISSIONARY'S MESSAGE

Jesus isn't Savior to all, but He is propitiation for all, taking God's anger away.

◄ ►

BACKGROUND Although today's lesson comes from Oswald Chambers' series of missionary studies (see September 4, *Companion*), it has a theological bent. Do you think Jesus took away God's anger against Adam's sin that had spread to the whole world? Why does it even matter?

Understanding the theological term *propitiation* is, according to Chambers, the key to the missionary message. And lest you think you don't have to learn the missionary message, Chambers added, in his original sermon, that by "missionary" he means "a doctor, a teacher, an industrial worker, or a nurse" or anyone else.

SCRIPTURAL CONTEXT Chambers uses two verses to suggest that Jesus' propitiation took upon himself *everyone's* original sin. First, 1 John 2:2 says that Jesus' propitiation is for the whole world. Pretty hard to argue against that! Second, John 1:29 says Jesus takes the whole world's sin away. Chambers likes to distinguish between *sin* and *sins*. Which word do these verses use?

The last verse Chambers quotes is 1 Corinthians 9:16, explaining that the "gospel" is Jesus' propitiation. Do you agree?

WHAT'S THE DEVOTIONAL SAYING?
To understand *Utmost*, it helps to know the spiritual climate that prevailed in Chambers' world. As we read through his *Complete Works*, we can find clues to this climate. For example, we read: "We have cheapened the doctrine of sin and made the atonement a sort of moral 'lavatory' in which men can come and wash themselves from sin, and then go and sin again and come back for another washing." Do you see signs of the same climate in our day?

Whenever Christians cheapen the doctrine of sin, the missionary message is ridiculed. What can you do to strengthen your understanding of sin and how God dealt with it? Don't give in to mental woolgathering (see August 23, *Companion*). Do the hard work it takes to learn theology!

APPLICATION
When you talk about God with other people, what is your focus? What is *not* limitless?
Why is it important to focus on the limitless thing? How does that message affect you?
Finish this prayer: "Jesus, you have remitted my sins—cancelled them completely. Now God's wrath is . . ."

OCTOBER 16
THE KEY TO THE MASTER'S ORDERS

Prayer is harder than work.

◄ ➤

BACKGROUND As we reach the halfway mark of our five-day series, we can take stock of what we've learned so far. First, we learned that our relationship to Jesus is the only basis for our work as missionaries. Second, we learned that our message must be based on Jesus' propitiation, since it's the only part of Jesus' work that was truly universal.

Today we turn to the issue of prayer. Oswald Chambers loves to talk about prayer, and he mentions it one hundred times in *Utmost* alone. In today's study, he says prayer is essential for missionaries, especially relative to what we typically think of as Christian "work."

SCRIPTURAL CONTEXT What prompted Jesus to speak today's theme verse? Have you ever felt like a sheep without a shepherd? The conviction of sin, and the crisis it produces, is what makes the harvest so plentiful (see also John 4:35).

Chambers also discusses John 13:16. He says that we are not to "dictate" our demands to Jesus. Have you been treating Master Jesus as lower than you and telling Him what you want Him to do? That's not how it works with Jesus!

WHAT'S THE DEVOTIONAL SAYING? Henry Blackaby's popular Bible study *Experiencing God* teaches us that our ministry is more effective when we go where we see God working. Today's lesson teaches the same thing. We must concentrate on God through prayer and look for the crises that occur in others' lives. Otherwise, we will be so busy doing our own thing that we will miss when God works in the lives of even our closest friends and relatives.

For whom do you pray? Do you pray that they will experience the conviction of sin? Spend more time in prayer today and less time in frantic, over-energized activities. Look for where God is working!

APPLICATION

Do you know anyone in distress, convicted of sin, and ready to be "harvested" for God? What work are you doing for God? Does it distract you from God? How is your prayer? Finish this prayer: "Lord of the harvest, please send out laborers—even me! I'm ready to pray and not . . ."

OCTOBER 17
THE KEY OF THE GREATER WORK

God's redemption makes us pray, and our praying redeems those around us.

BACKGROUND Today's lesson comes from "The Key to the Missionary Problem," the first of three "Key" lectures Oswald Chambers gave in his missionary series. What is the missionary problem? It's the problem of reaching the lost with the good news message that will save them.

All of us know lost people. Even some of the people around us who we think are Christians (including those who read *Utmost* every day) might not be saved. What is the key to this problem? Prayer! Chambers practiced what he preached. He was constantly praying for others.

SCRIPTURAL CONTEXT In John 14:9–10, Jesus replies to Philip. He then addresses all the disciples. Do you think they understood what He was saying? When did they finally get it? How do we know that "greater works" come from prayer (see verse 13)?

Chambers also quotes from Matthew 9:38, which we saw yesterday. Today he highlights the fact that God *commands* us to pray. Are you willing to follow God's orders?

WHAT'S THE DEVOTIONAL SAYING? How does God's miracle of redemption work in us? Chambers says "prayer is the working of the miracle of Redemption," but what does that mean? He explains that prayer is based on redemption's agony, not on any of our agonizing efforts. We don't work. God is the only one who works. And by our meeting with God in prayer, God connects His work into our lives.

Do you want to make God's ingenious plans come to fruition? Then pray. Prayer is the battle. Everything else we do is just the job of walking through the battlefield and picking up the spoils of war.

APPLICATION

Do you pray that God will bless your works for Him? Do you see prayer as a work? Why? When do you pray? Do you see it as an order? Are you willing to be a harvest laborer?

Finish this prayer: "Jesus, I want to be childlike in my prayers, using your agony, not mine, in asking you . . ."

OCTOBER 18
THE KEY TO THE MISSIONARY'S DEVOTION

God's love makes us faithful. Our faithfulness helps us love others.

◄

BACKGROUND As we finish our five-day series, we get to read a powerful lesson on loyalty to God. We are so loyal to our own interests that we can't be loyal to God. We are to be a conduit to others for God's ideas and interests. God is not our conduit.

Who has God placed in your life? Do you see those people as His sheep or yours? How will you feed them practically this week?

SCRIPTURAL CONTEXT We don't often read John's third letter. It has fewer words than a typical *Utmost* devotional! The people John mentions in verse 5 are good examples for us. They went out among strangers because of God's great name. What else do we know about them? Was there a danger that they would not be treated hospitably even by fellow Christians?

Now read 1 Corinthians 13 and John 21. We've seen these chapters many times before.

What do they teach us about practical love for God's sheep?

WHAT'S THE DEVOTIONAL SAYING? Some Christians in Oswald Chambers' day went overboard on piety. Chambers often talked about these "pi" people and how they separated themselves from the world in an unhelpful way. Jesus never told us to detach from the world externally. He wants us to detach internally. We shouldn't be aloof, just unhindered in our one internal attachment, which is to God.

Are you detached from the world externally? Are all of your friends Christians? Are you detached internally? Do you love the things that everyone else loves? Turn your heart completely to God today!

APPLICATION

How can you feed God's sheep? What is one quality of love (1 Corinthians 13) that you lack? To what are you attached? How can you be more faithful to Jesus? How would that look?

Finish this prayer: "Holy Spirit, you've poured out your love into my heart to make me faithful, so I will . . ."

OCTOBER 19
THE UNHEEDED SECRET

Gotten busy?
Soak up God or you'll snap!

BACKGROUND Today's lesson is a great description of what Oswald Chambers wanted the Bible Training College to be. The students at his college were never in the spotlight or "shop window" (Classic Edition). And that is why they had a big effect on the world. The fact that we are still reading *Utmost* is a tribute to their impact.

Are you spending time soaking before God? Do you read *Utmost* in a rush? Or are you able to think deeply about what you learn and talk to God about what He's doing in your life? What is hindering your soak?

SCRIPTURAL CONTEXT Jesus' conversation with Pilate in John 18 ends with Pilate's sarcastic question, "What is truth?" Nowadays, we often hear that kind of response from the people we meet. Why does Jesus shift the conversation from His kingdom to truth? Is this what Pilate needed to hear?

Something else we often hear today is that truth, God, or happiness (or any other such idea) "is within you." How is that different from the verses Chambers quotes (Luke 17:20–21)? What is Chambers' point?

WHAT'S THE DEVOTIONAL SAYING? Chambers knew his students would be sent by God to difficult places. He had seen firsthand how woefully unprepared most missionaries were for the "hand-to-mouth spiritual life," as he called it. Their only hope was to get steeped in the fact of God's redemption and what it means in their lives. Strain and stress were bound to come. But with a deep understanding of how God gives us His Spirit through the redemption, we can survive.

What "practical work" keeps you from soaking? What will you do today to spend time before God? Ask Him to engineer your circumstances to keep you from the spotlight. Ask Him for the courage to make a change in "the innermost of the innermost" (the most personal area) of your life. He has already given you the power to change; you just need to decide to do it. Ruthlessly cut out the activities that rob you of your soaking time!

APPLICATION

Does our culture focus on works over relationships? How? What about our churches?

How are you soaking in God's truth and rooting in Him? How can you do this more?

Finish this prayer: "Christ, my Lord, in my life there is only you, and in my death I'll gain more. Let me . . ."

Christ's atonement is dynamite. Do you want its sanctifying power in you?

BACKGROUND Did you ask God to fill and empower you with the Holy Spirit? What happened? It took four years from when Oswald Chambers started asking for the Spirit until he finally made up his mind to come to Jesus with nothing. The hymn ("Rock of Ages") he quotes from today says:

> *Nothing in my hand I bring,*
> *Simply to Thy cross I cling;*
> *Naked, come to Thee for dress;*
> *Helpless, look to Thee for grace;*
> *Foul, I to the fountain fly;*
> *Wash me, Savior, or I die.*

Does this attitude characterize your life? You won't experience the Spirit's sanctifying, empowering presence until you realize your nakedness and cling to the atoning work Jesus did on the cross.

SCRIPTURAL CONTEXT On July 22 we had the same theme verse as today. Why is our sanctification God's will? What else is God's will according to the Bible?

Chambers also points us to Romans 5:8 and 8:39. What do these verses teach us about the atonement and what it does for us?

WHAT'S THE DEVOTIONAL SAYING? Today's lesson is a call to be sanctified. It also gives us three ways of knowing that we are sanctified. First, we are humble. Ashamed, we realize that God loved us while we were still His sworn enemies. Second, we are one with Jesus. Our oneness with Him gives us oneness with the Father. Third, we are thankful. We adore God for His miraculous gift of the atonement.

Is your life characterized by humility, oneness, and thankfulness? If you have willed your heart to make a moral transaction with God, these three things will be evident. Downstream are obedience, service, and prayer. Upstream is atonement. The combination of humility, oneness, and thankfulness is your first clue that the atonement is real in your life.

APPLICATION

What would sanctification look like in your life? Do you want that? What will you do?

How will we respond as we receive sanctification? What keeps you from that response?

Finish this prayer: "Lord, I am so ashamed of how I've treated you, and yet you loved me despite all my . . ."

⟨⟩ OCTOBER 21 ⟨⟩
IMPULSIVENESS OR DISCIPLESHIP?

Feeling defensive?
God might be reigning in your natural impulsiveness.

BACKGROUND Today we return to the "Go" lectures we saw on September 24–28. Biddy Chambers took sections from the talk "The 'Go' of Sacramental Service" and created a lesson to help us with our impulsiveness.

Do you make rash decisions? When faced with a crisis, does your pride kick in to help you cope? God wants you to overcome with His power. That way you can make it through what is even harder than a crisis—the day-to-day drudgery of life.

SCRIPTURAL CONTEXT With the exception of the "Now to Him who is able to keep you from falling . . ." benediction, we don't often hear verses from Jude. Today's theme verse urges us to build ourselves up in most holy faith. How do we do that? How does our faith build us up? Doesn't God do that?

We build ourselves up *on* our faith the same way we pray *in* the Spirit. The Spirit empowers prayer. And our faith, which is our God-given link to the atonement, is the foundation of our "building up." Peter is a great example of someone who built himself up. He started off as impulsive, but he became humble enough to walk through the strain of ordinary life (see, for example, Galatians 2:14).

WHAT'S THE DEVOTIONAL SAYING?
The two paragraphs today both teach us about how God removes our impulsiveness. First, He "checks" (see June 3, *Utmost*) our impulsiveness, which at first makes us feel foolish and defensive but in the end turns our impulsiveness into intuition. Second, He gives us drudgery and then gives us His supernatural grace to get us through.

Has God disciplined the impulsiveness out of you yet? Or are you still following at a distance, as Peter did in Mark 14:54? Ask God for Jesus' calm strength so you can overcome drudgery and be His disciple!

APPLICATION

Did the Holy Spirit point out your impulsiveness? How did you feel? Did you change?

Are you spoiled? Who knows your spoiled side? How would they say to fix this side?

Finish this prayer: "God, I need your grace to get through the next twenty-four hours. For me, the 'dry land' of drudgery is . . ."

∽ OCTOBER 22 ∽
THE WITNESS OF THE SPIRIT

In a fog?
Abandonment is your lighthouse!

BACKGROUND In Oswald Chambers' day, just as nowadays, Christians put a premium on the witness of the Holy Spirit. That witness can come in many flavors: speaking in tongues and hearts "strangely warmed" are just two examples. Wouldn't it be nice to have these outward signs of God's inward work? That way we (and our friends!) could know for sure that God is blessing us.

Today's lesson warns against wanting a witness before we abandon to God. Once we abandon, God gives the witness. He doesn't give it to us. He gives it to His own life in us.

SCRIPTURAL CONTEXT Read Romans 8. It's a treasure trove of spiritual truth! What familiar verses can you spot? How does today's theme verse fit into this chapter? Have you ever cried "Daddy!" to God?

We also see two of Chambers' favorite verses: Matthew 11:28 and Luke 11:13. He uses Matthew 11:28 more than one hundred times in his *Complete Works,* and he had the words to Luke 11:13 written on a big banner on his YMCA hut in Egypt. In today's devotional, he says that *come* and *ask* are key words for us evil, weary, sin-laden people as we long for God's deliverance.

WHAT'S THE DEVOTIONAL SAYING? Do you long for God to deliver you? Chambers says to stop waffling. Trust that God can deliver, or tell Him plainly that He can't. And know that the reason He can't is because you are "in the road." *You* have become the god of your life; and as long as you are god, God Almighty can't reveal himself or His deliverance to you.

Why can't God give us some witness of His Spirit *before* we fully surrender? Wouldn't that make it easier for us to abandon all to Him? Chambers could have quoted Luke 16:19–31 to explain why God can't do that. Instead he says, "If you had the witness before the reality, it would end in sentimental emotion." Do you know anyone who ended up craving the spiritual highs the Holy Spirit gives? That's not what God wants for us. Therefore, He requires us to give all to Him first, before we get the witness of the Spirit.

APPLICATION

Do you ask for revelation? To you or to God in you?

What role should reason and common sense play? What role *do* they play? Why is that?

Finish this prayer: "Father, there are so many things I don't understand even though I should. Please help me seek . . ."

⚭ OCTOBER 23 ⚭
NOTHING OF THE OLD LIFE!

Don't cling to anything except Christ.

BACKGROUND In May 1914, the month before the assassination of Archduke Ferdinand set World War I in motion, Oswald Chambers gave today's lesson in lecture form. His message today is clear: We must totally throw out all our old ideas to make room for God's presence in us.

A key word today is *prejudice*. What does Chambers mean by this word? Elsewhere in his *Complete Works*, he defines it as "a judgment passed without sufficiently weighing the evidence." By *judgment*, he means any thought we have. Do you think things about God that you think are "all right" and come from Him? We all do!

SCRIPTURAL CONTEXT Today's theme verse is worth memorizing, if you haven't already. Have any old things passed away in your life? Notice how in some versions of the Bible the word *all* appears with the new things, but not with the old things. Do you think that difference is important?

Chambers adds another layer of meaning to this familiar passage by using verse 18: "All things are of God." He implies that when God fully has His way with us, all aspects of our life are of God—so much so that our love is really like 1 Corinthians 13. Are you there yet?

WHAT'S THE DEVOTIONAL SAYING? In Chambers' original lecture, he added "they are from Him" right after "He knows that my prejudices are all right." How scary! We think that our own selfish perspectives are actually from God.

Another scary thing about our prejudices and presuppositions is that we don't even know we have them. That's why God has to put them to death (have them "run straight across"—Classic Edition) by His providences.

Once providential circumstances reveal our prejudices, we have to decide not to use them anymore (see September 8, *Utmost*). This is how God kills them.

Have you sometimes wondered if your life will ever be what 1 Corinthians 13 describes? Chambers says it happens by watching God tear down our old self with its prejudices and by surrendering to Him unconditionally. Have you seen your old self come down? Are you ready to surrender?

APPLICATION

What are your prejudices (in other words, the things you think you know)? Will you let them die?

How has God removed past prejudices? Are you ready for God to withhold blessings?

Finish this prayer: "Lord, I need you more than your blessings, but so much of my old life relies on the . . ."

OCTOBER 24
THE PROPER PERSPECTIVE

We're Christ's spoils of war taken from the land of sin.

BACKGROUND Sometimes, the beauty of *Utmost* is how Oswald Chambers (with Biddy's skillful edits) perfectly describes a key concept. Today's key concept is our need to get God's perspective.

What is the essence of God's point of view? It's that we are His prisoners of war. We aren't fighting, He is. We are parading behind Him to display to the universe His amazing victory.

SCRIPTURAL CONTEXT Paul's paean of praise we read in today's theme verse comes right after he says he wasn't able to find his friend Titus. Do you praise God after things don't go as you had hoped? What does Paul thank God for? What does verse 18 say?

There are many verses that talk about captivity to Christ (Ephesians 4:8, 2 Corinthians 10:5, for example). But the only other passage Chambers quotes is Romans 8:37. How does Romans 8 demonstrate that Christ is the victorious conqueror?

WHAT'S THE DEVOTIONAL SAYING? Let's look at today's amazing lesson piece by piece. First, don't settle for a good viewpoint. Strive for God's view, although it will take you a long time. Second, God's view is of His Son as victorious warrior and us as His prisoners of war. Third, our own "good" viewpoints make us the warriors, and they are dead wrong. Finally, we have an opportunity to be God's favorite perfume: Eau de Jesus.

How can we smell like Christ? Do we steal his garments, as Jacob stole Esau's? Is our Christ-fragrance only external? No, if we smell anything like our Savior, it will be because of what's inside—Christ in us, as Colossians 1:27 says, "the hope of glory"!

APPLICATION

Have you felt alone in your battles? What is the proper perspective? Is it untouchable?

How will you keep the proper perspective every day? Are you glad to be led as Jesus' captive?

Finish this prayer: "Jesus, you conquered hell and made me a captive. Now I get to be led in your parade . . ."

ꙮ OCTOBER 25 ꙮ
SUBMITTING TO GOD'S AIM

Think you're ordinary?
God's aim transforms!

BACKGROUND If you go online right now and buy a copy of Oswald Chambers' *Complete Works*, your money will be well spent. Within days, your package will arrive. You will peel back the cardboard shipping container, open the glossy cover, and turn to the first lecture. Guess what you will read? The source material for today's lesson! The first chapter in that massive, 1,500-page tome comes from a talk Chambers gave during a sermon preparation class (see May 5, *Companion*). The title is "The Worker." The third section is headed "The External Crush of Things," which is today's title in the Classic Edition.

Do you submit to God's aim? What *is* God's aim? Read today's lesson and find out!

SCRIPTURAL CONTEXT Chambers' original talk focused on 1 Corinthians 9:11–27. He broke this passage into four sections: verses 11–15, 16–17, 18–19, and 20–27. Today's theme verse comes from the fourth of these pieces, but our lesson comes from all of them. What do the pieces have in common?

Chambers titled the second section of his talk "Amid a Creed of Powerful Things." What gives our creed its power and greatness? Jesus chose us, not the other way around (John 15:16).

WHAT'S THE DEVOTIONAL SAYING? When Chambers says, "He can plant men on the Rock as He has planted us," he's quoting *Positive Preaching and Modern Mind* by P. T. Forsyth, an author Chambers admired greatly. For example, the day he developed symptoms of appendicitis (see October 12, *Companion*) he wrote, "I certainly find Dr. Forsyth's *The Christian Ethic of War* the greatest book I have read for many a year."

So what *is* Chambers saying at the end of the second paragraph? The full quote from Forsyth is, "It is our genius to plant every man on the Rock and to plant the whole man there." In other words, we must let God have us completely if we want to help people make Christ their foundation.

Today's lesson says that we are ordinary, but God's aim ("matter" in the Classic Edition) makes us great. He must bend, break, and mold us to fit us for His aim. Once He does, woe to you if you turn aside! He will do amazing things with you. He will use you to plant others on the Rock. Don't worry where He puts you—even "amid a crowd of ignoble things."

APPLICATION

Where would you rather be? Why? What aim has God given you? Did it change you?
What was Jesus Christ's aim while on earth? How can you keep sight of that aim today?
Finish this prayer: "God, I'm in your hand; please use me to help others get planted on your
  Rock. Today . . ."

OCTOBER 26
WHAT IS A MISSIONARY?

We should be pushed by God, not pulled by needs as we do His work.

➤

BACKGROUND Once again we find ourselves in a series of missionary studies (see September 4, *Companion*). Today our focus is on the characteristic of missionaries. Tomorrow we will look at the method of missionaries.

What characteristics make for a true missionary? Compassion? A heart for the lost? Hard work? No. Oswald Chambers says it's the foolishness to trust and obey God's call. God calls us to "go and make disciples." Will you obey His command?

SCRIPTURAL CONTEXT Imagine being one of the disciples in John 20:19–23. Local leaders were after you. Your best friend and mentor had been brutally killed. Yet women were saying His grave was empty and they had seen Him alive again. Then suddenly, though the doors are locked, He's standing next to you, telling you He's sending you in the same way God sent Him!

Later, He meets you near your hometown and sends you out again (Matthew 28:19). After that, He takes you to a suburb near the capital you've been to many times before with Him, and He sends you out one more time (Luke 24:50 and Acts 1:12). Then quickly, He's gone! What is going on? How would you feel?

WHAT'S THE DEVOTIONAL SAYING? After these three "sendings," the disciples spent ten days continually praying and worshiping. They no longer feared the local leaders. They waited eagerly for the Spirit Jesus had promised. When He came, boom! They were on their way. It was God's power pushing them out, not their heart for the needs around them.

Do you want to follow in their steps? You need personal attachment to God and His viewpoint (see October 24, *Utmost*). Don't let God's "sending" call get buried in all the needs you see around you.

APPLICATION

Are you a missionary? In what sense are you sent? What might replace this "sending"?

Who is your spiritual hero? Why? Are you being as "foolish" as that person was? How so?

Finish this prayer: "Lord, I need your keen mind to guide me down 'foolish' paths as I . . ."

OCTOBER 27
THE METHOD OF MISSIONS

What's our call?
To trust God and feel the resulting power!

BACKGROUND "You cannot make disciples unless you are a disciple yourself." Such an obvious point, but how quickly we forget it! If we do any Christian work, we spend most of our energy thinking about how to do the work. We should spend far more of our energy focusing on being Jesus' disciples, in other words, His students.

What grade do you think you would get if you took a class and spent very little effort learning from the teacher? Even if you stayed up late teaching other people, wouldn't the teacher still give you a failing grade? Yet we expect to earn A's when we pour ourselves out for others and neglect our relationship with God. Today's lesson will reset our priorities!

SCRIPTURAL CONTEXT Yesterday we imagined what it would feel like to experience Jesus' three "sendings." Today's theme verse is the second of those three and the most comprehensive. What details do you see today that you haven't noticed before?

Oswald Chambers also quotes Matthew 9:28. What is the context for this question? Did the blind men believe? Did their actions show that they believed even before Jesus healed them? Why didn't they obey His command?

WHAT'S THE DEVOTIONAL SAYING?
Yesterday we explored a characteristic of missionaries. Today we look at their method: boundless confidence in Jesus. This confidence is constantly under attack. The greatest onslaught is from our own "passion for souls" and our own efforts to overcome people's "callous indifference." It takes our utmost vigilance to keep our confidence rooted in our relationship with God.

We all need this missionary method. Without it, we will crumble under the strain of everyday life. Tend your relationship with God carefully. He's given you the Holy Spirit, and when you live by the Spirit, He will energize your spirit to ruthlessly say "no" to everything that keeps you from God.

APPLICATION
Who do you want to see saved? Does it seem difficult? What is the real challenge?
Are you a disciple? What does that mean? Do you disciple others? Who? How?
Finish this prayer: "God, your only call is for me to embrace the power of trusting in you. I'll do that by . . ."

∾ OCTOBER 28 ∾
JUSTIFICATION BY FAITH

How can you brag?
God does it from first to last!

➤

BACKGROUND Today we are treated to another theological lesson in which Oswald Chambers really stresses the fact that God alone saves us. Why is it so important that we realize we don't do *anything* to earn a relationship with God?

Is there still a part of you that thinks God is lucky to have you on His "side"? When you have come to the end of your rope, do you admire yourself for how well you repent? Let today's lesson shake the last shred of self-satisfaction out of you!

SCRIPTURAL CONTEXT On October 24, Chambers told us how God made each "red-handed rebel" one of Christ's captives. Today, we read Romans 5:10, which in *The Voice* version of the Bible describes us as "in the heat of combat with God."

When did God capture us? John 19:30 records Jesus' words, "It is finished." Perhaps this marks the moment in time when Jesus sealed His victory.

WHAT'S THE DEVOTIONAL SAYING? Let's look carefully at what today's lesson says. First, we are not saved merely by believing. Instead, God reveals that when we receive His gift of salvation, our belief simply accepts this gift and gives us realization, which in turn gives us repentance. Second, our obedience doesn't put us right with God. Christ's death does that. Our turning to God in faith allows the Holy Spirit to bring rightness before God into our lives. Third, this plan of salvation is humanly illogical. It is all from God. The fact that we can't do anything to accomplish it (or even understand it!) means that it is completely secure.

Are your salvation, justification, and sanctification secure? Does it feel that way? Chambers took a lot of time to teach his students good theology because he knew that without it they would fail in the strain of real life. Apply yourself to these truths. Use your mind for all it's worth!

APPLICATION

What saves you? What roles do believing and repenting play? What is the atonement?

What is unconquerable about our lives? How does this help our relationship with God?

Finish this prayer: "Lord God, you have done it all. If I attribute my salvation to myself, I'm lost; instead . . ."

OCTOBER 29
SUBSTITUTION

Christ saves because of His obedience in becoming sin—not by His sympathy!

BACKGROUND Even while he was the live-in professor at the Bible Training College, Oswald Chambers kept up a busy schedule of evening lectures at other locations around London. At some of these extension classes, he spoke about substitution. He said, "It is being said nowadays that Jesus . . . was such a pure noble character and realized so keenly the shame and horror of sin, that He took our sin on Himself by sympathy. All through the Bible it is revealed that Our Lord bore the sin of the world by identification, not by sympathy. If Jesus only took on the sin and wrong of human nature by sympathy . . . all I can say is, 'Yes, I mourn over my sin and wrong-doing and I wish I were better; I do accept the life of Jesus as very beautiful and holy, but that holiness is not mine.' "

Do you see Jesus' life as yours or as something you can only appreciate sympathetically, from afar?

SCRIPTURAL CONTEXT On October 7, we talked about how today's theme verse is an apt summary of the gospel. How does it also refute the view that Jesus died out of sympathy for us? How do the previous verses, especially verse 15, relate?

Chambers points us to three places in John—1:29, 15:22–24, and 14:9. What do they say? If Jesus came to take the world's sin away, why is it still guilty of sin?

WHAT'S THE DEVOTIONAL SAYING? The picture we get as we read Chambers' theological writing is that Jesus died the death that Adam and all his offspring deserved. Thanks to Jesus' death, we can be put right with God, something that was impossible without His death. But not everyone knows about this possibility, and some who know reject the possibility. Those who don't know and those who reject are in the same boat: They're still not right with God.

Today's lesson tells us why Jesus died Adam's death: because God told Him to. Jesus *didn't* do it because He felt sorry for us. If we don't know this, we can't grasp that He offers His life to be fully *ours*. We will instead go around feeling sorry for ourselves and appreciating Jesus' life only from afar.

APPLICATION

What does Jesus do for the world? What does He do only for the saved? Why is this?

What can we say instead of "He died my death"? How does this distinction matter in your life?

Finish this prayer: "Lord Jesus Christ, I will never understand the full mystery of your death, but as I . . ."

Faith alone burns, common sense freezes. Warm hearts have both.

❮ ❯

BACKGROUND Amid his busy lecture schedule, Oswald Chambers taught a three-part series on faith. Portions of today's lesson come from this series, which is rich in important truths about our faith in God.

Do you understand the nature of faith? How does it relate to wisdom and common sense? Today we will see the difference between these concepts and, in doing so, strengthen our faith.

SCRIPTURAL CONTEXT Hebrews 11 is *the* chapter on faith. Verses 1 and 6 define faith, and the rest of the chapter illustrates it. What new things do you learn about faith as you read this chapter again?

As an example of putting Jesus first, Chambers refers us to Matthew 6:33. He also quotes Romans 8:28 and John 14:9. Do you *know* that all things work together for good? If you do, no matter what happens, your faith will be transformed into reality. Have you seen Jesus (John 14:9)? If so, you will "have something that is real."

WHAT'S THE DEVOTIONAL SAYING? The overarching message today is that faith must be turned into reality. What does this mean? It's a bit like Pinocchio. Geppetto creates him to be his son, but this doesn't happen for *real* until the end of the story. And just like our faith, it takes all kinds of troubles for him to become real.

What will become of your faith? Will it falter for trusting in the wrong people, as in the story of Pinocchio (before it was given a kid-friendly happy ending)? Or will it be educated by God's providence? Will you remain steadfast to God until He brings you through victoriously?

APPLICATION

How is faith alone fanatical? How is common sense cold? Which controls you most?

What commonsense detail did God use to prove your faith? Did it make faith real?

Finish this prayer: "Father, you care about all the commonsense things and use them to make my faith . . ."

THE TRIAL OF FAITH

God isn't blessing like before?
Chin up! He's perfecting you.

◄

BACKGROUND Was Abraham just as valuable when he was rescuing Lot and defeating five kings as when he was waiting in years of silence for a son? We think our heroic moments are more valuable to God than the times when we are waiting in silence. Today we learn that trusting God when we can't see His blessings can make us even more valuable in God's eyes.

Part of today's lesson comes from Oswald Chambers' series on the life of Abraham that he taught during his own trial of faith in early 1915 (see March 28, *Companion*). Are you facing a situation that seems to contradict God's character? Hold fast to what you know from Scripture to be God's unchanging character, no matter what comes your way from His hand.

SCRIPTURAL CONTEXT Looking at today's verse apart from its context is puzzling. But once we realize it's part of the story of the epileptic boy that we've seen many times (for example, October 1, *Companion*), the reason Biddy chose this verse is clear. The disciples experienced a trial of faith when they couldn't drive out the demon, and the father had been experiencing a trial all of his life. Did any of these people "pass" their trial? Did they continue to trust in God's character despite what the situation was telling them?

Besides Abraham, Job is another great example of faith. How did God "slay" Job (Job 13:15)? Do you think Job ever found out why God did what He did?

WHAT'S THE DEVOTIONAL SAYING? When you started following God, did He bless you for trusting Him? Have there been times when He seems to have had to "knock the bottom" out of your Christian life? How did that make you feel?

Chambers makes a distinction between trials of faith and ordinary life. The difference is that a trial of faith seems so contrary to what God has said that it makes you question God's character. In contrast, the ordinary discipline of life agrees with what God says, though it's still painful. For example, if we make a bad decision, the negative results we experience are true to what God said in Galatians 6:7, "A man reaps what he sows." This is the ordinary way that life disciplines us. But when the world comes crashing down, like it did for Job, it seems to go against everything God has said. *That* would be a trial of faith!

God uses both trials *and* ordinary life to shape us. Today's lesson focuses on the trials. Have you ever been through one? Ask God to prepare you for the next one!

APPLICATION
When you became a Christian, how did God reward your faith? How has that changed? How do you view God's character? Is He completely trustworthy in your mind? Why? Finish this prayer: "God, I need to know to the core how faithful you are even if . . ."

"YOU ARE NOT YOUR OWN"

God crashes pity parties.

BACKGROUND *Utmost* has already featured two of Alfred, Lord Tennyson's poems (see January 15 and March 10, *Utmost*). Today in the Classic Edition we see Tennyson's description of a womb as a "world within the world" ("De Profundis," 1852). Oswald Chambers says that we can't hope for a cozy womb of safety if we are in fellowship with Jesus' sufferings.

Are you sad that you can't have a private hideout? Are you tired of all the heartbreak and just want to call it quits? Think of the woman who compiled *Utmost*. She had more heartbreaks than most of us. But that didn't stop her from thanking God for bringing His purposes to pass through her broken heart.

SCRIPTURAL CONTEXT On March 4 and 18, July 15, and especially on September 4, we saw today's verse. What price bought us? If we hadn't been bought, who would own us? When God bought us, did that change our worth? Why?

When Paul wrote this verse, he was thinking about sexual sin in particular. But anything that dishonors God in our bodies falls under the exhortation of verse 20: "Honor God with your bodies." How will you honor God in your body today?

WHAT'S THE DEVOTIONAL SAYING? We shouldn't care what happens to us as long as God's plans are accomplished. But we *do* care. We throw ourselves pity parties when we don't like what happens to us or are just worried about what will happen.

Our own pity parties are not the only danger. We also can end up on our "deathbed" due to the pity and sympathy we get from others. If things aren't going well for you, if your heart is broken, rejoice! God is accomplishing His purposes through you.

APPLICATION

What is your "private life" that Chambers talks about? What breaks it up? How do you respond? Why?

What's been your heartbreak? Who sympathized? What did God do? Are you grateful?

Finish this prayer: "Jesus, let me never forget how your hands were pierced for my sin, and now you are . . ."

⌘ NOVEMBER 2 ⌘
OBEDIENCE OR INDEPENDENCE?

Does God's redemption flow through you?
Obey in little ways, and it will.

BACKGROUND In yesterday's lesson Oswald Chambers told us that God can use us any way He wants as He accomplishes His will through us. Today we see that God's redemption flows out of us as we obey Him. God doesn't insist we obey. He doesn't give us rules. He gives us a standard (for example, the Sermon on the Mount). When we have Jesus' life in us, His relationship with God lives up to that standard. Our job is to obey Jesus and let His life abide in us.

Is God's redemption flowing out of you? Those little things you do in obedience are the tiny windows that let His redemption shine out of your life.

SCRIPTURAL CONTEXT What commands did Jesus have in mind when He spoke today's theme verse? Look back at John 13:34 and ahead to 15:12–17. Why did Jesus focus on that command?

Chambers also points us to two verses on the cost of being Jesus' disciple. Read the context of Luke 9:23 and 14:26. Do you agree that Jesus doesn't insist and that He also sounds stern? Is Luke 14:26 only about being of value and not about salvation?

WHAT'S THE DEVOTIONAL SAYING? Besides reminding us that God never insists, today's lesson teaches us that our little acts of obedience add up to our close relationship with God and our impact on other people's lives. In your seemingly insignificant life, what little things do you think God wants you to do? Will you obey Jesus in them today?

At the end of the first paragraph, Chambers says we can't interpret Luke 14:26 apart from Jesus. Why is that? What if we tried to hate our family members on our own, without our "hatred" being based on an equally deep love and knowledge of Jesus? Disaster! Thankfully, God will keep sending us circumstances that draw us into a closer love and knowledge of His Son. He doesn't want us to hate our family or anyone else. He just wants us to hate anything that competes with our love for Him, because He knows that only our love for Him will help us truly love others.

APPLICATION

Does it scare you that God doesn't insist on obedience? Why? How will you obey?

What are some petty things in your life? How could God reveal himself through them?

Finish this prayer: "Lord, please shine your redemption light out of me today as I start by obeying you in . . ."

NOVEMBER 3
A BONDSERVANT OF JESUS

Have you thrown in the towel yet?
God is waiting!

BACKGROUND Today's final paragraph comes from one of Oswald Chambers' sermon preparation lectures (see May 5, *Companion*). The rest of the lesson undoubtedly is also from talks he gave at the Bible Training College. Imagine sitting in his lecture hall being trained to be an "iron saint" (Classic Edition). Would you want to keep attending? Or would you drop out?

Are you so focused on your idea of what it means to be a Christian that you still haven't given up your rights to God? Chambers says that God may have to put the decision before you 365 times. As we near the year's end, will today be the day you surrender?

SCRIPTURAL CONTEXT On March 8 and 21, Galatians 2:20 was our featured verse. Today Biddy quotes a bit more of the verse. Do you think she was trying to highlight something in particular?

How many times did Jesus say, "for My sake"? In Mark alone, He said it three times.

Chambers tells us that if we understand the loyalty to Christ this phrase implies, we will be saints who are as strong as iron. Is that what you would like?

WHAT'S THE DEVOTIONAL SAYING? Let's pull apart what today's four paragraphs tell us. First, we must break our independence with our own hands. We must surrender our independence—our wanting to be our own gods. Second, we can't put conditions on our surrender. Once we do, we get the witness of the Holy Spirit (see October 22, *Utmost*). Third, surrender means signing away our rights to ourselves. Fourth, we can either stick with our own ideas about how we should follow God, or we can let God have His way with us. Those are the only two options.

Which option will you choose? Have you gotten to the end of your rope yet? Once you have, what else is there to do but to surrender all to Jesus? He's waiting for you!

APPLICATION

How have you broken your independence? Are you sure? If not, are you willing now?

Do you want to be an "iron saint"? Do you want God to have His way with you? How so?

Finish this prayer: "Father, I surrender my life to you. It's all I have, and I hold on to it so tightly; but if . . ."

NOVEMBER 4
THE AUTHORITY OF TRUTH

Do you keep on turning back, or have you finally crossed over the line?

BACKGROUND Throughout *Utmost*, we are challenged to transact with God: to give up our rights and surrender to Him. Today, Oswald Chambers takes time to explain how we transact. How does our will make a decision? We need to understand this process so we can do it!

Are you in fights and quarrels? Are you more friends with the world than with God? Have you stopped resisting the devil? Then draw near to God! Today's lesson will show you how.

SCRIPTURAL CONTEXT On June 10, we looked at James 4 in some detail. But it's such a great chapter that we could look at it every day and always find more! Can you relate to the poison in verses 1–5 and 11–17? How can you apply the antidote (verses 6–10)?

Once again, Chambers quotes Matthew 11:28. This time he says that *come* means "transact" ("act" in the Updated Edition). What makes it so hard to transact with God, when we do it all the time with other people?

WHAT'S THE DEVOTIONAL SAYING? Chambers makes a distinction between existing and living. He says we merely exist before we transact with God, but after we transact we live. He implies that our transaction is not a one-time thing: "The moments [plural] when I truly live . . ."

Has this been your experience? Do you feel more alive after you have made up your mind about something, even if you haven't physically done it yet? The most important decision we act on is the decision to give up our rights to God (see November 3, *Utmost*). But there are also smaller decisions to act on God's truth. What truths must you act on today?

APPLICATION

Who do you evangelize? Do you give them space to act on their own? Why is that key?

What truth have you failed to act on? Why is action a step beyond mere confession?

Finish this prayer: "God, you're reminding me of a truth that I've ignored. In my will I take action by . . ."

NOVEMBER 5
PARTAKERS OF HIS SUFFERING

Don't know where you're heading?
No problem, that's God's business!

BACKGROUND Two seniors at Yale, Stoddard King and Alonzo Elliot, wrote, "There's a Long, Long Trail" in 1913. It soon became a popular World War I song. You can almost hear Oswald Chambers singing the final stanza with his soldier friends as he waited for Biddy and Kathleen to arrive in Egypt:

There's a long, long night of waiting
Until my dreams all come true;
Till the day when I'll be going down
That long, long trail with you.

In today's lesson, Chambers says that our walk with God is a "long, long trail" and full of suffering. Yet at the end of the trail, God brings us to the "luminous place"!

SCRIPTURAL CONTEXT First Peter 4:13 tells us we should rejoice as exuberantly as we suffer. That runs counter to common sense. We have the *least* desire to rejoice when we suffer.

Chambers makes the point that our sufferings differ from Christ's. Jesus suffered. It's hard to figure out the difference just by reading today's study. But elsewhere, we read that Jesus suffered "in connection with our salvation and in no other connection." We suffer for Jesus' name (which, like Jesus' suffering, is according to God's will). Sometimes we suffer for our own stupidity. But we never suffer for our salvation!

WHAT'S THE DEVOTIONAL SAYING?
If Chambers were alive today, he might use the phrase, "It isn't all about you!" Once we realize that God uses circumstances to shape us, we are tempted to think He does it all for our benefit. Today's lesson reminds us that He does it for His own benefit. He also does it so we can understand what He's doing in other people—so we can join in His work.

Has God put someone in your life you can't deal with? Suffer through it, and everything else God sends your way, and you will understand what God is aiming at. If you take a shortcut to know and do His aims, it will end in disaster, as it has for the church many times before. And no matter what, you'll never know God's aims exactly, or you will become proud and unusable in God's hands.

APPLICATION

Who is the most difficult person in your life? Have you gained understanding? How?

What suffering have you avoided? Are you willing to keep going without knowing why?

Finish this prayer: "Lord, I don't need to know why you do what you do. It's enough for me to know that . . ."

INTIMATE THEOLOGY

Trouble believing in Jesus?
Commit; and then trust is easy.

BACKGROUND We first saw today's title phrase, "Programme of Belief" (Classic Edition), on August 29. There we learned that as soon as we have our program of belief clearly in mind, God sends something that contradicts it, like a financial hardship right after we start believing that He will meet our needs. Why might God do this? Maybe because He knows that our faith is nothing until it's tested in reality.

Do you, like Martha, believe something for the future but have trouble with the right now? Today's study will lead the way.

SCRIPTURAL CONTEXT Martha often gets a bum rap. Read John 11 and see what you think. Is Oswald Chambers right in saying that her belief became a personal, intimate possession?

Chambers says that belief starts by commitment. It then goes from program, to personal, to particular—from mental, to moral, to spiritual.

At the first level, we abandon anything that doesn't match our commitment. Next, we have to resist the temptation to compromise. Finally, we make up our minds to let Christ dominate us in that area of our lives. Then this process repeats itself in every area of our lives!

WHAT'S THE DEVOTIONAL SAYING? Are you going through a personal crisis? Chambers says our program of belief can't become personal until we face a personal problem. If you can't answer Jesus' piercing questions with, "Yes, I believe this," then your faith is not yet personal.

We all struggle to trust God. We are all tempted to take shortcuts to what we think He wants for us. Often, He probably *does* want those things for us, but He knows how best to give them. Our shortcuts would give us what we want but in a way that ruins everything. Let God lead you along *His* way.

APPLICATION
Do you believe that Jesus has power to heal? What would make your belief more intimate? What causes you to doubt? Will this problem change your theology into personal belief?
Finish this prayer: "Jesus, I need to commit, mentally, morally, and especially spiritually. Please help me . . ."

NOVEMBER 7
THE UNDETECTED SACREDNESS OF CIRCUMSTANCES

Would you like to be a prayer warrior?
Let everyday events guide you.

➤

BACKGROUND Have you enjoyed having some lessons grouped into series? There are only a few series left as we approach the end of the year. Today we begin a two-day series on prayer. First, we learn how God puts circumstances and people in our lives so we will pray for them. Tomorrow we answer the question, "What is our role in prayer?"

Are you spending much time interceding for people? Do you pray for situations? God wants you to be a prayer warrior!

SCRIPTURAL CONTEXT Today's verse is so famous that it's amazing we've only seen it once before (October 30). We often see this verse in a selfish light—all things work for *me*. Oswald Chambers puts a different spin on it. All things work together to help us pray. Is this spin consistent with the context?

WHAT'S THE DEVOTIONAL SAYING? Often, the reason Chambers tells us to welcome painful circumstances is that they are God's tools to refine our character. But today we see that they can also help us pray. It is God's plan to reach the whole world through our prayers, so He puts us into various circumstances so we will pray for just the right things.

Chambers says it's not our job to "enter into the agony of intercession." The Updated Edition changes this to "not to agonize over how to intercede," which is certainly part of what Chambers meant. Do you wonder what you should pray for first, second, and third? Don't stress! Just pray for who and what God has placed in your life. As you bring them to mind, the Holy Spirit will do the work.

APPLICATION

Do your circumstances seem unnatural? Why? Can they help you intercede? How?

How can you make your life a sacred place for the Holy Spirit? What will change?

Finish this prayer: "Holy Spirit, I'm so often my own providence, which makes your work more difficult. Therefore, . . ."

THE UNRIVALED POWER OF PRAYER

Prayer unleashes God's pure power—it starts and ends with His perfect will.

◀

BACKGROUND Yesterday Oswald Chambers gave us the first aspect of our role in prayer—bringing before God the people and things He places in our lives. We also caught a glimpse of another part of our role—making our conscious lives a temple for the Holy Spirit. Today we will learn more about this second role and the duty we have to keep our lives holy.

Are you doing anything to keep your conscious life holy? Jesus was willing to offend everyone in order to keep God's temple of stone holy. In the same way, we should be willing to keep His temple of flesh and blood holy.

SCRIPTURAL CONTEXT We know we need the Spirit to help us pray, but His role in prayer is far deeper, as today's theme verse says. Have you ever let Him pray through wordless groans? As 1 Corinthians 6:19 implies, we let the Spirit do His work by keeping our bodies, His temple, holy and pure.

The way Jesus cleansed the temple is a good example for us. He didn't care if people got mad at Him, and He took drastic action. Do you think He had to clear the temple twice (John 2 and Mark 11)? What does that mean for us?

WHAT'S THE DEVOTIONAL SAYING? Just as God speaks His commands to the Holy Spirit in us, not to us (since we could never obey them), so too He listens to the Holy Spirit's prayers, not ours. Realizing this frees us from worry as we pray. We still have the big job of fighting off the competition for our prayer times—and we often fail at that task. But we don't have the job of figuring out *what* to pray. We just talk to God about the people and things He's put in our lives and then quiet our hearts to let the Spirit talk to God.

Ruthlessly cast out everything in your life that competes for the Spirit's work. Let Him have full rein of your life. Then your prayers will have unrivaled power!

APPLICATION
Do your prayers invoke the Holy Spirit's energy? Why does God search our hearts?

Why does the Holy Spirit's intercession depend on being incarnate in our bodies?

Finish this prayer: "Holy Spirit, all that I do, I do with my body, but I rarely think about how you'd like my body to . . ."

∽ NOVEMBER 9 ∽
SACRED SERVICE

Our relationship to Christ is central to everything.

BACKGROUND With all the controversy surrounding celebrity Christians these days, today's lesson is a refreshing antidote. These words are for Christian workers. But any of us can benefit. Most of us like to be the focus, especially for Christian things. Oswald Chambers tells us why putting the spotlight on ourselves can't accomplish God's purpose. On the other hand, simply preaching the facts about Jesus is what God uses to transform the world.

Who can you talk to about Jesus' life and death? Do you think everyone in your family and circle of friends knows all the facts? Ask God for a divine opportunity today!

SCRIPTURAL CONTEXT Colossians 1:1–23 concludes with Paul calling himself a slave of the gospel. Then, in verses 24–29, he describes what it's like to be a gospel-slave. What does our theme verse say about it? Do celebrity Christians have the kind of sufferings Paul had?

Chambers quotes John 12:32 to show what we should do rather than "glory in men." Who was Jesus' intended audience when He spoke these words? Where else did He talk about being lifted up? What Old Testament event did He connect to "lifting up" (John 3:14)?

WHAT'S THE DEVOTIONAL SAYING? We need constant reminders of today's lesson. Thankfully, Chambers returns again and again in *Utmost* to the message that we can't draw attention to ourselves if we are working for God. The two are not compatible.

But today's devotional is not just a warning. It also teaches us what we *should* do. We must become so identified with redemption that Jesus' life is what people see when they look at our lives.

Do you like people to say that you are fascinating or have great insight? Who doesn't? But God can't do anything with a life focused on those kinds of things. It's not in His realm. It's only in ours, so He can't empower it. Let Him work through you as you lift Him up!

APPLICATION

What are two reasons we need to identify closely with Christ? What things last forever?

Who looks up to you? Whom do you admire? Why is this dangerous in witnessing?

Finish this prayer: "Father, since the whole point of life is to worship and enjoy you and let others do the same, help me to . . ."

⚭ NOVEMBER 10 ⚭
FELLOWSHIP IN THE GOSPEL

Are you immersed in the gospel?
Self-immersed people are useless to God.

BACKGROUND What is your life goal? Many self-help seminars and books begin with that kind of question. Today we read that it's not for us to know the answer to that question. Instead, we are to let God use us for *His* goals, not ours.

This is such a simple concept and one that we've seen before in *Utmost*. But have you been able to apply it? Or are you still pursuing your own goals?

SCRIPTURAL CONTEXT Paul spent only three Sabbaths in Thessalonica. So his concern about the faith of the people was understandable. Imagine how relieved he was to hear from Timothy, his fellow laborer in the gospel, that they were standing firm in their faith! As you read 1 Thessalonians 2–3, can you see how Paul and Timothy embody today's lesson?

WHAT'S THE DEVOTIONAL SAYING? On November 1, we saw the same quote from "De Profundis": "a world within the world." Tennyson wrote this poem to celebrate his son's birth. Oswald Chambers paints a picture of someone who doesn't want to go along with God's plan and tries to stay inside a comfy "world within the world," like an infant who wants to stay inside the womb.

Do you ever feel like that? Like not joining in with God's plan? What would be the consequences of not letting God crush and crumple you as He chooses? As we have read many times in *Utmost*, we find true satisfaction only when we are identified with God's interests.

We have only about fifty more days in *Utmost*. The focus will be increasingly on what Chambers thought was most important: our fellowship with God.

APPLICATION

What's your life purpose? How can having a life goal block God from using you?

What has caused you heartache? How can indulging in self-pity make you useless?

Finish this prayer: "God, once and for all I give up my personal plans. Please take me from my plans and . . ."

Do not indulge in self pity

We don't know what our life goal is - we are to let God use us for His goals, not ours.
Are you pursuing your own goals?
Do you not want to join God's plan.
True satisfaction comes from identifying with God's interests. Our fellowship with God is most important

325

⟋⟍ NOVEMBER 11 ⟋⟍
THE SUPREME CLIMB

God has plans for you. Don't let them slip past your fingers!

BACKGROUND In the spring of 1915, two-thirds of the way through his class on Abraham (see May 25, *Companion*), Oswald Chambers gave a talk on Abraham's greatest test of faith. Meanwhile, Chambers himself faced a test of faith: what to do about the war. Should he head to the front or stay in London?

As we saw on January 8, he faced his trial of faith by relying on God, not his own restlessness or reaction to the needs he saw. And as today's lesson says, he acted on his decision immediately. He did not delay.

SCRIPTURAL CONTEXT The lesson on April 26 shares today's title and theme verse. Chambers pointed out how Abraham needed to change his view of God. Today, Chambers points to verse 33 and how quickly Abraham acted on God's command. As you read chapter 22, which aspect do you see more clearly?

Chambers makes more than fifty references to not conferring with "flesh and blood." Why did Paul think it was important that he didn't talk with the disciples after he left Damascus and Arabia?

WHAT'S THE DEVOTIONAL SAYING? The three paragraphs today walk us through Abraham's example of faith. First, Abraham committed to do what God asked before he actually performed it. Chambers doesn't cite any verse. But we know this is what Abraham did because *every* action first starts as a decision of the will. Second, Abraham climbed the "supreme climb" immediately—he "rose early" to do it. He also didn't seek advice, not even from his own understanding, before acting. Again, we know this because we know how human understanding, when consulted, *always* delays obeying God, and Abraham didn't delay. Third, Abraham didn't choose his sacrifice: not the one he thought he would sacrifice, nor the one he did.

Chambers is well aware that few of us will hear God's voice the way Abraham did. God more often speaks to us through circumstances. So Chambers talks about our "cup" being sweet or bitter. Are your circumstances comfortable? Enjoy them with grace. In other words, don't "rub it in" to people who don't have sweet circumstances, and remember that God could change yours to bitter whenever He sees fit. If your circumstances are already bitter, remember that He drinks the bitterness with you. He weeps when you weep and rejoices when you do. Often that is the only comforting thought in the midst of pain.

APPLICATION

What cup has God given you to drink? Are you procrastinating? Or switching cups?
Have you successfully climbed to God's revealed heights? Have you blamed God? How?
Finish this prayer: "Lord, I must go through each trial before I reach a verdict, and once I do . . ."

Enjoy the sweetness w/ grace + reme
God speaks to us through circumstances
God drinks the bitterness
us

NOVEMBER 12
THE CHANGED LIFE

What's new with you?
If your answer is "not much," then are you really saved?

BACKGROUND Are you patient and kind? Do you envy and boast? Are you proud, rude, or self-seeking? Do you get angry easily, keep track of wrongs, or delight in evil more than truth? Do you always protect, trust, and hope? Do you never fail?

When we put it this way, many of us can't stand in the light. We shuffle and squirm. Does it mean we aren't born again? It's good to consider that possibility. Today Oswald Chambers shows how we can know for sure if we really are.

SCRIPTURAL CONTEXT Did you memorize today's theme verse on October 23? Can you still remember it? Did it help you to learn it by heart? How so?

Remembering the words "the old has gone, the new has come!" won't help unless it's true.

If it's true, then reminding yourself about it will help when Satan tempts you to think you must to do all the things you used to do. Likewise, 1 Corinthians 13, 1 John 1:7, or any other verse will be useless if you are not born again.

WHAT'S THE DEVOTIONAL SAYING? So how can you be sure you are born again? Chambers says one good way to know you are is when your perspectives and desires are noticeably different, especially in a crisis. We are born again if we know beyond doubt that *we* didn't go through the crisis; *God* did.

But Chambers reminds us that these conscious signs of new birth are only the tip of the iceberg. The real changes are deeper than our consciousness. Do you believe that God is at work even there?

APPLICATION
What past things do you yearn for? What are your godly yearnings? Which dominates?
Read 1 Corinthians 13 out loud. Does it make you squirm? How do you know you're saved?
Finish this prayer: "Jesus, you are faithful, even when I'm faithless, but I want to see more evidence that . . ."

FAITH OR EXPERIENCE?

Faith can hold Christ's glory—experience can't.

BACKGROUND "Unbelieving and perverse generation! How long do I have to put up with you?" Do you ever feel like Jesus is a bit harsh with the father of the epileptic boy? Why did the father's description of how the disciples failed evoke Jesus' sharp rebuke? Was Jesus mad at the disciples, the father, or the whole situation?

Today Oswald Chambers explains why the Spirit is so impatient with our unbelief. It's the same reason Jesus was impatient with His disciples. His disciples' unbelief (or fear) was wicked because it came from their unwillingness to feed their faith and identify with Him. Are you in the same boat? Will the Spirit be impatient with you too?

SCRIPTURAL CONTEXT Galatians 2:20 is such a rich verse that each piece of it makes for a great lesson theme. On March 8 and 21, we focused on being crucified with Christ. On November 3, we looked at how Christ lives in us. Today we see that Christ gave himself for us.

If He gave himself for our profound, unutterable justification, how can we fear? He *himself* is our righteousness (1 Corinthians 1:30 and 2 Corinthians 5:21)!

WHAT'S THE DEVOTIONAL SAYING? Today's lesson is as much about our unbelief as it is about our moods. On May 20, we read that "Moods never go by praying, moods go by kicking." Today Chambers tells us to kick our complaints about not getting the experiences (or feelings) we think God should give us.

Do you think you should feel happy, useful, and on top of your game? Think again! God doesn't always or even usually want us to have those feelings. Read Ecclesiastes 7:2 if you doubt it. We are to be "grim faced" (like the archer who killed Smaug the dragon, see September 1, *Companion*) even while we are "carefully careless" (May 21, *Utmost*). Can you be grim-yet-careless? Have you been trying to do this? What would it look like in your life today?

APPLICATION

What gets you moody? How will you fight for holy devotion? What fact will you learn? What "sacrifices" have you made? What experiences do you seek? What do you fear? Finish this prayer: "Lord Jesus, it's no sacrifice serving you. Let me never forget how you saved me from . . ."

∽ NOVEMBER 14 ∽
DISCOVERING DIVINE DESIGN

God acts in tiny details. Can you see Him there?

BACKGROUND Oswald Chambers spoke on "Divine Designs" and Genesis 24 in his class on Abraham (see May 25, *Companion*). Today he deals with the general principle of divine guidance that is expressed in Genesis 24:27.

Have you ever asked God to lead you about a specific question: what job to take, whether to accept a new responsibility, or some other important decision? Did He lead you the way he led Eliezer's quest to find a wife for Isaac? If He didn't, why didn't He?

SCRIPTURAL CONTEXT Garry Friesen (see July 20, *Companion*), challenges the idea that Genesis 24 shows us how God frequently guides our decisions through special circumstances, which some call "fleeces" (Judges 6:37). Instead, Friesen says we should find our mate and make all our other decisions based only on God's moral will as revealed in the Bible. Anything beyond that is up to our wisdom (though God secretly works all the unknowns for our good).

Do you think God frequently leads us through circumstances and internal "checks"? Or does He want us to find our way through wisdom?

WHAT'S THE DEVOTIONAL SAYING? Ironically, Chambers and Friesen agree that we shouldn't keep asking God for guidance—for completely different reasons! Friesen believes God doesn't have a special plan in mind for us that He wants us to find; and Chambers says we should be so close to God that our common-sense decisions are directly in line with God's special plan for us.

But in the end, are these views different? Friesen says God works things out for our good. Maybe he would agree that God *does* have a special plan for us, just not one we can discover. And in that, Friesen is like Chambers, who has often said it's not for us to know what God has planned for us.

What about you? Are you hung up on asking God to help you make decisions? Why not move forward with your best common-sense guess for what to do next. If you choose disobedience, won't the Holy Spirit in you immediately react? (If He doesn't, reread the lesson from November 12!) Letting go of your hang-ups about God's guidance will help you focus on being faithful and loyal to God.

APPLICATION

When making decisions, do you ignore God, pester Him, or do something else? How should you decide?

When has the Spirit warned you? What did you do? How were Jesus, Paul, and others guided?

Finish this prayer: "Father, as your child I want to live in natural obedience. First, I need to be more aware . . ."

"WHAT IS THAT TO YOU?"

Are others floundering?
Turn to face God; it's the best way to help them.

BACKGROUND Today's lesson ends on a Buddhist-sounding note, "Most of us live . . . consciously serving . . . . All this is immature . . . the mature stage is . . . never conscious." Oswald Chambers seems to be pointing us to a nirvana of subconscious oneness with God. That sounds like blasphemy!

Thankfully, the links between today's lesson and Zen philosophy are superficial. We are one with a person (God), not an impersonal god (Brahman) or anything else. And that makes all the difference!

SCRIPTURAL CONTEXT We have looked at Peter's reinstatement in John 21 many times, but today's theme verse is new to us in *Utmost*. What is going on in this story? What happened to Peter by the time John wrote his gospel? Why did he include this story?

Chambers' point is that we don't need to be amateur providences (see January 30, *Utmost*) for our friends. Peter didn't need to worry about whether God would keep John alive until the second coming. Those who first read John's gospel didn't need to worry about other people, nor do we.

WHAT'S THE DEVOTIONAL SAYING? What is the connection between maturity being "never conscious" and not worrying about others? Chambers says we can give God's advice as long as we are rightly related to Him, or mature (one with Him).

Is this oneness never conscious? Do parents consciously think they are giving, loving parents when they scoop up their crying child? No! Do small children consciously think how obedient they are when they cheerfully do what their parents ask? Not at all! So it is in *this* way that mature Christians are never conscious. Are you heading in that direction?

APPLICATION *God's guidance + care of his creature on Earth*

Do you feel spiritually stagnant? Are you playing God to others? What should you do?

Does God use you? How do you know? How would it look to serve unconsciously?

Finish this prayer: "God, forgive me for being an amateur providence. I want to bless others instead by . . ."

NOVEMBER 16
STILL HUMAN!

Are you serving God as a human or as an other-worldly being?

BACKGROUND Oswald Chambers' talk "Still Human" was part of his series on Abraham (see May 25, *Companion*). In that talk, Chambers said, "Abraham is not the [archetype] of . . . sanctification, but of the life of faith." What does this mean? How is the life of faith different from being filled with the Holy Spirit through sanctification?

Chambers explains, "From . . . faith there is a natural human progress to a sanctified life." Our faith, demonstrated by how we keep our focus on God in the midst of drudgery, is what allows us to progress to a more Spirit-filled life.

SCRIPTURAL CONTEXT Biddy used 1 Corinthians 10:31 for today. (Oswald's original text was Genesis 22:20–24.) What is the context for today's theme verse? Was Paul talking about heroic actions or ordinary things?

Chambers won't quote Colossians 3:3 again until Christmas Eve, so now is a good time to take a close look at this verse. On January 23, April 28, and June 14, we thought about what "hidden with Christ" means. Do you have a better idea about it now? One analogy is that of an unborn baby who is hidden in his mother's womb while his mother's life is in him. In the same way, we are in Christ and yet Christ is in us. Do you ever think how Christ is actually in you? When you ask, "What would Jesus do?" do you realize that *you* don't have to do what He would do? You just have to let *Him in you* do what He would do.

WHAT'S THE DEVOTIONAL SAYING? Today's lesson is both a rebuke and an encouragement. First, it nails us for our hunger for human attention. Shouldn't the power of God flowing out of us be enough? Second, it encourages us that our drudgery is not an anticlimax but the main miracle of God's grace. We think anyone can peel potatoes or scrub kids' faces. But as Chambers said in his original talk: "*Anyone* cannot do these things; anybody can do the shining in the sun and the sporting in the footlights, but it takes God's incarnated Spirit to make you so absolutely humanly His that you are utterly unnoticeable."

Are you willing to be *His*? It means you won't be noticed, and no one will compliment your devotion to God. Your success won't be measured the way most people measure it, and you will always seem less successful than those around you. Are you still willing? "All to the glory of God"!

APPLICATION

How do real heroes and heroic actions differ? What is God using to make you a hero?

Are you absolutely God's in all human endeavors? Where do you still need to be His?

Finish this prayer: "Lord, I want to serve you in ways no one sees, but I'm so tempted to make sure . . ."

༄ NOVEMBER 17 ༄
THE ETERNAL GOAL

What is the reward of obedience?
God himself!

BACKGROUND Today Oswald Chambers quotes three of his most loved authors: Frederick Brook, George MacDonald, and Frederic W. H. Myers (for more about these authors, see the notes in *Companion* on July 12, August 15, and April 9, respectively). These men grasped what Chambers is saying: God is our everything; so at any cost we must lay hold of Him. The only obstacle is our own pettiness.

Have you grabbed hold of the hem of Jesus' garment? Do you know that there is none but He who can heal you? Let today's lesson refocus your heart on seeking God alone.

SCRIPTURAL CONTEXT Today's lesson comes from Chambers' Abraham class (see May 25, *Companion*). Chambers spent five lectures on Genesis 22. Why is this chapter so crucial? How does today's verse fit in?

Chambers also quotes 2 Corinthians 1:20, which we saw on April 20. Today he says our "yes" and "amen" are prerequisites to receiving the promise. Do you agree? Where is the line between our responsibility and God's faithfulness?

WHAT'S THE DEVOTIONAL SAYING? Once again the message is this: The more we obey, the more God reveals. Today we learn that obedience includes not telling God how He should bring us into His oneness, which is the "eternal goal." Are you tempted to choose how He does this?

God's road is slow—not because of Him but because of us. Realizing how slow we are is our first step in the right direction. We will be much quicker when it's not *us* listening to God's voice, but *His nature* in us!

Think back on the last thing God revealed to you. Was it because you obeyed? Even seemingly small acts of obedience can root out the self-love in us and open the doors for more of God's revelation!

APPLICATION

Initially, what was Abraham's goal? What did it become? How? What is your goal?

Is God's nature in you? How do you know? When has a verse become suddenly clear?

Finish this prayer: "Father, you say, 'Jump,' and I want to say, 'How high?' Please help me reach the point . . ."

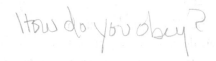
How do you obey?

Personality - the spiritual part of our being

WINNING INTO FREEDOM

Individuality - who we are but not renewed by the H S

God wants to break your individuality, not your spirit.

BACKGROUND Oswald Chambers uses the word *personality* to describe "the spiritual part of our being," as the Updated Edition helpfully puts it. Though we are already on day 323 of 366, Chambers mentions personality more in the next 43 days than he did in all the previous lessons.

Chambers contrasts personality with individuality. Individuality is the part of us that makes us who we are but that is not yet renewed by the Holy Spirit's presence. Chambers urges us today to let our old individuality give way to personality: "Stop listening to the tyranny of your individuality, and get emancipated out into personality." As we pay attention to Chambers' discussion of individuality and personality, we will learn how to stay close to God.

SCRIPTURAL CONTEXT John 8:32 ("You shall know the truth and the truth shall set you free") is a popular slogan in secular circles. Even Berkeley, California, has this verse emblazoned on the science building of its high school. Today's theme verse explains the meaning of "truth." The Son is the truth that sets us free.

On December 11, we will read that individuality is the husk of our personality. How does the Son set our personality free from its husk? Why doesn't the Savior do that?

WHAT'S THE DEVOTIONAL SAYING? Elsewhere in his *Complete Works*, Chambers says, "Never confound 'Savior' with 'friend.' Our Lord said, 'Ye are my friends' to His disciples, not to sinners." Today we see that sinners can't be set free by the Son. They need to be set free by the Savior before they can know the Son as their Friend. Do you think this is right? Is it also true of Galatians 2:20? Are we crucified with Christ the Son only after we are set free from our sin by our Savior?

Chambers says we are responsible to deliver ourselves from individuality by offering God our natural life. Then what is the *Son's* responsibility in setting us free from individuality if "we have to deliver ourselves," as today's lesson says?

The answer is that we have to offer our individuality to God the Son. Then He can crucify it, thus setting it free. We have to do this in "white funeral" fashion (see January 15, *Utmost*) every time God gives us a vision of a new aspect we need to surrender. But we also have to do this every moment, by disciplining our thoughts. Will you say "no" to the tyrant of your individuality and allow Christ to set you free?

APPLICATION

How has sin and individuality kept you from getting to God? What do *you* need to do?

How does freedom from sin and from self differ? When were you energized by Jesus?

Finish this prayer: "Lord Jesus, I need my individuality broken and my very core set free. My part is to . . ."

God is love, but love alone didn't redeem us—it took the blood of Jesus!

➤

BACKGROUND We've all done wrong things, and most of us know what it feels like to really feel bad about doing them. But today Oswald Chambers talks about a much deeper level of repentance: the conviction of sin.

Henry Blackaby (see October 16, *Companion*) says there are things only God can do. For example, when people are drawn to God, seek Him, and understand spiritual truth, only God could have caused these things. Likewise, only He can convict the world of sin, righteousness, and judgment. Have you felt the conviction of sin that Chambers describes?

SCRIPTURAL CONTEXT Can you find, in John 14 and 16, six things that only God can do? Why did Jesus tell the disciples this? How might it have changed their view of evangelism? Does it change yours?

We also read a famous quote from Psalm 51. What made David a man after God's heart? Would you like that to be true about you too? How can you start making it true today?

WHAT'S THE DEVOTIONAL SAYING? What should you do if you've never been convicted of sin the way Chambers describes? First, don't rest until you are. Second, don't minimize God's forgiveness. He doesn't overlook sin. He puts it on Jesus, and then He changes you into Jesus' image so you actually *deserve* heaven. If He didn't change you, His forgiveness would be an abomination. It would be like labeling a still-rabid bear "cured" and placing it in a room full of sleeping infants. Third, know the difference between remorse and the true repentance that comes from the conviction of sin.

Chambers once said, "We all experience remorse, disgust with ourselves over the wrong we have done when we are found out by it, but the rarest miracle of God's grace is the sorrow that puts an end forever to the thing for which I am sorry. Repentance involves the receiving of a totally new disposition so that I never do the wrong thing again." Have you repented, or did you only have remorse?

APPLICATION

When have you been disturbed by your wrongdoing? Convicted by your sin? How?

When you ask God to forgive you, do you think about the cost? Why does this matter?

Finish this prayer: "Father, your heart was broken so you could forgive my sin. I want to honor you by . . ."

THE FORGIVENESS OF GOD

Sanctification is easy—if you realize how hard forgiveness was for God.

◄ ►

BACKGROUND Today we continue a three-day series on forgiveness. The overarching theme is that God doesn't forgive the world because He loves it. Yes, He loves the world, as John 3:16 says. But His love didn't cause Him to forgive the world or befriend the world. James 4:4 says friendship with the world is enmity with God, and God can't be at enmity with himself!

Instead, God's love caused Him to send His Son to become our sin and suffer His full hatred of it. As Oswald Chambers said elsewhere, "God's love for the world is the kind of love that makes Him go to all lengths in order to remove the sin and evil from it . . . the stronger and more emphatic the love, the more intense is its obverse, hatred. God loves the world so much that He hates with a perfect hatred the thing that switched men wrong; and Calvary is the measure of His hatred."

Do you see the difference between God forgiving sin, and God fully expending His hatred of sin at Calvary? How do you think this distinction will change the way you live day to day?

SCRIPTURAL CONTEXT Read Ephesians 1. Do you get a sense for God's rich, lavish grace?

Read also 2 Corinthians 5. Can you tell that Paul grasped the distinction between God overlooking sin and God hating sin? How was Paul's life different as a result?

WHAT'S THE DEVOTIONAL SAYING? We know that God doesn't overlook sin, but would we be going too far to say that God "cannot forgive"? Chambers says it (Classic Edition, second paragraph). But what about Psalm 32:5, 65:3, 78:38, 85:2, 103:3, and 130:4, not to mention all the other books of the Bible? The solution to this paradox is that we get our sin *taken away*, which, from our point of view, is identical to forgiveness. Indeed, it is so much the same that even Chambers says "God can forgive" in the first paragraph—just four sentences before he says that God "cannot forgive." But from God's point of view, our sin is never merely forgiven. It is taken away from us, placed on Jesus, and punished to the last degree.

Isn't it interesting that Chambers, the champion of sanctification, says in today's final paragraph that sanctification pales compared to forgiveness? The Spirit in you, empowering you and making you into Christ's image, is just the outworking of forgiveness. Forgiveness truly is the mother of all miracles. Take time to thank God for all it cost Him to forgive you!

APPLICATION

What is your view of God the Father? Why? How do you understand the atonement?

What makes you grateful? How does gratitude (vs. ambition) compel/constrain you?

Finish this prayer: "God, your sacrifice overwhelms me with gratitude. Because of what Jesus did for me . . ."

NOVEMBER 21
"IT IS FINISHED!"

Don't preach a loving God until His wrath, borne by Jesus, is made amply clear.

◀

BACKGROUND As we end our three-day series, we see how preaching must reflect the distinction between God overlooking sin and God hating it. Not many of us have to preach sermons. But we all must preach to our own souls, as doctor-turned-pastor D. Martyn Lloyd-Jones urged everyone to do. And when we do, we need to preach the true picture of God's forgiveness.

The true picture is that Jesus is our ultimate hero, not that God is our sugar daddy. We live our lives as mini-heroes, pouring out for others to the utmost, not as spoiled children who never learn to correct their faults because their errors are simply overlooked.

SCRIPTURAL CONTEXT In John 17:4, how could Jesus say in His prayer that He had finished His work when He hadn't even gone to Gethsemane? Why does He say it again just before He dies (John 19:30)? Were there two different works God sent Him to do? Perhaps the key is the next verse, "And now, O Father, glorify me . . ." Jesus had finished His part before going to Gethsemane. From that point on, God was in charge of finishing the rest of His redemption plan. So when Jesus said, "It is finished!" in John 19:30, He was talking about what His Father had done.

In the end, does it matter precisely when Jesus finished the work God gave Him to do? The important thing is, as Hebrews 2:9 says, Jesus got glory *because* He died. His death was the whole reason God put Him on earth.

WHAT'S THE DEVOTIONAL SAYING? Are you obliterating God's holiness by not properly understanding the redemption? God forbid! Don't go another day with the wrong view of forgiveness. When you preach to your own soul, or talk with others, make sure you speak the truth: God so loved the world that He gave His only begotten Son to take on the full fury of His wrath against the sin that separated the world from His holy presence and to give the world a new nature so that whoever believes in Him shall not perish, but have eternal life.

No doubt you have memorized John 3:16, which tells us part of the story about how God takes our sin away. Will you also learn by heart, and teach to others, the full story of God's redemption?

APPLICATION

How was Calvary the playing out of God's mind? Is wrath God's main intent? Why?

What were Jesus' last three sentences on the cross? What is significant about them?

Finish this prayer: "Lord God, you planned Jesus' death from the very beginning. Yet often I lose sight of . . ."

NOVEMBER 22
SHALLOW AND PROFOUND

Lighten up—God says so!

BACKGROUND Do you have a favorite day in *Utmost*? If not, you may consider adopting today's devotional as your new favorite. It's a different kind of lesson from what we usually read, and it adds the perfect balance to the other 365 readings.

What's on your menu today? Seriously. What's for dinner? Do you think God cares? He does! And, as we read in today's lesson, so should you. Every detail matters to Him.

SCRIPTURAL CONTEXT First Corinthians 10:31 is one of six or so verses (Colossians 3:17 and 23, Ephesians 6:7, Romans 12:11, and Ecclesiastes 9:10) that talk directly about how we should do all that we do, deep or shallow, to God's glory and to our utmost.

Are there only six verses that commend life's "shallow" pursuits? Oswald Chambers quotes Luke 6:40. So we know that Jesus' actions also commend life's lighter side. What did Jesus care about? Weddings, hungry crowds, a fish breakfast, a fishing business. Pretty ordinary stuff! Then there are all the other examples in the Bible, such as when God miraculously restored a borrowed ax, when He created supernatural shade for an ornery prophet, and when He gave prophecy about missing donkeys! If these are the biblical examples of what God cares about, why are we "abominably serious"? Is it any mystery why some nonbelievers think Christians are sticks-in-the-mud?

WHAT'S THE DEVOTIONAL SAYING? "Lighten up" isn't just God's friendly suggestion. Chambers says the shallow part of life is our safeguard. If we ignore today's message about honoring the shallow as much as the deep, we do so at our own peril.

Today's lesson comes from Chambers' class on Abraham (see May 25, *Companion*) and Genesis 17:17. Have you laughed recently? Have you ever laughed like Abraham—because you believed in God's hilariously generous provision and knew beyond doubt that He was going to give you something you had always wanted? Think of what happens to a child when he first hears he's going to Disneyland. You can't fake that kind of exuberance. But you can keep serving God faithfully and joyfully in all the shallow things. One day you might fall on the floor laughing!

APPLICATION

What shallow things are you doing? How do you feel about them? How does God feel?

Do you take things too seriously? Do people feel rebuked being around you? How so?

Finish this prayer: "God, I want to take you 100 percent seriously, but often I neglect you and instead take seriously . . ."

THE DISTRACTION OF CONTEMPT

Life's worries and lust for approval breed an attitude set against God.

➢

BACKGROUND Today and tomorrow come from a series of lectures that Oswald Chambers gave after the Bible Training College closed (see July 31, *Companion*) but before he left for Egypt. The setting was a tiny antique shop owned by Chambers' friend. Each evening, former students would gather on the second floor and hear Chambers talk about the Psalms of Ascent (120–134). These short psalms were meant for singing on the road to Jerusalem. Chambers' own path was in that direction!

How about you? Where are you headed? Today's lesson helps us focus on God, so that when we get to our destination, and all along the way, we will be one with Him.

SCRIPTURAL CONTEXT Psalm 123 has one of the most eloquent descriptions of our relationship to God. It also contains today's verse, which we can't relate to quite as easily. Chambers applies it to our lives (in the original talk) by linking "contempt" to being annoyed at other people. We can all relate to that!

When did you last read Malachi? Read the first two chapters. How is 2:16 the key to avoiding wickedness? What wickedness do the first two chapters describe?

The parable of the sower tells us that God's Word loses its chance to bear fruit in our lives when the devil takes it from us, when we don't deepen it, or when we let cares choke it. Which one keeps it from producing Jesus' life in yours?

WHAT'S THE DEVOTIONAL SAYING? Today's lesson naturally breaks into four parts. First, pay no heed to human ingenuity. When you do, you lose your faith in God. Second, don't let little cares distract you. Refuse them! Third, don't try to explain why you were in the right. You might have been, but as soon as you try to clear your name, you are in the wrong. Let God clear it. Finally, don't let insight into other people's sins distract you. Pray for them, but don't criticize them in your heart.

We need to be ruthless with anything that distracts us from God. If we aren't, we will flounder on the way to our Jerusalem. There are plenty of people who annoy us, plenty of cares that need tending, plenty of sins we learn about. Don't let any of them move you one inch from your focus on God.

APPLICATION

When have you had the wrong attitude? What happened? How was Satan involved?

What distracts you? How will you avoid this next time? Who needs your intercession?

Finish this prayer: "Holy Spirit, I need you to fill me with the right attitude. Please help me to pray for . . ."

NOVEMBER 24
DIRECTION OF FOCUS

A little too eager for God?
Nonsense! Go for broke!

◄

BACKGROUND Yesterday we saw that when we put our trust in human ingenuity, we lose our faith in God. Today we see what it means to trust human opinion such as when we listen to our own humble-sounding thoughts about ourselves or to our friends' seemingly humble advice to us. For example, they might say, "Don't be such a spiritual super hero," which sounds like humble advice (and is similar to Oswald Chambers' warning on May 11 in *Utmost* against standing on "tiptoe").

We trust in human opinion whenever we try to love God with our own power. But if we are asking for God's power and come to Jesus when we are weary and heavy-laden, there is no limit to how long we can stand on our "tiptoes"; no height of love for God is too great.

Have you been heeding your humble-sounding thoughts or your friends' "advice"? Roughly brush them aside. Let today's lesson give you courage to completely ignore them.

SCRIPTURAL CONTEXT Today's verse is such a perfect way to describe how we ought to see our relationship with God. As Oswald Chambers said, "Am I a woolgatherer, or like a man looking for his Lord?" We ought to look to God as an attentive worker looks to his boss.

Isaiah 53, the famous chapter on the suffering servant, begins with a question: "To whom has the arm of the Lord been revealed?" Chambers answers that it is to those whose eyes are riveted on God. Do you want the strength of God's arm? Then keep your eyes fixed on Him. As soon as you lose focus, your strength "leaks," as Chambers likes to put it.

WHAT'S THE DEVOTIONAL SAYING?

How do we "remedy" spiritual leakage? Chambers says we have to do so immediately—but how, exactly? Obviously it has to do with looking to God and getting our focus back on Him. But to do that, our best approach is to do all the things people (and the feelings inside us) tell us we are foolish for doing. "Wasn't that too pretentious? Isn't this stand a bit too high?" Those are just the things we need to do in order to plug our spiritual leak!

In what ways are you relying on human ingenuity and opinion? How can you be over-the-top and even pretentious for God? What can you "readjust" today?

APPLICATION

Where are your eyes focused? What have you learned about God's countenance? How?
Do you feel drained? What can you do? What do friends say about your past victories?
Finish this prayer: "God, I'm focused on you right now. Help me to walk through this week continually . . ."

THE SECRET OF SPIRITUAL CONSISTENCY

What are you living for? Externals? Or the foundation of Calvary?

➤

BACKGROUND Today we start the third-to-last series in *Utmost*. For the next three days, we will learn about keeping our spiritual energy. Yesterday we learned about "spiritual leakage." This three-day series will tell us more about how to plug our leaks.

Oswald Chambers advises us to clearly think about what we believe. The next step is to throw out all the beliefs that don't have to do with the cross. One gets the impression that Chambers expects most of us will have to throw out some of our most treasured beliefs, since they often aren't firmly rooted in Christ and Him crucified.

SCRIPTURAL CONTEXT Second Thessalonians 3:17 indicates that Paul wrote something in his own hand on each of his letters. He had been plagued by forged letters (2 Thessalonians 2:2) and wanted to stop any further identity theft. The theme verse for the next three days comes from the section of Galatians 6 that Paul wrote in his own handwriting. Thus, it carries special significance.

What does the first half of Galatians 6:14 indicate? How does it relate to the second half, which we will look at next? Have you ever boasted about something Christian and felt justified because you were promoting Christianity? But were you boasting about the cross?

WHAT'S THE DEVOTIONAL SAYING? The main rebuke today is that we try to be put together *externally*, but we don't try to be *internally* consistent. Initially, God throws our external life into chaos. But we fight Him and try to get back the consistency we once had. Sure, we put a Christian veneer on it, but it's still the same crowd-pleasing consistency. Let the externals be in chaos, as God wanted! Then He can smash the idol of external consistency that you worship.

The cross is the key to everything. Chambers wants us to "brood" on the cross. Will you dwell on the topic of the cross today?

APPLICATION

List your beliefs. Which ones aren't based on the cross? How can you get rid of those?

What circumstance has affected your emotions? How can you become more like Paul?

Finish this prayer: "Holy Spirit, thank you so much for the new birth you gave me; I will be true to it by . . ."

THE FOCAL POINT OF SPIRITUAL POWER

Want God's power right now?
Consider His tragedy and victory at Calvary.

BACKGROUND Oswald Chambers says today that we must cut ourselves off from our "prying" personal interest in our own spiritual symptoms. If we constantly pry into our religious barometer ("Did I have my quiet time?" "Am I reading the Bible?"), we will pry ourselves away from God and begin to lose our spiritual power.

When you preach to your own soul or to others, do you focus on the cause (the cross) or the effects (living holy, healing)? Today's churches have lost their power even more than in Chambers' day. The culprit is loss of focus on Jesus and His cross.

SCRIPTURAL CONTEXT

Today we look at the middle of Galatians 6:14—nothing but our Lord's cross. Is that your attitude? Or do you focus on your spiritual symptoms (how you handled stress, whether you trusted God enough)? We must be on the lookout for spiritual leakage, but we can't let watchfulness become a distraction.

First Corinthians 2:2 says the same thing: nothing but Jesus and His crucifixion. How does this context differ from Galatians? What issues was Paul addressing?

WHAT'S THE DEVOTIONAL SAYING?

Chambers moves from the pastor (*you* cut off personal interests) to the congregation (the listening crowd seemed to pay no attention) to the church at large (we don't think about the cross enough). Few of us are pastors, but we all are part of the church and can see that our personal struggles are the same ones our small Christian communities face and the ones that plague Christendom. What is the cure? It is individuals who are focused on Christ and the cross and who encourage others to do the same. How can you brood on the cross today?

APPLICATION

Did you just now consider God's tragedy? Do you believe God's power is now in you?
Have you preached Christ and Him crucified? What happened? If not, why haven't you?
Finish this prayer: "God, this week I commit to dwelling on your tragedy, the cross of Christ.
   Each day, . . ."

ᕯ NOVEMBER 27 ᕯ
THE CONSECRATION OF SPIRITUAL POWER

Consecration (but not sanctification) is our job.

◄

BACKGROUND Two days ago we saw that brooding on the cross helps us plug any spiritual energy leaks we may have sprung. Today we learn more about how to brood without leaving behind the world.

But shouldn't we want to leave the world behind? Didn't we just read how James 4:4 tells us not to befriend the world? Oswald Chambers often discusses this puzzle of consecration. His advice, which we see today, is the same as Jesus' admonition in John 17—be in the world but not of it.

SCRIPTURAL CONTEXT "World" is mentioned twice at the end of Galatians 6:14. Paul was dead to the world: It had no claims on him. And the world was dead to Paul, since it held no attraction (in particular, the world's religious ceremonies, such as circumcision). But Paul, like Jesus, was very much in the world.

"Otherworldly" is what Chambers calls being in the world but not of it. This concept comes from John 17:15–16. Do you lean toward worldly, anti-world, or otherworldly? What can you do today to be more otherworldly?

WHAT'S THE DEVOTIONAL SAYING? The three paragraphs in today's lesson each teach different aspects of consecration. First, we don't leave the world and focus on our own holiness when we consecrate. We focus on Jesus, who is very much interested in the world. Second, we don't cut things out of our lives hoping that it will help us consecrate. The only thing we need to cut out, as we saw yesterday, is our hypersensitivity to how we are doing spiritually. This is why "shallow" things are our safeguard (see November 22, *Utmost*). Third, even though cutting things out of our life won't help us increase our spiritual power, we do still need to cut things out—not just our spiritual hypersensitivity but also anything Jesus wouldn't like.

Chambers always helps us clarify what part of the Christian walk is our job and what is God's job. Today, we see that consecration is our job, and the gift of the Holy Spirit (sanctification) is God's. Are you doing your job? How can you stay in the world while not being "of" all the things that would keep your heart from God?

APPLICATION

What are Jesus' interests in your life? What are Satan's? How can you be consecrated?

What do you avoid so as to be holy? Is that good or counterproductive? How so?

Finish this prayer: "Lord, you have redeemed me, set me apart from sin, and are making me holy. My job is to . . ."

ᕀᕀᕀ NOVEMBER 28 ᕀᕀᕀ
THE RICHES OF THE DESTITUTE

The biggest barrier to accepting the gospel is pride, not intellect.

BACKGROUND In April and May 1915, Oswald Chambers gave a series of lectures on the Holy Spirit. In his second talk, he introduced his students to Émile Boutroux's 1912 lecture "The Beyond That Is Within," which describes the intersection of finite and infinite within us. Today's lesson ends with an explanation of how God within puts the "beyond" in us and lifts us to the "above" where we see and enter God's kingdom.

All of this is the "bounty of destitution," which was the title of Chambers' third talk in his series. Have you reached the point of destitution? Or are you just depressed? Only God can help you see your poverty. Put aside your pride and ask for the Holy Spirit.

SCRIPTURAL CONTEXT The third chapter of Romans is the turning point in Paul's argument. Read Romans 1–3. How does 3:21–24 fit in? How do you define sin, glory, justification, and redemption?

Boutroux's title serves as a comment on Jesus' words to Nicodemus in John 3. As Chambers put elsewhere in his *Complete Works*: "The power to see is within; what is seen is without. . . . When the Holy Spirit comes in there is a new power of perception." Did Nicodemus ever understand this?

WHAT'S THE DEVOTIONAL SAYING? Most of today's devotional tells us we need the gift of seeing our spiritual poverty. The last few sentences explain what Nicodemus couldn't understand: The Spirit ignites Jesus' life in us, which gives us new eyes to see (and then enter) God's kingdom.

What is God's kingdom? Where is it? Many think of it as the afterlife, but Jesus said, "The kingdom is at hand!" We don't have to wait until we die to enter God's kingdom. We will realize we are citizens of His kingdom right now if we don't allow our pride and our reluctance to be humiliated get in our way.

APPLICATION

Did the gospel make you feel longing, or resentment? Where does your pride come out?

Are you hungry spiritually? How so? What does the Holy Spirit give us? To what end?

Finish this prayer: "Holy Spirit, thank you for putting God's nature in me. I want to stop seeing myself as . . ."

THE SUPREMACY OF JESUS CHRIST

What is the Holy Spirit's job?
He applies Christ's work to all who believe.

BACKGROUND Every era in church history has its problems. Churches in the developed world today are plagued with materialism, celebrity worship, and irrelevance to young people who believe more in ghosts than in God. In Oswald Chambers' day, the problems were pietism and holiness movements that put all the focus on fasting, prayer meetings, and times of personal devotion. Pastors today would love their parishioners to have *those* problems!

But as Chambers tells us today, they are real problems because they take the focus away from Jesus and His cross. Let today's lesson stir your heart to personal, passionate devotion to Jesus.

SCRIPTURAL CONTEXT Why does Jesus, not God the Father, give the Holy Spirit messages for us? Since Jesus received His messages from the Father (John 14:24), and the Spirit receives His messages from Jesus (today's verse), it makes sense that there is a division of labor within the Godhead.

Why is it helpful to know about this division of labor? We need to know, for example, to whom we pray. Requests to Jesus after the ascension are rare (see Revelation 22:21). And we never see people pray to the Holy Spirit. Instead, we are commanded to pray in Jesus'

name and in the Holy Spirit (Jude 20). The Spirit glorifies the Son, who glorifies the Father, by guiding us into all truth. And His truth is not mere head truth. He guides us into truth we live out each day.

WHAT'S THE DEVOTIONAL SAYING?
The holiness movement people Chambers refers to in today's study knew plenty of truths from the Bible. They even lived in a way that was different from non-Christians in how they spent their time and money. But that's not the kind of living out the truth God wants. He wants the "rugged reality" kind that costs the blood of Jesus.

We don't want a life that has Jesus as its figurehead, like the mascot of a sports team. We need lives invaded by His life. We become passionately devoted to His person because His Spirit is in us. The Holy Spirit is passionately devoted to the Son, just as the Father and Son passionately love one another.

Do you want people to look at you and say your life is "the work of God Almighty," like we say when we learn about Chambers' life? If so, commit yourself to the revelation of truth that is given in the New Testament. Let God order your steps as you simply follow Him to the next thing.

APPLICATION
What holiness movements have you heard about? What are their identifying features?
Who sees Christ as a mere figurehead? What is He to you? How is He glorified in you?
Finish this prayer: "Holy Spirit, you work Christ's death into my life by . . ."

NOVEMBER 30
"BY THE GRACE OF GOD I AM WHAT I AM"

God's power is effective in you. Are you willing to admit it?

BACKGROUND A few times in *Utmost*, we have been challenged to ask, "Am I even born again?" This is an extremely vital question. But some might ask this question in the wrong way and adopt an attitude that seems humble but is actually an insult to God.

It's not only our salvation we question. We also question our ability to do what God wants us to do. Again, this question is good in the appropriate setting. Asking ourselves whether we have enough ability can spark increased efforts to train and prepare ourselves. But this question is often a thinly veiled attack against God. Look at today's study so you can avoid insulting God in this way.

SCRIPTURAL CONTEXT The situation in Corinth forced Paul to constantly defend his apostleship. Today's theme verse comes at the end of Paul's defense of how he came to be an apostle. Why was it right for Paul to defend his apostleship? How is this different from defending *our* reputation and trying to clear *our* name (see November 23, *Companion*)?

Have you made sure that God's grace to you is not for nothing? How can you "work harder" and yet know that it is not you but God's grace within you?

WHAT'S THE DEVOTIONAL SAYING? The main theme today is that many of our statements about our drawbacks are "slander against God." Oswald Chambers also makes three related comments. First, he shows how true humility sounds prideful to others. Second, our relationship with God is the biggest thing in our lives. Finally, one life can be of huge value to God (see September 2, *Companion*).

Next time you are tempted to say out loud or to yourself, "I'm no saint," remember today's lesson. Your "humility" might actually be an insult to God!

APPLICATION

When did you last talk about your inabilities? How do you suppose God felt? Why?

Is God your all in all? Will you let Him be? What value might your life have to Him?

Finish this prayer: "God, I'm sorry for saying disparaging things about myself. I know that you can do all . . ."

⚭ DECEMBER 1 ⚭
THE LAW AND THE GOSPEL

p. 99 in complete BTC (handwritten)

Slam into God's Law—you'll see why Jesus died for you!

BACKGROUND Oswald Chambers' class on morality was one of his specialties. At the one-year anniversary of the Bible Training College, G. Campbell Morgan, the famous pastor of Westminster Chapel, specifically praised this class, which had been part of Chambers' core curriculum since the very first semester.

Today's lesson comes from the first lecture in *Biblical Ethics,* a 1947 book containing many of Chambers' talks on morality. Biddy edited it into a clear introduction to the law and the gospel. Will you read it and be convicted and encouraged?

SCRIPTURAL CONTEXT James understood the place of law and the gospel—of works and grace. So did Paul, whose writings were hard to understand even to their first audience (see 2 Peter 3:16). It is hard, for example, to understand how James 2:24 fits with Romans 3:38. Today's verse, though, is easy to understand, and it is similar to what Paul says in Galatians 3:10: We are cursed if we do not *continuously* do *everything* the law requires.

Paul's point in Galatians is that we can't hope to keep the law. (James would agree, though his point in today's verse is that we should live *as if* we are going to be judged by the law.) How do Romans 7:9 and 14 support Paul's point?

WHAT'S THE DEVOTIONAL SAYING? Today's lesson has at least two tricky bits. First, what does "less than alive" mean? Chambers points to Romans 7:9, which says that when we are alive we will eventually slam into God's law. If we are not realizing the absolute nature of the law, it's because we aren't even "alive" yet.

Second, what does "it comes with an 'if'" mean? In the original lecture, Chambers added that it means, "I have the power not to obey it." By giving us the choice not to obey, God infuses the law with power. If He forced us to obey, like we sometimes want Him to do (whenever we're not wanting Him to leave us alone), the law would be pointless and powerless. And here is where the encouraging part of today's lesson comes in: When we choose to obey, God taxes the remotest star to help us be successful in our obedience. All we have to do is set our wills in motion!

APPLICATION

When have you realized the demanding nature of God's law? How did you respond?

How can we obey to absolute perfection? How is this related to our initial obedience?

Finish this prayer: "Lord, it's good you don't force me to obey, even though I want you to force me. Instead, you . . ."

Romans 3:38 ...neither death nor life angels nor demons... will be able to separate us from the love of God

James: 2:24 Those who truly trust in God's naturally end up participating in good works

DECEMBER 2
CHRISTIAN PERFECTION

God's the boss. He decides.

BACKGROUND What would you do if you had to preach on Genesis 25:1–4? The difficulty is not that this passage is controversial or hard to understand. It's just that it's so irrelevant.

You might say it only *seems* irrelevant, and that (since it's in the Bible) it must be somehow relevant. If you said that, you'd be right, but only half right. This passage *is* irrelevant—and that's exactly what makes it relevant! As Oswald Chambers said in his talk on this passage, "One of the most striking features in Abraham's life is its irrelevancy. . . . The irrelevant things in Abraham's life are evidences of that half-conscious living which proves that his mind was not taken up with himself. . . . The whole trend of his life is to make us admire God, not Abraham."

Today's lesson comes from this talk on Abraham. It teaches us not to see ourselves as the main point. God is always the main point. So we must only be "half-conscious" about our own life.

SCRIPTURAL CONTEXT Philippians 3:12 winds up Paul's attack against (and antidote for) legalism. What can we learn from verses 1–11?

How is Paul's admission in verse 12 not defeatist, but triumphant?

We read Isaiah 53 for its clear prophecies about Jesus. But have you put *yourself* in the shoes of the suffering servant? Are you (as Chambers asks today) surprised that God treats you like He treated His Son?

WHAT'S THE DEVOTIONAL SAYING? Chambers definitely thought we could be perfected. He gave a talk in 1914 titled, "You Need Not Sin." But he never said sinlessness was the goal. On the contrary, he often warned that putting the emphasis on not sinning would always lead us away from God, whereas focusing on God could (and should) lead us to sinless Christian perfection.

Are you sinless yet? Don't try to be! Just focus on God. He might decide to put you in circumstances that exacerbate your temptation to sin. But if you keep your focus on Him, He will do what He likes with you. In the process, you will grow ever closer to Him, and your desire to sin will melt away.

Just focus on God NOT on being Sinless. Let him do what he wants with you.

APPLICATION

Does part of you want to be a trophy in God's showcase? How is this a misguided wish?

How has God bruised you? What seems pointless in your life? Whose life seems great?

Finish this prayer: "God, I will stop working on being a super saint and start working on my relationship . . ."

Put God first

Don't try to be a super saint!

Base faith in the perfect atonement of Christ. Does the atonement exert a dominating influence in your life? Have you sacrificed your body to God? Sin does not belong to human nature as God created it. Sin = your right to yourself. Let Christ rule, Sin demand from the outside obedience on the inside.

DECEMBER 3
"NOT BY MIGHT NOR BY POWER"

Be secure in God. Stand firm on the redemption!

BACKGROUND "Some trust in chariots, and some in horses, but we trust in the name of the LORD our God." So says Psalm 20:7, and so says today's lesson.

What do you trust in? Your knowledge of how to be saved? Your clear explanations? There is only one thing that is secure: God himself!

Did you notice that *Utmost*, the world's most popular devotional, breaks all the rules about successful devotionals? There are no personal stories, very few illustrations, and the language (even in the Updated Edition) is hard to follow! But it does one thing very well. It focuses on Christ's redemption. And it comes from a man and a woman who relied on the Holy Spirit.

SCRIPTURAL CONTEXT Paul had much to tell the church in Corinth. He first rebukes the denominational fights of the people. Then he attacks the prideful intellectualism that is at the root of their divisions. At the end of this attack is today's theme verse. If you were in Corinth and God opened your heart to receive Paul's rebuke, how would today's verse have made you feel? Are you like the Corinthians in some ways?

"Sanctification must . . . be sanctified." What does Oswald Chambers mean by this statement? He cites John 17:19, but that still leaves us scratching our heads. He may have been paraphrasing the chapter "Sanctification, Which Needs Sanctifying" from F. E. Marsh's 1908 book *Pearls, Points and Parables*. If so, Chambers means that our view of our sanctification is always in need of more clarification from the Spirit. As he suggests in the final sentence, we must continuously set apart our already sanctified (set apart) life so God can use it.

WHAT'S THE DEVOTIONAL SAYING?
Today's lesson likely comes from one of Chambers' sermon preparation classes (see May 5, *Companion*). He tells his listeners to put their confidence in the power of the gospel when they preach. Where is your confidence today? Has God placed you in situations that upset your faith and made you realize that your confidence was in the wrong thing?

Move into personal contact with Jesus. Only a relationship with Him will keep you from being shaken. "Not by might, nor by power, but by My Spirit, says the LORD" (Zechariah 4:6).

APPLICATION
How did you feel after telling others about God? What stood out? What should have?
What is sanctification? How will it look? Why must our sanctification be sanctified?
Finish this prayer: "Holy Spirit, I have trusted in my own wisdom and efforts. Please help me refocus on . . ."

DECEMBER 4
THE LAW OF OPPOSITION

Are you struggling?
No strain, no gain!

BACKGROUND "The Shadow of an Agony" is a line from one of Oswald Chambers' favorite book-length poems, and it is also the title of a compilation of his lectures—the first such compilation that Biddy published after his death. Part of today's reading comes from one of the final lectures, which he gave in Egypt on August 25, 1917, a few months before he died.

Chambers says that struggling is the basis of our physical, mental, moral, and spiritual life. Where are your battles today? Will you face them with eyes open to how God uses them, or are you going into your struggles blind to what God could be doing?

SCRIPTURAL CONTEXT Revelation 2–3 features letters to seven churches. Each letter includes the words, "to him [or he] who overcomes" followed by blessings that Jesus will give the overcomers. Which one of these blessings makes the most sense? Which one makes the least?

John faithfully recorded Jesus' messages to the seven churches. He also recorded what Jesus said the night He was betrayed. The two messages have some similarities, such as what John 16:33 says about tribulation. What other connections can you find?

WHAT'S THE DEVOTIONAL SAYING? Let's look at what Chambers tells us about struggles in each area of life. Physically, our body struggles against externals (decay, sickness, and other problems). When the tug-of-war is balanced, we call it *health*. Mentally, we struggle to maintain the balance, which we call *thought*. Morally, our fighting produces the balance called *virtue*. Spiritually, our tribulations produce *holiness* when we fight.

The key to all of this balance is that we fight. If we stop fighting, we lose the balance. Health turns to illness. Thought turns to mental wool gathering (see August 23, *Utmost*). Virtue turns to vice. Holiness—being set apart to God—turns into spiritual narcissism.

Most of today's lesson comes straight out of Chambers' class on Abraham (see May 25, *Companion*). When did Abraham struggle and overcome? How did overcoming struggles shape his life? How will you overcome today? Which area (physical, mental, moral, or spiritual) do you need to focus on first?

APPLICATION

Are your daily struggles like a war? What elements sustain you but also spell death in the end? How is holiness like health (and thought and virtue)? How will you achieve balance?

Finish this prayer: "God, you've created me for physical, mental, moral, and spiritual war. Today I'll strive to . . ."

⚬⚬⚬ DECEMBER 5 ⚬⚬⚬
"THE TEMPLE OF THE HOLY SPIRIT"

Need a reason to do right?
The Holy Spirit is in you!

BACKGROUND Sometime in early 1915, Oswald Chambers gave a three-part talk on "The Temple of God." The third part focused on 1 Corinthians 6:19, and it mirrors much of what we read in today's lesson.

Have you ever been "sterner with others" (from the Classic Edition) than with yourself? Do you make excuses for the things in your life and condemn the things you see in others? Are you smugly confident that you would *never* do what they did? (Isn't it only because you prefer other sins?) If you answered, "yes" to any of these questions, today's lesson will help you get back on track.

SCRIPTURAL CONTEXT What an odd theme verse! Who spoke these words? How do those words relate to today's lesson? For Chambers, Pharaoh represents Jesus; and Joseph, the "prime minister" of Egypt, represents each of us. As Chambers wrote elsewhere, "Take Pharaoh as a picture of Jesus Christ; the soul that is born again . . . is prime minister of his own body under Jesus Christ's dominion. That is the ideal, and it is not an ideal only, but an ideal which Jesus Christ expects us to carry out— all the powers of the soul working through the body in an express personality, revealing the Ruler to be the Lord Jesus Christ."

To better explain how this works, Chambers quotes some of his favorite verses (Galatians 2:21, Philippians 2:12, 1 Corinthians 9:27, and Romans 12:1). Which helps you more, the analogy of Pharaoh and Joseph or the verses?

WHAT'S THE DEVOTIONAL SAYING? In the last sentence today, Chambers says that the law for the body is summed up in the truth that your body is "the temple of the Holy Spirit." Does this match what the Bible says? Jesus said that the Golden Rule "is" the law and the prophets. And the law and the prophets depend on, according to Jesus, loving God and neighbors. Paul said loving neighbors sums up and fulfills the law. How do all of these statements fit together?

The key is that Jesus came to fulfill the law. If we try to find the one command (for instance, love God or love your neighbor,) that we need to do, Jesus will ask us to do the one thing we can't do (for example, sell all your possessions or love your enemy), and we will walk away dejected. Instead, we need to have His life—the Holy Spirit—in us so we can love as He did. Then He will fulfill the law using our body, just as He fulfilled the law when He was in His earthly body. Let your body be His temple today!

APPLICATION

How are we like Joseph? How does this authority make you feel? What must you do? Who are you judging severely? Why? How are you doing in your thoughts and desires? Finish this prayer: "Holy Spirit, my body is your temple. There are things I need to . . ."

DECEMBER 6
"MY RAINBOW IN THE CLOUD"

Every rainbow, every communion, reminds you to transact with God.

BACKGROUND In the last year of the Bible Training College, Oswald Chambers gave lectures on Genesis. We already saw some of his lectures on Abraham, which he gave in the early spring of 1915. He covered the chapters before Abraham in the fall of 1914. Today's lesson comes from one of the last of his autumn lectures.

Can you picture yourself sitting in Chambers' class? All around you the world is at war. The quick victory you had hoped for never materialized. It's clear that your life will never be the same, no matter what you do. And there is Oswald Chambers, preaching about Noah—but really about how you must turn your life over to God. Will you do it?

SCRIPTURAL CONTEXT In his original lecture, Chambers painted a vivid picture of the ark sitting atop Mt. Ararat with no dry land in sight. Then "at last" the waters receded. What a triumph! Noah had no hope except the hope he had in God. And God came through just as He promised, in a way that exceeded all expectations. You can be sure of God's promises. When He says, "Look to Me, and be saved" (Isaiah 45:22), the very next thing He does is to promise that "every knee shall bow, every tongue shall swear allegiance" (verse 23, ESV) to Him. We do well to trust His promise and turn to Him before it's too late!

After the miracle of the fulfilled promise, God gave a covenant and marked it with a beautiful sign. Have you stepped into God's covenant? What *is* His covenant (Luke 22:20, Hebrews 8:13)?

WHAT'S THE DEVOTIONAL SAYING? God's covenants are always given to help us get into "moral relationship" (Classic Edition) with Him. We know that *moral* means "of the will." The main reason God gives us a covenant, according to Chambers, is so we have the opportunity to exercise our will to choose Him over anything else in our life.

Do you think someone can choose God before being born again? No way! But once we're born from above, we need to exercise our new "roused" will (see June 6, *Utmost*). Noah exercised his will by planting a vineyard and being fruitful, just as God's covenant had said to do. How will you exercise your will to fulfill the new covenant? Every time you take communion, remind yourself of your need to exercise your will.

APPLICATION

What or who has deceived you? When were you disillusioned by this deception? How?

Who do you love? Do you demand more perfection than the person you love is able to give? Why?

Finish this prayer: "God, I want to be true to the facts about others—not my ideas of them. But I need you to . . ."

DECEMBER 7
REPENTANCE

Repentance is a gift that the memory of Christ's sacrifice helps us receive.

BACKGROUND On November 19, we learned about the conviction of sin. Today Oswald Chambers quotes a hymn from 1863, which begins:

> *My sins, my sins, my Savior!*
> *They take such hold on me,*
> *I am not able to look up,*
> *Save only, Christ, on Thee;*
> *In Thee is all forgiveness,*
> *In Thee abundant grace,*
> *My shadow and my sunshine*
> *The brightness of Thy face.*

Have you come to this point? Are you so sad that your sins fall on Jesus that you say, "My God, *I* should be there on that bitter cross"? Today's lesson helps us understand that this is true repentance.

SCRIPTURAL CONTEXT Did the church in Corinth truly repent between the two letters we call 1 and 2 Corinthians? Paul indicates that they did. And he writes today's theme verse to teach them about repentance so they can continue to truly repent. What can you learn about repentance from verses 2–16?

Chambers quotes Psalm 51—another great chapter on repentance. How did David respond when confronted with his sin? How did that compare to Saul's response? The difference is that David had God's heart (1 Samuel 13:14). It was God's heart in him, and his strength in God (see 1 Samuel 30:6), that gave him this response.

WHAT'S THE DEVOTIONAL SAYING?

Chambers calls conviction of sin rare. Conviction occurs when our pain over hurting God is so great it eclipses our sorrow for hurting others by our sins. This pain crashes into our respectability, as it did to Chambers (see January 16, *Companion*). Then we enter God's kingdom, and Jesus' life grows in us. This new life causes continuous, true repentance in us. We are conscious of the repentance, but not the holiness it produces.

Are you continuously repenting? If not, pray for the "gift of tears." God can give you the rare gift of conviction of sin, which will form Jesus' life in you and make repentance continuous again.

APPLICATION

When was the last time you felt repentant? How is this different from "self-disgust"?

Has God forgiven you? How do you prove you're forgiven? What specifically will you do?

Finish this prayer: "Holy Spirit, please convict me of my sin; only you can do it. And I can only be holy if . . ."

DECEMBER 8
THE IMPARTIAL POWER OF GOD

God doesn't look at your résumé. Everyone must enter through the Cross.

BACKGROUND Are you holy? Do you live in a holy, sinless way—the way God lived when He came to earth? If not, how do you know you are saved? Oswald Chambers says God is just and justified "in saving bad people only as He makes them good." If you are not good (and only God in you is good—see Mark 10:18) then are you really saved from sin and destined for God's eternal presence?

These are unsettling questions. But we need to ask them. Yesterday's lesson ended with the charge, "Examine yourself." Today let us do that bravely!

SCRIPTURAL CONTEXT Did Jesus' one-time sacrifice make us perfect forever? If so, why are we still "being made holy" as today's theme verse says? The subsequent verses help us. We have opportunities to "shrink back" (verse 38), but when we persevere, we are not set aside for destruction. Instead, we are set apart (made holy) for salvation.

Chambers helps us further understand this by quoting several verses: 1 Corinthians 1:30, Acts 4:12, and Ephesians 1:7. How does Jesus' becoming our sanctification help us understand how we are "being made holy"? Why does it make salvation "boundless" that Jesus has the only name by which we may be saved? How is God's forgiveness "lavish"?

WHAT'S THE DEVOTIONAL SAYING? Let's look at each paragraph in today's rather difficult lesson. First, God can't forgive us just because we are sorry. Someone has to repair the damage. The same is true in human forgiveness. No one forgives just because the other person is sorry. If he or she is genuinely sorry, that person will try to do something to clean up the mess.

Second, God can't forgive us just because Jesus asks Him to—Jesus actually had to die. And God doesn't care who we are or what amazing things we've done with our life. He requires us to come as sinners and accept (identify with) Jesus' death. Identifying with His death means this: Everything in our life that is not in Christ dies.

Third, God can't forgive us just because He says we're "right" even though we aren't. For one, God can't lie, and He can't pretend something is true when it's not. Instead, He calls our nonexistent holiness into existence (Romans 4:17).

Do you think God is heartless or boundless in His "impartial power"? Thank Him for saving even you!

APPLICATION

Do you imagine that your tears earn forgiveness? Why is that offensive? What is true? God forgives—and what else? How does that make you feel? What's the catch? Why? Finish this prayer: "Father, if you were to forgive me and not fix me, you would be unjust. I praise you that . . ."

∽ DECEMBER 9 ∽
THE OPPOSITION OF THE NATURAL

Sin isn't the danger; our gifts are a worse threat.

➤

BACKGROUND The lessons for today and tomorrow come from one of Oswald Chambers' lectures on Abraham (see May 25, *Companion*) and from a paragraph's worth of a lecture he gave in 1917. Chambers looked at the relation of Ishmael and Isaac. Both boys had ordinary faults and merits. But one wasn't part of God's plan, and he had to be cast aside.

What part of your life is not God's plan? If it's one of your natural gifts and virtues, you'll fight your biggest war to cast it aside—the good against the best.

SCRIPTURAL CONTEXT Galatians is the only book of the Bible other than Genesis that mentions Hagar. So it's not surprising that Chambers quoted from Galatians several times in his original lecture. And Biddy used, for today's theme, a verse that follows the "fruit of the Spirit" passage. How does crucifying our flesh lead to the Spirit's fruit?

Chambers also quotes Matthew 16:24. Do you think the disciples would have been ready to hear this verse earlier in Jesus' ministry? How are you denying yourself?

WHAT'S THE DEVOTIONAL SAYING? What is the natural life? Chambers says, "We mean by the 'natural' life, the ordinary, sensible, healthy, worldly minded life." Chambers says that it's not sinful; the disposition that rules the natural life is the problem. As a result, we need to lay our natural life on the altar so God can put a new ruling disposition in it. We have the hardest time sacrificing the most "sensible, healthy" parts of our natural lives—all the things in us that represent the highest natural good.

What are your strengths? How can you give up your rights to them? The first step is to consciously relinquish your rights to use them. Decide today that only God has that right.

APPLICATION

Which of the two extreme views about natural life plague you? How does God see it?

Though not sinful, why is natural life so dangerous? Where do you see this in your life?

Finish this prayer: "Lord, I give, with my own hands, my rights, self-will, and independence to you. Take . . ."

ᏬᎺᎧ DECEMBER 10 ᏬᎺᎧ
THE OFFERING OF THE NATURAL

Is your natural life good for anything?
Yes, as long as it's been sacrificed.

◄

BACKGROUND As we saw yesterday, this two-day series comes from the story of Isaac and Ishmael. We hear a lot about Abraham's sacrifice of Isaac but often forget that Abraham had prior "training" when God asked him to send away Ishmael. Today Oswald Chambers explains the significance of these two boys, and Paul confirms what we learn.

SCRIPTURAL CONTEXT Read Galatians 4. Who does Ishmael represent? Have you been a slave to the law? What strikes you most about Paul's interpretation of the story of Isaac and Ishmael?

Chambers moves beyond Paul's use of this story. Compare what Chambers says in the final paragraph to Genesis 21:15–19. Now imagine your best gifts (see December 9, *Companion*). Will God take care of them if you "send them away"?

WHAT'S THE DEVOTIONAL SAYING? Not only must we send away our natural life and gifts so we'll be ready to offer up our spiritual life, but we must also do it to protect our spiritual side. Our old habits—not the bad or sinful ones, just the ones that get along fine without God—will prevent us from going God's way. Our old gifts and how we use them are like ruts made by wagon wheels. If we don't violently turn to the side, we will just keep going the same old way.

In his *Complete Works*, Chambers says that God intended for Adam and Eve's natural life to steadily evolve into a spiritual life by their obedience. But since they failed to obey, we have to sacrifice everything about our natural life to God. Only then can it be turned into the spiritual as it was supposed to from the beginning. Will you sacrifice your natural life to Him today?

APPLICATION

What are your natural interests? How do you sacrifice them? What have they become?

What is your plan to discipline yourself? Who will help you? What's your motivation?

Finish this prayer: "Lord, I haven't had to sacrifice like Abraham, but I want to have his faith. Please . . ."

DECEMBER 11
INDIVIDUALITY

Individuality protects our real life until it's ready for salvation; then it must go!

➤

BACKGROUND We first discussed individuality versus personality on March 1 and then dug deeper into this contrast on November 18. What is the point of thinking about the difference between these two terms? For starters, it helps us fight off our unbelief. If we realize it's our natural "individuality" that can't believe and that our spiritual "personality" can't help *but* believe, we can understand the source of our lack of faith.

A second benefit of examining the differences between these two words is that it helps us understand people who haven't allowed God to break their personality out of its protective covering (their individuality). Today's lesson will help you have patience with others and with yourself.

SCRIPTURAL CONTEXT What is the "self" Jesus asks us to deny in Matthew 16:24? It's none other than the individuality that Oswald Chambers describes. In what context did Jesus ask this? Was this the first time He mentioned His death?

Chambers gives us a specific example of when we have to deny ourselves. Matthew 5:23–24 tells us we have to reconcile with those who have things against us. This is hard to do! Will you deny yourself in this specific way and in any other way God shows you?

WHAT'S THE DEVOTIONAL SAYING?
If you're reading in the Classic Edition, the following words might jump out at you and help you understand the lesson: *husk, elbows, shell, lust, independence, self-assertiveness, margins, surrender,* and *emerge.* As you trace these words through the text, what picture comes into focus? How would you describe individuality?

The key is to look for what the Holy Spirit wants you to do, and then surrender to Him. This will cause your personality to emerge the way it was created to do. Write a declaration of denying your independence!

APPLICATION
What is your individuality? Where do you notice it? What does Chambers say to do with it?
What is your new spirituality? Where did it come from? How can you help it grow?
Finish this prayer: "God, it was your will for my spirit to obey you and transform my natural life into . . ."

DECEMBER 12
PERSONALITY

Salvation frees personality from individuality. Our sacrifice helps it grow.

◄

BACKGROUND Today we learn the difference between spiritual life and personality. Personality is the "incalculable" part of our spiritual life that makes us who we are. Each of us has a spiritual life, and we can talk about spiritual life in a general, generic way. But if we talk about personality, we can't forget that everyone's personality is made differently from everyone else's.

Oswald Chambers also explains that Jesus sets personality free from the protective "husk" of individuality, which itself is "transfigured." It ceases to exist as "individuality," because once personality is released and merges in love with Jesus, it's no longer solitary but is joined with another life. These are the deep, amazing truths that we learn about today!

SCRIPTURAL CONTEXT The only two verses Chambers quotes are John 17:22 and 10:30. Read them and compare what they say. Does Jesus seem to back down from this claim in 10:34–36? How does the context of the two verses differ? How do we become one with Him, God, and one another? Do we just imitate Jesus?

WHAT'S THE DEVOTIONAL SAYING? Both personality and individuality are unique to each person. However, while individuality can be understood by a close friend or spouse, personality is so profound we can't even understand it for ourselves. Only God can plumb the depths.

Why is Jesus defined by personality and not individuality? Chambers says it's because He is one with the Father. If Jesus didn't need individuality, we don't need it either. We had it, as Adam and Eve did, to protect our personality until personality was ready to be freed. Give up your individuality—all the worldly gifts, characteristics, and rights that make you who you are—and be made one with God. Give up all your worldly rights. Let love completely transform you.

APPLICATION

Can you find the twelve references to "personality" (in the Classic Edition)? What does this term mean?

Have you merged with another person? With God? How can you be more devoted?

Finish this prayer: "Jesus, thank you for setting my personality free. Now I must devote my natural life to . . ."

DECEMBER 13
INTERCESSORY PRAYER

Have you lost your nerve in prayer?
Buck up! Redemption is the key.

BACKGROUND Beginning when he was thirty-one years old, Oswald Chambers made a habit of praying for a list of people. Ten days before he turned thirty-two, he wrote, "What a blessed habit I have found my prayer list, morning by morning; it takes me via the Throne of all Grace straight to the intimate personal heart of each one mentioned here, and I know that He Who is not prescribed by time and geography answers immediately." Two years later, he wrote: "I have a greatly increased prayer list. I believe more and more that this is His way—intercessory prayer, this is the way He makes us broken bread and poured-out wine for other people."

Do you have a list of people you pray for morning by morning? Even if the list is short and you have it in your head, you can still have it and use it daily in prayer—as today's lesson encourages us to do.

SCRIPTURAL CONTEXT We agree that we should "pray and not faint," but how? Luke 18 says that Jesus' parable of the persistent widow will help us pray without giving up. Does this parable have the promised effect on you?

How do Christ's afflictions (Colossians 1:24) link to intercession? His afflictions on the cross brought *us* before God. In bringing others before God, we are filling up to God's predetermined fullness all that Jesus accomplished in His earthly affliction. (Jesus planned for others to be reached through our lives on earth after He had already ascended.) That is how we participate in Jesus' sufferings—as Paul describes in Philippians 3:10.

WHAT'S THE DEVOTIONAL SAYING? What do the four paragraphs tell us about prayer? First, we need to believe in redemption. Nowadays, we say "the gospel"—it's whatever you call the truth that God made us right with himself through His Son's sacrificial death. Once we put the redemption first, all our prayers fall into place. Second, we don't need to pry into the lives of the people on our prayer list. We've already learned what we can handle, so we should just pray for them and not look for more information. Third, don't let quantifiable Christian work stop you from praying for others. We love numbers (how many prayed to receive Jesus as their Savior, for example), but numbers can keep us from coming into contact with God. Finally, God has decided to do some things only through our prayers for others. Which of those things will never be done because you aren't praying?

APPLICATION

Who or what is crashing on you? How do you pray? What role does redemption play?

Do you know too much? Are you a gossip? A busybody? What should you be doing?

Finish this prayer: "Lord, the one thing I know I need to do is to intercede. Please fill me with the Holy Spirit and help me to . . ."

ᏙᏙᏙ DECEMBER 14 ᏙᏙᏙ
THE GREAT LIFE

Want peace?
Obey God!

BACKGROUND Are you stressed? (We discussed that question in *Companion* on April 1, and it's a good one to revisit!) For today's lesson, Oswald Chambers gives us *two* theme verses and both are antidotes to our stress and worry.

He also gives us a devotional that comes straight from his own experiences. For example, the first paragraph ends in a sentence about how we "usurp" the Holy Spirit's authority. This is what Chambers did in his years of "clouds and darkness" when he wanted the Spirit's power in his own hand (see February 2, *Companion*).

The other two paragraphs also seem drawn from Chambers' personal experiences. You can imagine him preaching the second paragraph to himself when he was deciding whether to go to Egypt and the third paragraph when his first student at the Bible Training College fled the house in the middle of the night. "The Great Life" describes the life Chambers lived. Will it describe yours too?

SCRIPTURAL CONTEXT Today is the only time in *Utmost* that we get two theme verses (Classic Edition). In the Upper Room Discourse, the disciples were clearly troubled. A half-dozen times, Jesus comforts them with words about grief, peace, and being troubled.

Perhaps Biddy included two verses so we would see both the command not to worry and the reason we don't need to worry (because Jesus gives us His peace). Does reading John 13–17 increase your peace? Does it help you more than, say, Psalm 27 or 91 or Matthew 6?

WHAT'S THE DEVOTIONAL SAYING? The three paragraphs in today's lesson, which are rooted in Chambers' own struggles and victories, each teach a different facet of the great life. First, reaching an impasse reminds us we have to deny ourselves. Chambers gives the specific example of when we pray for the Holy Spirit and don't get any power. The reason? We wanted the Spirit for our own purposes. Second, when we hit an obstacle, we have to wait for God's peace. That gives God time to show us how our actions may have been our own impulsive decision and not His. Third, doubts and roadblocks are the result of not obeying. But obedience brings God's peace. Then even the problems and blockades will bring us joy, not worry.

What hurdles are in your life? Do they come between you and God? If so, are you not obeying in some area? Make it right, and live the great life!

APPLICATION

What in your life is difficult? Are you blaming God, even a little? Are you obeying?

When have you felt deep peace? What problems arose, and how did God solve them?

Finish this prayer: "God, I want more peace than I have right now. Please show me where I'm disobeying . . ."

DECEMBER 15
"APPROVED TO GOD"

Want to teach others?
First struggle with truth.

BACKGROUND On January 28, we saw that the slogan, "What thou hast not by suffering bought, presume thou not to teach" influenced Oswald Chambers' teaching. In today's lesson, we read a similar statement, "Our position is not ours until we make it ours by suffering."

Chambers was an advocate of studying hard. As a student at Edinburgh (see February 2, *Companion*), he wrote, "God . . . shows me the necessity of long arduous study." As a teacher, his enemy was "spiritual laziness and intellectual sloth" along with "fixed ideas . . . and utter ignorance of God's book." Does this characterize the life of your mind? Today's lesson will challenge you!

SCRIPTURAL CONTEXT A big motivator for hard study, ironically, is bad teaching. Read 2 Timothy 2 and see what motivated Paul to write today's theme verse. How do soldiers, athletes, and farmers embody the kind of hard study that Chambers advocated?

This is a good time to look at the scriptural context, not just for today's lesson but also for all of life. Are you well-versed enough in the Bible to connect what you experience to specific verses, their context, and how they fit into the whole story of God's redemptive plan? If not, plan on reading the whole Bible next year. (A particularly good way is through *The Daily Devotional Bible*, which has an accompanying devotional; see August 7, *Companion*.) Whatever you decide to do, do it now, or you risk sinking deeper and deeper into intellectual laziness.

WHAT'S THE DEVOTIONAL SAYING? In two paragraphs, Chambers sounds the charge for careful study. First, we must struggle to properly understand and explain our belief. God will use our hard-won explanations to bless others. Second, our goal is not to tell people new things but to tell them what they know to be true but can't explain, even to themselves.

When Chambers talks about being wine poured out for others, we think of serving in menial tasks and working long hours. Today we see that studying to figure out how to express spiritual truth is how we "go through the winepress of God." If you teach the Bible to anyone, you are robbing him or her of God's blessing if you don't study hard. Don't be a thief!

APPLICATION
List ten truths of God. Which ones are hard to express? Will you struggle with them?

What author has taught you the most about the Bible? Why? Have you taught others? In what ways?

Finish this prayer: "Father, your truths are so rich. It takes a life of struggle to grasp them even partially . . ."

DECEMBER 16
WRESTLING BEFORE GOD

Want to pick a good fight?
Grab what keeps you from God and beat it to death!

BACKGROUND Yesterday we saw that Oswald Chambers was a zealous champion of studying hard. He was equally a champion of prayer, as we have seen many times in *Utmost*. Today he tells us not to squat "lazily" and give up in prayer. Instead, he urges us to put up "a glorious fight" and not be spineless jellyfish as we wrestle *against* things and *for* other souls, and do all that *before* God.

Are you wrestling before God or with God? Or not wrestling at all? We must work hard in prayer. It is the work, not just preparation for the work.

SCRIPTURAL CONTEXT Surprisingly, we haven't looked yet at the famous "Armor of God" passage of Ephesians 6. Why are these verses so famous? How do they relate to prayer (see May 3, *Utmost*)? Which part of the armor will you focus on today?

Chambers uses the story of Jacob in Genesis 32 to describe people who pray incorrectly. Do you think this is the correct interpretation of this story? Would Jacob have been crippled if he had wrestled *before* God instead of *with* Him?

Chambers quotes Romans 8:28, explaining how it refers to people who are faithful to God's ultimate plan. Do you agree with this way of interpreting the verse?

WHAT'S THE DEVOTIONAL SAYING? There are three key parts of today's lesson. First, as Chambers pointed out in a lecture on January 8, 1917, that mirrors today's lesson, "We are spiritual 'Jacobs,' men wrestling with God," which forces God to make us limp, since we are asserting our own will. Second, we need to be complete in Christ to have the power to wrestle correctly and prevail in prayer. Third, "permissive" and "passive" in the Classic Edition are identical and are contrasted with God's perfect will. We *must* wrestle with things in His passive will. This is our job as His children.

Are you putting God in a headlock to force Him to answer your prayers? Go ahead and wrestle, but not with *God*. Wrestle with the people and things He puts in your life. Don't back down until you have brought them before God's throne, have understood His mind about them, and have taken on His perspective as your own.

APPLICATION

Has God worked in a way you didn't like? Did you fight him? How should you fight?

How do God's perfect and permissive wills differ? Where have you seen each one?

Finish this prayer: "God, your permissive will has sent me tricky situations today. Please use them to reveal that I . . ."

⌘ DECEMBER 17 ⌘
REDEMPTION—CREATING THE NEED IT SATISFIES

Free will versus predestination
is a false dichotomy; by God's plan, they both are true.

BACKGROUND To the Bible Training College students, Oswald Chambers gave a talk on the "Highest Good." His points in the third section of this talk match closely the first part of today's lesson and give us some extra insight. For example, he adds ritualists and rationalists to the list of people who don't sense their need of the gospel.

Who are the people you would most like to see accept the gospel? Are they moralists? Or do they see a need for a Savior? Today's lesson shows us how people are free to reject God's grace—and free to ask for it. But people don't ask for it until God creates a need in their hearts.

SCRIPTURAL CONTEXT Today's verse is not often used in debates about free will and predestination. It tells us that apart from God people don't receive what God offers. Why don't they? Does the context help you?

How do we know that Chambers is right about who can't see the gospel? Does 2 Cor-inthians 4 help us? We actually have to infer his point from other places (see Mark 2:17). He also quotes Matthew 7:7, John 12:32, and 6:63. We've seen all these before. How do they relate to free will and predestination?

WHAT'S THE DEVOTIONAL SAYING? The final paragraph today is priceless when it comes to sharing the good news with your friends. Don't talk about yourself, even though God may have done great things for you. Talk about Jesus. God can mystically create a need in your friends that wasn't there before. If they trust in their morality, rituals, rationality, or anything else, God can strip away their idols and expose the gaping hole in their hearts. Just preach Jesus and Him crucified. That story has power you will never understand. God's great redemption plan is what always carries the day.

APPLICATION

When did you first ask God for help? Can you see how this set His process in motion?

To whom do you talk about God? Do you share your experiences or Jesus Christ? Why?

Finish this prayer: "Spirit of God, thank you for making me aware of my need for Christ. Help me to tell . . ."

❦ DECEMBER 18 ❦
TEST OF FAITHFULNESS

Do you believe God is in control?
He'll test you to make sure you do!

BACKGROUND "For Christ's Crown and Covenant" was emblazoned on seventeenth-century Scottish war banners. Oswald Chambers used this slogan to capture the essence of the Bible Training College, just as many Reformed churches in his day used it to capture theirs. In a talk he gave to his students, he said this motto "comes nearer to the New Testament conception of loyalty to Christ than any other all down the centuries." And he said our job is to "translate it into terms which fit our own day and generation." What can you do to prove your loyalty to Christ's crown and covenant today?

SCRIPTURAL CONTEXT Today's lesson uses Romans 8:28 as a litmus test for loyalty. Those who are loyal to Jesus believe that God works all circumstances for good, even the trying ones. Those who are not loyal do not. Is this a correct use of today's theme verse? Why or why not?

In his "For Christ's Crown and Covenant" talk, Chambers said, "We are baptized with the Holy Ghost not *for* anything at all, but entirely, as Our Lord puts it, to be His witnesses, those with whom He can do exactly what He likes." Is that how you feel about your life?

WHAT'S THE DEVOTIONAL SAYING? Although the theme of loyalty spans all three paragraphs, they each say something a bit different. First, God breaks up our "parties"—those areas of our life that are going well—so we realize that *He* was the one who threw the party and is the only party planner. Second, full-time Christian workers are the worst offenders of loyalty to Jesus. They put their work first and only ask Jesus to bless what they are doing. Third, God can use us without explaining anything about what He is doing. As Chambers put it, "To imagine that Jesus Christ came to save and sanctify *me* is heresy: He came to save and sanctify me *into Himself*, to be His absolute bondslave."

Are you Christ's slave? Are you out on the battlefield fighting under His command for the honor of His crown and covenant? When you see yourself as nothing but His slave, you will have the right attitude about anything He sends your way.

APPLICATION

What's going on in your life? Is God in control? How do you know? Will you worship?

When have things fallen apart? Did it show your lack of trust in God's control?

Finish this prayer: "God, do your work through me this week; I will try hard not to complain. Please help . . ."

⌘∽ DECEMBER 19 ∽⌘
THE FOCUS OF OUR MESSAGE

Do you want God to be someone's good cop?
Then take the role of bad cop!

➤

BACKGROUND The lessons for today and tomorrow come partly from a sermon preparation lecture titled, "The Right Lines of Work." In Oswald Chambers' sermon preparation class (see May 5, *Companion*), he emphasized the need to be stern with people so God can be gracious. How should we take this emphasis when, at other times, Chambers taught us not to force truth down people's throats?

Chambers says the right way to balance being stern with letting God reveal truth is to focus on the standard Jesus set forth. A great example of Jesus' standard is His Sermon on the Mount. Once people come to see the gap between what they have and what Jesus wants, Chambers says we should let them stew on it for a while. Then, after they have seen there is no way at all for them to live up to the standard, we should tell them about the Holy Spirit's power available to them.

SCRIPTURAL CONTEXT Chambers' original lecture focused on Paul's letters to Timothy. Skim 1 and 2 Timothy. Can you find where Paul (as Jesus does in today's theme verse) talks about the confrontational nature of preaching the gospel?

Today is the last time in *Utmost* where we see Chambers' life verse (Luke 11:13). Why is this verse so vital to his message? Have you claimed its promise this year?

WHAT'S THE DEVOTIONAL SAYING? In the first paragraph, Chambers tells us that some people look like they're sorry about their sin but aren't willing to give it up. In the next paragraph, he says we should meet people where they are until they realize they're not living up to Jesus' standard. Once they understand how far they've fallen short, our job gets a lot easier. In the final paragraph, Chambers explains why we sometimes have to be so tough. If we aren't, those who hear us will ask, "What's the point?" They see their lives as already very good and don't feel they need the truth of God that we preach.

Have you tried talking about Jesus' sacrifice with those who don't seem to care? Why don't they care about it? Could it be that no one has taken the time to "erect the standard of Jesus" to them?

APPLICATION

Can you deal firmly and ruggedly with others? Are these attitudes from you or from God?

Reread the first sentence of the devotional. Stop and pray for someone who is facing a harsh situation.

Finish this prayer: "Thank you, Jesus! Even 'happy pagans' aren't safe from you. Now help me to . . ."

THE RIGHT KIND OF HELP

Do you want your friends to believe?
Then know why Christ had to die!

◄

BACKGROUND As we read yesterday, today's lesson comes partly from a sermon preparation lecture at the Bible Training College. It continues the theme we started yesterday on how to share the gospel with others.

Has anyone turned to God after you talked with him or her about Jesus? Has God used you to share about His Son with anyone recently? The point today is that your relationship with God is the basis of any help you can give people. If your focus is not on that relationship, you won't have "The Right Lines of Work" as you preach the good news.

SCRIPTURAL CONTEXT Oswald Chambers' original talk ended with today's theme verse. He called the image of Jesus being lifted up on the cross a "standard they [the lost] never saw before." *We* are the standard lifters, holding high the flag of God's love for all to see. Does the original context of John 12:32 (see John 3:14 and Numbers 21:4–9) fit with the idea that we lift up the standard?

Six times in *Utmost,* Chambers mentions Christ crucified (1 Corinthians 2:2) as the essence of our message. Is that what you preach? Do you preach anything?

WHAT'S THE DEVOTIONAL SAYING? Today's lesson fights against the notion that our message to the lost is based on sympathy and understanding for their broken condition. How dishonoring to Jesus' sacrifice! If all people needed was our sympathy, the cross would be a huge waste of effort.

Instead, our message is based on what needed to be accomplished, and was accomplished, on the cross. Jesus surgically removed the disposition of sin (see June 13, *Companion*). If we have a personal relationship with God, and we know it is only possible thanks to this surgical operation, then the people we "talk to *must* be concerned" (see Classic Edition).

Is this the basis for any conversations you have with others about God? If it is, God will cause you to have a huge effect on people. If not, you probably will give up even trying to talk with people about Him. What will it be? Will you focus on God's redemption and sternly expose sin—first of all in your own heart?

APPLICATION

Are you willing and prepared to confront *yourself* with God's Word before confronting others? What will you say?

How would you explain to others *why* Jesus died? Why is sympathy the antithesis of His death?

Finish this prayer: "Jesus, thank you for letting God put His wrath on you instead of on me. Please help . . ."

Disposition of sin - self realization - I am my own god - my claim to my right to myself

ᥬᥭ DECEMBER 21 ᥬᥭ
EXPERIENCE OR GOD'S REVEALED TRUTH?

At rebirth, we are whisked away to Christ; thereafter, He helps us fill in the gap.

➤

BACKGROUND The lessons for today and tomorrow follow the flow of a series of lectures Oswald Chambers gave on "Christian Thinking." The following quote from that lecture helps us as we try to understand today's lesson: "I must be careful not to confound the reality of my experience with reality itself. For instance, when I am born again I am not conscious of the redemption of my Lord, the one thing that is real to me is that I have been born again; but if I watch the working of the Holy Spirit I find that He takes me clean out of myself till I no longer pay any attention to my experiences, I am concerned only with the reality which produced those experiences, viz., the redemption."

What was your experience of being "born again"? Is this experience what you preach to others when you preach the good news? Or has the Holy Spirit made you impatient with your experience and made you cling only to God?

SCRIPTURAL CONTEXT Anything that God gives us is our "experience." In today's verse, Paul says that the Spirit helps us "know" these things. Have you been content to merely receive experiences from God, or are you letting the Holy Spirit help you know the reality behind those experiences?

WHAT'S THE DEVOTIONAL SAYING?
Reading the Classic Edition gives us an excellent mental picture of the wrong way to handle experience. Chambers says, "If you try to dam up the Holy Spirit in you to produce subjective experiences, you will find that He will burst all bounds and take you back again to the historic Christ." We dam up rivers to produce energy. Some people try to dam up the Spirit to produce experiences. What happens to these people? Has that ever happened to you?

Today's lesson puts experience in its proper place. It doesn't say that experiences are bad. They serve an important role. Your experience of a particular truth allows that truth to speak to your conscious life. Without these conscious experiences, the truth would be still there, but it wouldn't *mean* anything to you.

Chambers gives the example of the experience of rebirth. We experience a conscious whisking away of our life from sin into God's kingdom. Later, we understand more fully what happened. Can you think of other examples where the Spirit helps us more fully understand and know spiritual realities? Ask Him for more understanding today.

APPLICATION

When you were saved, how did the Holy Spirit lift you from where you were to Christ?

Do you keep going back to Christ, or do you now focus on your "spiritual growth"?

Finish this prayer: "Holy Spirit, you want my focus to be on Christ, even as I'm working out redemption . . ."

DECEMBER 22
THE DRAWING OF THE FATHER

Where is God leading you?
Resolve to follow Him anywhere He goes!

◀

BACKGROUND As we saw yesterday, today's lesson comes from Oswald Chambers' lectures on Christian thinking that he gave at the Bible Training College. Chambers always challenged his listeners to commit their lives completely to God. Today's lesson is a perfect example.

Have you committed to follow God wherever He goes? Or is your "faith" merely intellectual? Listen to Chambers' words. Give yourself completely to God.

SCRIPTURAL CONTEXT John 6 records the feeding of the five thousand and how the crowd's response unfolded. How does today's theme verse fit into their response? Picture a grumbling mob arguing with each other. How would they have understood Jesus' words?

Jeremiah 31 is the "new covenant" chapter. But in verse 3, God tells us that he will draw us with His unfailing kindness. Have you seen instances where God's love has won you over? Do you win other people's hearts with love or by your persuasive power?

WHAT'S THE DEVOTIONAL SAYING? In three short paragraphs, Chambers teaches us about the interaction of God's irresistible grace and free will. First, he asks if we will "dump" ourselves down on God (Classic Edition). Will

we, without sorting out our life, throw the whole of it down at God's feet? Second, Chambers urges us to preach commitment of will, not intellectual assent, and to preach without trusting in our persuasive power. Commitment of will causes violent upheaval, but it's the only way to truly *believe* in God. Third, our will to believe and God's miracle combine to give us a personal relationship with God.

Eighteenth-century theologian John Gill, writing in his commentary on today's theme verse said, "This act of drawing is an act of power, yet not of force; God in drawing of unwilling, makes willing in the day of His power: He enlightens the understanding, bends the will, gives an heart of flesh, sweetly allures by the power of His grace, and engages the soul to come to Christ, and give up itself to Him; He draws with the bands of love. Drawing, though it supposes power and influence, yet not always coaction and force: music draws the ear, love the heart, and pleasure the mind." This aptly describes the interplay between free will and irresistible grace. One wonders if Chambers—musician, lover, and thinker—read this section of Gill's commentary before teaching his class on Christian thinking. Will you be God's instrument for drawing others?

APPLICATION
What is the role of will in following God? How do you emphasize this to nonbelievers?
Do you reach beyond your grasp? How? Is God inspiring this? Are you grasping Him?
Finish this prayer: "Father, you drew me to Jesus, and you are drawing me to . . ."

<small>∽</small> DECEMBER 23 <small>∽</small>
SHARING IN THE ATONEMENT

Do you feel like dying?
Probably not! But that's what God requires of you.

BACKGROUND On May 29, we imagined what it would have been like for Oswald Chambers to preach at the annual League of Prayer autumn conference. Today we see a lesson that comes partly from the talk Chambers gave the following year at the same venue.

You have a choice. Will you choose God or yourself? As you near Christmas and dramatically change your schedules, will you give yourself time to stand before God? Make time today!

SCRIPTURAL CONTEXT Galatians 6:14 was our featured verse for the November 25–27 lessons. The power in this verse lies in the cross. Paul explained throughout Galatians that the cross is central to our faith. What competes for this central importance? Have you bragged about anything lately?

Chambers also quotes John 15:5. Did the disciples believe they couldn't do anything without Jesus' Spirit (the Holy Spirit)? How do you know? What do you believe?

WHAT'S THE DEVOTIONAL SAYING? Like Socrates, Chambers taught by asking questions. Answer his first three questions as best you can. If you can immediately answer "yes" to each one, get alone with God and pray that God will draw you closer to Him (see December 22, *Utmost*). Then tell Him you want to be identified with Jesus' death at all costs, such that everything in you that is against Him (your "old man") will die.

This is the time of year when Christians and non-Christians love others in out-of-the-ordinary ways. Will you listen to the voice of Jesus Christ today to hear how He wants you to love? Or will He have to show you, as the ghosts of Christmas had to show Scrooge, what your life would be like if it were not for Him? He wants you to identify with Him in His death and resurrection. Tell Him you want that right now!

APPLICATION

Did God reveal how you would be if not for Him? Do you want to identify with Him even more?

What are your interests? How can you die more to interests in self, the world, and sin?

Finish this prayer: "Lord, thank you for the joy you gave when I was young in Christ. Now I realize that . . ."

Perfect inner strength only comes from God.

BACKGROUND The theme "hid in Christ," or "hidden saints," is a reoccurring theme in *Utmost* (see January 23, April 28, May 1, June 2, 7, and 14, August 31, September 10, October 19, and November 16). Biddy Chambers' introduction to the book included a quote by Robert Murray McCheyne: "Men return again and again to the few who have mastered the spiritual secret, whose life has been hid with Christ in God. These are of the old-time religion, hung to the nails of the Cross." She saw her husband as one who had been hidden with Christ in God.

Are you hidden with Christ in God? What does that even mean? Today's lesson describes this life. After reading it, decide if you have this hidden life.

SCRIPTURAL CONTEXT In addition to the theme verse, which we saw before, Oswald Chambers also quotes two verses (and alludes to several others). First, he applies Psalm 18:36 to the secure, hidden life. Then he quotes John 14:27. Has Jesus given you His peace by letting you "see" Him (April 9, *Utmost*)? You'll know He has if you aren't troubled by doubts.

WHAT'S THE DEVOTIONAL SAYING? Can we really live as Chambers describes? Reading his biographies and hearing his wife talk about him, we have to conclude that at least *he* was able to live like that. We know that his mind was "unrelieved" (March 28, *Companion*) at least once, but that is not the same as doubt. After his time of "darkness" (see January 3, *Utmost*), he never doubted that God was leading him. He felt a sense of suspense only as he waited for God to clear things up.

There's no way to live the hidden life in your own power. Don't even try! Today, focus on loving God and treasuring Him in your heart moment by moment. He can and will bring you to the "plateau" where living a holy life is easy. Don't despair. The life He wants you to live is coming. Wait in suspense for it. Soon your mind will no longer be unrelieved!

APPLICATION
Why is a "hidden life" so secure? How do we walk in the light? Where do you doubt?
When has your life in God been easy? What was the key? How could it be easier now?
Finish this prayer: "God, you made birds to fly, the sun to shine, and me to live with you. Help me to see . . ."

DECEMBER 25
HIS BIRTH AND OUR NEW BIRTH

Let Jesus be born in you!

BACKGROUND Today's lesson comes from one of the chapters of *The Psychology of Redemption* (April 5, *Companion*). This material came from Biddy's notes in 1915 and 1916, and Oswald Chambers gave the same lectures at a League of Prayer convention in Perth, Scotland. These were lectures that Chambers thought about often and deeply.

Today's lesson is also one of two that match a holiday (New Year's Eve is the other). So have a Merry Christmas today! Enjoy Oswald and Biddy's gift to you: a devotional about how Jesus came from outside the world and wants to be born into your life.

SCRIPTURAL CONTEXT The Christmas story is found in Matthew and Luke. Chambers quotes from both. What is more amazing to you: the virgin birth, God with us, "the holy thing which shall be born of [Mary]" (Luke 1:35, KJV), or that Jesus is the Son of God? They all point to the redemption, which is *the* miracle. Can you find other signposts in the story of Jesus' birth that point to redemption?

Chambers brings in two other verses that show how God can be born in us. Read Galatians 4:19 and John 3:7 with a Christmas perspective. How do their meanings change?

WHAT'S THE DEVOTIONAL SAYING? Are you puzzled by the sentence, "Our Lord's birth was an advent"? *Adventus* is Latin for "arrival." When a new baby arrives, we know that a stork didn't drop her from above, but that she came from natural processes and is part of the human line that started with Adam. But when Jesus arrived, His birth really was an arrival, like an airplane arriving from another place. The importance of this is that when His life is formed in our lives, it comes from another place, not from our own goodness.

In all the hubbub of Christmas, have you lost sight of the main point—Christ in you? Now is a good time to refocus. Let Jesus' life shine out of your life. Let Him live out the perfect, otherworldly life that He lived when He was on earth.

APPLICATION

How do you see God's role in history? Why does how Christ relates to history matter?

Is your life a "Bethlehem"? How do you know? How can Christ be born in you today?

Finish this prayer: "Lord Jesus, thank you for leaving the Father's side to appear in history and in my life . . ."

DECEMBER 26
"WALK IN THE LIGHT"

Atonement draws us into God's light. Stay there!

BACKGROUND Ah, the day after Christmas! Time to look forward to the year ahead. Today's lesson and the next five are all we have left. Have you decided whether to do the year in *Utmost* again? Did you find a Bible reading plan (see December 15, *Companion*)?

Today's lesson comes from a talk called "Cleansed from Sin." In this talk, Oswald Chambers said, "If you make the experience of conscious freedom from sin the test, you make hypocrites. Sin enough and you will soon be unconscious of sin." Are you a hypocrite who says (and believes!) that you are free from sin? You might think you are free from sin because you sinned enough to sear your conscience (1 Timothy 4:2). Today's lesson will point you to the Spirit's work of revealing your sin nature.

SCRIPTURAL CONTEXT We use John 1:9 far more than we quote today's theme verse. Why is that? Could it be that we like the idea of *just* confessing our sins? Isn't that a lot easier than walking in the light? But we don't get to decide which verse describes how God purifies us from sin. They both do! So if we are "confessing" but not walking in the light, we can be sure that we aren't truly confessing.

WHAT'S THE DEVOTIONAL SAYING? Look at today's study paragraph by paragraph. First, truly understanding our sinful state is the final miracle of the atonement. Second, our conscious sin—the nature of sin we know we have—is only the tip of the iceberg. There is a far more ugly side of our sin nature that we don't even know we have. Third, our walking in the light is as much helped by our love for God's holy light as it is by our hatred of darkness.

If you were to drive at night in a parking lot, avoiding potholes along the edges, you would use the contrast between darkness and light to keep you in the well-lit, pothole-free zone. You need *both* the light and the darkness to create the contrast. It's not that darkness is just as important as light. But hatred of a God-shaped void *is* just as important as clinging to the good (see Romans 12:9).

Let's make this specific. If you are prone to lying, you may have lied so much that you are unconscious of your sin. Your only hope, which is everyone's only hope, is that the Spirit will apply the atonement to you and show you your sin nature. When as an act of free will you decide not to lie, you will be heeding God's warnings and walking in the light (see December 24, *Utmost*).

APPLICATION

What is sin? Are you able to understand the full extent of your sin? Who will help you?

What do you hate? What are you hiding from God? How will you walk in the light?

Finish this prayer: "Lord, I know what sin is better than I did in the past, but I don't fully understand . . ."

DECEMBER 27
WHERE THE BATTLE IS WON OR LOST

Want to win?
Fight in secret using your will.

BACKGROUND Before World War I, Oswald Chambers taught a class about the four major prophets. Today's lesson comes from his discussion of Jeremiah 4:1–2. Have you read Jeremiah recently? It's a difficult book to absorb without more context. (*The Daily Devotional Bible*—see December 15, *Companion*—helpfully provides the context.) But if you understand today's theme verse and lesson, you will be well on your way to learning the main thrust of Jeremiah's prophecies.

SCRIPTURAL CONTEXT For today's theme verse, read chapters 3 and 4. Who was king when God sent this message? Was he a good king (see 2 Kings 23:25)? Why does today's verse address Israel? Was Israel still a nation at that point?

The main point of Jeremiah 4:1 is that God's people must first have the *will* to return to God. That's where the real battle is. In chapter 3, God calls His people; then, in chapter 4, He asks them if they have decided with their will to return. Is God calling you? Have you committed in your will to come to Him?

WHAT'S THE DEVOTIONAL SAYING? Today is the fifth and final time we see the phrase "My Utmost for His Highest." What has this statement come to mean to you as you have read through *Utmost*? Do you agree that the battle to be your utmost for God is in the area of will, not in externals?

One key to winning the battle of the will is to "get alone with God." Do you get alone with Him when He grabs you by the collar about something in your life? Make the effort today to spend some time with Him. Wrestle before Him with your circumstances and with the people He put in your life. Don't quit until you commit your will!

APPLICATION

What battle are you fighting? Has your will battled internally before God? How so?

When was a big turning point in your life? Did you win or lose? Did it correlate to a battle of will?

Finish this prayer: "God, I must fight, using all my willpower, to renounce my rights to myself. Right now . . ."

DECEMBER 28
CONTINUOUS CONVERSION

We receive new birth in weakness, not strength.

BACKGROUND Today's devotional is the last one that comes from Oswald Chambers' talks on Abraham (see May 25, *Companion*). In this talk, he explained that our natural life, not our sin, is what gets "converted." We have to convert our natural life continually. It's hard to do! Just because we did it once doesn't mean we will do it again. That's why Chambers says we are being fanatics if we say, "I will never do anything natural again."

What's the difference between natural and sinful? Chambers implies that we can do things that are not of God but are not sinful. Do you agree? Whether you do or not, today's lesson will inspire you to let God, not your natural life, rule you.

SCRIPTURAL CONTEXT It seems the disciples were always jockeying for position in God's kingdom. How does today's verse help counteract this attitude? Do you like being higher than others? Do you look up to and "welcome" people who are powerful or people who are like children? Naturally, we like to be in control. So we really have to be converted and turn from our natural ways if we will become children and enter God's kingdom.

Chambers also quotes Ephesians 4:24. What is the "former way of life" (verse 22)? How is it different from the "deceitful desires" it has? Is this the same as the distinction Chambers makes between natural life and sin?

WHAT'S THE DEVOTIONAL SAYING? Into which new conditions and situations has God brought you? In which ones did you make sure your natural life submitted to God? Chambers says the one thing we don't like to do is to convert our natural life into spiritual life. Do you think that's true for you?

To Chambers, sin is not *having* a natural life but *refusing to convert* natural into spiritual in each new situation. Converting and becoming like a child might seem like weakness, and refusing to be made low seems like strength. But in God's eyes, it's the other way around. Will you be made low today?

APPLICATION

What new situation has God sent? How will you respond? What's your first impulse?

Do you see obedience in the same light as conversion? How so? Where must you obey?

Finish this prayer: "Lord, I submit to you now as a little child, casting off the independence that I called . . ."

༺ DECEMBER 29 ༻
DESERTER OR DISCIPLE?

We backslide if we don't live up to revealed truth.

BACKGROUND We don't talk much about backsliding nowadays. It's embarrassing that there are many of us who stop living the Christian life. In today's study we face the topic of backsliding head-on and learn how it gets started. People who knew Jesus in the flesh stopped following Him, and people today do too. The reason is still the same: Not doing what God shows us to do.

SCRIPTURAL CONTEXT We've read the end of John 6 many times this year. Did you notice the different groups that responded to Jesus' teaching? Oswald Chambers lists how Jesus was treated by "the crowd, by the Pharisees, and by the disciples, and . . . the handful left." All but the last group left Jesus (see verses 40, 60, and 66). Jesus brought each of these groups to a decision point, and three out of four of them decided to leave. What decision points have you faced? What did Jesus ask you to do at each of these points?

Can you imagine being the man immortalized in Luke 12:13? What was he thinking, asking Jesus to help him sort things out with his brother? We ask Jesus to do this kind of thing for us all the time, and He loves it! He knows that when we ask Him for help—even for foolish, selfish things—we will get to know His heart from what He tells us. A good example is what He told the man in verse 15. How about you? Is there a sense of "personal right" developing in you?

WHAT'S THE DEVOTIONAL SAYING?
We love to disagree with other Christians on all kinds of issues. Today we see that God gives each of us different visions for what He wants, and it's not our job to compare ourselves to others or to judge them. Our job is to obey what He shows us. If we don't, we start backsliding.

It's great when we have abandoned to God in one area of our life, but today's lesson warns us that we can't bask in the memory of that victory. God will soon give us another vision of what we need to abandon; and if we fail to abandon at that point, we will slide backwards to the very beginning. Don't let that happen to you. Decide today to throw it all on Jesus in every new situation.

APPLICATION
What truths has God given you? How did you respond? What were the consequences?
Who has views contrary to Christ? Do you imitate them? Do you debate God on this?
Finish this prayer: "Jesus, I want to follow you and not turn back. Please help me to have your way of . . ."

DECEMBER 30
"AND EVERY VIRTUE WE POSSESS"

Natural gifts are from Eden, not from heaven.

BACKGROUND *Biblical Psychology* (see July 8, *Companion*) is the longest of three books Oswald Chambers published before he died. The other two were *Baffled to Fight Better* (see March 21, *Companion*) and *Studies in the Sermon on the Mount* (see May 18, *Companion*). Today we see part of chapter 11, section 3 (about virtues and vices) of *Biblical Psychology*. Here Chambers quotes a line from the hymn "Our Blest Redeemer, Ere He Breathed": "And every virtue we possess, . . . [is] His alone."

What are your virtues? Did you have them before you were born again? Today's lesson says that your confidence in old virtues must wither. They can't be rebuilt into born-again virtues. The new virtues—*spiritual* love, *spiritual* patience, *spiritual* purity—all come from Jesus' life, not yours.

SCRIPTURAL CONTEXT We saw today's verse, in the same translation, on May 16. How does the wording differ from your Bible? Does Chambers make the same point he made in the earlier lesson?

Interestingly, our natural virtues wither, but our natural human life doesn't. Instead, it puts off the old man that used to run the show. And it puts on the new man (Jesus) and all of His new virtues. Do you think that's what Ephesians 4:24 means?

WHAT'S THE DEVOTIONAL SAYING? Natural virtues motivate evangelism. We see a non-Christian with natural gifts (natural love, natural patience, natural purity), so we say, "Wouldn't it be great if those gifts could be used in the kingdom?" Suddenly we share the gospel with that person, even though we are usually reluctant to do so. But today's lesson says this motivation is based on a falsehood. The gifts we see in non-Christians are not the same as the ones they would use once they become believers and have Jesus' life in them. They would use Jesus' gifts, which are infinitely better.

Are you still confident in your natural gifts? Ask God to send you a drying-up experience. Such an experience might be painful, since everything that used to be so easy for you will go disastrously wrong. But you will thank God for your experience even while you go through it!

APPLICATION

What are your natural virtues? Have they failed? Do you still put confidence in them?

What are the virtues of Jesus' resurrection life? How are you drawing from that spring?

Finish this prayer: "Jesus, thank you for providing an ever-flowing spring of virtues for me. Please help . . ."

YESTERDAY

Anxious about tomorrow because of yesterday?
"I AM" will keep you strong.

BACKGROUND You finally made it! If God has used a daily dose of *Utmost* to change your heart over the past year, you probably feel like celebrating. If He only used a part of *Utmost*, you still can celebrate the end of a year and the beginning of a new one. Oswald and Biddy Chambers' custom was to seek God together on New Year's Eve. On December 31, 1914, they waited before God, and Oswald received 2 Timothy 4:6, which gave them assurance that God was calling them to something new.

Will you wait before God today? Will you ask Him to give you a verse for what He wants you to do next? Today's lesson will help you put in perspective the past and future so you can live in the present and in His presence.

SCRIPTURAL CONTEXT One sad thing about *Utmost* is that there aren't enough lessons to cover each verse of the Bible. Today we get our last theme verse. Why is it such a good verse for New Year's Eve?

For our "security from yesterday," Chambers quotes Ecclesiastes 3:15. How do the different parts of this chapter fit together? Do verses 9 and 10 make sense with what comes before and the verse that follows? How do verses 11 and 14 relate to today's verse? What are verses 12 and 13 doing there?

WHAT'S THE DEVOTIONAL SAYING? Tomorrow is a new year! There is so much promise. Is your excitement about what you could do dampened by your regrets over what you could have done differently this year? Today's lesson says to let God remind you of your past in order to keep your "security for today" from being shallow.

Are you less excited because you are afraid of making the same mistakes in the future? Chambers' words are encouraging: "God will garrison where we have failed to." Of course, we are to prepare the best we can. That's what *Utmost* has urged us to do again and again. But we aren't living up to the full measure of what God has in mind for us, so there will be places where we fail to "garrison," putting our troops in the right places ahead of time.

Remember, God loves you so, so much. That's why He sends people like Oswald and Biddy to help you get closer to God. It's never about the people God uses. Oswald and Biddy would never want you to think about them. They would want you only to think about God, which is what they've been telling you to do all year. Will you do that today and for the rest of your life?

APPLICATION

What are you anticipating in the coming year? What mistakes did you make this past year? How does God use past mistakes? Will you be invincible next year? How do you know? Finish this prayer: "God, thank you for carrying me through this year. Next year I . . ."

ACKNOWLEDGMENTS

We are grateful for so many who have helped us along our journey. We thank our family, who gave us an early appreciation for wrestling with the big questions of life. We are thankful for all the amazing people at Discovery House, especially Miranda Gardner, Carol Holquist, Dave Branon, John van der Veen, Alyson Kieda, Anne Bauman, and freelance designer Michelle Espinoza. Moreover, we thank our friends, especially Mrs. Finke, and all those who tested early versions of this study guide. We also thank Jim Reimann (1950–2013) whose Updated Edition has helped millions better grasp *Utmost* and who encouraged us when this study guide was no more than a series of short summary sentences, questions, and unfinished prayers.

We would also like to acknowledge three important books, without which we would not have been able to complete *A Daily Companion*:

The Complete Works of Oswald Chambers (Discovery House, 2000) allowed us to see many of the daily *Utmost* readings in their original context. For anyone who seeks deeper understanding of Oswald Chambers' thinking, *The Complete Works* is absolutely essential.

David McCasland's award-winning biography, *Abandoned to God* (Discovery House, 1993), was our principal source of historical information. While *A Daily Companion* provides the background about Oswald and Biddy Chambers that is relevant to each *Utmost* reading, *Abandoned to God* tells their story in a beautiful narrative. This is a must read! Moreover, we deeply appreciate the time David McCasland took to help us get certain historical details correct. We know of no other individual alive who knows more about Oswald and Biddy Chambers.

Carolyn Reeves wrote a helpful set of questions to go along with each day of *Utmost*. Her book, *My Daily Journey* (Discovery House, 1995), was instrumental in helping us write many of the questions in the Application section of *A Daily Companion*. We are grateful to her for her work and commend this now-out-of-print book as an additional source of study questions for *Utmost*.

Finally, we would like to thank our children, to whom this book is dedicated. We have learned so much from them about God, His character, and what really matters in His eyes. We are so thankful for them and for the love they shine each day.

NOTE TO THE READER

The publisher invites you to share your response to the message of this book by writing Discovery House Publishers, P.O. Box 3566, Grand Rapids, MI 49501, U.S.A. For information about other Discovery House books, music, or DVDs, contact us at the same address or call 1-800-653-8333. Find us on the Internet at dhp.org or send e-mail to books@dhp.org.

ABOUT THE AUTHORS

Jed and Cecilie met in a chemistry lab and have been married for twelve years. They have five children. Jed, a physics professor, holds a BS from Massachusetts Institute of Technology (MIT) and a PhD from University of California, Berkeley. Cecilie earned her undergraduate degree from Princeton and her MD from Wake Forest University. *My Utmost for His Highest* has helped them through many seasons of their lives, joyous and difficult. They are inspired by reading how Oswald and Biddy Chambers loved working as a team and having fun. They also admire the way the Chambers viewed both spiritual truth and secular truth—including truth in physics and medicine—as all part of God's overarching truth.

For daily thoughts on *Utmost*, follow the authors at twitter.com/dailyutmost (@dailyutmost).

T. Odom Photographics